IPT's GUIDE
to
BLUEPRINT
INTERPRETATION

by

Grant E. Jacobs

Published by
IPT PUBLISHING AND TRAINING LTD.
BOX 9590
EDMONTON, ALBERTA, CANADA   T6E 5X2

Web site: www.iptbooks.com
Email: info@iptbooks.com
Phone (780) 962-4548   Fax (780) 962-4819
Toll Free 1-888-808-6763

Printed in Canada by
Elite Lithographers, Edmonton, Alberta

The material presented in this publication has been prepared in accordance with recognized trade working practices, codes, and procedures, and is for general information only. In areas of critical importance the user should secure competent engineering advice with respect to the suitability of the material contained herein, and comply with the various codes, standards, regulations or other legal obligation. The crane setup and hookup drawings are examples only, and the information should not be transposed to an actual similar lift. Anyone using information in this book assumes all responsibility and liability arising from such use.

IPT's GUIDE to BLUEPRINT INTERPRETATION

First Printing March 2001

Second Printing January 2004

Third Printing November 2007

Fourth Printing April 2010

Fifth Printing February 2013

Sixth Printing April 2015

Seventh Printing May 2017

Eighth Printing September 2020

Ninth Printing May 2022

ISBN 13: 978-0-920855-42-3
ISBN 10:   0-920855-42-3

ACKNOWLEDGEMENTS

The author and publisher wish to thank the following for their assistance in developing this publication:

Illustrations: Ian Holmes – Holmes Consulting
                Cassandra Strumecki – CAS Consulting Services
                Cindy Joly and Ken Jurina – Top Draw

Layout and coordination of illustrations:
                Sincere thanks to Ian Holmes, Cindy Joly, and
                Cassandra Strumecki for their work organizing
                this book into its present format.

Editing and Proofreading: Ronald Garby – IPT PUBLISHING

Crane Lift Data: Procrane Engineering (A Division of Sterling Crane) for providing crane hoisting examples.

Concrete Drawings: Bruce Healy P.Eng. (Structural Design Instructor - Northern Alberta Institute of Technology) for providing sample drawings and text for this section.

ABOUT THE AUTHOR

Grant E. Jacobs: Adult Education Diploma - University of Alberta, has over thirty years experience in industrial fabrication and construction. This includes working as a journeyman boilermaker, structural steel plate fitter and welder, construction and maintenance supervision and management, instruction of several apprenticeship programs and seminars concerning various topics. He was Assistant Program Head of Steel Construction and Hoisting Trades, Northern Alberta Institute of Technology. His current position is National Training Coordinator (Canada) for the Boilermakers Joint Training Trust Fund.

METRIC CONTENT

This publication is primarily designed for Canada and the United States. Canada has adopted the Metric system, although the inch-foot system is still extensively used in some applications. The inch-foot system is most often used in the United States, with the Metric system being widely used in certain industries. However, the degree of use is not consistent in either country. The application of Metric units to the wide range of blueprint use varies widely, as some structures and components are designed and built using the Metric system only, or the inch-foot system only, while others may have a combination of both. Individuals performing specific tasks requiring blueprints will have their own preferences, however, being able to interpret drawings in either system will certainly be an advantage. Therefore example drawings using both the Metric and the inch-foot systems are shown.

TABLE OF CONTENTS

i

SECTION ONE

BASIC BLUEPRINT THEORY

Types of Drawings

This section is intended to give the reader a familiarity with drawings used for fabrication, construction or installation projects, and the purpose for each.

Architectural Drawings

Architectural drawings are the first set of drawings to be made for most projects. When there is a need to have an office complex built, an architectural firm is engaged to design a structure that will meet the customer's requirements, look good in its surroundings, and meet all building codes to make it safe for the occupants. The architect will assess the client's needs and based on their budget, will start the designing process. Architectural drawings show the building elevations and general floor plans. After the client has chosen the best design, the engineers will begin the process of designing the structure from an engineering perspective.

Engineering Drawings

The engineering drawings will be used to design the building's skeleton structure and mechanical systems including electrical, ventilation, plumbing, and other related systems. These drawings will be used to tender the project to firms who will submit bids. Using a building as an example of how this process might work if the building skeleton structure was made of steel, companies who fabricate structural steel buildings would bid on the job using the engineering drawings of the building's structure. In most cases these engineering drawings could not be used by the companies to fabricate the steel, but would give them the necessary information to be able to estimate the amount of steel required, the size of the beams and columns, and other related steel work.

After one of the bidding steel fabricating companies is awarded the job, they will then develop, from the engineering drawings of the building, another set of drawings which are commonly called shop or fabrication drawings.

This same process will be used by all the various companies who bid on the other building systems, such as the plumbing, electrical, heating and ventilation.

Shop Drawings

Shop drawings or fabrication drawings (again using the building's steel frame as an example), will give the tradesperson the necessary information to select the steel from stock and fabricate the beams, columns, stairs and other steel required to complete the skeleton frame of the building. The information contained on these shop drawings give the size of the beams, their lengths, details for connections, and the piece mark number and job number. After the steel is fabricated it will be shipped to the site for erection. Generally, on larger steel buildings, erection drawings are used to position the steel components in their proper location.

Erection Drawings

When the steel arrives on site it will have to be erected into position. Erection drawings are drawn so that the site erecting crew can locate the steel to its correct place. The shop drawings would have included a mark number for each fabricated steel member. This mark number would have been placed on the steel component before it left the shop. This same number is also on the erection drawing and is now used to locate the steel member in its correct position.

This allows the building to be assembled like a jigsaw puzzle. If everyone has done their job correctly, and quality control personnel have been checking for errors and having them corrected, the erection of the building will go ahead very smoothly.

Other components of the building are designed much the same way as the steel structure, although not much prefabrication for the electrical is done in a shop, as most of the electrical work will be started and completed on site.

Each of the building systems are completed in the same way until the building is ready for occupancy.

Assembly Drawings

Assembly drawings are used to show parts of an object and how they fit together in their assembled position. Each part is identified by an item number enclosed in a circle. These item numbers are referenced to a parts list. Assembly drawings are not commonly used in the construction industry, however they may be included with parts needed in the overall project.

Alphabet of Lines

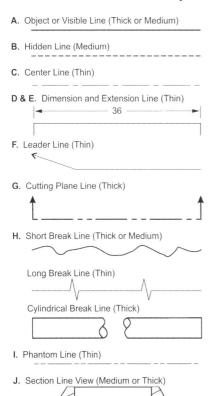

A. Object or Visible Line (Thick or Medium)

B. Hidden Line (Medium)

C. Center Line (Thin)

D & E. Dimension and Extension Line (Thin)
36

F. Leader Line (Thin)

G. Cutting Plane Line (Thick)

H. Short Break Line (Thick or Medium)

Long Break Line (Thin)

Cylindrical Break Line (Thick)

I. Phantom Line (Thin)

J. Section Line View (Medium or Thick)

Illustration #1-1 — Line Description & Function

Approximately ten types of lines are commonly used to develop a drawing. These lines are often referred to as the 'alphabet of lines'.

Each line serves a particular purpose and is used to show such things as the object drawn, surfaces which are hidden from the viewers sight, the geometrical center of the object, and dimension lines of the object. An explanation and an example of each type of line is shown in illustration #1-1. These lines are drawn on prints using various line weights and shades for clarity purposes. No explanation of line weights will be shown in this book. If the readers would like more information about this topic, they should consult a drafting textbook.

Visible Lines

The most common line is the visible line. It is also called the object line. Visible lines are drawn as wide continuous lines and are used to represent all edges and surfaces of the object being drawn. See illustration #1-1A.

Hidden Lines

Hidden lines are used to represent surfaces, edges, or features that are concealed by part of the object, or interior details which cannot be seen by the observer from the outside of the object. Hidden lines are drawn as a series of consecutive, short, medium-weight dashes, approximately $1/8$ in. (3 mm) in length, and are most often used when their presence would help clarify the view. The use of hidden lines will often be omitted if they clutter the drawing and serve no useful purpose. Hidden lines are commonly used to illustrate the thickness of a part, holes, countersunk holes, interior threads and other details that will help the viewer interpret the drawing. See illustration #1-1B.

Center Lines

Center lines are used to designate the geometrical center of holes, circles, arcs, or symmetrical objects. They are drawn as a light-weight line made up of a series of long and short dashes approximately $3/4$ in. (20mm) in length for the long dash and $1/8$" to $1/4$ in. (3 mm to 6 mm) in length for the short dash. The symbol used for centerline ($\cent$) is sometimes drawn either on the line or beside it. See illustration #1-1C.

Dimension Lines

Dimension lines are used to show direction of a dimensional value. The dimension line is drawn as a thin, solid, light weight line that is interrupted (usually in the middle) for the insertion of a dimension. The terminal points of the dimension line are most often shown with arrowheads on each end. See illustration #1-1D.

Extension Lines

The extension line extends down from the object's edges or surfaces. It is drawn as a thin light-weight continuous line about $1/4$ in. (6 mm) in length. The purpose of the extension line is to refer the dimension value and dimension line back to the object. The extension line is drawn so that it does not touch the object's edge, and accurately lines up with the edge or surface it extends down from. See illustration #1-1E, depicting the combined use of the dimension line and extension line.

Leader Lines

Leader lines are used to relate to a feature on a drawing requiring a reference note, for example the stated diameter of a circle, or the radius of an arc. They are drawn as a solid light-weight line, either straight or bent and ending with a dot or an arrowhead pointing to the surface the note refers to. See illustration #1-1F.

Cutting Plane & Viewing Lines

Cutting plane lines are used to locate the exact plane of the section where an object will be imagined to be cut, or when the draftsperson wants to indicate that another view of the object will be shown. When this line is used to indicate the location of a section view it is called the cutting plane line. When it is used to indicate another view of an alternate surface of the object, but does not cut through the object, the line is called a viewing line. Cutting plane lines are commonly drawn as a thick long dash, followed by two short dashes, then repeated. The ends of the line will be bent 90°, and terminated with arrowheads. The arrows on the line ends indicate the direction in which the section is observed. See illustration #1-1G.

Break Lines

Break lines are used to 'break out' a section for purposes of clarity, or to eliminate unimportant sections, therefore allowing the important portions to be drawn to a larger scale. There are three types of break lines, called short break line, long break line, and cylindrical break line. Short break lines are often drawn as fine, ragged lines done freehand. See illustration #1-1H.

Phantom Lines

The phantom line is used to indicate an alternate position, such as the open or closed position of a handle, a door, or a moving part. The phantom line is often used to indicate the location of an existing part or object in relationship to the new one, or to indicate the repeated detail of an object or part when it is not necessary for clarity purposes to draw it in. See illustration #1-1I.

Section Lines

Section lines or section lining is used to give tone to sectioned surfaces. Section lines are most often drawn as thin parallel lines at an angle of approximately 45° to the principal surfaces or axis of the part. See illustration #1-1J. Different section lining denotes the conventional symbol of the material being cut. Different symbols are used to represent different materials including wood, concrete or steel, to name a few.

Note: In practice, draftpersons use each of these lines to develop a drawing. For hand drawn prints the styles will vary and therefore the lines or the use of the lines will vary as well. With electronic drafting, these lines, symbols and arrowheads will vary somewhat from program to program.

Symbols and Abbreviations Used on Drawings

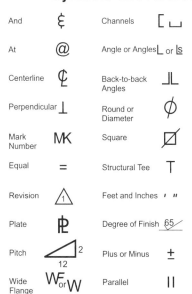

Symbols and abbreviations are used on drawings to save time and conserve space. Abbreviations are used extensively in the bill of materials to describe the different materials and parts that will be used to make the object as specified on the drawing. As well as the bill of materials, symbols and abbreviations are used in the drawing notes, the revision chart, the specifications, and title block of the drawing. The reader of the drawing must be able to comprehend the symbols and abbreviations used, or difficulty may be experienced in understanding the drawing. Some of the more common symbols are shown in illustration #1-2.

Illustration #1-2 — Common Symbols

List of Abbreviations

Abbreviations are commonly used on drawings to help simplify a drawing and conserve space, for example, in the bill of materials. If all the information about the material was written out in its full form, the bill of materials would be two to three times larger than necessary.

Table #1 is a comprehensive list of abbreviations that are used on drawings. Each trade will have specific abbreviations from this list. Some abbreviations will be widely used, while others will be less frequently used.

List of Abbreviations

AB	Anchor Bolt		CWB	Canadian Welding Burcau
ABT	About		CPLG	Coupling
AISI	American Iron and Steel Institute		CS	Carbon Steel
			C/W	Complete with, comes with
ANSI	American National Standards Institute		CYL	Cylinder
AUX	Auxillary		DIA	Diameter
AVG	Average		DIAG	Diagonal
ASME	American Society of Mechanical Engineers		DIM	Dimension
			DO	Ditto or Same
ASTM	American Society for Testing Materials		DWG	Drawing
API	American Petroleum Institute		EA	Each
			EL or ELEV	Elevation
BB or B/B	Back to Back		EST	Estimate
BC	Bolt Circle		EXP	Expansion
BBE	Bevel Both Ends		EXT	External
BCD	Bolt Circle Diameter		ELL	Elbow
BOE	Bevel One End		E to E	End to End
BE	Both Ends			Edge to Edge
BL	Baseline or Bendline			
BM	Beam/Bench Mark		F/F	Face to Face
B/M	Bill of Material		FF	Flat Face
Btm	Bottom		FLG	Flange
BP	Base Plate		FS	Far Side
B/P	Blueprint		FW	Fillet Weld
BLD	Blind		F & D	Flanged and Dished
C/C	Center to Center		Ga	Gauge, Gage
CA	Corrosion Allowance		Galv	Galvanized
COL	Column		GDR/GIRD	Girder
CONN	Connection		GOSL	Gauge Outstanding Leg
CSA	Canadian Standards Association			
			HD	Head
CSK	Countersink		HVY	Heavy
CuFt	Cubic Feet			

Table #1 — List of Abbreviations

HH	Hex Head		OSL	Outstanding Leg, Protruding Leg
HR	Hot Rolled		O/O	Out to Out
HT	Heat Treatment		OPP	Opposite
HLS	Holes		OPPH	Opposite Hand
HSS	Hollow Structural Steel or High Speed Steel			
			PAT	Pattern
ID	Inside Diameter		PBE	Plain Both Ends
IN	Inches		PCS	Pieces
INT	Internal		POE	Plain One End
INSP	Inspection		PSI	Pounds per Square Inch
INCL	Include, Inclusive		PROJ	Project or Projection
ISO	Int. Standards Organization			
			RD	Running Dimension
KP	Kick Plate		R or RAD	Radius
			RD	Round
LH	Left Hand		REF	Reference
LAT	Lateral		RP	Reference Point
LR	Long Radius		REQ'D	Required
LOA	Length Overall		REV	Revision
LG	Long		REPAD	Reinforcing Pad
LWN	Long Weld Neck		RF	Raised Face
			RH	Right Hand
MB	Machine Bolt			
MS	Mild Steel		S or SCH	Schedule
MW	Man Way		SI	Int. System of Units
MIN	Minimum		SPA	Spacing, Spaces
MAX	Maximum		SPECS	Specifications
MAT'L	Material		SPL	Splice
MISC	Miscellaneous		SQ	Square
			SE	Semi-elliptical
NC	National Coarse		SF	Straight Flange
NF	National Fine		SM	Seam
NL	Nosing Line		SMLS	Seamless
NS	Near Side		S/S	Seam to Seam
NO	Number		SO	Slip On
NOM	Nominal		SEC	Section
NTS	Not to Scale		STR	Straddle, Straight
NPS	Nominal Pipe Size		SR	Short Radius
NPT	National Pipe Thread		STD	Standard
			SS	Stainless Steel, Shop Stock
O/C	On Center		SYM	Symmetrical
OA	Overall			
OD	Outside Diameter			
OR	Outside Radius			

Table #1 — List of Abbreviations con't.

T	Top			
T & B	Top and Bottom		VERT	Vertical
T & C	Threaded and Coupled		WD	Working Drawing
THD	Threaded or Thread		WL	Working Line
TBE	Threaded Both Ends		WP	Working Point
TOE	Thread One End			or Wear Plate
THK	Thick		WT	Weight
TOL	Tolerance		W	Wide Flange
TOC	Top of Concrete		WN	Weld Neck
TOS	Top of Steel		W/O	Without
TS	Tube Sheet			
TYP	Typical		XH	Extra Heavy
T/T	Tan to Tan		XXH	Double Extra Heavy
			XS	Extra Strong
U/N	Unless Noted		XXS	Double Extra Strong

Table #1 — List of Abbreviations con't.

Dimensioning Systems Used on Drawings

Probably the most important information contained on a drawing are the dimensions of the various components. The dimensions used on a drawing indicate the size of the object and location of its various parts or components. Standard drafting practices help keep consistency in the dimensioning of drawings. When followed, they make it easier to read and interpret what the draftsperson has listed for dimensions. However, it should be understood that each draftsperson develops their own style of printing. These variations in style can sometimes be confusing. Thus, computerized drafting programs are being used more and more with resulting increased consistency.

Dimensions are placed on a drawing by using a system which incorporates extension lines, dimension lines, leader lines, and arrowheads (see Alphabet of Lines, in this section, for an explanation).

Unidirectional System of Dimensioning

The unidirectional system of dimensioning, shown in illustration #1-3A, results in all the dimensions on a drawing being oriented or read from left to right, and placed in the horizontal position. The unidirectional system is the preferred system of showing dimensions because it is easier to read for the person viewing the drawing.

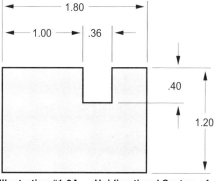

Illustration #1-3A — Unidirectional System of Dimensioning

Symbols/Dimensioning Systems 9

Aligned System of Dimensioning

In the aligned system, the dimensions are placed on the drawing from the bottom or right side of the print. The dimensions are aligned or written so that they are oriented in the direction the dimension lines are running. This results in dimensions being either horizontal, vertical, or at an angle. As a result it is slightly more difficult to read the dimension, although interpretation does not present any problem. See illustration #1-3B.

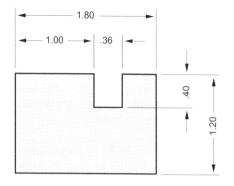

Illustration #1-3B — Aligned System of Dimensioning

General Guidelines for Dimensioning

Some general guidelines for dimensioning a drawing will help present the drawing measurements in a way which eliminates confusion for the reader. Each drawing must be dimensioned according to its individual requirements, as what is acceptable in one situation may not work in another. Some general guidelines will help eliminate confusion.

• Place dimensions so the reader will not have difficulty determining which surface or edge is being defined.

• Do not place dimensions too close to the edge being defined. Keep a distance of about $3/8$ in. (9 mm) from the objects surface. See illustration #1-4.

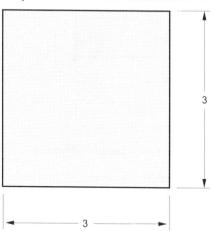

Illustration #1-4 — Dimensions Away From Edge

• Space dimensions evenly, as this gives the drawing a neat appearance and makes it easier to read. See illustration #1-5.

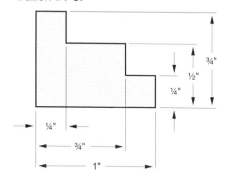

Illustration #1-5 — Space Dimensions Evenly

• Avoid using different units of measure. Dimensions should be in either metric or the inch-foot system of measure. Don't mix fractions and decimal dimensions unless it is necessary for a closer tolerance. See illustration #1-6.

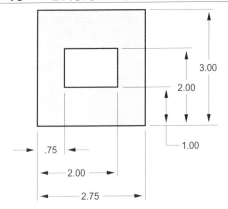

Illustration #1-6 — Decimal Dimensions

- Use either the unidirectional or the aligned system, not both.
- Avoid running extension lines or dimension lines through other extension or dimension lines. See illustration #1-7.

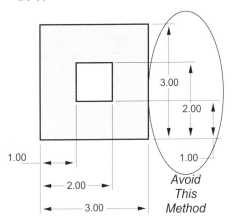

Illustration #1-7 — Extension/Dimension Lines

- Always include overall dimensions such as length, width, and height on objects. Do not make it necessary for the reader to add or subtract dimensions to obtain basic measurements.
- Always indicate the size of a hole by specifying its diameter. Curves and arcs are specified by indicating their radius. See illustration #1-8.

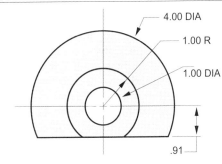

Illustration #1-8 — Extension/Dimension Lines

Linear Units of Measurement

Construction drawings and shop drawings are dimensioned using either the metric or the inch-foot system of dimensions. See illustration #1-9.

With the metric system, the unit of measurement commonly used is millimeters, and with the inch-foot system the unit of measurement is inches, or feet and inches.

It is not unusual to have large number values when using millimeters to dimension a drawing. It is standard practice to avoid the use of a comma to separate groups of three numbers. The number 14065 would be shown as 14 065, not 14,065, and the abbreviation for millimeters (mm) would not be used. Examples of metric measurements are shown in illustration #1-9A.

It is standard practice for shop drawings or construction drawings dimensioned using the inch-foot system to use inches, or the feet and inch format. Dimensions under 12 feet are normally written in inch and fractional measurement (see illustration #1-9B), while dimensions greater than 12 feet are written in feet and inches (see illustration #1-9C), with parts of an inch given as common fractions. It is preferred to use a dash to separate the feet and inches, and if no inch value is needed, a '0' is placed after the dash in the inch location.

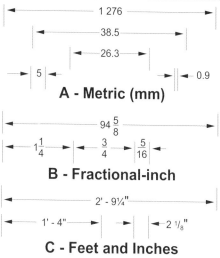

A - Metric (mm)

B - Fractional-inch

C - Feet and Inches

Illustration #1-9 — Dimensioning Systems

Decimal Dimensions

Other types of measurements are often needed to dimension blueprints. For example, if a part requires a higher tolerance (such as a drilled and reamed hole), then the decimal-inch system may be used. Decimal dimensions are expressed on blueprints in hundredths of an inch (.01"), thousands of an inch (.001"), or ten thousands of an inch (.0001").

Blueprints seldom require this level of tolerance for the heavy construction trades.

Angular Dimensions

The size of an angle is expressed on a blueprint in terms of degrees. For example, an angle can be shown as 30, 45, or 60 degrees. Degrees can be further broken down into minutes and seconds, 60' (minutes) to a degree, and 60" (seconds) to a minute. However, there is very little requirement for this tolerance on shop or construction drawings.

Angles for weld bevels are normally shown in degrees. In many instances the degree of a weld bevel is included in the welding symbol and is not shown otherwise on the drawing.

When a surface has a corner cut at an angle, the degree of the corner angle is shown by using a circular dimension line drawn with a compass. The compass point is located at the vertex of the angle, as shown in illustration #1-10A. Sometimes the angle is not shown in degrees but is indicated by using linear dimensions, resulting in the correct angle being formed. This method of using measurements is easier than using degrees to lay out angled corners. See illustration #1-10B.

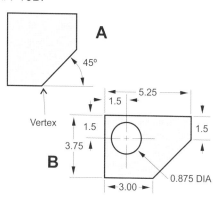

Illustration #1-10 — Angular Dimensions

Dimension Tolerances

Tolerance is the permissible variation in the size of a part. Without a tolerance specification there would be no room for small variations to occur, which are essentially inherent in any type of manufacturing, especially with items that are welded. The natural expansion and contraction resulting from joining steel components by welding is difficult to predict accurately every time. Therefore dimensional tolerances allow for variations to occur during fabrication. Tolerance also helps keep the cost of constructing an item in line. If a carpenter were required to frame a house to within $1/16$ of an inch or within 1 mm, the cost of construction would be much higher. The tolerance allowed on an item takes into consideration the manufacturing capabilities, customer requirements, usage requirements, material properties, and cost constraints.

Tolerance is usually specified as a maximum (upper limit) and a minimum (lower limit). The tolerance of a part is commonly included in with the dimension and most often stated as a plus/minus value. For example a dimension could be stated as 10' - 3 $3/4$" ($\pm 1/8$"). The tradesperson would know they have a variation limit of 10' - 3 $5/8$" to 10' - 3 $7/8$". Tolerance values for inch-decimal dimensions are stated as a plus/minus value in tens, hundreds, or thousands of an inch. For example 2.5 in. $\pm$ .010. If metric dimensions are used, then the plus/minus tolerance is stated in millimeters and commonly placed beside the dimension.

Tolerances for angular dimensions are stated as a plus/minus value expressed in degrees, degrees and minutes, or degrees, minutes and seconds, depending on the required accuracy.

An example would be a weld bevel of 30 degrees. It could have a tolerance of 2 degrees with little effect on the finished product. The tolerance could then be stated as 30° ($\pm 2°$). Brackets around the tolerance make it easier to interpret.

If no tolerance value is shown on a drawing, this implies that a standard tolerance is to be used. Some trades or industries have a plus/minus tolerance that is practiced as the standard for that trade or industry.

Accumulative error is a term used to describe poor lay out practices that can occur when several small errors are compounded. A tolerance should never be included in a dimension when laying out. Always measure the exact dimension as stated on the drawing. If for instance, the tolerance on a job was ± 3 mm for overall dimensions, then the tradesperson could not allow 3 mm error on each dimension laid out. Such practice would result in a larger error than the overall tolerance of 3 mm.

Linear Dimensioning Systems

Linear dimensions are commonly shown on drawings by using one of three methods:
• Conventional dimensioning
• Baseline dimensioning
• Group dimensioning

Conventional Dimensioning

Conventional or standard dimensioning systems show the overall dimensions of the part or object. See illustration #1-11.

Some addition and subtraction of dimensions may be required to obtain location measurements and care must be taken not to make a mathematical mistake. For this reason it is common practice to use conventional dimensions along with baseline or group dimensioning systems.

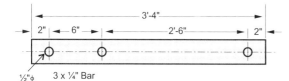

Illustration #1-11 — Standard Dimensioning

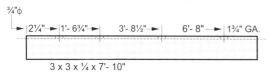

Illustration #1-12 — Baseline System

Baseline or Datum Dimensioning

With the baseline system all dimensions along the same plane originate from the same point or line. See illustration #1-12. This point or line is called the baseline, reference line, or datum line. This method of dimensioning is much more accurate and trouble-free than the conventional system. A reference point could be the end of a beam, a head to shell seam on a pressure vessel, or the tangent point of a pressure vessel's head. Other common reference points are the top of the base plate for a steel column or the top of a storage tank floor.

It is not necessary to add or subtract dimensions to establish any location points because the dimension can be read directly off the print. From illustration #1-12, note that each dimension is progressive, which means they are added up as they extend from the reference point.

Baseline dimensioning eliminates the possibility of accumulative errors, or tolerance buildup from one dimension to the next, and makes it easier for those who check the work.

This system is readily adapted to the requirements of computer controlled shop machines.

Common practice on prints using the baseline system is to use a short dimension line that touches the extension line. The dimension line uses only one arrow head running in the direction the dimension is going. The dimension is placed in front of the dimension line which originates from the fixed reference point. Another method, as shown in illustration #1-13, is to place the dimension on the extension line representing the location point and not use a dimension line at all.

The baseline system is easily recognizable to the tradesperson reading the drawing, however, it is common practice to indicate it in the drawing notes. A typical note may read, "All dimensions for clips, nozzles, or holes originate from a fixed reference point". This reference point will be indicated on the drawing.

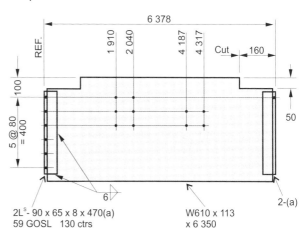

Illustration #1-13 — Baseline System

Running dimensions (R.D.) is another term used to define the baseline system often used on structural steel shop drawings. The reference point will be noted on the drawing and represents 0' - 0" for drawings dimensioned using inch-foot units of measure, and 0 mm for drawings using metric units of measure.

Group Dimensioning

The group system of dimensioning is most often used when repetitive locations points, such as the layout of holes on the same plane with the same center to center distance is needed (see illustration #1-14), or when clips or brackets are located on the same plane and are the same distance apart. Another example would be the distance between ladder rungs on steel ladders used to access manways or platforms on towers, stacks, and tanks.

6 SPA @ 4" = 2'- 0"

3"[4.1# x 2'- 8"

Illustration #1-14 — Group Dimensioning

To explain this type of dimensioning system, a steel ladder is used as an example. The dimensions for the ladder rungs start with the distance from the bottom of the ladder side rails to the first ladder rung. Then the group dimension would be placed between the first and last rungs of the ladder. For example, 10 spaces @ 12" c/c = 10' - 0". This group dimension states the number of spaces between the first and last rungs, then the center to center distance between each space (ladder rung), and finally the center to center or overall distance between the first and last rungs.

To complete the dimensions, the distance from the last ladder rung to the top of the side rails is shown.

The number of ladder rungs in the example is 11, and there are 10 spaces, as there is always one more rung (or hole) than there are spaces. To explain this think of a line of holes all on the same plane. If the group dimension stated: 6 spaces @ 8 in. c/c = 4 ft. - 0 in., there would be 7 holes along the line.

Group dimensions are easy to check for accuracy. Using the steel ladder as an example, the tradesperson can back-check the layout by using the overall distance stated in the dimension. If the distance between the first and last rungs measures 10 ft. - 0 in. after the spaces have been laid out, then it is correct. Or in the example of the holes, if the distance between the first and last hole is 4 ft. - 0 in., then the layout is correct.

Other Dimensioning Methods

Dimensioning Holes

Illustration #1-15 shows several methods used to dimension holes. Holes are dimensioned by indicating their diameter. This is because drill bits, punches, and boring tools are labeled or marked in terms of diameter.

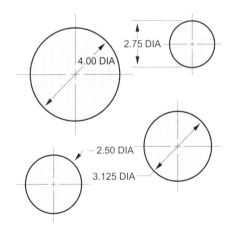

Illustration #1-15 — Dimensioning Holes

It is common practice to locate the center of the hole with a set of linear dimensions then specify the hole diameter. On drawings where all the hole diameters are the same, a note may be placed on the drawing indicating their size instead of dimensioning each hole. An example of a note is "all holes to be $^{13}/_{16}$ inches diameter unless otherwise noted". If there are holes that are different, then their noted size will be indicated on the drawing.

Bolt Circles

When a bolt hole pattern is circular and the hole center to center is the same distance apart (measured as the chord distance or arc distance between bolt hole centers) then the term bolt circle is used. The chord is the straight center to center distance. See illustration #1-16. The most frequent method used to dimension bolt circles is to state the bolt circle diameter, the number of holes required , and the bolt hole diameter (or drill size) of the holes. Usually the center of the bolt circle is also the center of the part, such as a circular plate or flange. When a bolt circle is not part of a circular part, the center of the bolt circle will be shown by using linear dimensions.

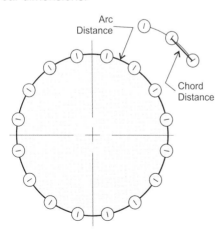

Illustration #1-16 — Bolt Circles

Curved and Radius Dimensions

The length of a radius is usually shown by using a leader line, and then indicating the length of the radius and placing an R beside it. See illustration #1-17. Linear dimensions will be used to indicate the location of the center point of the radius. The same is true for curved surfaces or arcs. The length of the radius required to form the correct curve or arc is given, and the location of the center of the radius is shown using linear dimensions.

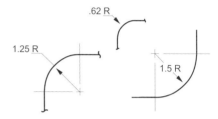

Illustration #1-17 — Dimensioning Arcs

It is common practice to indicate the diameter when a complete circle is required, and to indicate the radius for a partial circle. In the latter case the terminal point of the partial circle would have to be shown. This is done by stating the degrees of the partial circle. An example would be a 90 degree corner.

In some instances a surface which has a large curve, for example the camber in a long beam, cannot be shown by stating the radius of the curve. This would not be practical because of the length of the radius. These curves can be shown by dimensioning points which define the curved line. In this case equal distances are spaced out along a horizontal base line, then a vertical distance is indicated along each of these spaces. Each distance increases until the top of the curve is reached, then decreases to form the other half of the curve. An example of this system can be seen in illustration #1-18.

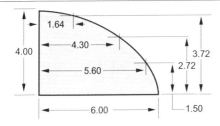

Illustration #1-18 — Dimensioning an
Irregular Curve

Bevel; Slope; Pitch

The terms bevel, slope and pitch are used to describe the incline or slope of a surface to either a horizontal or vertical plane. See illustration #1-19A for an example of an 8 to 12, and 12 to 8 slope.

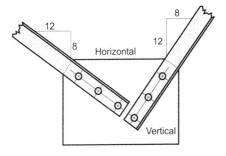

Illustration #1-19A — Bevel, Slope or Pitch

The angle or slope is stated as a rise-over-run ratio rather than in degrees. This is easier to layout for tradespeople, as they simply use a two foot (or metric) square to achieve the angle or slope. An example is the pitch of a house roof being 4 in 12, which means a 4 inch vertical rise for every 12 inches of horizontal run.

This method of indicating a sloped surface is based on the right triangle. A fixed dimension, such as 12 inches or 250 mm, is used as a rise or run. The other leg dimension will vary.

This method of expressing the slope of a surface is commonly used on structural drawings. See illustration #1-19B.

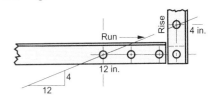

Illustration #1-19B — Rise and Run

Degree of Finish

The degree of finish on the surface of a part indicates its specified smoothness. To compare production surface finish, a cold rolled round bar has a much smoother surface than a hot rolled round bar. Most steel products produced by the hot rolled process will have an acceptable surface finish for many applications. A smoother surface can be obtained by machining or grinding the part when the end application so requires.

The degree of finish symbol, which looks like a check mark, is shown in illustration #1-20.

Illustration #1-20 — Degree of Finish Symbol

The symbol will be located on the surface to be finished, and the roughness stated as a number of micrometers or microinches. An example of a specific surface finish is the gasket surface of a pipe flange. To create a good gasket surface, the flange must be finished to within 125 and 250 microinches or 6.3 to 3.2 micrometers. A skilled operator using a hand oxy-fuel gas cutting torch will typically produce a surface finish of about 1000 to 800 microinches or less, depending on the operator.

Thread Designations on Drawings

Threaded fasteners are used in the joining of many fabricated items. Fasteners used in the heavy construction trades are machine screws, bolts, and stud bolts. The thread specifications (or thread call off), of fasteners is easier to understand with a familiarization of thread types and classes.

Types of Threads

Unified Standard Thread

The Unified Standard Thread System is common for fasteners used in North America. The Unified Standard Thread series consists of the following thread types:

- **Coarse Threads:** These threads are designated as NC. Coarse thread fasteners are used in general applications requiring rapid assembly and disassembly.
- **Fine Threads:** These threads are designated as NF. Fine thread fasteners are used for many automotive applications where greater resistance to vibration is required, or where greater holding strength is needed.
- **Extra-Fine Threads:** Another thread type in the Unified Standard Thread is the Extra-Fine Thread, designated as UNEF.

Metric Screw Threads

ISO metric threads are also used for general fastening purposes. ISO metric screw threads come in three standards: coarse, fine and constant pitch.

The coarse series is often used for industrial applications and is specified by stating the fastener diameter in millimeters. For example a common diameter used for structural steel bolting is 20 mm.

Screw Thread Nomenclature

Illustration #1-21 depicts the system of names used to describe the basic parts of a fastener. For the purpose of interpreting fasteners specified on drawings, only those terms most often associated with drawing practices are highlighted.

- **Internal Thread:** Threads produced by tapping nuts or drilled holes.
- **External Thread:** Threads produced on the outside surface of bolts or threads made by threading stock material with a threading die.
- **Major Diameter:** The major thread diameter, which is often referred to as the nominal diameter of the fastener, is the root to root distance for internal threads and the crest to crest distance for external threads.

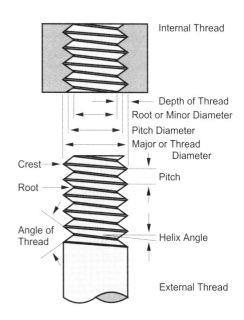

Illustration #1-21 — Screw Thread Nomenclature

- **Pitch:** Thread pitch is the center to center distance of the thread crests. When specifying inch designated fasteners, the thread pitch is expressed as the number of threads per inch. This is abbreviated as TPI. The pitch of a thread will determine if it is a fine or coarse thread fastener. Metric thread pitch is specified by stating the pitch in millimeters. A common pitch, center to center of the thread crests is 1.5 mm.
- **Length of Fastener:** The method of stating the length of bolt required to secure a grip is to specify the distance measured from the inside of the bolt head to the end of the threads. For stud bolts it is the total length of the fastener.

Thread Classes

Thread classes refers to the tolerance of the mating surfaces between two threaded parts. The unified inch thread is designated by a number followed by the capital letter 'A' for external threads and 'B' for internal threads; three classes of external threads are '1A', '2A', and '3A'; and three classes of internal threads are '1B', '2B', and '3B'. The most common tolerance is '2A' and '2B'.

For ISO metric threads the tolerance grade is designated by numerals 3 through 9 for external threads and 4 through 8 for internal threads.

It should be noted that these tolerances are not usually included on the drawing when specifying the size and length of the fastener.

Metric Thread Designation

To simplify metric thread designation it is standard practice to include only the diameter, pitch and length of the fastener. Thus a bolt with a 12 mm diameter, a pitch of 1.75 and a length of 75 mm would be specified as M12 x 1.75 x 75. In many cases the pitch is excluded and only M12 x 75 would be shown.

Inch Thread Designation

With the inch thread designation, it is standard practice to include only the diameter, pitch and length. A bolt which is 3/4 of an inch in diameter with 10 TPI and is 3 inches long, would be indicated as ¾ - 10 UNC - 3. In some cases the pitch is excluded in the designation and only ¾ - 3 is shown.

Thread Representation

Internal and external threads and threaded parts are represented on a drawing by using one of three methods. These are: detailed representation, schematic representation, and simplified representation.

A - Detailed Representation

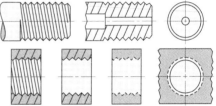

B - Schematic Representation

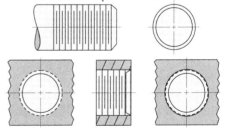

C - Simplified Representation

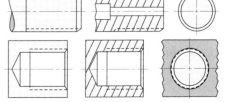

Illustration #1-22 — Thread Representation

- *Detailed representation* is a close approximation of the actual appearance of the fastener. See illustration #1-22A.
- *Schematic representation* uses staggered lines which represent the crests and the roots of the fastener. This is easier to draw than detailed. See illustration #1-22B.

- *Simplified representation* is the easiest of the three to draw. See illustration #1-22C.

These representations are not used to designate fasteners on drawings unless there is a special need to show them. It is common practice to list the quantity, diameter, pitch, and length of fasteners in the bill of materials of the drawing.

Welding Symbols

Welding symbols are used on drawings that require parts to be joined by welding. The welding symbol is made up of lines and symbols that convey the required information from the designer to the welder. Welding symbols have sometimes been described as a universal language, which means it is a standardized system that anyone can understand if they know how to interpret the symbols.

Welding Terminology

In order to better understand welding symbols it is helpful to have some familiarity with terms used in welding. Many of these terms define the type of joint preparation and welding that the symbol will describe.

Welding is the process of joining two pieces of metal together by fusion so that they can withstand the imposed designed loads.

Gas welding consists of joining metal by melting the two weld edges with the heat of a gas flame. The addition of a filler wire is used to add molten metal to the weld pool to maintain full joint thickness. The wire is also melted by the heat of the flame.

Arc welding is similar to gas welding because the two weld edges are joined by fusion, the difference being that the heat is created by an electric arc.

Similar to gas welding, a filler wire is used to fill the joint, however, the wire may be in the form of either a flux coated electrode or a bare wire continuously fed into the molten puddle by an automatic process.

Symbols describe the various welds used for joining metals for both the gas welding and arc welding processes.

As well as symbols, information contained in the completed welding symbol describes the actual design of the joint and how it is to be prepared.

A brief review of welding terms will make it easier to understand the requirements of the welding symbols presented on drawings, as shown in illustration #1-23.

- *Base Metal:* The metal to be welded. It is often called parent metal.
- *Backing:* A strip of metal placed at the root of a weld joint to support the molten weld metal. Also called a back-up bar, backing strip, or welding ring in the case of pipe joints.
- *Back Weld:* A weld deposited from the root (back) side of the joint.
- *Bead:* Narrow weld or layers of weld beads deposited on the base metal.
- *Bevel Angle:* The angle at which the edge of a plate (base metal) is to be prepared. This is normally 30° for plate joints and 37½° for pipe joints.
- *Fillet Weld:* A triangular weld joining two pieces of metal positioned to form a perpendicular weld joint.

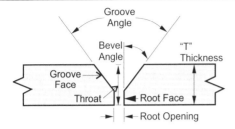

Groove Weld Preparation

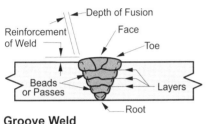

Groove Weld

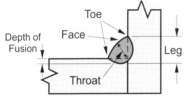

Fillet Weld

Illustration #1-23 — Groove & Fillet Weld Terms

- *Intermittent Welding:* A technique where the continuity of a weld is broken by staggering sections of the weld along the seam. These sections of weld are referred to as weld increments.
- *Groove Angle:* Is the included angle of two beveled members to be joined by welding. This is normally 60° for plate preparations (2 times the 30° plate bevel).
- *Groove Welds:* Types of welds made between two members to be joined.
- *Root Face:* Unbeveled portion of a joint member at the root of the joint. This is also referred to as the land.

- *Root Opening or Root Gap:* The separation at the base of the joint between members to be joined.
- *Weld Face:* The top portion of the weld or exposed surface.
- *Weld Joint:* Position of two or more weld members to be joined.
- *Weld Leg:* Distance from the root of a weld to the toe. This term is used to describe the leg size of fillet welds.
- *Weld Size:* The thickness of the weld from the face to the root of the weld. This is described as the throat of a weld.
- *Weld Toe:* The point at which the face of the weld joins the parts being welded.
- *Flange Weld:* A weld made on the edges of two members, one of which is flanged. See illustration #1-24.

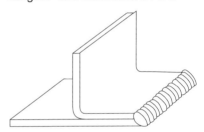

Illustration #1-24 — Flange Weld

Basic Weld Types

For ease of interpreting weld symbols it is helpful to understand the basic types of welds. Essentially most welds fall into one of the following categories: these are butt welds, fillet welds, plug or slot welds, and surfacing welds. See illustration #1-25.

Fillet welds are used to join parts that are essentially 90° to each other. It should be noted that welding codes specify the degrees at which a joint can be out of perpendicular and still be classified as a fillet weld. The most common types of joints for fillet welds are: tee joint, corner joint, and lap joint.

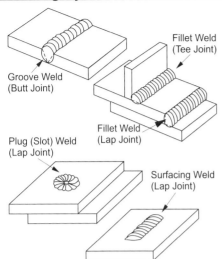

Groove Weld
(Butt Joint)

Fillet Weld
(Tee Joint)

Fillet Weld
(Lap Joint)

Plug (Slot) Weld
(Lap Joint)

Surfacing Weld
(Lap Joint)

Illustration #1-25 — Basic Welds

Butt welds or groove welds are used
to join two parts or members together,
such as plate, tube, and pipe. There are
several basic groove weld types: square
groove, bevel groove, vee groove,
J-groove and U-groove welds. With the
exception of the square groove, which requires no bevel, the parts to be joined will
have the edges prepared to a specified
bevel angle.

Plug or slot welds are used to join overlapping parts together. Welds of this type
are used when the necessary joint
strength can be achieved without the
joint being welded full length. This re-
duces the cost of welding and helps eliminate weld distortion. One of the
overlapping members will have round or
slotted holes.

The welding will be contained within
these holes or slots and will fuse the two
plates together.

Surfacing welds are used to build up a
surface's thickness or to overlay a
surface.

Basic Weld Joints

The weld types mentioned previously are
utilized on five basic kinds of weld joints,
as shown in illustration #1-26. They are:
butt, corner, lap, tee, and edge or flange.

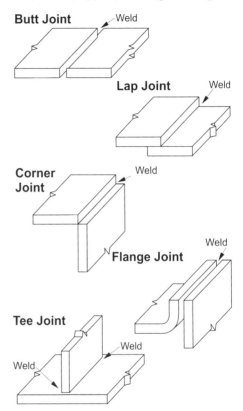

Butt Joint   Weld

Lap Joint   Weld

**Corner
Joint**   Weld

Flange Joint   Weld

Tee Joint

Weld

Weld

Illustration #1-26 — Basic Weld Joints

Basic Weld Symbols

Symbols are used in conjunction with the
welding symbol to identify each of the basic weld types. Illustration #1-27 shows
the symbols used to illustrate these
welds.

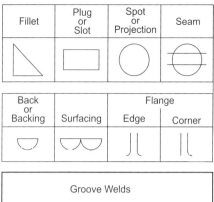

Fillet	Plug or Slot	Spot or Projection	Seam

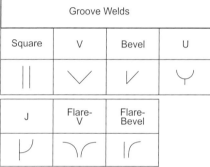

Back or Backing	Surfacing	Flange Edge	Corner

Groove Welds			
Square	V	Bevel	U

J	Flare-V	Flare-Bevel

Illustration #1-27 — Basic Symbols

Basic Welding Symbol

The main foundation of a welding symbol consists of a reference line with an arrow at one end. The tail of the welding symbol is used if additional data is required in the welding symbol. See illustration #1-28.

Illustration #1-28 — Welding Symbol Arrow

Note: It is customary for weld symbol standards to differentiate between the weld symbol and a welding symbol. Essentially the weld symbol is used to indicate the desired type of weld.

The welding symbol is the assembled symbol which includes the weld symbol and all other information necessary to prepare and weld the joint.

Illustration #1-29 shows each type of weld and the corresponding symbol used with the basic welding symbol.

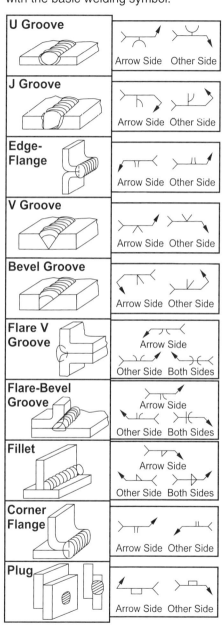

Illustration #1-29 — Types of Weld Symbols

Supplementary Symbols

Supplementary symbols are used in conjunction with basic weld symbols. See illustration #1-30. These symbols are used for such things as specifying welding all around the joint and field welds. The field weld symbol means that the assembly or part of it will not be welded until assembled on site (away from the shop).

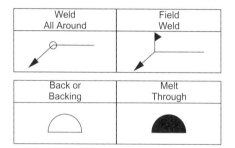

Weld All Around	Field Weld

Back or Backing	Melt Through

Contour		
Flush	Convex	Concave

Illustration #1-30 — Supplementary Symbols

The back weld symbol is used for full penetration welds that will be back gouged and filled as part of the welding procedure. If a full penetration weld is done from only one side of the joint, as is frequently the case for small diameter pipe, then the melt through symbol is used. The contour symbols indicate the required shape of the face of the weld after welding is completed.

Elements of a Welding Symbol

Illustration #1-31 shows an assembled welding symbol and the location of all of the information that can be included. Besides the basic weld symbol and supplementary symbols, other data including the size of welds, length and pitch of welds, degree of bevel for groove welds, root opening, and the effective throat of a weld may be added to the reference line of the symbol.

The standard location of the weld symbol and related data on a welding symbol is also shown in illustration #1-31. If the tail and the arrow are reversed, the information on the reference line remains in the same location. This standardization eliminates confusion on the part of the reader.

Information on the reference line is read from left to right. This is standard drafting practice.

By studying this illustration, you can become familiar with the location of data, for instance, where the size of a weld is shown, where the groove angle of a weld joint is indicated, and other data relating to the weld joint and welding requirements.

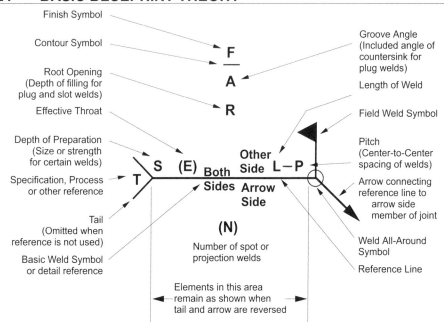

Finish Symbol

Contour Symbol

Root Opening
(Depth of filling for
plug and slot welds)

Effective Throat

Depth of Preparation
(Size or strength
for certain welds)

Specification, Process
or other reference

Tail
(Omitted when
reference is not used)

Basic Weld Symbol
or detail reference

Groove Angle
(Included angle of
countersink for
plug welds)

Length of Weld

Field Weld Symbol

Pitch
(Center-to-Center
spacing of welds)

Arrow connecting
reference line to
arrow side
member of joint

Weld All-Around
Symbol

Reference Line

F
A
R
S   (E)   Both   Other
T   Sides   Side   **L−P**
Arrow
Side

(N)
Number of spot or
projection welds

Elements in this area
◄── remain as shown when ──►
tail and arrow are reversed

Illustration #1-31 — Elements of a Welding Symbol

The direction of the arrow is not important, in that it can be on either the right or left side of the reference line and point up or down. The arrow side of the joint is always the side the arrow is pointing to, and the other side is always the opposite.

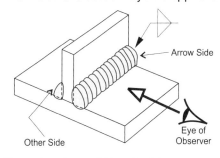

Arrow Side

Eye of
Observer

Other Side

Illustration #1-32 — Sides of a Joint

See illustration #1-32.

Basic Rules for Interpreting Welding Symbols

Location Of Weld Symbols

One of the essential requirements for interpreting welding symbols is the method used to indicate on which side of the joint the weld is to be made. The terms 'arrow side' and 'other side of the joint' are used to designate the side of the joint on which the weld is to be made.

The Arrow Side of the joint is the side that the arrowhead of the welding symbol is pointing to, or touching. On the welding symbol the arrow side designation is always indicated below or on the bottom of the reference line. See illustration #1-33A. This means that when any weld symbol, such as the symbol for fillet weld is shown on the bottom side of the reference line, it indicates a fillet weld to be made on the arrow head side of the joint.

The welder would then interpret the arrow side of the joint to be the side that the arrowhead of the welding symbol is pointing to.

The Other Side of the joint is the side opposite to which the arrowhead is pointing. Other side of the joint is indicated on the welding symbol by placing the weld symbol on the top side of the reference line. See illustration #1-33B.

When both sides of the joint are to be welded, as in the case of a fillet weld, then the fillet weld symbol would be placed on both sides of the reference line. The welder would interpret this to mean that both sides of the joint would require a fillet weld. See illustration #1-33C.

Illustration #1-33D indicates the welding symbol when welding is required on both sides of a solid member. However the drawing may be simplified by using only one welding symbol and another arrow from the reference line to the other joint, or the word *'typical'* may be included in the tail of the welding symbol.

Perpendicular Leg

For standardization, the fillet, bevel, J-groove, flare-bevel and corner-flange weld symbols are drawn with the perpendicular leg on the left side, regardless of whether the arrow points left or right. See illustration #1-34.

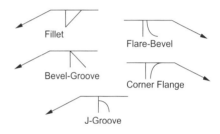

Illustration #1-34 — Perpendicular Leg on the Left

Fillet Welds

The Leg Size of fillet welds is shown to the left of the weld symbol and is expressed in fractions of an inch or millimeters. See illustration #1-35. If the fillet weld symbol appears on both sides of the reference line then both should be dimensioned. If the weld on the arrow side of the weld symbol is a different size than the weld on the other side, both will be dimensioned to indicate the difference.

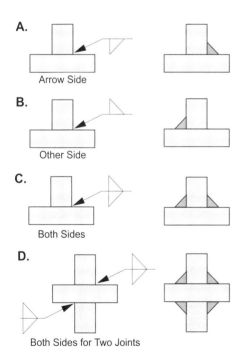

Illustration #1-33 — Weld Locations

Where a note appears on the drawing that specifies the size of the fillet welds, no dimensions are usually shown on the symbol unless their size is different than what appeared in the note.

Unequal leg fillet welds have their size placed to the left of the weld symbol and placed in parentheses. See illustration #1-35. It is common practice to indicate by the use of a drawing the orientation of the leg size for unequal leg fillet welds.

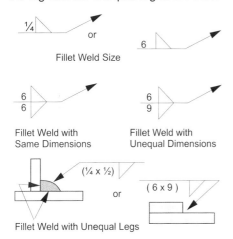

Illustration #1-35 — Size of Fillet Welds

The Length of the fillet weld increment is shown to the right of the weld symbol, except when the weld is to extend the full length of the joint. See illustration #1-36. For a full length weld, the length measurement is omitted. If the fillet weld does not extend the full length of the joint, then the starting point of the weld will be shown on the drawing and the length of the weld will be shown on the welding symbol.

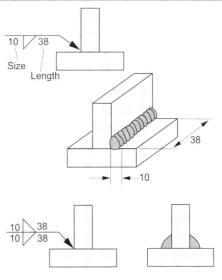

Illustration #1-36 — Length of Fillet Welds

Intermittent Fillet Welding

Intermittent welding is used when the strength of a joint does not require the whole joint to be welded.

Three methods of intermittent welding are:

- **Stitch Intermittent Welding:** This type of weld is used when only one side of the joint requires welding. See illustration #1-37A.
- **Chain Intermittent Welding:** This type of weld is used when intermittent welding is required on both sides of the joint. With chain intermittent welding the weld increments are placed opposite each other on both sides of the joint. See illustration #1-37B.
- **Staggered Intermittent Welding:** This type of weld is when the welds alternate on each side of the joint. The welds are not opposite each other but are offset. See illustration #1-37C.

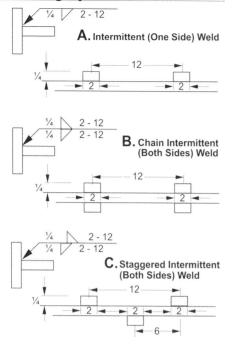

Illustration #1-37 — Intermittent Welds

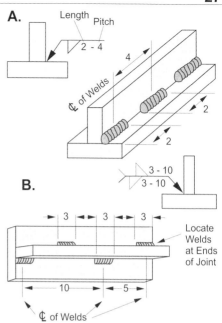

Illustration #1-38 — Length and Pitch of Intermittent Fillet Welds

The size and length of fillet welds are indicated in the same location on the welding symbol, but in the case of intermittent welding another dimension called pitch is shown to the right of the length measurement.

Pitch, as it relates to this type of fillet welding, is the center to center spacing between intermittent weld increments. Illustration #1-38A shows the pitch when one side is welded, and illustration #1-38B shows the pitch for staggered intermittent welding.

Groove Welds

The names of the various groove welds are as follows: square, vee, bevel, J-groove, U-groove, flare vee and flare bevel.

Groove welds are used when full penetration welds or full strength welds (effective throat) cannot be achieved without chamfering (beveling) the plate ends.

The symbol for the groove weld is located on the reference line in accordance with the usual arrow side, other side, or both side positioning.

The depth of preparation of groove welds is shown to the left of the groove weld symbol on the same side of the reference line. When no dimension is placed to the left of the symbol it indicates that the groove weld is to be prepared the full thickness of the joint.

The effective throat refers to the depth of root penetration or the actual material included and fused into the weld. This dimension is shown in parentheses and to the immediate left of the groove weld symbol. In cases where the depth of preparation and effective throat are shown together, the depth of preparation is located to the left of the effective throat size as shown in illustration #1-39.

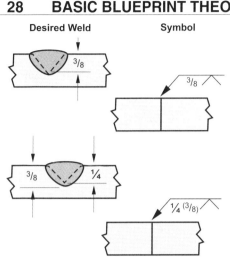

Illustration #1-39 — Dimensions Showing Groove Bevel Depth

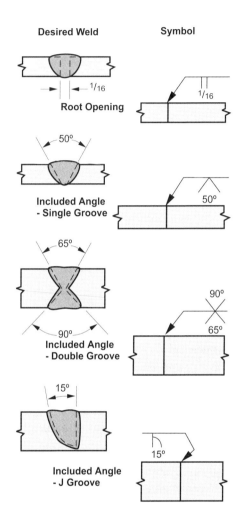

Illustration #1-40 — Root Opening and Included Angle for Groove Welds

The root face or land size is determined by subtracting the depth of preparation for the required groove weld from the actual thickness of the metal being prepared. For instance, if a $^1/_4$ inch (6 mm) bevel weld is indicated on the welding symbol and the metal thickness is $^3/_8$ inch (9 mm), then the land will be $^1/_8$ inch (3 mm) thick after the bevel is prepared.

The root opening or gap refers to the distance between the pieces to be welded, and is shown by placing the dimension inside the groove weld symbol. See illustration #1-40.

The bevel or groove angle is the angle formed by the members to be welded. This dimension is given in degrees and is placed just outside of the groove weld symbol. See illustration #1-40.

Welding Symbols

29

Broken Arrow Line
When using the bevel or J-groove weld symbol, the arrow line must have a definite break and point towards the member of the joint that is to be prepared, as shown in illustration #1-41. When it is obvious which member is to be prepared, the broken arrow line may be omitted.

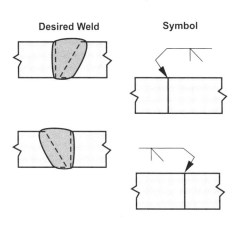

Desired Weld   **Symbol**

Illustration #1-41 — Break in Arrow Showing Member to be Beveled

Plug or Slot Welds
The same symbol is used for both plug and slot welds, the difference being that plug welds are round and slot welds are elongated. Their weld symbol is located on the reference line in accordance with the usual arrow side, other side or both side positioning.

The size of plug welds is shown to the left of the weld symbol using either fractions or millimeters. If the plug or slot will not be filled to the top of the opening then a dimension showing the depth of filling is placed inside the symbol.

The center to center spacing (pitch) between the plug or slot welds is placed to the right of the symbol, and the included angle of countersink (if any) will be shown below the symbol. See illustration #1-42.

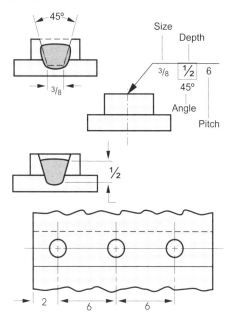

Illustration #1-42 — Dimensions for Plug Welds

To avoid confusion, slot welds are usually dimensioned using a special detail on the drawing, or by the use of a note.

Combined Weld Symbols
Combined weld symbols are used for joints that require more than one type of weld. An example would be a groove weld covered by a fillet weld for extra reinforcement. When this happens a symbol is used for each weld. See illustration #1-43. Standard dimensioning practices remain the same for each weld symbol.

Desired Weld   **Symbol**

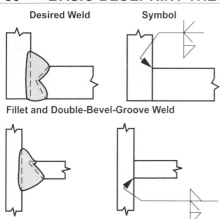

Fillet and Double-Bevel-Groove Weld

Single-Bevel-Groove and Double-Fillet Weld

Illustration #1-43 — Combined Weld Symbols

Use of Supplementary Symbols
Weld All Around

The weld all around symbol is indicated by an open circle placed where the arrow joins the reference line. See illustration #1-44.

Desired Weld   **Symbol**

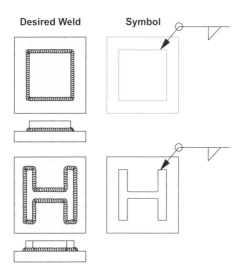

Illustration #1-44 — Weld-All-Around Symbol

Field Weld

The field weld symbol is indicated by a flag positioned where the arrow joins the reference line. See illustration #1-45.

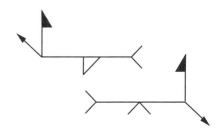

Illustration #1-45 — Field Weld Symbol

Contour Symbols

Contour symbols are used to indicate the desired shape of the weld face. The contour symbols most often used are: flush, convex, and concave. They are placed on top of the weld symbol to indicate the shape of the weld face.

Illustration #1-46A shows the contour shapes and illustration #1-46B shows the contour symbols.

Finish Symbols

Finish symbols are used in conjunction with the contour symbols as they indicate how the face of the weld is to be finished. If no finishing symbol is used, then the contour is achieved by welding only. Three typical finishing symbols are:

• **M** - the weld is to be finished by machining.
• **C** - the weld is to be finished by chipping.
• **G** - the weld is to be finished by grinding.

Illustration #1-46 shows some examples of the use of contour and finishing symbols.

A. Contour Shapes

Flush   Convex   Concave

B. Contour Symbols

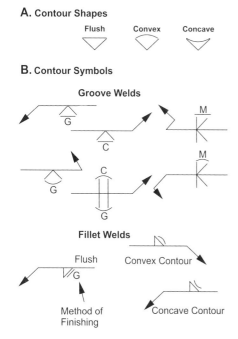

Illustration #1-46 — Contour & Finish Symbols

Back or Backing Welds

A back or backing weld refers to a weld made on the opposite side of a single groove weld. A half moon symbol is placed on the other side of the groove weld symbol. The height of reinforcement is the only dimension shown on the welding symbol for back welds. See illustration #1-47.

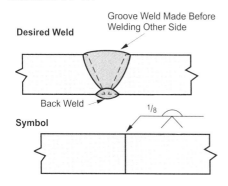

Illustration #1-47 — Back Weld Symbol

Melt Through Welds

A melt through weld indicates full joint penetration, as well as reinforcement on the root side of the joint, and will be completed by welding from one side of the joint only. This symbol is similar to the back weld symbol (half moon) except it is shaded, and is placed on the other side of the groove weld symbol. See illustration #1-48.

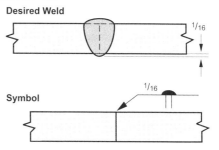

Illustration #1-48 — Melt-Thru Symbol

Surfacing Welds

Surfacing welds are used to overlay or build up a surface by using single or multiple pass welding. The depth of the weld overlay is indicated by placing the dimension to the left of the surface weld symbol. If the entire surface will not be built up, then the length of the weld and location of the area of the overlay will be shown on the drawing or a detail of the required weld area will be included on the drawing. See illustration #1-49.

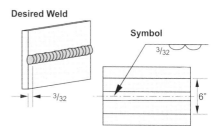

Illustration #1-49 — Surfacing Symbols

Types of Drawing Views

One-View Drawings

When drawing an object, occasionally only one view is necessary. The view would be of the object as seen looking from one direction at one of its surfaces. This view is not drawn in three-dimensional form. One-view drawings are often used when parts or objects are uniform in their other dimensions, such as circular flanges. In this case a view of the flange could be shown as seen looking directly at it. The outside and inside diameters of the flange could be easily dimensioned, as well as any bolt hole locations and their size. The thickness of the flange could be stated as a note. No other dimensional information would be necessary for fabrication.

Multiview Drawings

For clarification and ease of interpreting the actual shape of an object, multiview drawings are most often used for fabrication or construction drawings.

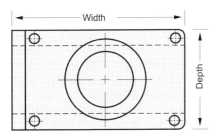

Illustration #1-50A — Top View Drawing Showing All Features

This type of drawing presents the object in two or more views when looking directly at it from a specific direction. See illustrations #1-50A, B and C for examples of three views of a drawing. This method is called the direct view method. With these types of drawings, a part is imagined as if it were held and moved or rotated in different positions to view each face of the object.

To illustrate this method, think of a toy car. Hold the car in your hand and view it at eye level looking at the front of the car. This would be how the car would appear on the drawing. It is a front view. Now rotate the car 90° so that you are looking at the top of the car. This is the top view and would be drawn as seen from the top.

Now rotate the car back into the front position, and then 90° clockwise so that you are looking at the driver's side.

This would be called the right hand side view and would be drawn as seen from this side. This process could be repeated for the left side, the back and the bottom. The number of views used will be determined by the complexity of the object being drawn. The views are organized in a systematic way so that the reader can develop a three-dimensional image of the object as a completed assembly. Each view is a true view either drawn full size or to scale, and therefore can be dimensioned accurately.

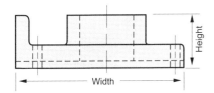

Illustration #1-50B — Side View Drawing Showing All Features

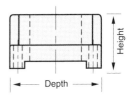

Illustration #1-50C — End View Drawing Showing All Features

Orthographic Projection

Another method of drawing that uses multiviews is called orthographic projection. The part is drawn as viewed from different directions looking at each face of the object, as shown in illustration #1-51A.

Three principal views are common with orthographic projection. These are: front view, top view, and right hand side view. The part to be drawn is imagined to be enclosed in a glass box and suspended in the middle of it, and each surface is projected onto the face of the glass box. See illustration #1-51B.

These sides of the imagined box can swing open as if they were on hinges. This is how the part would look when drawn using orthographic projection. See illustration #1-51C.

There are a number of ways orthographic projection can be drawn, as there are a number of ways to look at an object. However, the six normal views are: front, top, bottom, right side, left side, and rear. Illustration #1-51D shows these six views of the object.

Six views are not generally required because most objects can be completely defined in the three views previously mentioned, which are, front, top, and right side. These three correspond to height, width, and depth. Drafting conventions require these views to be placed on the drawing in a specific order, and any variance is an error.

The view alignment is important and is always consistent in orthographic projection. The top view, or plan view, is situated vertically over the front view. Situated to the right of the front view is the right side view. The views are labeled; front, top, bottom, right side, left side, and rear to avoid confusion. These views are aligned with, and interconnected to each other using vertical and horizontal projection lines, called construction lines, that are erased after the drawing is completed. At no time should the alignment of the views be altered, as this could cause confusion for the viewer.

The front view of the object is usually the first view drawn, then each view is taken at right angles to the front view. It is not a picture as observed in a three-dimensional drawing but a two dimensional representation which has given up perspective for the sake of technical accuracy. There is no attempt to picture the object, as each view presents only one face or piece of the total object. Orthographic views are dependent on each other for a complete depiction of the object. This is why it is so important to maintain the correct alignment of the views. In this manner the observer can put together the views, and develop a mental picture of the object. If the part being drawn has no natural front to it, one face of the part will be chosen to be the front, especially if it conveys some identifiable feature of the object.

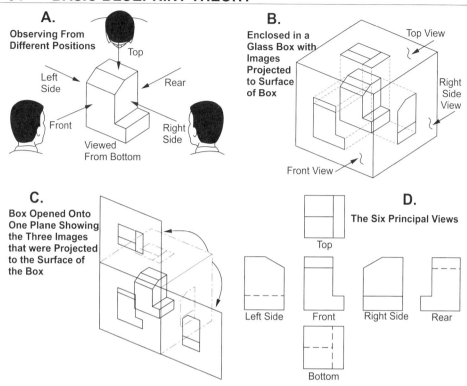

A.
Observing From Different Positions
Top
Left Side
Rear
Front
Right Side
Viewed From Bottom

B.
Enclosed in a Glass Box with Images Projected to Surface of Box
Top View
Right Side View
Front View

C.
Box Opened Onto One Plane Showing the Three Images that were Projected to the Surface of the Box

D.
The Six Principal Views
Top
Left Side   Front   Right Side   Rear
Bottom

Illustration #1-51 — Orthographic Projection

Advantages of Orthographic Projection

Most construction drawings will be developed using orthographic projection. Three-dimensional drawings make it easier for the viewer to envision the part; however, they are time consuming and difficult to draw. Some of the advantages of orthographic projection, as compared to three-dimensional drawings, are:

- They show all features of the object.
- They allow ample space for complete dimensioning.
- Each view is a true view either drawn to a scale or to full size.
- Distortion of scale or angle is eliminated.
- They are easier and quicker to draw.

Guidelines for Viewing in Orthographic Projection

When studying an object drawn in orthographic projection, certain procedures will be helpful in visualizing the object. Look at each of the views and note any projection, hole, or irregularity that might be included in another view, then look for these features in the other views. This will help develop a mental picture of the part. It is best to start by scanning the front view for shape description, and then move to another view, looking for features that describe the intersection of the same surfaces, as well as edges or lines coordinating with the front view.

If it is still difficult to visualize the object, then study one feature at a time in several views and begin to picture the shape of the object.

Try sketching the object by putting the views into a in three-dimensional form. In order to visualize an object, one combines features from its different surfaces or views. Once you have a mental picture of the object, it is usually much easier to proceed with the construction of it.

Often the visualization of the object drawn is not difficult because the viewer is familiar with it. If it is too difficult to sketch and visualization is still a problem, try drawing one view at a time until the shape becomes clearer.

Practical Exercises in Orthographic Projection

Using graph paper sketch the top, front, and right side view of the four blocks shown in illustration #1-52.

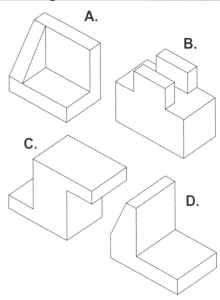

Illustration #1-52 — Third-Angle Orthographic Projection

Pictorial Drawings

A pictorial drawing gives the reader a three dimensional view of the object being shown. This allows the viewer to see the object in three-dimensional form, which makes it much easier to visualize the object as it would look when built. On some working drawings, a pictorial view of the object would be used to reveal information that would be difficult to show using only orthographic views. Other circumstances may require a pictorial drawing merely to supplement a major view.

With the aid of computer generated drawings, a pictorial view can be included on the drawing with little difficulty.

In fact, an increasing number of drawings are being produced which include this feature along with the orthographic views.

Three types of pictorial drawings, which are, isometric, oblique and perspective, are shown in illustration #1-53.

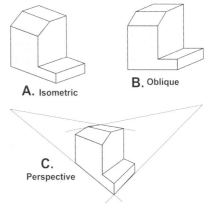

Illustration #1-53 — Pictorial Drawings

Isometric Drawings

Isometric drawings are one of the more common methods of developing pictorial drawings. This type of drawing is based on the concept of a cube with its three axis exposed in an angled position, which allows three sides to be shown. The height, width, and depth of the object can then be seen in one view, as shown in illustration #1-53A. One axis is a vertical line and the other two are sloped lines placed at 30° angles to a horizontal line. Often this is enough to dimension the object and to show other important information so that hidden lines are unnecessary.

These axis and all lines drawn parallel to them are drawn full size or scaled. This places the three dimensional view at angles which take full advantage of the equal foreshortening of all the sides of the object. No attempt is made to adjust the length of any line to improve the appearance of the drawing (e.g. provide perspective). Therefore all sides of the object appear proportional to the viewer because they are drawn to their actual size or scale.

Oblique Drawings

Oblique drawings are drawn so that the viewer can see three sides of the object with the most important side as the frontal plane or front view. The receding top and sides of the object are drawn with parallel oblique lines at an angle, commonly 30 or 45 degrees, to the horizontal plane of the drawing. See illustration #1-53B.

The front of the object appears similar to an orthographic view while the oblique lines provide the appearance of depth. These oblique sides are foreshortened, which allows the object drawn to look proportional to the viewer, otherwise oblique drawings would appear distorted.

For this reason it is not practical to dimension oblique drawings and therefore they are commonly used to create an illusion of three dimensions.

Perspective Drawings

The perspective method of showing an object in three-dimensional form gives the best representation of how the eye sees it, therefore perspective drawings look realistic to the viewer. The image is seen on the drawing similar to the way we would see it as viewed in a photograph. The reason for this is that the horizontal features receding from the observer appear to converge at a distant point. If the object is drawn at an angle the receding lines will disappear at two distant points called vanishing points. These vanishing points fall on the horizon line (more or less the same level as the observer's eye) thereby giving it perspective. See illustration #1-53C.

This type of drawing is generally unsatisfactory for showing technical information, as it is difficult to dimension because the sides of the object are not proportional. However, perspective drawings are useful for architectural presentations and construction display drawings. The viewer sees the object much the same as it would look after completion.

Guidelines for Interpreting Drawings

Interpreting drawings requires two principal elements, which are the ability to visualize, and the ability to interpret what is being drawn and written. Understanding how a drawing is designed gives the reader an idea of how the various views are coordinated. Knowing how to interpret the meaning of the various lines, symbols and abbreviations completes the task.

The drawing should be studied carefully before beginning any work. The reader should attempt to establish a visualization of what is being shown on the drawing and how it will be built. Mistakes can be made when the tradesperson does not take the time to become fully familiar with the drawing. Simple drawings should be studied as carefully as complicated ones, as it is easy to overlook details when one is familiar with the drawing, or type of drawing and is over confident with what has to be done. Just because one drawing appears to be similar to another, there may be an easy-to-miss detail that makes it different.

The following information is a guideline to follow each time a new drawing is observed:

- Look at the title block to familiarize yourself with the item being built and other information specified. The title block will sometimes contain design information (such as the overall size of the item) giving the tradesperson an idea of shop floor space or working area that will be required to built it.
- Read through the general notes on the drawing to familiarize yourself with any design or fabrication information.
- Look at the bill of materials and determine what items can be build as sub-assemblies to the main job.

- Familiarize yourself with the grades of material and quantities. Some items may be stored as standard stock while others may require a special order.
- Look through all of the design specifications to become familiar with any design criteria such as tolerances or other limitations in the design. Note any welding specifications or heat treatment requirements, and be familiar with any code specifications listed that you are unsure of.
- Familiarize yourself with the weights and size of components to determine hoisting capacities and special requirements for blocking and securing the item.
- Generally look over the drawing and look at welding symbols and bolting or fastening requirements. Look at the revision chart and familiarize yourself with any design changes made to date. Look for any seemingly obvious errors that may require checking or correction before fabrication of the item begins. If errors are found, they should be noted and the supervisor informed.
- Check the bill of materials and make a cut list specifying the correct grade of material, quantity and length. These can often be cut prior to the start of the job.
- If you are unclear about any details, check with your supervisor or the draftsperson to clarify before beginning.
- Make note of any detail which is to be done later, to avoid missing or forgetting to do them.
- As parts of the project are built, it is helpful to mark these off on the drawing to avoid any repeat work being done by another shift or crew.

Basic Layout of a Drawing

The layout of most drawings is similar in that the drawing format has some standard features or components for the convenience of interpreting the print, and being able to find or locate information needed to proceed with the job. A typical drawing format will include some or all of these features:

• Title block
• Bill of materials or material list
• Area where the job specifications are listed
• General notes
• Reference drawing list
• Revision chart

These drawing components are common for some types of drawings, however, other components may be used to show the necessary information for the complete design.

An example of additional information would be the nozzle schedule and welding detail section of a pressure vessel drawing. This specific section of the drawing lists the information necessary to fabricate, install, and weld the nozzles that will be part of the vessel. Drawings used to fabricate structural steel components do not usually have a specific section to list the various welding requirements. Welding symbols are used to supply all the necessary information.

Each of the listed drawing components serve a specific purpose and contain information about the job and its specifications. See illustration #1-54.

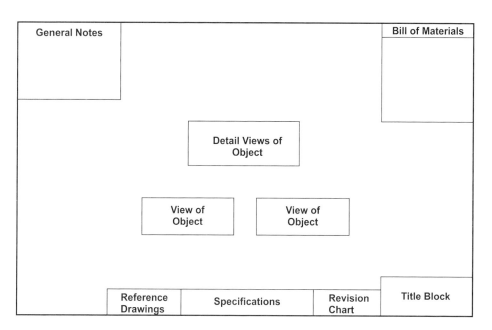

Illustration #1-54 — Drawing Format

Title Block

The title block is located in the lower right corner of the drawing and is separated from the main drawing. See illustration #1-54. The contents of the title block will vary from company to company and often differs from drawing to drawing by the same company. As a standard feature, a company will have its name and logo in the title block along with other standard company information, plus particular information, for instance the customer's name.

The following information can be located in the title block, however, it should be noted that not all of the items listed below are necessarily included:

• Name of the item to be fabricated or installed
• Name of the company who will build or install the product
• Name of the customer
• Name of the designing engineer or firm
• Name or initial of draftsperson
• Date drawn
• Drawing number
• Contract number or job number
• Number of revisions, if any, for the drawings
• Scale of the drawing

Bill of Materials

The bill of materials is usually located in the upper right corner of the drawing, above the title block. See illustration #1-54. As with the title block, the bill of materials is separated from the rest of the drawing and is essentially a table with partitioned rows into which information can be inserted. These rows will have column headings to identify the type of information.

Some of the more common column headings are:
• Item Number or Mark Number
• Quantity
• Material Description
• Material Grade
• Material Weight
• Remarks

The Item or Mark Number is the identification number for each piece of material, or can be the line number on the bill of materials. When it takes several pieces to fabricate a component a line by line listing is needed. An example would be a nozzle for a pressure vessel. A nozzle is made of a piece of pipe and a flange. Therefore the two items required to make the nozzle are each given a line in the bill of materials. The nozzle neck (pipe) would be on one line and the nozzle flange would be on another, and each would be given an item number in the bill of materials. However, in the remarks column, a piece mark number (such as N1) would be assigned to this nozzle, and it is understood that these two items make up nozzle N1. This piece mark number, N1, is the actual identification mark for the completed fabricated part. In some cases the actual piece mark number of the item is used instead of the item number. This is a common practice on structural drawings in which only one item is needed to make the complete piece. For example, a gusset plate or base plate.

The Quantity or Number column heading simply identifies how many items or pieces are required to be made.

The Material Description Column is the area of the bill of materials where the dimensions are specified. An example would be an angle iron, 3 x 3 x $\frac{1}{4}$ x 3'-4" long. The size, thickness, and length required are all given. The items in the material description section are often abbreviated because of space considerations. For example, a flange used in a piping system may be abbreviated: 150# RFWN, flg. std. bore. This is read as a 150 pound, raised face weld neck flange with a standard wall thickness or bore.

For this reason the person reading the drawing must be familiar with abbreviations in order to interpret this type of information.

The Material Type or Grade column is the area of the bill of materials where the grade of material is specified. This information is very important to ensure that the correct material is used in the fabrication of the item.

The grade numbers marked on the material must match the numbers specified on the drawing.

The Material Weight column specifies the weight of the item. In the case of multiple items, it is common practice to give the total weight of all of the items required.

The Remarks column of the bill of materials specifies the end use of the item. For example the heads for a pressure vessel would have the word 'heads'; and in the case of rolled shell plates for a pressure vessel, the word 'rings or cans' may be found.

Companies may use additional columns for specific uses. A purchase order number would be an example.

Revision Chart

The revision chart, shown in illustration #1-54, is often located to the left of the title block and is bordered off from the rest of the drawing. The revision chart, like the bill of materials, is divided into columns. These columns identify the revision number, give a general description of the revision change, state who approved the revision, who checked the revision, and the date of the revision. Abbreviations are often used to describe the revision, and the reader must be familiar with them to make it easier to interpret the chart.

Drawing Specifications

The specification section of a drawing is used to list all the design information of the item being built or installed. This section is often located to the left of the revision chart. If drawing space is a problem it may be located elsewhere. A common location is the area below the bill of materials.

The type of information listed will relate to design specifications such as the governing code body or standard it is built to, the material specifications, paint specifications, preparation requirements, design pressures, welding requirements, and any other information specific to the fabrication.

Drawing Notes

Drawings will often contain two types of notes. These are general notes and specific notes. The general and specific notes should not be confused with the information found in the bill of materials, title block, revision chart, or the drawing specifications.

The general notes are usually located in the upper left corner of the drawing. A general note is information about the fabrication that refers to similar items or procedures. For instance, on a tank or pressure vessel with inlet and outlet nozzles, a general note could read *"All nozzles shall be installed with bolt holes straddling the vessel centerlines."* The fabricator would know from this note that all the nozzles are installed exactly the same way. A common general note on structural drawings is "all bolt holes $13/_{16}$ in. diameter (20 mm), unless noted otherwise (U.N.O.)." On the drawing, the location of the hole centerline would be shown and the fabricator would know the hole size is $13/_{16}$ in. (20 mm).

Specific notes on a drawing are notes referring to specific items or procedures that may not affect other similar items on the drawing.

For instance, if the general notes indicated the hole sizes were $13/_{16}$ in. (20 mm) but a larger diameter was required for another item, then the specific note would indicate the hole size for that item. Specific notes are not located on any particular area of the drawing, but could be found anywhere as needed.

Specific notes are most often written with a leader line pointing to the relevant part or area.

Reference Drawings

A job requiring more than one drawing is called a drawing set and contains two or more drawings.

It is a common practice with a set of multiple drawings to list the names of individual drawings on the first drawing of the set. This listing is referred to as the reference drawings for the project.

Each drawing in the set will have its own title block and drawing name, usually referring to the items drawn.

There is no set area where the reference drawings are listed, however, two locations are near the bottom of the print on the far left hand side, or just below the bill of materials.

The Drawing Itself

The drawing itself is the focal point of the print. It will be made up of various views of the object, dimensions, notes, symbols and abbreviations. The complexity of the job being drawn determines how much information must be included for fabrication purposes and how many separate blueprints will be required to display all the information needed.

Right and Left Hand Views

In many instances components are shown on prints as exact opposites of each other, or as a mirror image. Right and left hand details are used on many types of drawings including pipe drawings, vessel drawings and structural drawings, although the practice is more common on structural drawings.

A simple explanation of right and left hand imaging is to hold both your hands in front with your palms facing away from you.

With your thumbs pointing towards each other, your left hand is an exact opposite of your right hand.

It is common practice for the drafter to draw the right hand view of the piece on the drawing and label it with the letter 'R', for right hand, and then note when a left is also required.

The piece which is made as a left hand will be labeled using the letter 'L'. See illustration #1-55. Because computerized drawing has made the opposite hand drawing very easy to create, many drawings now show both the right and left hand views.

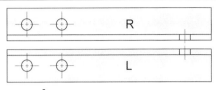

A. Right and Left Angles

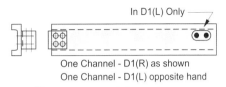

In D1(L) Only

One Channel - D1(R) as shown
One Channel - D1(L) opposite hand

B. Right and Left Channels

Illustration #1-55 — Right and Left

Supplementary Views

Supplementary views on drawings help the draftsperson clarify details of the drawing that cannot easily or clearly be shown on normal views. They are used in addition to the main views on the drawing. Two supplementary views used frequently on drawings are section views and auxiliary views.

Section Views

It may be necessary to show interior construction of an assembly to provide a complete understanding of design detail not revealed, or confusing if included in the regular views. Hidden lines show interior features of a project, however these can often be confusing. Section views are used to provide a direct view or a cross-section of the interior details of the assembly.

There are no set rules concerning when or where a section view should be used.

The decision usually remains with the draftsperson. More than one section view is often used on a drawing.

With section views, the object is cut by an imaginary cutting plane, as shown in illustration #1-56. The location of the cut is indicated by using the cutting plane line (refer to the section of this book on Alphabet of Lines) and labeling the line for identification purposes. In this way the reader can identify the cutting-plane line with the section view. For clarification purposes the section's surfaces are often highlighted using section lining or crosshatching. The section view is often drawn to a larger scale than the regular view it was taken from. This allows the drafter to show a better detail of the interior, thereby making it easier to dimension and understand.

There are several types of section views used on drawings, each for a specific purpose.

Illustration #1-56 demonstrates a portrayal of a section view, consisting of a split pictorial 'isometric' representation.

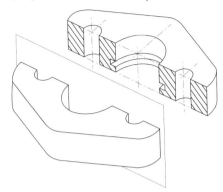

Illustration #1-56 — Imaginary Cutting Plane Showing Sectional View

- **Full Section** is the most common type of sectional view. The term full section is used whenever the cutting plane passes fully through the object resulting in it being cut in half. Arrows are placed at the ends of the cutting-plane line to show the direction of sight. See illustration #1-57. The reader should pay particular attention to the direction of the arrows as this is the direction the section view would be interpreted from. When reading any print with sectional views the rules of orthographic projection should be followed. The section will be identified in capital letters and noted on the drawing as 'Section A-A', 'Section B-B' and so on.

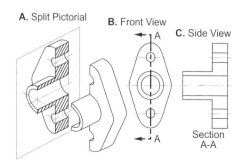

A. Split Pictorial   **B.** Front View   **C.** Side View

Section A-A

Illustration #1-57 — Side View in Full Section

- **Half-Sections** show interior details of objects that are symmetrical or where a full section is not necessary. One half of the part is shown in section up to the centerline, and the remainder is seen as an external view. See illustration #1-58. The cutting plane line is drawn halfway through the object stopping at the axis or centerline indicating that only one quarter of the object is shown in section.

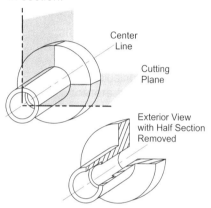

Center Line

Cutting Plane

Exterior View with Half Section Removed

Illustration #1-58 — Half-Section

- **Offset Sections** are used in situations where internal details of an object, such as holes, do not lie in a single plane (or straight line), the drafter may use an offset cutting plane line. The line is drawn through the desired part, which is then shown on one plane as a sectional view. The direction from which the object is to be viewed is indicated by the arrows marked A-A, as shown in illustration #1-59.

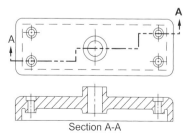

A

A

Section A-A

Illustration #1-59 — Offset Section

• *Broken-Out Section* shows how the inner detail of an object may sometimes be revealed by the removal of just a small section. A broken-out section is used in cases where the drafter wants to reveal some inner detail at a location on one of the regular views. The boundary of the section is shown using a freehand break line, and no cutting plane line is used. The inner details are shown with solid lines at the location of the section. See illustration #1-60.

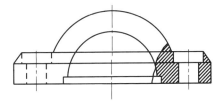

Illustration #1-60 — Broken-Out Section

• *Revolved Sections* are used to show the cross section of bars, spokes, ribs, chain hooks, shackles and many other items. At the location where the drafter wishes to show a cross section, a centerline is used instead of the cutting plane line. At this location the part of the object is rotated 90 degrees on the centerline. The revolved section now reveals details of the part at that location. See illustration #1-61.

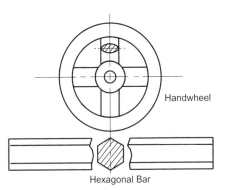

Handwheel

Hexagonal Bar

Illustration #1-61 — Revolved Section

• *Removed Sections* differ from revolved sections in that the section is removed to an open area on the drawing, or in the case of a symmetrical part, it is placed on an extension of the center line. See illustration #1-62.

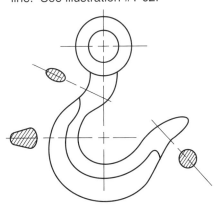

Illustration #1-62 — Removed Sections

• *Removed Views* show some detail of an object that will not be sectioned out. The cutting plane lines indicate the views desired, and the arrows show the direction they will be shown in. The views are then redrawn elsewhere on the drawing and labeled. See illustration #1-63 to compare removed sections A-A and B-B, to end view C-C.

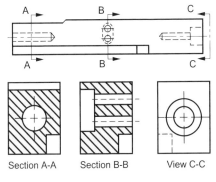

Section A-A   Section B-B   View C-C

Illustration #1-63 — Removed Sections and Removed View

Auxiliary Views

Auxiliary views become necessary when details of the slanted or sloped surface of an object have to be shown. The problem is shown in illustration #1-64A.

The top and the right side views show a distorted detail of the slanted surface.

However, as shown in illustration #1-64B, when another view is projected perpendicular (90°) to that surface, the drafter can detail the auxiliary view without distortion.

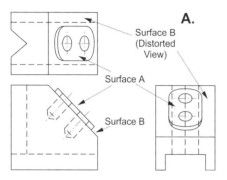

Regular Views Do Not Show True Features
of Surfaces A and B

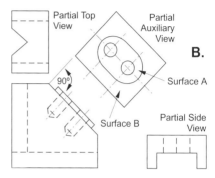

Auxiliary Views Added to Show
True Features of Surfaces A and B

Illustration #1-64 — The Need for and Use of Auxiliary Views

Scale Drawings

Drawing to Scale

Almost all blueprints, whether shop drawings, construction site drawings, or architects' drawings, are drawn to scale. The idea of drawing objects to scale is not unique to drafting, for example children draw representations of people, animals, and houses, and artists will paint landscapes to scale. A road map is another example of a drawing made to scale.

Scale drawings are made large enough to be easy to read but not so large that handling the drawings would be cumbersome.

Reduced Scales are used to draw large objects to a smaller than actual size (reduced).

Reduced scale drawings are common for the fabrication and construction trades because most of the work being performed is much larger than the drawings detailing the job.

Enlarged Scale is another type of scale. This scale is more common for mechanical trades, such as machinists, where the objects they produce could be very small in size, and require the drawing to be enlarged for ease of interpretation.

Full Scale drawings portray the actual size of the object, and are neither reduced or enlarged. These drawings are used when the size of the object drawn is such that it fits on standard drawing paper, is convenient to draw, and can be read easily.

The instrument used to draw scaled drawings, called a scale ruler, is shown in illustration #1-65. These rulers are designed in a triangular shape with six ruled faces, each designed to measure in a different ratio. A scale rule allows the user to avoid having to calculate each measurement as the scale ratio shown on the face of the rule is in direct proportion to the scale being used.

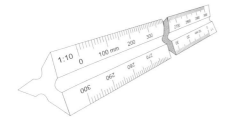

Illustration #1-65 — Metric Triangular Scale

Inch-Foot Scale Rulers: This is a scale used on drawings that have the inch-foot system of measurement. It is a reduced scale. Each scale on the ruler is divided into fractions of an inch with each fractional division representing one foot, for example 1" = 1'-0" (illustration #1-66A) and ¼" = 1'-0" (illustration #1-66B). Using the ¼" = 1'-0" scale, an object four feet in length would have a size on the drawing of one inch. At the beginning of each scale the fractional part is further divided into parts of an inch so that measurements of less than a whole foot can be obtained.

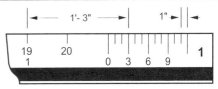

A. 1" = 1'- 0" SCALE (1:12 SCALE)

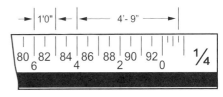

B. ¼" = 1'- 0" SCALE (1:48 SCALE)

Illustration #1-66 — In-Foot Scale Ruler

Metric Scale Rulers: This scale is used for drawings with the metric system of dimensioning. Scales on the metric ruler are 1:2, 1:5, 1:10, and 1:50. This means that if the 1:50 scale is used then each division of 1 mm is equal to 50 mm of actual object size. See illustration #1-67.

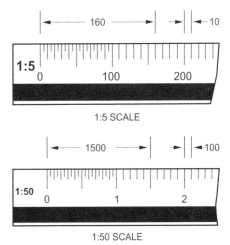

Illustration #1-67 — Metric Scale Rulers

Measuring Blueprints to Obtain Dimensions

As an absolute last resort, a scale rule can be used to measure dimensions directly from a drawing if a dimension is missing. If a scale rule is not available, then a tape measure can be used for measuring provided the scale is known.

For instance, if the scale was 1:50, and a line on the drawing measures 30 millimeters in length, then to calculate the actual object length, you would multiply 30 x 50 = 1500 mm. However, it is never considered a reliable practice to obtain a missing dimension by measuring directly from a drawing.

There are several reasons for not directly measuring a blueprint:

- When a drawing is reproduced from the original, shrinkage may occur resulting in the reproduced drawing being somewhat inaccurate.
- The drawing originals are made as accurate as possible. However, in the event that a dimension change is made, the draftsperson may not necessarily change the actual drawing other than altering the dimension number.

For handling purposes, drawings may be photo reduced, which would make measuring from them totally inaccurate. It is always best to consult the draftsperson for the dimension of a missing measurement.

Detail and Assembly Drawings

To manufacture equipment or buildings made of structural steel, a set of drawings is necessary to provide all the details necessary to fabricate and assemble the item.

Detail Drawings

The first drawing in a set is the general plan and it would show the general arrangement or plan of the whole piece of equipment or structure.

However, because of a lack of space or too small a scale the general plan would likely not have enough detail included to be able to fabricate the whole item.

The usual practice is to include additional drawings that would show specific parts of the equipment or structure in greater detail, hence the term detail drawing.

These detail drawings supply information including:

- The name of the part.
- The various views needed to describe the shape.
- Dimensions of the part and its features.
- Notes detailing required materials, specifications for finish, and other information.

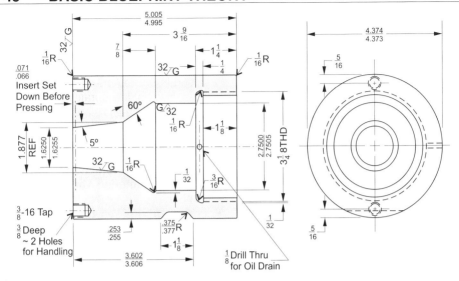

Illustration #1-68 — Detail Drawing Example

Only one detail drawing is used for the manufacture of several items that are exactly the same, such as the columns and beams used to build a steel structure. That one drawing would show the detail of the beam or column including all measurements and sizes, and it would also indicate how many are required. More than one part may be included on the same drawing, but it is more common to make single sheet drawings for each part to be detailed.

Illustration #1-68 shows a detail drawing of the housing for a piece of equipment. Not shown in illustration #1-68 are the title block, list of materials, and a specification section that are usually included with the detail drawing.

Assembly Drawings and Erection Drawings

Assembly drawings show the arrangement of various parts for a piece of equipment, and are referred to when assembling the parts.

The term erection drawing is more often used to describe drawings used to erect buildings or other large structures.

Assembly drawings and erection drawings will provide the following information:

• Name of the equipment or structure.
• Visual relationship of one part to another in order to enable correct assembly.
• List of all the parts required.
• Overall size and location dimensions for checking clearances when mating to other parts, or for foundation positions.

Assembly drawings often show the general outline of the parts of the complete assembly, thus making it easier to visualize how everything fits together. These are called exploded pictorial assembly drawings. An example is shown in illustration #1-69.

A diagram assembly drawing (control system schematic) uses symbols and single line drawings to show the relationship of the various parts of the complete assembly. These types of assembly drawings are used for piping, heating, ventilation and electrical systems. See illustration #1-70.

Installation assembly drawings (erection drawings) are used in the installation or erection of large pieces of equipment, such as boilers and structural steel buildings. They will include the general shape of the equipment, and will often use single lines to indicate the location of parts and components.

The structured steel section of this book shows examples of drawings used to erect building steel.

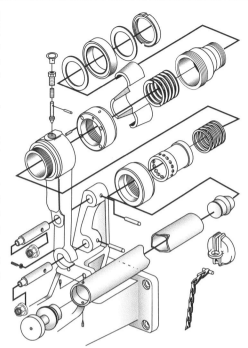

Illustration #1-69 — Exploded Pictorial Assembly

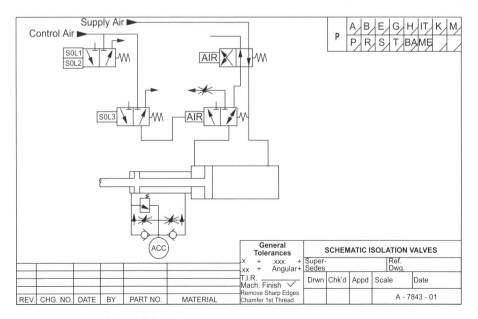

Illustration #1-70 — Control Schematic

Care of Drawings

Drawings are valuable documents and should be treated with proper care. The drawings that are used on the shop floor or in the field are not the originals. If a drawing does get damaged it usually can be replaced, however, the drawing user should treat them with consideration. Some general use and care rules are:

- Never write on a drawing. The exceptions to this is making an authorized change, or when checking off items as a record of items that have been built. For various reasons, for example poor drafting practices or poor quality reproduction, certain letters, numbers and lines can be difficult to interpret on the drawing. Adding writing to a poor quality drawing will only make it worse. If two or more people are working off one drawing, one person's common sense notes may be meaningless to someone else.

- Keep prints free from stains such as oil and grease from dirty hands or gloves, coffee stains, or stains from lunch tables. The drawings should be kept away from sharp tools, or objects that may be laid on top of them.

- Drawings should be protected from the elements. If they are to be used outside, they must not be exposed to direct sunlight or rain.

- They should never be stored in a tool box unless they are the last items to be placed inside at the end of a shift and will be removed first at the start of the next shift.

- Drawings should be carefully folded and unfolded. This is especially true if they are continually being folded and unfolded. Drawings can be rolled up or folded in the same manner as a map. When folding a drawing, make sure that the title block and print number remain visible. A method of folding is shown in illustration #1-71.

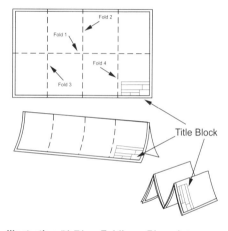

Illustration #1-71 — Folding a Blueprint

Freehand Sketching

Why Sketch

Freehand sketching is a very useful skill that can be mastered by anyone with a little practice by following a few guidelines. The ability to interpret drawings is complemented by the ability to sketch information from a drawing to reflect the requirements of the job.

Also valuable, when no drawing is available, is the ability to sketch the required job so that it can be understood correctly by others. The old phrase, "a picture is worth a thousand words" is very appropriate when it comes to explaining job requirements. Often a hand sketch will reveal all that needs to be said, and will present a clear picture of what must be done.

All that is required to produce a freehand sketch is a pencil, a piece of paper or a good smooth surface to work on. Many a sketch has been drawn on a concrete floor, a steel plate, or a piece of plywood to convey the information needed.

To practice freehand sketching, use graph or grid paper. This type of paper is made with horizontal and vertical lines permanently printed onto its surface. A common type of graph paper has its lines spaced at ¼ in. (6 mm) increments.

Using squared paper helps in plotting out the sketch dimensions and keeps the sketch looking square and straight.

Sketching Techniques

By observing a few basic techniques the quality of freehand sketches and the ability to draw them will be improved dramatically.

- The pencil used to produce the sketch should have a lead with a hardness of H, or HB, and have a sharp conical point.
- The proper technique to hold the pencil is to let it rest on the second finger while being held loosely with the thumb and index finger. The pencil is held about ¾ to 1 inch (19 to 25 mm) from the point. As you begin to draw, use an easy arm motion, pivoted about the forearm muscle. At first make very light lines, then when you are satisfied with what you have done you can trace over these lines to make them stand out. Light sketching lines are easy to erase.
- Only provide the detail that is needed to interpret what the job requires. Try to keep everything in the sketch to the same proportion or scale. The use of graph paper will help make the sketches fairly accurate.

- Make the sketches large enough so they are easy to read. Allow sketching lines to intersect and pass each other at the corners. Remember you are not trying to produce a perfect drawing, as the idea is to avoid spending a lot of time making them perfect. You will discover that as you practice sketching, it becomes easier and faster.

Sketching Straight Lines

Probably one of the most difficult things about freehand sketching is being able to draw straight lines. However, a few basic techniques will help to make this easier.

- When sketching a straight line, do not look at the point of the pencil, but learn to look slightly ahead of the pencil point. If the lines are relatively short in length, concentrate on where you want the pencil point to end, or the termination point of the line. It takes a little practice and you must learn to trust your instincts, but it works.
- Another technique which helps to draw straight lines is to mark the starting and the end points of the line with dots. See illustration #1-72A. This will make the task of drawing a straight line easier because it gives something to aim for. For a long line, place intermediate dots between the first and last. This will help as a guide as you sketch the line. You can then glance ahead to the next dot as you sketch the line. Before you actually sketch the line make a few trial motions between the dots. Then, make a light line with a few sweeping motions, and make any necessary corrections before you draw the final line.

With a little practice the procedure will become routine.

Sketching Horizontal Lines

- When sketching horizontal lines it may be convenient to arrange the paper so that it is at an angle, making it easier to draw the line. Generally speaking, you arrange the paper so that you are drawing the line at a slight upwards angle. This makes it easier to see the line as you draw it, and compensates somewhat for the natural arc of the circle, centered at the elbow.

- When drawing horizontal lines right-handed people should start from the right side of the line and draw from right to left. Left-handed people do the opposite.

- As with any straight line, it is easier to place dots along the proposed line to help keep the line straight. After your skill level develops you will find it unnecessary to use dots.

Sketching Vertical Lines

When sketching vertical lines, it is generally considered best to start from the top and move towards the bottom of the line. See illustration #1-72B. As with the horizontal line, dots may be placed at the start and end points of the line. If it is easier, for longer lines, the paper can be turned so that vertical lines can be drawn in the horizontal position.

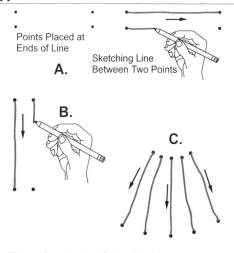

Points Placed at Ends of Line

A. Sketching Line Between Two Points

B.

C.

Illustration #1-72 — Sketching Lines

Sketching Slanted Lines

Sketching slanted lines is similar to horizontal and vertical lines. The slant line may be drawn either from the top down or from the bottom up, whichever feels more natural. For convenience, dots can be used at the starting and ending points on the line. See illustration #1-72C.

Sketching Arcs Connecting Straight Lines

Arcs which connect two straight lines can be drawn in several easy steps. The method that is usually most satisfactory is called the triangle-square method.

To sketch this arc, follow the steps, shown in illustration #1-73.

- Connect the two straight lines so they intersect and form a corner (Step 1).
- On each line, measure back from the corner a distance equal to the desired arc radius. Sketch the square (Step 2), and form the center of the desired radius.
- Sketch a diagonal line connecting the two points previously established on the straight lines and form a triangle. Locate the center point of the triangle with a dot (Step 3).
- Using short, light strokes, sketch a curved line which starts at the point marked on the vertical line and ends on the point marked on the horizontal line. This line should pass through the dot placed in the center of the triangle (Step 4).
- The arc line can then be traced more heavily and the other lines erased as desired (Step 5).

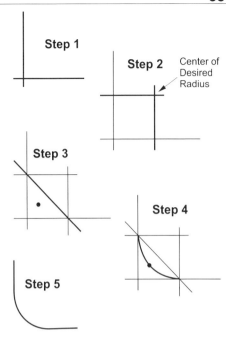

Illustration #1-73 — Sketching an Arc

Sketching Circles

Circles are sketched in a similar manner to the arc using the triangle-square method. Circles can be sketched accurately by following the few easy steps shown in illustration #1-74.

- Locate the center of the circle. Sketch the horizontal and vertical centerlines. On these centerlines, establish the diameters in relationship to their center point (Step 1).
- Using light construction lines, sketch horizontal and vertical lines at each of the respective diameter ends. A square with sides equal to the circle diameter will be formed. (Step 2)
- Join opposite corners of this square with two lightly drawn diagonal lines and locate the mid-point of each triangle (Step 3).
- Using short, light strokes, sketch in the circle curve within each quarter making sure it passes through the mid-point dot of each triangle and joins smoothly with the square at the diameter ends (Step 4).
- Darken in the construction lines to form a smooth circle. Erase any other lines as desired (Step 5).

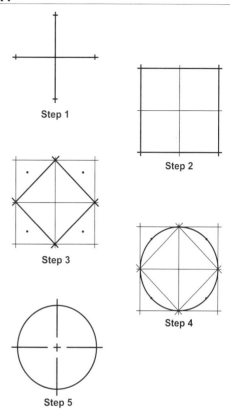

Step 1

Step 2

Step 3

Step 4

Step 5

Illustration #1-74 — Sketching a Circle

Section One Questions

1. Structural steel used in a building is usually fabricated from what type of drawings?
   - ❏ architectural
   - ❏ engineering
   - ❏ heating and ventilation
   - ❏ shop drawings

2. Drawings used to assemble components on a jobsite that have been fabricated elsewhere are called:
   - ❏ architectural drawings
   - ❏ fabrication drawings
   - ❏ heating and ventilation drawings
   - ❏ erection drawings

3. What type of line has a series of dashes and also has an arrow at each end angled 90 degrees to the line?
   - ❏ hidden line
   - ❏ center line
   - ❏ cutting plane line
   - ❏ break line

4. A component that is too long to be shown in full length on a drawing can be shown by using a (an):
   - ❏ object line
   - ❏ center line
   - ❏ section line
   - ❏ break line

5. What important symbol, consisting of a triangle containing a number or letter, is often found in various places on a drawing?
   - ❏ mark number
   - ❏ revision symbol
   - ❏ centerline sign
   - ❏ size of material symbol

6. What is the name of the symbol that is drawn as a circle with an angled line drawn down through it?
   - ❏ mark number
   - ❏ round or diameter
   - ❏ degree of finish
   - ❏ centerline

7. The abbreviation for "thread one end" would be:
   - ❏ THD
   - ❏ TBE
   - ❏ TOE
   - ❏ TOL

8. Blueprint dimensions often use a combination of feet and inches, and millimetres.
   - ❏ true
   - ❏ false

9. Steel fabrication drawings almost always require drawing measurements to be accurate within ten thousands of an inch.
   - ❏ true
   - ❏ false

10. A component measurement, in millimetres, shown as 785 mm (+/- 2), would allow the component dimensions to vary from 784 to 786.
    - ❏ true
    - ❏ false

11. With baseline dimensioning, all measurements originate from a common reference point.
    - ❏ true
    - ❏ false

12. How many rungs would there be on a ladder if a print indicated the rungs with the measurement note "12 spaces @ 1'-0"?

Answer: _____

13. The bolt holes on a circular flange are positioned on which of the following?
    ❏ inside diameter
    ❏ outside diameter
    ❏ bolt hole diameter
    ❏ bolt circle diameter

14. The chord distance between bolt holes on a circular flange is the same as the arc distance.
    ❏ true
    ❏ false

15. The pitch or slope of a surface to a horizontal plane (such as the roof of a building), is known as rise over run.
    ❏ true
    ❏ false

16. The pitch of a bolt thread is the factor that determines whether the bolt will be fine thread or coarse thread.
    ❏ true
    ❏ false

17. One steel plate overlapping another plate would be welded with what type of weld?
    ❏ edge weld
    ❏ butt weld
    ❏ fillet weld
    ❏ overlay weld

18. Two plates fitted together to form a tee would have what type of weld?
    ❏ surface weld
    ❏ fillet weld
    ❏ edge weld
    ❏ butt weld

19. A weld symbol placed below the reference line would indicate welding on the "arrow side" of the joint.
    ❏ true
    ❏ false

20. What welding procedure is indicated by a flag positioned where the reference line and the arrow join together on a welding symbol?
    ❏ weld in the field
    ❏ weld in the shop
    ❏ weld completely around joint
    ❏ grind joint after welding

21. What welding method or procedure is indicated by a small circle drawn where the reference line and the arrow line join on a welding symbol?
    ❏ weld in the field
    ❏ weld in the shop
    ❏ weld completely around the joint
    ❏ grind joint after welding

22. What symbol is NOT one of the usual welding finish symbols?
    ❏ C
    ❏ G
    ❏ M
    ❏ W

23. Which view is NOT one of the three most commonly used views associated with orthographic projection?
    ❏ section view
    ❏ top view
    ❏ front view
    ❏ side view

24. A perspective view is not suitable for dimensioning as the sides are not drawn to equal length and it is not drawn to scale.
    ❏ true
    ❏ false

25. The company name and drawing number are found in what area of a print?
- ❏ general notes
- ❏ specifications
- ❏ bill of material
- ❏ title block

26. Which of the following is NOT usually found in the Bill of Materials?
- ❏ item or mark number
- ❏ quantity of pieces required
- ❏ welding process for components
- ❏ description of material

27. Two "mirror image" components are said to be:
- ❏ left and right
- ❏ section views
- ❏ top and side views
- ❏ non of the above

28. The interior construction of an object can be shown with what type of view?
- ❏ top
- ❏ side
- ❏ detail
- ❏ section

29. The details of a sloped surface are best shown using which of the following?
- ❏ front view
- ❏ side view
- ❏ top view
- ❏ auxiliary view

30. What would be the drawing line length of an object 18 ft. 6 in. long, drawn to a scale of ¼ inch = 1 foot.
- ❏ 9 ft. 3 ¼ in.
- ❏ 9 ¼ in.
- ❏ 4 5/8 in.
- ❏ 2 5/16 in.

31. If the 1: 50 metric scale is used, what is the drawing line length of an object 2.5 metres in length?

Answer: _____

32. Blueprints stored in a toolbox should be first in and last out.
- ❏ true
- ❏ false

SECTION TWO

PRESSURE VESSELS

Pressure Vessel Components

Pressure Vessels are containers for pressurized liquids and gases that are designed under the ASME code (American Society of Mechanical Engineers). The most common design of pressure vessel is a cylindrical shell with two formed end closures called heads. The head geometry results in the end of the vessel having a curved surface, formed in two directions, resulting in a much stronger design than a flat end. In order to help interpret pressure vessel drawings, the reader should have a basic understanding of the typical pressure vessel components. The various service requirement of pressure vessels make it difficult to include all possible internal components, but some of the more typical ones will be mentioned in this text. Refer to illustration #2-1 for location of the following external components.

Other designs allow for the use of conical heads and even flat heads, although these are not as common as the hemispherical, ellipsoidal, or flanged and dished heads.

For vessels of small and medium diameter, ellipsoidal heads are usually used, while large diameter vessels are most often built with hemispherical or flanged and dished heads. Heads are usually made of one piece construction which means they are formed from a flat, round sheet of plate. The plate may be heated to make it easier to press it into the forming dies, resulting in a two directional curved surface. Some heads are certified to have had no heat applied in forming.

Another common feature of heads is the straight flange portion (abbreviated as SF on drawings), see illustration #2-2.

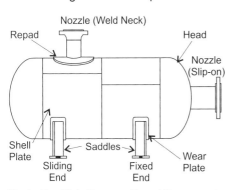

Illustration #2-1 - Pressure Vessel Components

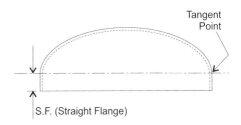

Illustration #2-2 - Head with Straight Flange (S.F.)

Heads

The heads are located on each end of the pressure vessel. The three most common types of heads are hemispherical, ellipsoidal, and flanged and dished. Flanged and dished heads have the least strength. See illustration #2-2 for a head example.

Codes governing the design and construction of vessels require that formed heads butt welded to the shell of the vessel have a straight flange portion. The exception to this is the hemispherical head. The minimum required length of the straight flange is specified in the design codes. For ellipsoidal heads it is usually 2 inches (50 mm) and for flanged and dished it is usually 1-1/2 inches (38 mm).

Shell

A pressure vessel shell is made from flat steel plate that is rolled into a cylinder or from steel pipe. Rolling machines vary in the width of plate they can roll, with eight and ten foot widths being standard in the industry.

Vessels shorter than the capacity of the rolls can be made using only one cylinder. This is called a one course shell.

For longer vessels the shell will have two or more courses. This is referred to as a two, three or more course shell. An example would be the towers in gas processing plants and oil refineries. These vessels can be hundreds of feet in length requiring many courses to make up the vessel shell.

The shell of small diameter vessels can be made from pipe, although this is not the standard practice. Shells made from rolled flat plate will have a longitudinal welded seam (long. seam for short form) that will run the length of the shell course. The name of the seam where two or more shell courses join together or where the heads join the shell is called the circumferencial seam (abbreviated circ. seam for short). See illustration #2-3 for seam terminology.

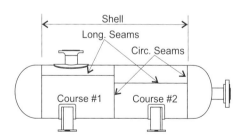

Illustration #2-3 - Courses and Seams

Saddles

Saddles are used to support horizontal vessels. The pressure vessel code (ASME - American Society of Mechanical Engineers) requires that whenever possible, two saddles shall support the vessel rather than a multiple support system. The saddles are designed to cradle the vessel for a minimum of one third (120 degrees) of the shells circumference and be placed at the statically optimum location. Because the heads provide a stiffening effect, saddles are located as close to the heads as possible on thinner walled vessels.

The main parts of a typical saddle are the wear plate the vessel will sit in, the web plate, the base plate, the end plates, and web plate stiffeners. See illustration #2-4 for a saddle detail.

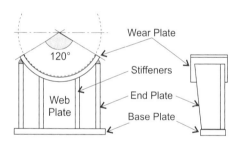

Illustration #2-4 - Supporting Saddle

For expansion and contraction purposes, one saddle is designed with slotted anchor bolt holes. This is called the sliding saddle, and the other is called the fixed saddle. See illustration #2-5.

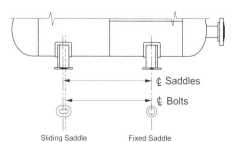

Illustration #2-5 - Fixed and Sliding Anchors

Skirts

A skirt is the most common type of support for a vertical vessel. See illustration #2-6. The skirt is attached to the bottom head of the vessel by a continuous weld, and in most cases it looks like part of the shell or an extension of the vessel itself. The skirt is designed to be the same diameter as the vessel shell.

The pressure vessel code states that the minimum wall thickness of the skirt shall be one-quarter inch (6 mm).

Openings, including manways, piping, and vent holes are incorporated into the skirt when necessary. See illustration #2-6.

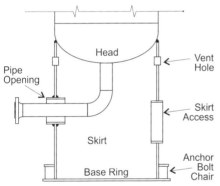

Illustration #2-6 - Typical Skirt

The bottom of the skirt sits on a base ring that has holes drilled in it for the anchor bolts. The base ring for a tall tower may be stiffened by using gusset plates, or another ring welded to the skirt above the base ring with stiffener plates joining the two rings on each side of the anchor bolt hole. This design, called an anchor bolt chair, is shown in illustration #2-7 and allows for stronger anchorage of the vertical vessel.

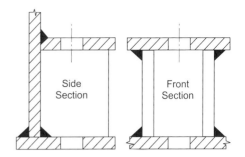

Illustration #2-7 - Anchor Bolt Chair

Nozzles

Nozzles are openings in the vessel used for cleaning, inspection and access, attaching external piping to the vessel, or for joining vessel internals to exterior piping. Nozzles are made from a piece of pipe, called the neck, and a pipe flange. See illustration #2-8.

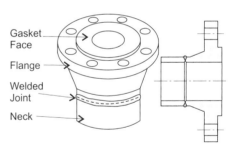

Illustration #2-8 - Weld Neck Flange

The flange welds to the neck and has a gasket surface on top. The neck of a nozzle welds into the opening cut for it in the vessel shell. The flanges used for nozzles are the same size as those used to connect them to any external piping. There are several types of flanges but two are very common. They are the raised face slip on flange, and the raised face weld neck flange. These are commonly abbreviated on vessel drawings as RFSO for raised faced slip on, and RFWN for raised faced weld neck.

Manways and Davit Arms

A manway is used on a vessel for access. The manway is actually a nozzle in the vessel that is large enough for a worker to pass through. It has a blind flange cover to seal off the pressure contained in the vessel. Manways are usually 24 inch (600 mm) O.D. or larger, and for this reason the blind flange cover is very heavy. A device called a davit arm is used to support the cover when it is being removed.

The most common design for a davit arm is a bent pipe. The arm sleeve is welded to the manway neck or the vessel shell and has an eyebolt that is secured to the manway cover. This allows the cover to swing out of the way while the manway is open. For an example of a horizontal and a vertical davit see illustration #2-9.

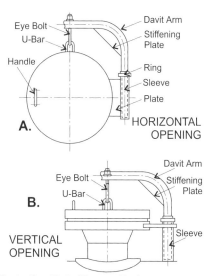

Illustration #2-9 - Manway Davits

Reinforcing Pads

Reinforcing pads (re-pads) are used around manways and nozzles. Their primary function is to compensate for the loss of strength in the shell of the vessel after cutting an opening for a nozzle.

Not all nozzles require a reinforcing pad, as the pressure vessel code allows for design variations that do not require a re-pad. See illustration #2-9B and illustration #2-10 for a cross-section view of a re-pad and nozzle.

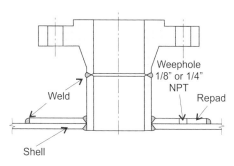

Illustration #2-10 - Re-pad (Reinforcing Pad)

Ladders and Platforms

A platform on a vertical vessel is shown in illustration #2-11. It serves as a deck for workers to open the vessel manways, service control devices, or for maintenance of the vessel.

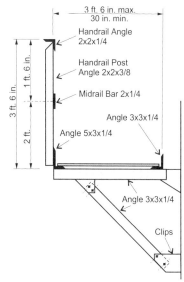

Illustration #2-11 - Handrail and Platform Dimensions

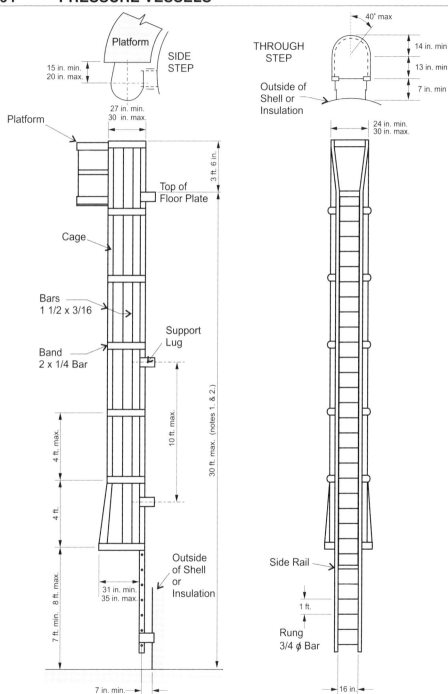

Illustration #2-12 - Ladder and Cage

The ladders are attached to the vessel shell with clips. The clips are normally welded to the vessel and the ladder is bolted to the clips. The ladder siderails, ladder rungs, and ladder safety cage are designed according to the pressure vessel code. The vessel fabrication drawings may state dimensions other than those shown in illustration #2-12.

The pressure vessel codes state the height of the platform handrails and other platform detail dimensions. Most platform railing details are fairly standard throughout North America.

Either pipe or angle iron can be used for handrail posts and rails.

Nameplate

The pressure vessel code requires a nameplate for each vessel manufactured to the code specification.

The minimum required information that must be on the nameplate is:
- manufacturer's name
- maximum allowable working pressure of the vessel
- test pressure
- design temperature
- year the vessel was built

Manufacturers of pressure vessels often design the nameplate to have more information about the vessel than the code minimum requirements.

Illustration #2-13 shows a typical nameplate for a pressure vessel built in accordance with the ASME Boiler and Pressure Vessel Code.

Most of the information is abbreviated, and the reader must be familiar with the abbreviations in order to interpret them correctly.

Trays

A typical feature at any gas processing plant or oil refinery are the tall vertical columns. These are pressure vessels and are referred to as process towers.

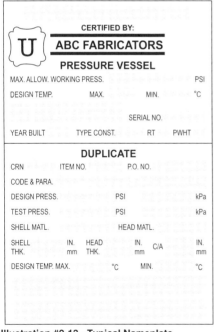

Illustration #2-13 - Typical Nameplate

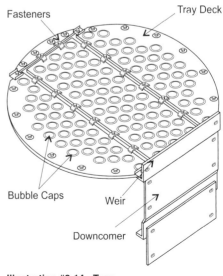

Illustration #2-14 - Tray

Their primary function is separation of the various products produced from crude oil or natural gas. Inside these columns are trays spaced approximately 18 to 24 inches (450 to 600 mm) apart.

The trays are made of carbon steel or light gauge stainless steel. They are supported in the tower by tray rings welded directly to the inside of the shell. The design of the tray varies considerably and depends upon the actual use. Illustration #2-14 depicts one type of tray deck.

The trays are designed to be bolted together inside the tower, and therefore must be made of pieces that will fit through the small manway openings. The tray will be assembled inside the tower at its correct elevation.

Demisters

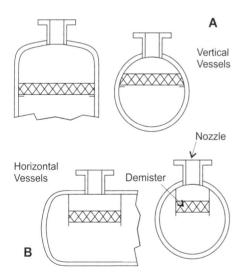

Illustration #2-15 - Demisters

Demisters or mist extractors are another type of common pressure vessel internal. These devices separate undesirable liquids from vapors that would carry over in the vapor stream as it leaves the vessel.

There are varying designs of demisters, but they are usually made of stainless steel or plastic screen mesh which is enclosed in a cage. Demisters are usually mounted over a nozzle opening. See illustration #2-15 for several cross-section views of demisters.

Vortex Breakers

Vortex breakers are used to stop the swirling action of the liquid at the point of inlet, or exit from the vessel. There are several designs that are widely used.

These include cross plate baffles or a single plate baffle located in front of the nozzle opening on the inside of the vessel.

The vortex breaker is welded directly to the inside of the shell. Illustration #2-16A shows the vortexing action of a liquid in a vessel. Illustration #2-16B shows the cross-section of cross plate and single plate baffles.

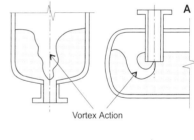

Vortex Action

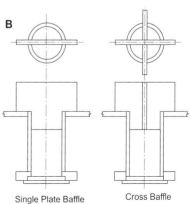

Single Plate Baffle   Cross Baffle

Illustration #2-16 - Vortex Breakers

Longitudinal and Circumferencial Seams

The shell of a pressure vessel made by rolling flat plate into a cylinder will have a weld seam that runs along its length. The term describing this weld seam is longitudinal seam (abbreviated long. seam). The weld seam that joins a head to the shell, or joins shell courses together, is called the circumferencial seam (abbreviated circ. seam or girth seam).

Illustration #2-17 shows longitudinal seams and circumferencial seams for a horizontal vessel.

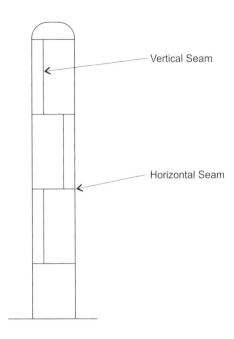

Illustration #2-18 - Seams on a Vertical Vessel

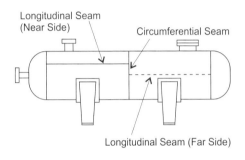

Illustration #2-17 - Seams on a Horizontal Vessel

If a vessel sits in the vertical position, then the terms describing the shell seams change to horizontal seams and vertical seams (or verts).

In other words the longitudinal seam becomes the vertical seam and the circumferential seam becomes the horizontal seam. See illustration #2-18 for a vertical vessel example.

Vessel Drawing Views

Orientation View

The orientation is a view looking at a vessel from one end. This view is used to establish the orientation of the nozzles, longitudinal seams, other attachments such as the nameplate, and to show the saddle location around the shell perimeter.

The orientation view shows the location of these items in degrees based on zero degrees as the starting point, then moving in a clockwise direction around the vessel to three hundred and fifty nine degrees (360 degrees in a circle). This sequence is based on the orientation view being positioned on either the right or left end of the elevation view.

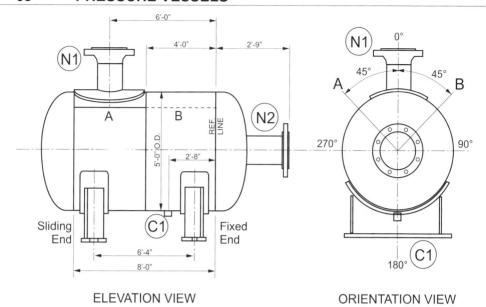

ELEVATION VIEW   ORIENTATION VIEW

Illustration #2-19 - Horizontal Elevation and Orientation

If we consider nozzle "N1" as shown in the orientation view of illustration #2-19, we can see that the nozzle center is positioned at the top or the zero degree centerline of the vessel. The orientation of nozzle N1 is zero degrees.

This vessel has two longitudinal seams, called long. A and long. B. Longitudinal seam A is located 45 degrees anti-clockwise of the zero degree centerline and longitudinal seam B is located 45 degrees clockwise from the zero degree centerline.

Most vessel drawings use zero degrees as the starting point and any attachments are orientated from the zero degree centerline and progress clockwise.

Rather than referring to long. A as 45 degrees anti-clockwise from the zero degree centerline it is more often labeled as 315 degrees.

To see if you understand how to interpret the orientation view shown in illustration #2-19 , answer the following question: What is the orientation of coupling C1?

If you said that coupling C1 is located on the 180 degree centerline you would have answered the question correctly.

It is common practice to divide the vessel orientation view into quarters with four centerlines (top, bottom, and each side). Therefore, the orientation view as shown in illustration #2-19 would show 0 degree, 90 degree, 180 degree and 270 degree quarter lines (centerlines).

Note: The orientation view can be shown on the right or the left side of the elevation view for horizontal vessels. Therefore it is extremely important when laying out nozzles and fittings on a horizontal vessel that the layout person make sure which end of the vessel the orientation view is taken from (left or right end).

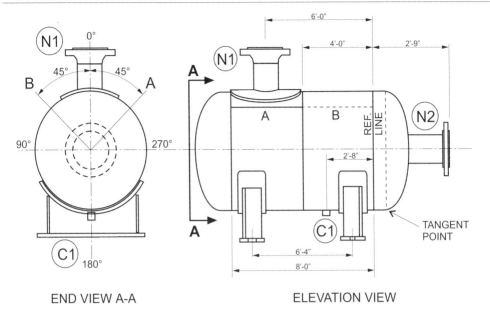

END VIEW A-A   ELEVATION VIEW

Illustration #2-20 - Horizontal Elevation and Orientation

It is also important to note which end the reference line is on to avoid laying out the vessel backwards. This can be an easy mistake, and a common one for inexperienced layout people.
As a comparison, see illustration #2-20, the left hand end view of the same vessel. Note the locations of the 90 degree and 270 degree centerlines. Also note the location of seams A and B.

The 270 degree centerline on the elevation view of this horizontal vessel is on the near side, while the 90 degree centerline is on the far side. However, there are exceptions as some companies position the orientation view on the left end, which means the 90 degree centerline is on the near side of the elevation view. See drawing 2-28A.

Note: Always be aware of the centerline positions in relation to the two views, orientation and elevation.

Note: An end view is not necessarily an orientation view.

If the vessel is standing in the vertical position, the orientation view is always viewed as if looking down from the top of the vessel. This view is shown in illustration #2-21.

Elevation View
The elevation view shows the location of nozzles, saddles, and other attachments from a reference point. This reference point is either the head to shell seam or the tangent point on the head. The reference point could be on either the right or left on a horizontal vessel. The tangent point is a point on the head where the curved portion of the head becomes the straight flange. The tangent point can be measured back from the seam end along the straight flange. It is usually 1-1/2 or 2 inches (38 or 50 mm) from the weld seam. The straight flange portion on the head is generally listed with the head description found in the bill of materials. It may be shown on the elevation view.

As stated earlier, the elevation view shows the location of various attachments as measured from a given reference point.

The reference point for the elevation view shown in illustrations #2-19 and #2-20 is the right end head to shell seam.

To see if you understand what has been written so far about elevation views, answer the following question by reference to illustrations #2-19 and #2-20.

What is the measurement from the reference (abbreviated ref.) seam line to the center of nozzle N1?

If you answered 6 ft. 0 in. you would have answered correctly.

Coupling C1 is 2 ft. 8 in. from the seam reference line. Nozzle N2 measures 2 ft. 9 in. from the seam reference line to the raised face of the flange.

How do the orientation and the elevation views go together to correctly layout a nozzle or any other attachment on the shell?

It works as follows: Refer to illustration #2-19 to establish the orientation and elevation of nozzle N1.

The center of nozzle N1 is located on the zero degree centerline and a distance of 6 ft. 0 in. from the right end head to shell seam. This locates the center point of the nozzle. At this point the layout person would mark out the diameter of the hole in the shell for this nozzle.

Note: A point to remember is that on a horizontal vessel elevation view, the centerline shown through the middle, left to right is either the 90 degree or 270 degree centerline, depending on the orientation view position; and on a vertical vessel, with the orientation view shown above the elevation, the centerline through the middle, top to bottom, is usually the 180 degree centerline.

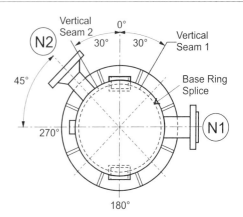

ORIENTATION VIEW

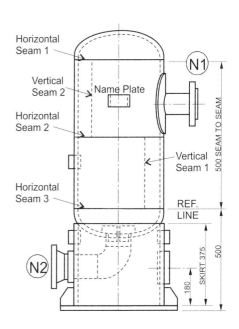

ELEVATION VIEW

Illustration #2-21 - Views of a Vertical Vessel

Vertical vessel drawings also have elevation views. For tall vessels the elevation view may be shown with the vessel laying on its side.

The manufacturer will almost always build vertical vessels on their sides and ship them to the jobsite the same way.

Dimensions on the elevation view for vertical vessels are given from a reference point originating on the bottom head. As with the horizontal vessel, this reference point is generally the bottom head to shell seam or the tangent point on the bottom head.

Detail and Section Views

Most vessel drawings will also have detail views and section views. Detail views are used to illustrate the required information to fabricate an item such as a saddle. See illustration #2-22.

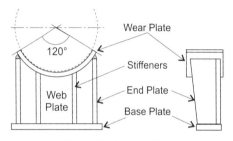

Illustration #2-22 - Typical Saddle

Section views are often used to show interior details of the vessel for items such as demisters or trays.

Vessel Drawing Layout

Various manufacturers of vessels use a somewhat similar format to draft their drawings. The layout may vary slightly from manufacturer to manufacturer but the information contained in each of these areas is the same. Each drawing will contain a:

- title block
- bill of materials
- revision chart
- area to list the specifications, for example, type of steel, paint and corrosion requirements, codes, and other information.

There will be a separate area for listing:

- general notes or shop notes
- schedule for the nozzles and welding details
- separate area to list the reference drawings if there are any

GENERAL NOTES	NOZZLE SCHEDULE AND WELDING DETAILS	BILL OF MATERIALS
Instructions for Reading the Drawing and Carrying Out the Construction	Detailed Fabrication Requirements of the Vessel Nozzles	List and Description of Items Required to Carry Out the work
	Views of the Finished Vessel	

List of Related Drawings	SPECIFICATIONS	Descriptions and Dates of Revisions to the Drawing	TITLE BLOCK
	References to Codes and Standards, Design and Operating Pressures, Temperatures, Testing, Weight etc.		Company Name, Client Identification, Drawing Description, Number, Date

Illustration #2-23 - General Layout of Vessel Drawings

Illustration #2-23 depicts the layout of a typical vessel drawing. It should be understood that the location of some of the information may vary from manufacturer to manufacturer.

Using illustration #2-23, look for each of the areas listed and scan them to identify the type of information each contains.

Where the draftsperson decides to list the reference drawings is often a matter of convenience as they will be included where there is room on the drawing. Common locations are above the title block or next to the specifications.

Interpreting Vessel Drawings

Vessel drawings, as a minimum, will use at least two views to show all of the necessary details to fabricate the vessel. These two views are the orientation view and the elevation view.

As an example, the Air Receiver drawing (drawing 2-26), being of a basic design, uses these two views and one other detail view, plus the nozzle schedule and the bill of materials to illustrate this vessel.

Nozzle Schedule

A nozzle schedule specifying the details about the various vessel nozzles is often shown in chart form. One important item shown is the nozzle projection, which is a term commonly used to describe how far a nozzle will protrude out of, or inside a vessel. This term is used to describe the distance a nozzle will project from the shell of the vessel. The projection of the nozzle will be given in inches or millimeters. The measurement is the shortest distance measured from the outside surface of the shell to the top of the gasket surface of the nozzle flange. This is called the outside projection or external projection of the nozzle. Illustration #2-24 shows the external projection for a weld neck flange and a slip on flange.

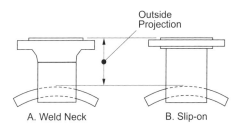

A. Weld Neck   B. Slip-on

Illustration #2-24 - Outside Projection

The term inside or internal projection describes how far the nozzle will protrude inside the shell of the vessel. The terms flush and set flush are used to describe whether or not the pipe will be cut to the curvature of the shell, and are shown in illustration #2-25.

If a nozzle is used as a drain it is usually cut to the curvature of the shell, otherwise it is set flush. It saves time and money in the fabrication of the vessel if nozzles do not have to be trimmed. Two other methods of internal projection are minimum and maximum extension, as shown in illustration #2-25.

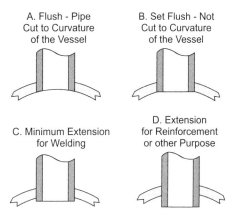

A. Flush - Pipe Cut to Curvature of the Vessel

B. Set Flush - Not Cut to Curvature of the Vessel

C. Minimum Extension for Welding

D. Extension for Reinforcement or other Purpose

Illustration #2-25 - Inside Projection

General Pressure Vessel Questions

1. Flat plate heads, rather than ellipsoidal or hemispherical, are more commonly used on pressure vessels?
   - ❏ true
   - ❏ false

2. The seam where a vessel head is welded to the shell on a vertical vessel is what type of joint?
   - ❏ longitudinal
   - ❏ vertical
   - ❏ circumferential
   - ❏ horizontal

3. The supports for a horizontal pressure vessel are called:
   - ❏ saddles
   - ❏ skirts
   - ❏ nozzles
   - ❏ davit arm

4. The anchor bolt chair is welded to the:
   - ❏ top head
   - ❏ skirt
   - ❏ manway
   - ❏ demister

5. What is used to seal off a manway opening?
   - ❏ hemispherical head
   - ❏ blind flange
   - ❏ wear plate
   - ❏ nozzle neck

6. The orientation view shows the position of items such as nozzles around the vessel circumference in relation to degrees of a circle.
   - ❏ true
   - ❏ false

7. The orientation view centerlines usually run in the same clockwise order, 0-90-180-270, regardless of whether the view is positioned on the left or right end of a horizontal vessels elevation view.
   - ❏ true
   - ❏ false

8. The first step when laying out a vessel shell is to determine which end to start from.
   - ❏ true
   - ❏ false

9. The starting point to lay out a horizontal vessel shell, after determining which end is the reference line, and the order of the centerlines is:
   - ❏ find the position of the largest nozzles first
   - ❏ find how many nozzles are the same size
   - ❏ establish 0 degrees in relation to the shell weld seam
   - ❏ establish the length of the skirt

10 An elevation view reference line, established on a vessel head at the point of curvature, is said to be at what point.
   - ❏ reference point
   - ❏ end point
   - ❏ tangent point
   - ❏ nozzle point

Air Receiver Drawing 2-26

The following questions refer to the Air Receiver drawing. The answers can all be found on the drawing. Try to find the answers in the appropriate section of the drawing.

For instance to answer question one, the best area to locate this answer is in the title block. Some answers can be located in more than one area.

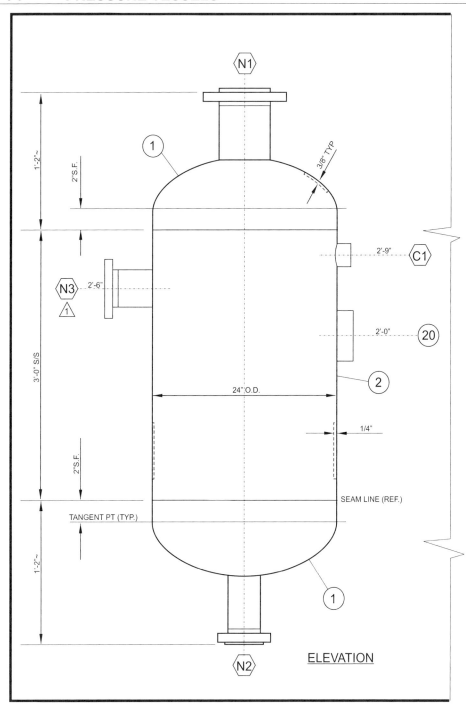

ELEVATION

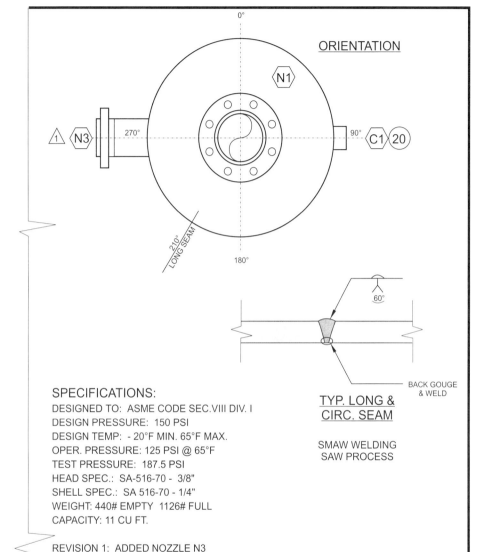

ORIENTATION

N1

0°

270°

90° C1 20

1 N3

180°

210° LONG SEAM

60°

BACK GOUGE & WELD

TYP. LONG & CIRC. SEAM

SMAW WELDING
SAW PROCESS

SPECIFICATIONS:
DESIGNED TO: ASME CODE SEC.VIII DIV. I
DESIGN PRESSURE: 150 PSI
DESIGN TEMP: - 20°F MIN. 65°F MAX.
OPER. PRESSURE: 125 PSI @ 65°F
TEST PRESSURE: 187.5 PSI
HEAD SPEC.: SA-516-70 - 3/8"
SHELL SPEC.: SA 516-70 - 1/4"
WEIGHT: 440# EMPTY 1126# FULL
CAPACITY: 11 CU FT.

REVISION 1: ADDED NOZZLE N3

IPT FABRICATION COMPANY
Air Receiver
DATE: JAN.2001   DRAWING 2-26A 1 of 2

NOZZLE SCHEDULE AND WELDING DETAILS

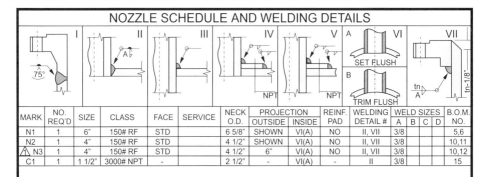

MARK	NO. REQ'D	SIZE	CLASS	FACE	SERVICE	NECK O.D.	PROJECTION OUTSIDE	PROJECTION INSIDE	REINF. PAD	WELDING DETAIL #	WELD SIZES A	B	C	D	B.O.M. NO.
N1	1	6"	150# RF	STD		6 5/8"	SHOWN	SHOWN	NO	II, VII	3/8				5,6
N2	1	4"	150# RF	STD		4 1/2"	SHOWN	SHOWN	NO	II, VII	3/8				10,11
N3	1	4"	150# RF	STD		4 1/2"	6"		NO	II, VII	3/8				10,12
C1	1	1 1/2"	3000# NPT	-		2 1/2"	-		-	II	3/8				15

BILL OF MATERIALS

	ITEM	QTY.	DESCRIPTION	MATERIAL	REMARKS	O/S	REQ. / P.O.
	1	2	24" O.D. x 3/8" NOM 24 S.E. ASME HD. W/2" S.F.	SA 516 70	HEADS		
	2	1	24" O.D. x 1/4" ℀ (R & W) x 3'-0" LG.	SA 516 70	SHELL		
	5	1	6" - 150# ANSI RFSO FLG	SA-105	N1		
	6	1	6" - SCH STD SMLS PIPE x 6 3/16" LG	SA 106B	N1		
⚠	10	2	4" - 150# ANSI RFSO FLG	SA-105	N2, N3		
	11	1	4" - SCH STD SMLS PIPE x 6 1/16" LG	SA 106B	N2		
⚠	12	1	4" - SCH STD SMLS PIPE x 6 1/2" LG	SA 106B	N3		
	15	1	1 1/2" - 3000# NPT CPLG	SA 105	C1		
	20	1	NAME PLATE c/w BRACKET				

GENERAL NOTES:

1. VESSEL TO BE THOROUGHLY DRAINED AND CLEANED WITH ALL OPENINGS COVERED BEFORE SHIPPING.

2. ALL BOLT HOLES TO STRADDLE NATURAL VESSEL CL'S UNLESS NOTED OTHERWISE NOTED.

3. EXPOSED INSIDE EDGES OF NOZZLES TO BE ROUNDED TO 1/8" MINIMUM RADIUS, MANWAYS TO 3/16" MIN. RADIUS.

4. ALL DIMENSIONS ON ⬡— ARE TO REFERENCE LINE UNLESS NOTED OTHERWISE.

5. ALL DIMENSIONS ARE IN INCHES UNLESS NOTED OTHERWISE.

IPT FABRICATION COMPANY

Air Receiver

DATE: JAN.2001   DRAWING 2-26B 2 OF 2

If you were looking for the thickness of the shell, it could be found in two locations. One is in the bill of materials, the other is on the drawing.

11. In what area of the drawing is the print number found?
Answer: _____

12. In what area is the grade of material found?
Answer: _____

13. Where is the following information found? "All bolt holes to straddle natural vessel centerlines unless noted otherwise."
Answer: _____

14. What change does revision one refer to?
Answer: _____

15. What section of the ASME code is referenced for the fabrication of this vessel?
Answer: _____

16. What section of the drawing shows the outside diameter (O.D.) of the nozzle neck for N1?
Answer: _____

17. What is the approximate empty weight of this vessel?
Answer: _____

18. Calculate the difference between the operating pressure and the hydrotest pressure.
Answer: _____

19. What reference line do the location dimensions originate from to dimension the drawing and layout the vessel shell?
Answer: _____

20. The revision is referenced in the nozzle schedule.
   ❏ true
   ❏ false

21. Determine the shell thickness of this vessel.
Answer: _____

22. List all the areas of the drawing that show the thickness of the head.
Answer: _____

23. Calculate the inside diameter of this vessel.
Answer: _____

24. Coupling C1 is how many degrees from the zero degree centerline?
Answer: _____

25. How many degrees is the longitudinal seam from the 180 degree centerline?
Answer: _____

26. Calculate the overall length of this vessel from the flange face of N1 to the flange face of N2.
Answer: _____

27. How far does nozzle N3 project out from the side of the shell?
Answer: _____

28. Determine the weld seam to weld seam length of the shell only.
Answer: _____

29. What is the pressure rating for each of the flanges used on nozzles N1, N2, and N3?

Answer: _____

30. What is the design corrosion allowance for this vessel?
   - ❏ 1/4 inch
   - ❏ 1/8 inch
   - ❏ 1/32 inch
   - ❏ not shown

31. What is the orientation of the name plate?

Answer: _____

32. Calculate the length from tangent to tangent between the two heads.

Answer: _____

33. What is the distance from the seam reference line to the center of the hole for nozzle N3 on the elevation view?

Answer: _____

34. Nozzle N3 is located on which of the vessel's quarter lines.

Answer: _____

35. What is the outside diameter of the pipe used for the neck of nozzle N1?

Answer: _____

36. Does nozzle N3 have a reinforcing pad?

Answer: _____

37. Describe the inside projection requirements for nozzles N1, N2, and N3.

Answer: _____

38. What is the material grade of the raised face slip-on flanges for nozzles N1 and N2.

Answer: _____

39. What is the nominal pipe size (NPS) of coupling C1?

Answer: _____

40. Will the item installed in C1 be welded or threaded into the coupling?

Answer: _____

41. Describe what will be done to the inside edge of each nozzle installed in the vessel.

Answer: _____

42. What is the projection from the seam line for nozzles N1 and N2?

Answer: _____

43. The included angle of the weld preparation for the longitudinal and circumferencial seams is 60 degrees.
   - ❏ true
   - ❏ false

44. Write out the abbreviations of the two welding processes used to complete the welding requirements for this vessel.

Answer: _____

45. What is the O.D. of the neck for nozzle N3?
   - ❏ 4 inches
   - ❏ 4-1/2 inches
   - ❏ 6 inches
   - ❏ 6-5/8 inches

Water Column Drawing 2-27

Several points to note concerning this drawing are:

- It is a vertical vessel.
- It has a semi-elliptical head on the bottom end, and instead of a head on the top end it has a weld neck flange with a blind flange for a cover.
- The vessel does not use a skirt for support, but has three legs made of angle iron.

The orientation view, which is a view of the vessel looking down on the top, shows the location of the nozzle, and other attachments to the vessel shell, in their position relative to the circumference (360 degrees) around the shell. The elevation view shows the reader the location of the same nozzles and attachments relative to their position from the reference line. Which, in this case, is the tangent line on the head. This reference line is abbreviated T.L. on the elevation view and establishes the 0 ft. 0 in. mark for the vessel.

The true position of the nozzles as indicated on the orientation view do not necessarily coincide with their apparent location as seen in the elevation view. For example, find nozzle 4N in the orientation view. It is located on the 0-degree centerline. Now find 4N in the elevation view. It is located on the left-hand side of the vessel close to the middle. The reason for this is the draftsperson will show the location of nozzles and other attachments on the elevation view in a location which is convenient for clarity and measurement purposes. This practise is common for all vessel drawings.

Note: One point which must be remembered to avoid any confusion as to the exact location of a nozzle is the following: The orientation view is used to show the location of components which are located on the shell in relationship to their placement around the shells circumference (360 degrees); while the elevation view is used to show the location of the same parts in relationship to a fixed reference line, such as a head seam or the tangent point on the head. These two dimensions will establish the exact center location of the nozzle.

Drawing 2-27 uses several other views to detail some of the vessel parts. It has a section view called Section A-A, which shows the layout of the base plate and its location on the support legs.

The Grating and Support Ring Detail shows how this internal is fabricated and welded. The 2N Nozzle Neck Weld Detail shows how this nozzle is fitted to the shell and welded in place. The remainder of the drawing is similar to the style used to develop many vessel drawings. This includes a Nozzle Schedule and Nozzle Welding Detail table which depicts the information about the nozzles and graphically displays the welding procedures for each of the nozzle configurations. This drawing has a bill of materials with many abbreviations common to vessel material bills. One item to note is the name plate stamping. This shows the required information stamped on the name plate which will then be fixed to the shell of the vessel.

Note: Most vertical vessel prints will show the orientation view directly over the elevation, similar to Illustration #2-21. However, if space does not allow this, the orientation will be shown to the side.

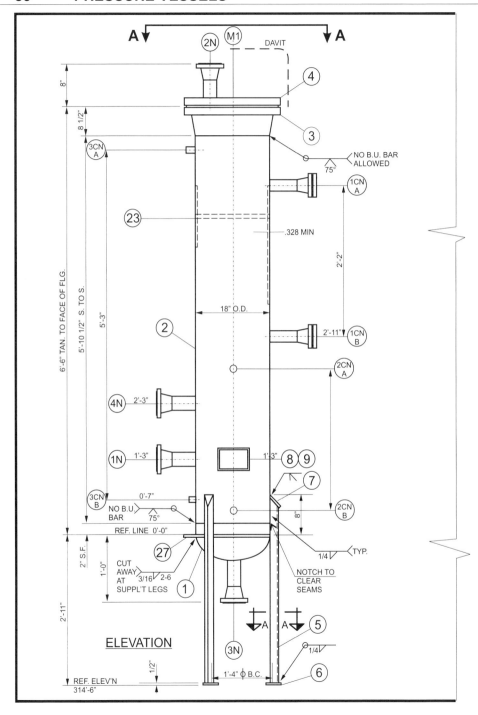

A

2N M1 DAVIT

4

8"

8 1/2"

3

3CN A

NO B.U. BAR ALLOWED
75°

1CN A

23

.328 MIN

2'-2"

18" O.D.

2'-11" 1CN B

2

2CN A

4N 2'-3"

1N 1'-3"

1'-3" 8 9

8"

7

3CN B 0'-7"

2CN B

NO B.U. BAR
75°

REF. LINE 0'-0"

1/4 TYP.

27

6'-6" TAN. TO FACE OF FLG.

5'-10 1/2" S. TO S.

5'-3"

2" S.F.

1'-0"

CUT AWAY AT SUPPL'T LEGS

3/16 2-6

1

NOTCH TO CLEAR SEAMS

2'-11"

ELEVATION

A A 5

3N

1/2"

1'-4" ⌀ B.C.

1/4

6

REF. ELEV'N
314'-6"

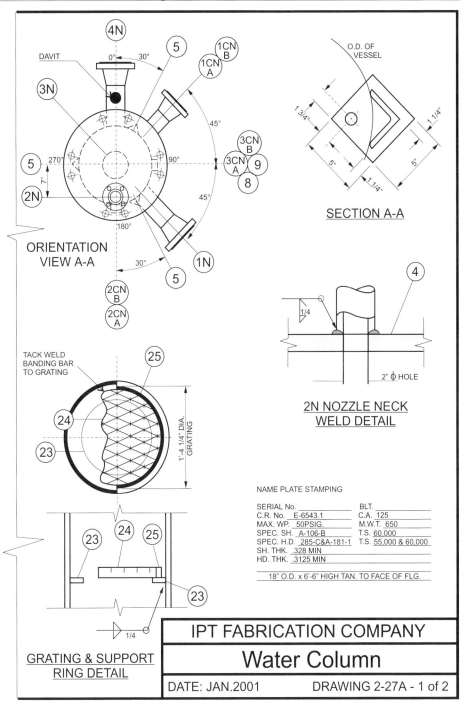

ORIENTATION
VIEW A-A

SECTION A-A

2N NOZZLE NECK
WELD DETAIL

2" φ HOLE

1/4

TACK WELD
BANDING BAR
TO GRATING

1'-4 1/4" DIA.
GRATING

NAME PLATE STAMPING

SERIAL No.	BLT.
C.R. No. E-6543.1	C.A. 125
MAX. WP. 50PSIG.	M.W.T. 650
SPEC. SH. A-106-B	T.S. 60,000
SPEC. H.D. 285-C&A-181-1	T.S. 55,000 & 60,000
SH. THK. .328 MIN	
HD. THK. .3125 MIN	

18" O.D. x 6'-6" HIGH TAN. TO FACE OF FLG.

GRATING & SUPPORT
RING DETAIL

IPT FABRICATION COMPANY
Water Column

DATE: JAN.2001   DRAWING 2-27A - 1 of 2

NOZZLE SCHEDULE & NOZZLE WELDING DETAILS

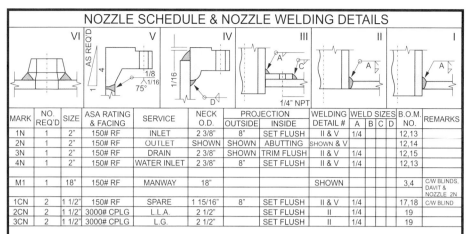

MARK	NO. REQ'D	SIZE	ASA RATING & FACING	SERVICE	NECK O.D.	PROJECTION OUTSIDE	PROJECTION INSIDE	WELDING DETAIL #	WELD SIZES A	B	C	D	B.O.M. NO.	REMARKS
1N	1	2"	150# RF	INLET	2 3/8"	8"	SET FLUSH	II & V	1/4				12,13	
2N	1	2"	150# RF	OUTLET	SHOWN	SHOWN	ABUTTING	SHOWN & V	1/4				12,14	
3N	1	2"	150# RF	DRAIN	2 3/8"	SHOWN	TRIM FLUSH	II & V	1/4				12,15	
4N	1	2"	150# RF	WATER INLET	2 3/8"	8"	SET FLUSH	II & V	1/4				12,13	
M1	1	18"	150# RF	MANWAY	18"			SHOWN					3,4	C/W BLINDS, DAVIT & NOZZLE 2N
1CN	2	1 1/2"	150# RF	SPARE	1 15/16"	8"	SET FLUSH	II & V	1/4				17,18	C/W BLIND
2CN	2	1 1/2"	3000# CPLG	L.L.A.	2 1/2"		SET FLUSH	II	1/4				19	
3CN	2	1 1/2"	3000# CPLG	L.G.	2 1/2"		SET FLUSH	II	1/4				19	

BILL OF MATERIALS

ITEM NO.	PART NO. OR REQ. NO.	QTY.	DESCRIPTION	MATERIAL
1	REQ.# 42856	1	HEAD 18" O.D. x 5/16" MIN. 24 S.E. 2" S.F.	A-285-C
2	REQ.# 42857	1	18" - STD (.375 WALL) SMLS. PIPE x 5'10 1/2" LG (BBE)	A-106-B
3	REQ.# 42862	1	18" - 150# ANSI. RFWN FLG. W/.375 WALL BORE	A-181-1
4	REQ.# 42862	1	18" - 150# ANSI. RF. BLIND FLG.	A-181-1
5	REQ.# 43600	3	3 x 3 x 5/16" ANGLE x 3'-6 1/2" LG.	A-36
6		3	PL 5" x 1/2" x 5"	A-283-C
7		3	PL 3 1/4" x 1/4" x 5" LG. (TRIM TO SUIT)	A-283-C
8	09-CU-938	1	NAME PL BRKT.	A-283-C
9	09-CS-1301	1	NAMEPLATE	S.S
12	REQ.# 42862	4	2" - 150# ANSI. RFWN FLG. W/XHY. BORE	A-181-1
13		2	2" - XXHY. SMLS. PIPE x 6 1/4" LG. (BOE POE)	A-53-B
14		1	2" - XHY. SMLS. PIPE x 4 1/2" LG (BBE)	A-53-B
15		1	2" - XXHY. SMLS. PIPE x 6 1/2" LG. (BOE POE)	A-53-B
17	REQ.# 42862	2	1 1/2" - 150# ANSI. RFWN FLG. W/XHY BORE	A-181-1
18		2	1 1/2" - XXHY. SMLS. PIPE x 6 1/4" LG. (BOE POE)	A-53-B
19		4	1 1/2" - 3000# COUPLING	A-105-11
23		1	F. BAR 2" x 3/8" x 4'-6" LG. (ROLL ON EDGE TO 1'-5 3/16" O.D.)	C.S.
24	REQ.# 43600	1	GRATING 1'-4" DIA. x 3/4" THK. W/3 1/2" RIVET SPACING 3/4 x 1/8	C.S.
25		1	F. BAR 3/4" x 106 x 4'-2 13/16" LG. (ROLL ON FLAT TO 1'-4" I.D.)	C.S.
27		1	BAR 3/4" x 3/16" x 5'-3" LG. (ROLL ON EDGE TO 18" I.D.)	C.S.
			FURNISH & INSTALL	
FOR		1	GSKT. FOR 18"-150# RF. FLG.	JM-60
M1	REQ.# 43600	16	1 1/8" Ø x 5 3/4" LG. STUDS c/w HEX. NUTS	A-193-B7 A-194-2H
FOR		2	GSKT. FOR 1 1/2" - 150# RF. FLG.	JM-60
1CN		8	1/2" Ø x 2 3/4" LG. STUDS c/w 2 HEX. NUTS	A-193-B7 A-194-2H
	REQ.# 42862	2	1 1/2" Ø -150# ANSI. RF. BLIND FLG.	A-181-1

IPT FABRICATION COMPANY

Water Column - Details

DATE: JAN.2001   DRAWING 2-27B - 2 of 2

Elevation View of Water Column Drawing 2-27

46. Calculate the distance from the bottom of the base plate (item #6) to the top of nozzle 2N.

Answer: _____

47. At the intersection points of number 27 and the support legs, which item is cut away?

Answer: _____

48. What is the distance from the reference line to the centerline of nozzle 4N?

Answer: _____

49. What is the projection of nozzle 3N from the reference line?

Answer: _____

50. What is the seam to seam distance from the seam of the bottom head to the weld seam of item #3?

Answer: _____

51. Determine the distance from the top of item #3 to the top of 2N.

Answer: _____

52. What is the distance from the reference line to the bottom of the support legs?

Answer: _____

53. What type of weld is used to attach the support legs to the shell of the vessel?

Answer: _____

54. What is the leg size of the weld attaching the support leg to the vessel shell?

Answer: _____

55. Calculate the elevation from the reference line to the center of nozzle 1CNA.

Answer: _____

56. What is the weld detail describing item 2 being welded to item 3?

Answer: _____

57. Refer to the weld that joins #3 to the shell. The bevel angle for the shell and the flange is 37.5 degrees.
   - ❏ true
   - ❏ false

58. Describe how the support legs will be prepared to clear the weld seam?

Answer: _____

59. What is the center to center distance between items #3CNA and 3CNB?

Answer: _____

60. The type of weld used to join the bottom head to the shell is called a:
   - ❏ fillet weld
   - ❏ bevel weld
   - ❏ vee groove weld
   - ❏ lap weld

Orientation View of Water Column Drawing 2-27

61. Nozzles 2CNA and 2CNB are orientated at 90 degrees.
   - ❏ true
   - ❏ false

62. Nozzle 1N is how many degrees from the 0 degree centerline:
   - ❏ 45 degrees
   - ❏ 90 degrees
   - ❏ 135 degrees
   - ❏ 180 degrees

63. Nozzle 2N is located on what center line?

Answer: _____

64. Nozzle 2N is how many inches off the 90 - 270 degree centerline?

Answer: _____

65. What is the number of support legs (item #5) shown in the orientation view?

Answer: _____

66. Which of the following shows the location of each leg in degrees from the 0 degree centerline?
   - ❏ 0, 90 and 270 degrees
   - ❏ 30, 90 and 270 degrees
   - ❏ 30, 120 and 270 degrees
   - ❏ 30, 150 and 270 degrees

67. The davit arm is located on the 0 degree centerline.
   - ❏ true
   - ❏ false

68. What type of line represents nozzle 3N on the orientation view.
   - ❏ hidden line
   - ❏ object line
   - ❏ section line
   - ❏ broken line

69. The name plate bracket is located on the:
   - ❏ 0 degree centerline
   - ❏ 90 degree centerline
   - ❏ 180 degree centerline
   - ❏ 270 degree centerline

70. How many nozzles are located on the 45 degree centerline?
   - ❏ 1
   - ❏ 2
   - ❏ 3
   - ❏ 4

Nozzle Schedule and Nozzle Welding Details Drawing 2-27

71. Nozzle 1N is designated as an inlet nozzle for this vessel.
   - ❏ true
   - ❏ false

72. What nozzle is designated as a spare?

Answer: _____

73. What nozzle is used as a level gage?
   - ❏ 2N
   - ❏ 2CN
   - ❏ 3CN
   - ❏ 4N

74. The pressure rating of the couplings is:
   - ❏ 150#
   - ❏ 300#
   - ❏ 3000#
   - ❏ not shown

75. What two nozzles are supplied with blinds?

Answer: _____

76. What is the outside diameter of the pipe that is used for the neck of the manway nozzle?

Answer: _____

77. What is the outside projection for nozzle 4N?

Answer: _____

78. List the Bill of Material item numbers that make up nozzle 1CN.

Answer: _____

79. As indicated in the weld detail, what is the leg size of the fillet weld required on Nozzle 1N?

Answer: _____

80. As shown in the weld detail, how much gap is required between the flange and the neck of 3N?

Answer: _____

Bill of Materials for Water Column Drawing 2-27

81. What is the wall thickness of the pipe used for the shell of this pressure vessel?

Answer: _____

82. The end preparation of item 2 is:
- ❏ square cut one end
- ❏ bevel one end
- ❏ bevel both ends
- ❏ square cut both ends

83. What is the leg size and thickness of the angle iron used for the support legs?

Answer: _____

84. Write out the following abbreviations.

XXHY _____

RFWN _____

SMLS. _____

FLG. _____

B.O.E. _____

P.O.E. _____

85. The nameplate is made of stainless steel.
- ❏ true
- ❏ false

Propane Storage Vessel Drawing 2-28

This is a horizontal pressure vessel used to store propane gas. Horizontal vessels are supported by saddles. The saddles are located close to the ends of the vessel because of the stiffening effect of the heads. This helps give the shell rigidity. Saddles are designed to cradle the vessel for about one third of its circumference. The saddles will sit on concrete footings or a steel structure, with the vessel cradled in the saddles which are fastened down with anchor bolts.

Locate the elevation view of this vessel. As with any vessel elevation view, the location of the nozzles as shown on the view are not necessarily their correct location on the outside circumference of the vessel. The elevation view only shows where the nozzles are located in relationship to the length of the vessel. The nozzles are shown in their correct position on the outside circumference of the vessel on the orientation view.

Some of the parts of the vessel are dimensioned using what is termed in drafting textbooks as conventional or standard dimensions. For instance the location of the saddles can be laid out from either end of the vessel.

NOZZLE WELDING DETAILS

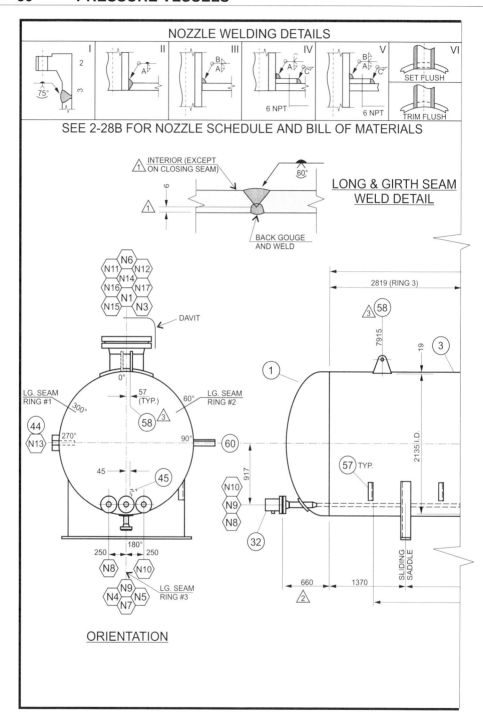

I

2

3

75°

II

A

III

B
A

IV

A
C

6 NPT

V

B
A
C

6 NPT

VI

SET FLUSH

TRIM FLUSH

SEE 2-28B FOR NOZZLE SCHEDULE AND BILL OF MATERIALS

1 INTERIOR (EXCEPT
ON CLOSING SEAM)

6

1

60°

BACK GOUGE
AND WELD

LONG & GIRTH SEAM
WELD DETAIL

N6
N11   N12
N14
N16   N17
N1
N15   N3

DAVIT

LG. SEAM
RING #1

0°

57
(TYP.)

300°

58   3

60°

LG. SEAM
RING #2

44

N13

270°

90°

60

45

45

180°

250   250

N8   N10

N9
N4   N5
N7

LG. SEAM
RING #3

ORIENTATION

2819 (RING 3)

3   58

7915

19

3

1

N10
N9
N8

917

32

57   TYP.

2135 I.D.

SLIDING
SADDLE

660   1370

2

GENERAL NOTES:

1. VESSEL TO BE THOROUGHLY DRAINED AND CLEANED WITH ALL OPENINGS COVERED BEFORE SHIPPING.

2. ALL BOLT HOLES TO STRADDLE NATURAL VESSEL CL'S UNLESS OTHERWISE NOTED.

3. EXPOSED INSIDE EDGES OF NOZZLES TO BE ROUNDED TO ____ MINIMUM RADIUS, MANWAYS TO ____ MINIMUM RADIUS.

4. ALL DIMENSIONS ON ⬡—— ARE TO REFERENCE LINE UNLESS NOTES OTHERWISE.

5. ALL DIMENSIONS ARE IN MILLIMETRES UNLESS NOTED OTHERWISE.

6. NOZZLES AND ATTACHMENTS PROTRUDING PAST INSULATION: PAINT (1) COAT LIGHT GRAY CONVERTED EPOXY RESIN, 5242/5243, 3.0 MILS D.F.T.; PAINT (1) FINISH COAT WHITE CONVERTED EPOXY RESIN 5240/5242, 3.0 MILS D.F.T.

7. BOLT HOLES IN STRUCTURAL MEMBERS TO BE DRILLED OR PUNCHED ONLY.

8. COVER ALL FLANGES WITH 13 MM THICK PLYWOOD COVERS C/W SOFT GASKET AND ADEQUATE BOLTING PRIOR TO SHIPMENT.

9. PAINT P.O. NUMBER AND ITEM NUMBER IN 76 MM HIGH LETTERS ON OPPOSITE SIDES OF VESSEL IN CLEARLY VISIBLE AREA.

10. ELECTRIC HEATERS AND EXCESS FLOW VALVES SHALL BE SHIPPED INSTALLED.

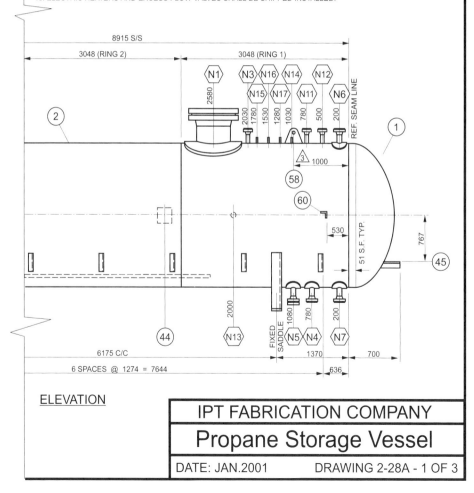

ELEVATION

IPT FABRICATION COMPANY

Propane Storage Vessel

DATE: JAN.2001   DRAWING 2-28A - 1 OF 3

NOZZLE WELDING SCHEDULE

MK	NO.	SIZE	CLASS	FACE	SERVICE	NECK OD	PROJECTION	
							INSIDE	OUTSIDE
N1	1	20"	150#RF	STD	MANWAY	508	330	VI(A)
N3	1	2"	150#RF	STD	RELIEF VALVE	60	230	VI(B)
N4	1	3"	150#RF	STD	INLET	89	230	INTERNAL
N5	1	3"	150#RF	STD	DRAIN	89	230	INTERNAL
N6	1	3"	150#RF	STD	INSTRUMENT COL	89	230	INTERNAL
N7	1	3"	150#RF	STD	"	89	230	INTERNAL
N8	1	3-2"	150#RF	STD	HEATER	60	SNC WN	INTERNAL
N9	1	3-2"	150#RF	STD	"	60	SNC WN	INTERNAL
N10	1	3-2"	150#RF	STD	"	60	SNC WN	INTERNAL
N11	1	2"	150#RF	STD	OUTLET	60	230	INTERNAL
N12	1	2"	150#RF	STD	VAPOR RETURN	60	230	INTERNAL
N13	1	1"	6000#NPT	STD	THERMOMETR	57	100	INTERNAL
N14	1	1"	6000#NPT	STD	PRESS.GAGE	57	100	INTERNAL
N15	1	1"	6000#NPT	STD	PRESSURE SWITCH	57	100	INTERNAL
N16	1	1"	6000#NPT	STD	PRESS.SW LOW	57	100	INTERNAL
N17	1	1"	6000#NPT	STD	PRESS SW. HI	57	100	INTERNAL

MK	REINF. PAD	WELDING DETAIL	WELD SIZES				BILL OF MATERIALS	REMARKS
			A	B	C	D		
N1	YES	I,VI	10		14		5 THRU 11 (INCL)	C/W DIVITED BLD
N3	NO	I, II	10				17, 18	
N4	YES	I, V	10	6	9		21, 22, 23, 24, 25	C/W CPLG &EXCESS FLOW VALVE
N5	YES	I, V	10	6	9		13, 14, 15, 21 - 25	C/W CPLG
N6	YES	I, V	10	6	9		21, 22, 23, 24, 25	C/W CPLG &EXCESS FLOW VALVE
N7	YES	I, V	10	6	9		21, 22, 23, 24, 25	
N8	NO	I, III	10	6			27 THRU 35 (INCL)	C/W HEATER & DISTRIBUTOR
N9	NO	I, III	10	6			27 THRU 35 (INCL)	
N10	NO	I, III	10	6			27 THRU 35 (INCL)	
N11	NO	I, III	10	6			36, 37, 38, 39	C/W CPLG &EXCESS FLOW VALVE
N12	NO	I, III	10	6			36, 37, 38, 39	C/W CPLG &EXCESS FLOW VALVE
N13	NO	I, III	10	6			40	
N14	NO	I, IIII	10	6			40, 42	C/W EXCESS FLOW VALVE
N15	NO	I, III	10	6			40, 42	C/W EXCESS FLOW VALVE
N16	NO	I, III	10	6			40, 42	C/W EXCESS FLOW VALVE
N17	NO	I, III	10	6			40, 42	C/W EXCESS FLOW VALVE

GENERAL NOTES

1. VESSEL TO BE THOROUGHLY DRAINED AND CLEANED WITH ALL OPENINGS COVERED BEFORE SHIPMENT
2. ALL BOLT HOLES TO STRADDLE NATURAL VESSEL CL's UNLESS NOTED OTHERWISE
3. ALL DIMENSIONS ON ⬡ ——— ARE TO REFERENCE LINE UNLESS NOTED OTHERWISE
4. ALL DIMENSIONS ARE IN MILLIMETERS UNLESS NOTED OTHERWISE

SPECIFICATIONS

DESIGNED TO: ASME CODE SECT.VIII, DIV I
DESIGN PRESS: 1723 kPa
DESIGN TEMP: - 29°C MIN, 49°C MAX
OP. PRESS: 862 kPa @ 16°C
RADIOGRAPHY: PARTIAL

JOINT EFFICIENCY: 100%
HYDRO TEST: 2856 kPa
HEAD SPEC: SA - 516 - 70, MIN 2:1 SE
SHELL SPEC: SA - 516 - 70, 19 PL
EMPTY WEIGHT: 12430 kg
FULL WEIGHT: 47215 kg

BILL OF MATERIALS

ITEM	QTY	DESCRIPTION	MATERIAL	REMARKS
1	2	2135 I.D. X 16.89 MIN.2:1 S.E. HD W/S.I B.F.	SA 516-70	HEADS
2	2	2135 I.D. X 19 PL (R & W) S.E. 3048 LG	SA 516-70	RING #1, #2
3	1	2135 I.D. X 19 PL (R & W) S.E. 2819 LG.	SA 516-70	RING #3
5	1	DAVIT F/20" ISO # R.F. FLG	C.S.	)
6	1	20" - 150 R.F. BLIND FLG.	SA-103	)
7	1	GSKT. F/20"RFWN FLG.W/SCH STD BORE	FLEXITALLIC 304 SS/ ASB	)
8	1	20" - 150 ANSI RFWN FLG. W/SCH.STD. BORE	SA-105	) N1
9	20	29 DIA. x 152 LG STUD C/W (2) HEX NUTS EA.	SA 52-LT SA 194 -4	)
10	1	20" SCH STD SML8 PIPE x 238 LG.	SA-106 B	)
11	1	845 O.D. x 514 I.D. x 19 PL (REPAD)	SA-516-70	)
13	1	3" - 150 ANSI R.F. BLIND FLG.	SA - 105	)
14	1	GSKT. F/3" - 150 ANSI R.F. FLG.	FLEXITALLIC 304 SS/ ASB	)FOR N5
15	4	16 DIA. x 89 LG STUD C/W (2) HEX NUTS EA.	SA 52-L7 SA 194 -4	)
17	1	2" - 150 ANSI R.F.W.N FLG. W/SCH.80 BORE	SA - 105	)N3
18	1	2" SCH 160 SMLS PIPE x 235 LG (NECK)	SA - 106 - B	
21	4	3" - 150 ANSI R.F.W.N. FLG. W/SCH 80 BORE	SA - 105	)
22	4	3" SCH 80 SMLS PIPE x 235 LG (NECK)	SA - 106 - B	)
23	4	191 O.D. x 92 I.D. x 12.7 PL (REPAD)	SA - 516 -70	) N4, N5, N6, N7
24	4	3" - 6000# SCR'D FULL CPGL	SA - 105	)
25	4	3" NPT EXCESS FLOW VALVE REGD A7539R6F (150 gpm)	STEEL	)
27	3	3" - 150 ANSI R.F.W.N. FLG. W/SCH 160 BORE	SA - 105	)
28	3	3" - 2" SCH STD.SMLS CONC. RED	SA - 243 - WPB	)
29	3	3" SCH 160 SMLS PIPE x 408 LG (NECK)	SA - 106 - B	)
30	3	2" SCH STD.SMLS PIPE x 6596 LG (INTER.PIPE)	SA - 106 - B	)
31	3	2" SCH STD. WELD CAP	SA - 243 - WPB	)
32	3	3" - 150# RF FLG'D HEATER CHROMALOX TMP-3-111-2 OR EQUAL		)N8, N9, N10
33	3	GSKT F/3" - 150 ANSI R.F. FLG.	FLEXITALLIC 304 SS/ ASB	)
34	12	16 DIA. x 89 LG STUD C/W (2) HEX NUTS EA.	SA 320-LT SA-194 -4	)
35	3	2" WIDE x 1/2" PL (REPAD)	SA - 516 -70	)
36	2	2" - 150 ANSI R.F.W.N FLG. W/SCH.160 BORE	SA - 105	)
37	2	2" SCH 160 SMLS PIPE x 225 LG (NECK)	SA - 106 - B	) N11, N12
38	2	2" - 6000# SCR'D FULL CPGL	SA - 105	)
39	2	2" NPT EXCESS FLOW VALVE REGD A2137 (50 gpm)	STEEL	)
40	5	1" - 6000# SCR'D FULL CPGL - 7" LG	SA - 105	N13, N14, N15, N16, N17
41	4	1" N.P.T. NIPPLE	STEEL	)N14, N15, N16, N17
42	4	1" NPT EXCESS FLOW VALVE REGD A1519-A2 (25 gpm)	STEEL	)
44	1	NAME PL & BRCKT W/100 PROJ.	SS NAME PL SA - 516 - 70BRKT	
45	1	153 x 5 PL x 340 LG (BEND INTO 475 x 75 x 340 LG AND FIT)	SA - 516 - 70	

IPT FABRICATION COMPANY

Propane Storage Vessel

DATE: JAN.2001   DRAWING 2-28B - 2 of 3

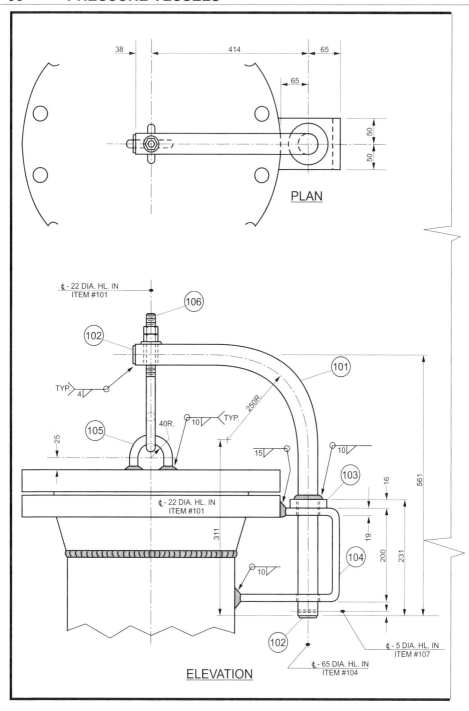

PLAN

ELEVATION

BILL OF MATERIALS

ITEM	QTY.	DESCRIPTION	MATERIAL	REMARKS	O/S	REQ. / P.O.
51	2	272 x 95 ℔ x 2320 LG. (ROLL ON FLAT TO 2173 I.D.)	SA 516 70	WEAR ℔		
52	2	796 x 9.5 ℔ x 2207 LG. (BEND)	SA 36			
53	4	162 x 9.5 ℔ x 322 LG.	SA 36	RIBS		
54	2	172 x 12.7 ℔ x 1902 LG.	SA 36	BASE ℔		
55	1	100 SQ x 6.4 ℔	304 SS.	GRD. WG		
101	1	2" SCH XXH PIPE x 906 LG (BEND)	SA 106 8	ARM		
102	2	48 O.D. x 5 ℔	SA 36			
103	1	90 O.D. x 63 I.D. x 16 ℔	SA 36	STOP		
104	1	100 x 19 ℔ x 526 LG. (BEND & TRIM TO CURVE)	SA 516 70	BRKT		
105	1	19 ø BAR x 205 LG (BEND)	SA 36	HOOK		
106	1	19 ø BAR x 452 LG (FORM EYE BOLT)	SA 36	EYE		
		c/w (2) N.C. HEX NUTS & (1) FLAT WASHER	SA 307	BOLT		

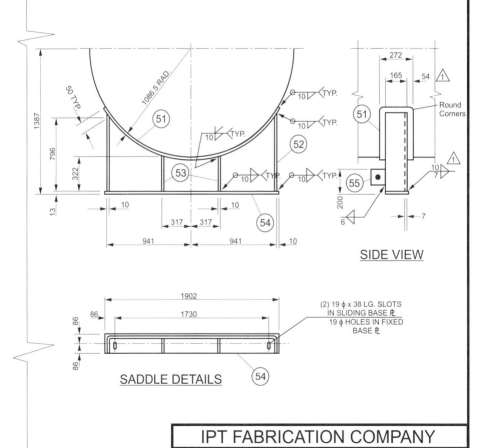

SIDE VIEW

SADDLE DETAILS

(2) 19 ø x 38 LG. SLOTS
IN SLIDING BASE ℔
19 ø HOLES IN FIXED
BASE ℔

IPT FABRICATION COMPANY

Propane Storage Vessel

DATE: JAN.2001   DRAWING 2-28C - 3 OF 3

However, the nozzle location dimensions all start from a common reference point, which in this case is the right hand seam line. The dimensions shown for the nozzles are to each of their centers and are written on each nozzle extension line. The person laying this vessel out in the shop would measure all the nozzle centers from the seam reference line on the right hand side of the vessel.

This system, called baseline dimensioning, is very accurate and does not require any mathematical calculations to obtain the measurement. This is because the exact dimension for each nozzle is written on the extension line for that nozzle.

Another type of dimensioning system, called group dimensioning, is used on the elevation view. Item numbers 57 have been dimensioned using this system. This method works well with dimensions which are the same and are repeated. Items 57 will be used to support a pipe that will be attached to the side of the vessel.

There are seven items 57 and each has the same spacing between them. The tradesperson simply locates the first one then repeats the spacing six times. If the last space laid out measures 7644 millimeters from the first one, they are laid out accurately.

Elevation View of the Propane Storage Vessel Drawing 2-28

86. What is the center to center (c/c) distance between the anchor bolt holes of the fixed saddle and sliding saddle?
Answer: _____

87. Determine the heel to heel distance between any two of item #57.
Answer: _____

88. The heel to heel distance between the first and last pipe support brackets (item #57) is:
Answer: _____

89. The length of the shortest ring section of the shell is:
❏ 2819 mm
❏ 3048 mm
❏ 6096 mm
❏ 8915 mm

90. What is used as the reference line for the elevation view dimensioning of the nozzles?
❏ tangent point
❏ circumferencial seam
❏ right hand head seam
❏ left hand head seam

91. What is the distance from the left end head seam to the center of the left end lifting lug?
❏ 1000
❏ 2000
❏ 2819
❏ 8915

92. Calculate the distance from the tangent point of the right end head to the center of N1.
Answer: _____

93. Determine the distance from the horizontal centerline to the center of nozzles N8, N9, and N10.
Answer: _____

94. What is the center to center distance between the holes in the lifting lugs?
❏ 1000
❏ 3048
❏ 6915
❏ 7915

95. How far is the heel of item #45 from the horizontal centerline of this vessel?
- ❏ 767
- ❏ 817
- ❏ 919
- ❏ 1092

96. The outside diameter of this vessel is:
- ❏ 2135 mm
- ❏ 2154 mm
- ❏ 2173 mm
- ❏ 2182 mm

97. What is the distance from the reference line to the first of items #57?
- ❏ 530 mm
- ❏ 636 mm
- ❏ 1274 mm
- ❏ 1370 mm

98. What is the length of ring #1?

Answer: _____

99. The overall length of the shell rings, not including gap, is 8915 millimeters.
- ❏ true
- ❏ false

100. The location of N13 as shown in the elevation view can be described as:
- ❏ near side to the viewer
- ❏ far side to the viewer

Orientation View of the Propane Storage Vessel Drawing 2-28

101. How many nozzles are located on the 0 degree centerline?

Answer: _____

102. The longitudinal seam for ring #3 is located on the:
- ❏ 0 degree centerline
- ❏ 60 degree centerline
- ❏ 180 degree centerline
- ❏ 300 degree centerline

103. Calculate the number of degrees apart between longitudinal seam #2 and longitudinal seam # 1, starting from ring #2 and rotating in a clockwise direction.
- ❏ 60 degrees apart
- ❏ 120 degrees apart
- ❏ 180 degrees apart
- ❏ 240 degrees apart

104. The lifting lugs are offset on each side of the 0 degree centerline. What is the distance between them?
- ❏ 57 millimeters
- ❏ 114 millimeters
- ❏ 45 millimeters
- ❏ 90 millimeters

105. How far is the center of nozzle N10 from the 0 - 180 degree centerline.

Answer: _____

Manway Davit Detail for the Propane Vessel Drawing 2-28

106. What type of weld is required to join item #103 to item #101?
- ❏ bevel weld
- ❏ vee groove weld
- ❏ corner weld
- ❏ fillet weld

107. What is the diameter of the hole in item #101 to install the eye bolt?

Answer: _____

108. The davit arm will be bent to a radius of 500 millimeters.

    ❏ true
    ❏ false

109. The length of the lower straight section of pipe on the davit arm, measured from the bottom of the pipe is:

    ❏ 231 millimeters
    ❏ 311 millimeters
    ❏ 561 millimeters
    ❏ 906 millimeters

110. Referring to the top part of the davit arm, calculate the length of the straight section of pipe measured from the end of item #102 to the start of the bend.

Answer: _____

Saddle Details of the Propane Vessel Drawing 2-28

111. What is the diameter and length of the slotted holes in the saddle base plate?

Answer: _____

112. What is the center to center distance between the slotted holes in the base plate?

Answer: _____

113. The wear plate will be rolled to a radius of 1086.5 millimeters.

    ❏ true
    ❏ false

114. The distance from the horizontal centerline to the upper side of the base plate is:

    ❏ 1387 millimeters
    ❏ 1374 millimeters
    ❏ 1065 millimeters
    ❏ 591 millimeters

115. Which of the following statements best describes the type of weld required to join item #53 to item #51?

    ❏ 10 millimeter fillet (typical)
    ❏ 10 millimeter fillet weld arrow side with a vee groove weld on the other side
    ❏ 10 millimeter bevel groove weld arrow side and a fillet weld on the other side
    ❏ 10 millimeter fillet weld arrow side with a bevel groove weld on the other side

SECTION THREE

STORAGE TANKS

Introduction to Tank Drawings

The layout of a tank drawing is similar to a pressure vessel drawing as it usually consists of an orientation view, an elevation view, as well as any detail views needed for fabrication and erection purposes. Tank orientation views show the location of nozzles and other components around the tank in relation to the zero degree centerline. The elevation view of the tank shows the position of the same nozzles and other tank components from either the bottom side or the top side of the floor, up to the centerline of that part on the tank shell.

Other views shown on tank drawings are the floor plate layout, roof type and layout detail, tank shell seam orientation, location of nozzles and fittings, ladder(s), and any platform details. Large diameter storage tank drawings also show the erection sequence of the individual floor and roof plates. The complexity of the detail views will vary with the size of the tank.

Types of Tanks

Tank design varies, but essentially the shape of a tank is cylindrical with a relatively flat bottom and roof. Larger storage tanks sit in the vertical position while smaller diameter tanks are either vertical or horizontal. Tanks are not pressure vessels and are not built to conform to the ASME Boiler and Pressure Vessel code. The ASME Boiler and Pressure Vessel code only includes containers that operate at pressures greater than 15 psi. Tanks seldom operate at a pressure above atmospheric pressure, other than the static pressure from the weight of the liquid they contain. The American Petroleum Institute (API) code is the governing code body most often referenced relating to the fabrication and construction of storage tanks.

Tanks are not pressure vessels, therefore the thickness of the steel shell plates for smaller tanks will average about $1/4$ to $5/16$ inches (6 to 7.5 mm) thick. The shell for larger tanks may vary from about 1 to $1 \, 1/4$ inches (25 to 32 mm) at the bottom to $1/4$ to $3/8$ inches (6 to 7.5 mm) at the top. Two roof designs are fixed roof and floating roof. Fixed roof tanks are common, while floating roof tanks are usually larger in diameter and used primarily for bulk storage of petroleum products. Floating roof tanks are much more complex in design than fixed roof tanks.

Unlike pressure vessels, most tanks are designed so the floor plates sit on an earthen base, instead of using separate saddle or skirt type supports. The earthen base made for the tank to sit on is most often gravel or a gravel and sand mixture. The tank base and the floor may be flat or the center may have a small concave or convex shape for drainage.

Fixed roof tanks usually have a conical roof. This type of roof may be self-supporting or have an interior steel structure made of beams and columns to support it. A floating roof tank is designed for the roof to float on the liquid in the tank and will rise or fall according to the liquid level. Some tanks have a combination of a floating roof and a fixed roof.

Tank Components

Floor: The tank floor or bottom is made of steel plates joined by welding. The individual floor plates for larger diameter tanks will be placed on the prepared tank base. After the first plate is correctly aligned, the next plate is positioned to overlap that plate. See illustration #3-1A. This allows for easy fit-up and welding of the floor plates.

A. Overlapped Floor Plates

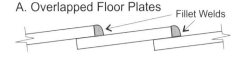

B. Butt Welded Floor Plates

Illustration #3-1 - Tank Floor Plate Welds

Another design method used to fit-up and weld the floor plates requires the use of back-up bars under the floor seams. These seams are then butt welded together. See illustration #3-1B.

Illustration #3-2 shows one method of how the floor plates may be positioned for a larger diameter storage tank. These plates are usually overlapped and fillet welded, but are occasionally butt welded together to create a leak tight seal.

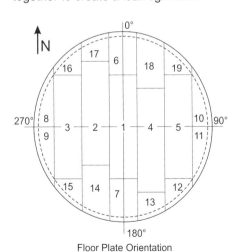

Floor Plate Orientation

Illustration #3-2 - Tank Floor Layout

Self Supporting Roof: The design of the roof will vary according to the tank diameter and the type of liquid in the tank.

The roof plates for a small diameter fixed roof tank are usually butt welded together on the shop floor. The plates are rectangular, and after being fitted together the overall rectangular size is larger than the roof diameter. Then a circular disk, again larger in diameter than the tank, is cut from these plates. A radial cut (a cut from the center out to the outside edge) is then made in the circular disk. When the center is lifted, the radial cut overlaps itself and a cone is formed. See illustration #3-3A. The overlapped edges are welded. The roof is then lifted on top of the tank and fitted to the tank shell.

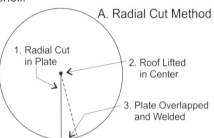

B. Sector Cut-Out Method

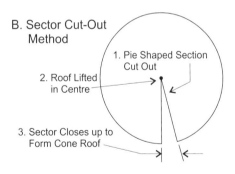

C. Flat Roof Plates

D. Roof Lifted Into Cone

Illustration #3-3 - Forming Conical Roofs

Another method of forming the cone roof for a smaller diameter tank is to cut a pie shaped sliver out of the circular roof. When the center of the tank roof is lifted, the pie shaped sliver closes and a cone is formed and welded. See illustration #3-3B.

Supported Roof: Larger diameter tanks with fixed roofs may require a separate steel structure including a column, or a number of columns, and rafter beams to support the roof plates. The rafter beams are attached (bolted or welded) to clips welded to the inside of the tank shell. The other end of the rafter beam sits on the column. The tank roof plates are then positioned on top of the rafter beams. There are numerous types of fixed roof tank designs, depending on the diameter of the tank. See illustration #3-4 for an example of a supported roof tank.

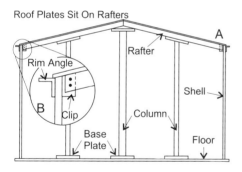

Illustration #3-4 — Supported Roof Tank

Floating Roof: A floating roof tank is designed to allow the roof of the tank to rise and fall with the liquid level in the tank. This type of roof has a pontoon welded to the tank roof. The pontoon is similar in appearance to a flat-sided doughnut, and it floats on the liquid in the tank. See illustration #3-5.

The pontoon for a floating roof must have an elaborate seal built in to protect against the release of hydrocarbons.

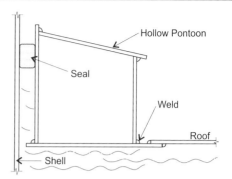

Illustration #3-5 - Floating Roof Pontoon

Floating roof tanks are designed for snow load in heavy snowfall areas.

A ladder, or a stairway spiraling up around the outside of the shell from bottom to top is necessary. A rolling access ladder pivoting at the top of the shell, which moves as the roof raises and lowers, is also necessary to permit access down onto the roof.

A rim angle on small tanks or a heavier stiffening plate around the tank rim is necessary to support the tank against wind damage. See illustration #3-6 for the basic design of a floating roof tank.

Again, the design of floating roof tanks will vary, with their design depending on the diameter, the contents, and where it is located.

Shell: The tank shell is made of steel plate rolled to the correct diameter of the tank. For small diameter tanks a cylinder is formed from flat plate and then the longitudinal seam is welded. One, two or more cylinders are fitted together to make the tank.

Larger diameter tanks are made by forming individual shell plates to the correct radius, then fitting them together to make one ring of the tank shell. On very large tanks this can amount to dozens of long shell plates.

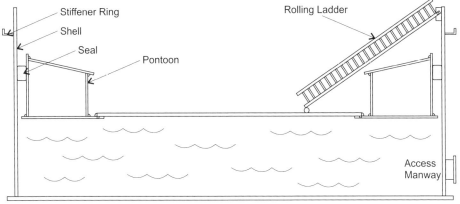

Illustration #3-6 - Floating Roof Tank

For example, a 200 foot (60.5 m) diameter tank is approximately 628 feet (190.2 m) in circumference and would require 20 to 30 separate plates for one ring, depending upon their length.

Illustration #3-7 indicates the terminology used to describe the tank weld joints.

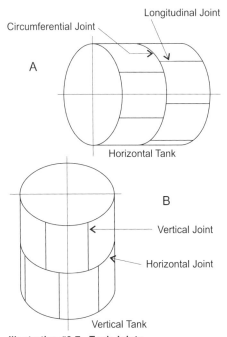

Illustration #3-7 - Tank Joints

The vertical (or longitudinal) weld joints for these shell plates must be offset from each other. The minimum offset distance is specified by code.

Storage Tank Questions

1. Most tanks are similar to pressure vessels in that they:
   - ❏ have two hemispherical heads
   - ❏ sit horizontal on two saddles
   - ❏ operate at high pressure
   - ❏ are cylindrical with an elevation and orientation view

2. Most tanks are vertical with floors that are:
   - ❏ flat
   - ❏ slightly concave
   - ❏ slightly convex
   - ❏ any of the above

3. For convenience, what is the usual method of laying out the floor of a tank for welding?
   - ❏ butt joints
   - ❏ lap joints
   - ❏ vertical joints
   - ❏ tee joints

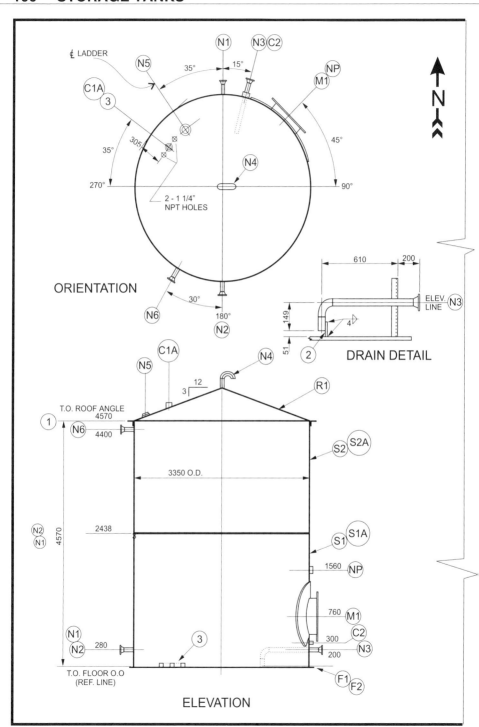

ℓ LADDER

N5

C1A
3

35°

305

35°

270°

2 - 1 1/4"
NPT HOLES

N1

N3 C2

15°

NP
M1

45°

N4

90°

ORIENTATION

N6

30°

180°

N2

N

610   200

149   4

51   2

ELEV.
LINE N3

DRAIN DETAIL

C1A   N4

N5

3 12

R1

T.O. ROOF ANGLE
4570

1
N6   4400

3350 O.D.

S2 S2A

2438

S1 S1A

N2
N1

4570

NP
1560

M1
760

C2
300

N3
200

N1
N2   280

3

T.O. FLOOR O.O
(REF. LINE)

F1
F2

ELEVATION

Tank Drawing 3-8

101

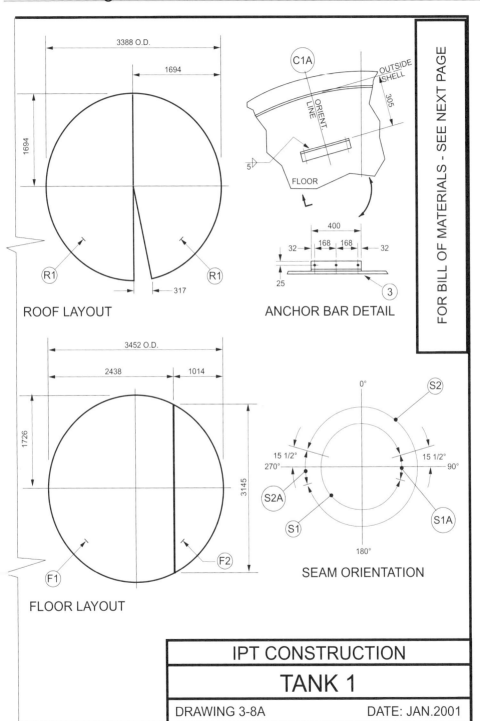

ROOF LAYOUT

ANCHOR BAR DETAIL

FLOOR LAYOUT

SEAM ORIENTATION

FOR BILL OF MATERIALS - SEE NEXT PAGE

IPT CONSTRUCTION

TANK 1

DRAWING 3-8A   DATE: JAN.2001

BILL OF MATERIALS

Mark No.	No. Reqd	Description	Service	Total Wgt.	Weld Type
S1	1	SHELL 6 (1/4") PL x 2438 x 9601 LG (3350 OD)		1271	S2,S5
S1A	1	SHELL 6 (1/4") PL x 2438 x 903 LG (3350 OD)		120	S2,S5
S2	1	SHELL 6 (1/4") PL x 2122 x 9601 LG(3350 OD)		1106	S2,S5
S2A	1	SHELL 6 (1/4") PL x 2122 x 903 LG (3350 OD)		104	S2,S5
R1	2	ROOF 4.76 (3/16") PL x 1694 x 3388 LG		372	S1,R2
I	1	ROOF ANGLE L 2"x 2" x 1/4" x 3337		49	T1
F1	1	FLOOR 7.94 (5/16") PL x 2438 x 3452 LG		443	B1,S4
F2	1	FLOOR 7.94 (5/16") PL x 1014 x 3145 LG		184	B1,B4
N1	1	FLG 60 (2") -150 RFWN x SCH XH BORE	INLET	3	F1
	1	NECK 60 (2") SCH XH PIPE x 168 LG		1	N5
N2	1	FLG 60 (2") -150 RFWN x SCH XH BORE	OUT-LET	3	F1
	1	NECK 60 (2") SCH XH PIPE x 168 LG		1	N5
N3	1	FLG 60 (2") -150 RFWN x SCH XH BORE	DRAIN	3	F1
	1	NECK 60 (2") SCH XH PIPE x 168 LG		5	N5
	1	ELBOW 60 (2") 90° LR x SCH XH		1	F1
	1	PIPE 60 (2") SCH XH x 76 LG		1	
N4	1	GOOSENECK 60 (2") 180° RETURN LR x SCH STD C/W 304 SS	VENT		
		BIRDSCREEN #4 x 2" DIA		3	F1
	1	NECK 60 (2")SCH XH PIPE x 203 LG		1	N2
N5	1	THIEF HATCH 8" F/G 54" CLAY BAILEY C/W STUDS & GSKT		68	
N6	1	FLG 60 (2") -150 RFWN x SCH XH BORE	BY-PASS	3	F1
	1	NECK 60 (2") SCH XH PIPE x 670 LG		1	N5
M1		MANWAY (SEE IPT-332-1-4 TYPE 1)		101	
2	1	SUPPORT ¼" x 1 ½" FB x 76 LG		1	
3	1	ANCHOR BAR L 2' x 2" x ¼" x400 LG		1	
C1A	1	CPLG 1" - 3000	LEVEL GAGE	1	C2
C2	1	CPLG 1" - 3000	T1	1	C5
NP	1	NAMEPLATE C/W BRACKET			
		TOTAL WT = 3847 kg			

IPT CONSTRUCTION

TANK 1

DRAWING 3-8B   DATE: JAN.2001

4. What type of tank roof is fabricated in a flat position, has a radial cut made in it, and is lifted in the center and welded into a cone shape?
 - ❏ self supporting
 - ❏ supported
 - ❏ floating
 - ❏ pressurized

5. The beams that extend from a center column out to the tank shell to hold up roof plates are called:
 - ❏ girders
 - ❏ davit arms
 - ❏ rafters
 - ❏ none of the above

6. A rolling ladder is found on what type of tank?
 - ❏ floating roof
 - ❏ self supporting
 - ❏ column supported
 - ❏ all of the above

7. On a very large tank, two vertical joints and a horizontal joint can all be positioned together in a cross shape.
 - ❏ true
 - ❏ false

8. What protects a floating roof tank against wind damage?
 - ❏ pontoon
 - ❏ column and rafters
 - ❏ reinforcing plate
 - ❏ stiffening ring

9. What is the name of the two items that hold up the roof of a supported roof tank?
 Answer:_____

Tank Drawings

Tank 1 - Drawing 3-8

Storage tank drawing 3-8 depicts a small diameter tank with a fixed conical roof. Because it is a small diameter tank, the roof is self-supporting.

The following questions refer to the orientation view and elevation view of Tank 1 - Drawing 3-8A.

10. What is the inside diameter of the tank?
 - ❏ 3350 mm
 - ❏ 3344 mm
 - ❏ 3338 mm
 - ❏ 3336 mm

11. What does the abbreviation "T.O. Floor 0-0" mean?
 Answer:_____

12. Specify the orientation and the elevation of nozzle N1.
 Orientation in degrees_____
 Elevation in millimeters_____

13. What is the elevation of the roof angle?
 Answer:_____

14. What is the slope, or pitch of the tank roof?
 Answer:_____

15. Determine the elevation to the top of the first shell ring.
 Answer:_____

16. How many individual shell plates are required to fabricate the two shell rings?
   ❏ 1 plate per ring
   ❏ 2 plates per ring
   ❏ 2 plates in total
   ❏ 4 plates in total

17. The orientation to the ladder center-line in a clockwise direction from the 0 degree centerline is 325 degrees.
   ❏ true
   ❏ false

18. Describe the orientation and elevation to the manway centerline.
Orientation in degrees_____
Elevation in millimeters_____

19. In what direction does nozzle N2 face?
   ❏ north
   ❏ south
   ❏ east
   ❏ west

20. This tank is classified as a floating roof type.
   ❏ yes
   ❏ no

21. The floor of this tank is:
   ❏ concave
   ❏ convex
   ❏ flat
   ❏ sloped

The following questions refer to the roof and floor layout and drain details of Tank 1 - Drawing 3-8A.

22. How many plates make up the tank floor?
   ❏ 1 plate
   ❏ 2 plates
   ❏ 3 plates
   ❏ 4 plates

23. The diameter of the floor is exactly the same as the outside diameter of the tank.
   ❏ true
   ❏ false

24. For the purpose of laying out the pie cut out for the tank roof, the length of the chord is 317 millimeters.
   ❏ true
   ❏ false

25. After fit-up to the top of the shell, what is the outside diameter of the tank roof?
   ❏ 3388 millimeters
   ❏ 3452 millimeters
   ❏ 3350 millimeters
   ❏ 3344 millimeters

26. What is the distance from the top of the tank floor to the center of the drain nozzle?
   ❏ 200 millimeters
   ❏ 149 millimeters
   ❏ 51 millimeters
   ❏ 40 millimeters

27. Which of the following nozzle flanges is a 4 inch, 300 RFWN?
   ❏ N1
   ❏ N2
   ❏ N3
   ❏ none of the above

28. The neck for nozzle N2 and N6 are both the same length.
   ❏ true
   ❏ false

29. The "level gage" is item:
   - ❏ N1
   - ❏ N2
   - ❏ C1A
   - ❏ C2

30. What is the diameter of the access manway?
   - ❏ 18 inch
   - ❏ 24 inch
   - ❏ 30 inch
   - ❏ not shown

Tank 2 - Drawing 3-9

Tank drawing 3-9 is a large diameter fixed roof tank. Included on drawing 3-9 is the roof and the floor layout. This shows how the roof and floor plates are marked and how they are positioned during the construction of the tank.

Unlike the self-supporting fixed roof tank in drawing 3-8, the roof for Tank 2 requires a steel structure for support. This roof structure is shown on a separate detail in drawing 3-9B.

The following questions refer to Drawing 3-9A orientation and elevation views and the Bill of Materials.

31. This tank has three manways. What is the piece mark number for the roof manway?
   - ❏ M1
   - ❏ M2
   - ❏ M3
   - ❏ M4

32. Which nozzle is designated for use as a sump?
   Answer:_____

33. Which manway is designated as the clean-out?
   Answer:_____

34. Referring to the orientation view, what will be the center to center distance between nozzles N14A and N14B after they are installed?
   Answer:_____

35. What will be the center to center distance between nozzles C1 and C6 after they are installed?
   - ❏ 203 mm
   - ❏ 1015 mm
   - ❏ 1676 mm
   - ❏ 2017 mm

36. By how many millimeters do each of the roof plates overlap each other?
   Answer:_____

37. Nozzle N2 is how many degrees clockwise from the zero degree centerline?
   Answer:_____

38. State the roof slope as a rise over run ratio for this tank?
   Answer:_____

39. Which drawing note refers to the nozzle projection?
   - ❏ note 1
   - ❏ note 2
   - ❏ note 3
   - ❏ note 4

40. Determine if this statement is true or false. "All 6 inch nozzles shall project from the outside of the shell to the face of the flange not less than 178 millimeters."
   - ❏ true
   - ❏ false

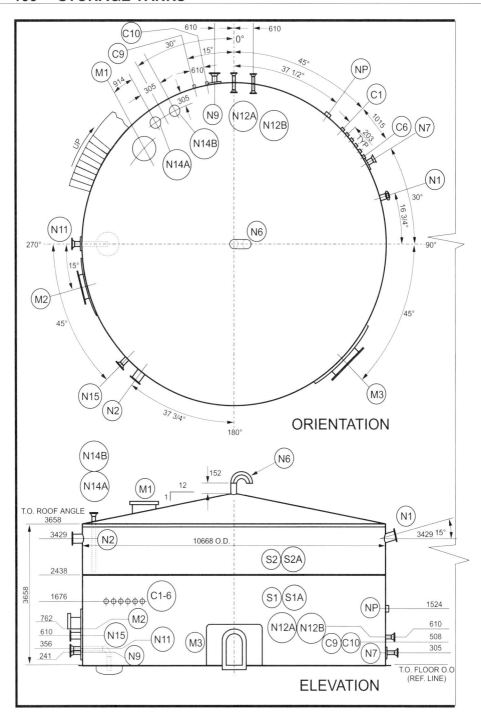

ORIENTATION

ELEVATION

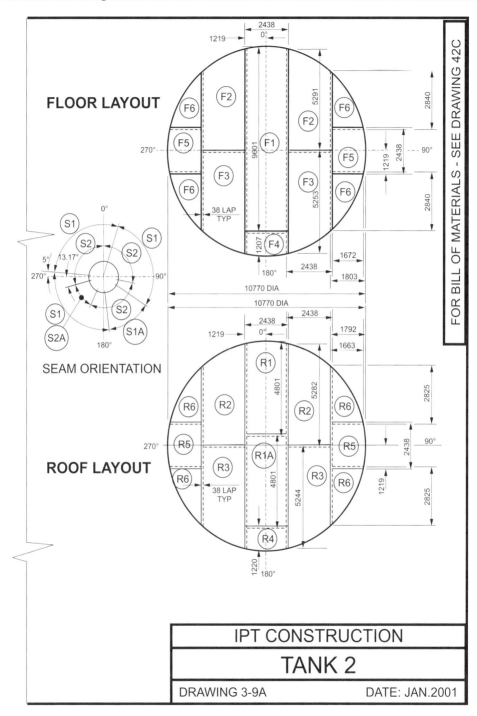

FLOOR LAYOUT

SEAM ORIENTATION

ROOF LAYOUT

FOR BILL OF MATERIALS - SEE DRAWING 42C

IPT CONSTRUCTION

TANK 2

DRAWING 3-9A   DATE: JAN.2001

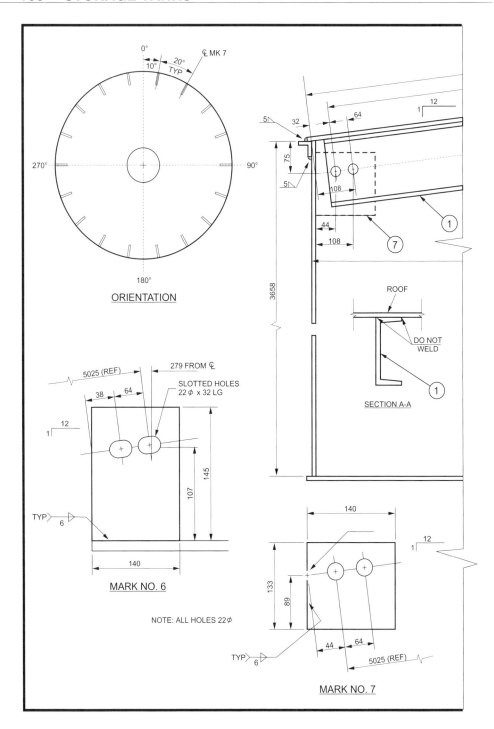

0°
10°
20° TYP
℄ MK 7
270°
90°
180°
ORIENTATION

12
1
5
32
64
75
5
108
44
108
7
1
3658

ROOF
DO NOT WELD
SECTION A-A
1

5025 (REF)
279 FROM ℄
SLOTTED HOLES
22 ∅ x 32 LG
38
64
12
1
145
107
TYP 6
140
MARK NO. 6

NOTE: ALL HOLES 22∅

140
12
1
133
89
44
64
5025 (REF)
TYP 6
MARK NO. 7

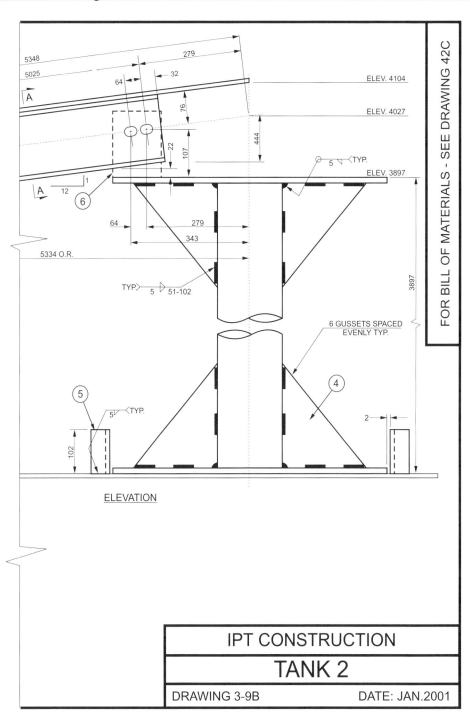

FOR BILL OF MATERIALS - SEE DRAWING 42C

5348
5025

A

279

64   32

ELEV. 4104

76

22   107

64

444

ELEV. 4027

5   TYP.

ELEV. 3897

A   1
12

6

64   279
343

3897

5334 O.R.

TYP   5   51-102

6 GUSSETS SPACED
EVENLY TYP.

5   4

5   TYP.

2

102

ELEVATION

IPT CONSTRUCTION

TANK 2

DRAWING 3-9B   DATE: JAN.2001

		Bill of Materials - (TANK 2 - DRAWING 3-9A)			
Mark No.	No. Reqd	Description	Service	Total Weight	Weld Type
S1	3	SHELL 3/16" PL x 2438 x 9601 LG (10 668 OD)		2860	S2,S5
S1A	1	SHELL 3/16" PL x 2438 x 4696 LG (10 668 OD)		466	S2,S5
S2	3	SHELL 3/16" PL x 1169 x 9601 LG (10 668 OD)		1430	S2,S5
S2A	1	SHELL 3/16" PL x 1169 x 4696 LG (10 668 OD)		233	S2,S5
R1.R1A	2	ROOF 3/16" PL x 2438 x 4801 LG		953	R1,T4
R2	2	ROOF 3/16" PL x 2438 x 5282 LG		1048	R1,T4
R3	2	ROOF 3/16" PL x 2438 x 5244 LG		1041	R1,T4
R4	1	ROOF 3/16" PL x 2438 x 1220 LG		121	R1,T4
R5	2	ROOF 3/16" PL x 2438 x 1792 LG		336	R1,T4
R6	4	ROOF 3/16" PL x 1663 x 2825 LG		763	R1,T4
F1	1	FLOOR 3/16" PL x 2438 x 9601 LG		1854	B1,B3,B6
F2	2	FLOOR 3/16" PL x 2438 x 5231 LG		2044	B1,B3,B6
F3	2	FLOOR 3/16" PL x 2438 x 5253 LG		2029	B1,B3,B6
F4	1	FLOOR 3/16" PL x 2438 x 1207 LG		233	B1,B3,B6
F5	2	FLOOR 3/16" PL x 2438 x 1803 LG		646	B1,B3,B6
F6	4	FLOOR 3/16" PL x 1672 x 2840 LG		1505	B1,B3,B6
N1	1	FLG 10" -150 RFSO		20	F2
	1	NECK 10" SCH XM PIPE x 246 LG		20	N7
	1	PAD 3/16" PL x 276 ID x 718 OD		9	
	1	BLD FLG C/W STUDS, NUTS & GSKT			
N2	1	FLG 10" -150 RFSO		20	F2
	1	NECK 10" SCH XM PIPE x 246 LG		20	N7
	1	PAD 3/16" PL x 276 ID x 718 OD		9	
	1	BLD FLG C/W STUDS, NUTS & GSKT			
C1-C6	6	CPLG 1 ½" - 3000		3	C3
M1		ROOF MANWAY (SEE IPT-326-1-1 TYPE 2)		82	
M2		SHELL MANWAY (SEE ST-380-1-4)		101	
N6	1	GOOSENECK 10" - 180° RETURN LR x SCH STD C/W 304 SS	VENT		
		BIRDSCREEN #4 x 10" DIA		76	F1
	1	NECK 10" SCH STD PIPE x 203 LG		20	N2
N7	1	FLG 3" 150 RFSO		4	F3
	1	NECK 3" SCH XM PIPE x 197 LG		3	N7
	1	PAD 3/16" PL x 92 ID x 343 OD		2	
N14		SEE DWG. IPT-3884-4			
N9	1	FLG 6" - 150 RFSO	outlet	9	F2
	1	NECK 6" SCH XH PIPE x 223 LG		9	N7
	1	PAD 3/16" PL x 171 ID x 495 OD		4	
C9	1	CPLG 1 ½" -3000	TI	1	C4
C10	1	CPLG 1 ½" -3000	TIC	1	C4
N11		SEE DWG. IPT-3884-4	SUMP		

	Bill of Materials - (TANK 2 - DRAWING 3-9A)					
Mark No.	No. Reqd	Description	Service	Total Weight	Weld Type
M3		MANWAY CLEANOUT (SEE DWG IPT-3883			
NP	1	NAMEPLATE C/W BRACKET			
N12		SEE DWG. S-3884-4			
N15	1	FLG 6" - 150 RFSO	INLET	9	F2
	1	NECK 6" SCH XH PIPE x 223 LG		9	N7
	1	PAD 3/16" PL x 171 ID x 495 OD		4	
		TOTAL WT = 17,998 kg			

NOTES (FOR TANK 2 - DRAWING 3-9A)

1. DIMENSIONS TO BE IN MILLIMETERS UNLESS OTHERWISE STATED

2. NOZZLE PROJECTION FROM OUTSIDE OF SHELL TO FACE OF FLANGE UNLESS OTHERWISE NOTED TO BE

SIZE	PROJECTION
3"	178
6"	203
10"	229

3. BOTTOM OF TANK TO BE TESTED PER API 650 PAR 5.3.2 (a)
4. TANK TO BE INSULATED BY OTHERS
5. HYDROTEST (WATERFILL)

	BILL OF MATERIALS - (TANK 2 - DRAWING 3-9B)		
Mark No.	No. Reqd	Description	Total Weight
1	18	RAFTERS 6 C @ 8.2 X 5088 LG	1118
2	1	COLLAR 6" SCH STD PIPE x 3827 LG	109
3	2	DOLLAR PLATES 1/2" PL x 16 DIA	96
4	12	GUSSETS 1/2" PL x 254 x 254	81
5	4	SUPPORTS L 2"x 2" x 1/4" x 102 LG	2
6	18	CLIPS ¼" PL 140 x145 LG	15
7	18	CLIPS ¼ PL 133 x 140 LG	14
	72	BOLTS ¾" DIA x 38 LG C/W NUTS	9
8	1	TOP L 2" x 2" X 3/16 X 10668 ID	121
		TOTAL WT. 1565 kg	

IPT CONSTRUCTION

TANK 2

DRAWING 3-9C   DATE: JAN.2001

41. State the code and paragraph that specifies the method that will be used to test the bottom of this tank.

Code:_____

Paragraph:_____

42. Determine if this statement is true or false: "The orientation of the first shell plate S1 is 275 degrees clockwise from the 0 degree centerline."

❏ true
❏ false

43. Which of these shell plates is the longest, S2 or S2A?

Answer:_____

44. How many shell plates are required to make the first ring of this tank?

❏ 1 plate
❏ 2 plates
❏ 3 plates
❏ 4 plates

45. State the requirements for hydrotesting this tank.

Answer:_____

Tank 2 - Drawing 3-9B

This drawing shows a typical steel structure used to support the roof of a large diameter fixed roof tank. It consists of clips welded to the shell of the tank and column in the middle of the tank sitting on the tank floor. Rafter beams are attached to the shell clips and the center column. The tank roof plates will lay on the rafter beams, however, for expansion and contraction, the roof plates are not welded to the rafters. The roof plates will be welded together and to the outside rim angle to make a leak tight seal.

The following questions refer to the Tank 2 - Drawing 3-9B, Roof Supports.

46. How many rafters in total are required to support this tank roof?

Answer:_____

47. What structural shape is used to make the rafters?

❏ angle iron
❏ channel iron
❏ wide flange beams
❏ flat bar

48. What is the clockwise orientation in degrees from the 0 degree centerline to the first rafter clip?

❏ 10 degrees
❏ 20 degrees
❏ 45 degrees
❏ 90 degrees

49. What is the center to center distance in degrees between each rafter clip?

Answer:_____

50. What is the elevation from the top of the tank floor to the top of the center column?

❏ 4104 mm
❏ 4027 mm
❏ 3897 mm
❏ 3877 mm

51. What type of weld is used to attach the column gusset plate (item #4) to the column center post?

❏ 5 mm. butt weld
❏ square groove weld
❏ seal weld
❏ 5 mm. fillet weld

52. How many gusset plates (item #4) are spaced evenly around the top of the column?
    - ❏ 6 gusset plates
    - ❏ 12 gusset plates
    - ❏ 18 gusset plates
    - ❏ 24 gusset plates

53. What is the slope of the slotted holes in the rafters clips stated as a rise over run ratio?

Answer: _____

54. What is the height to the top of the rim angle (item #8) from the top of the tank floor?
    - ❏ 4104 mm
    - ❏ 4027 mm
    - ❏ 3897 mm
    - ❏ 3658 mm

55. Refer to the chain intermittent fillet welding of the gusset plates to the column. What is the required length of each of the welds?
    - ❏ 5 mm
    - ❏ 51 mm
    - ❏ 102 mm
    - ❏ 125 mm

56. What is the radius from the center of the column to the outside of the tank shell?
    - ❏ 5334 mm
    - ❏ 5348 mm
    - ❏ 5025 mm
    - ❏ 5279 mm

57. Refer to section A-A. Write out the specific note regarding the welding of the rafter beams to the roof plates.

Answer: _____

58. What dimension would be used to position the column rafter clips from the center of the column to the center of the gusset plate hole?
    - ❏ 64 mm
    - ❏ 107 mm
    - ❏ 279 mm
    - ❏ 444 mm

59. What is the center to center dimension between the two outside holes in the rafter beams?
    - ❏ 4993 mm
    - ❏ 5025 mm
    - ❏ 5348 mm
    - ❏ 5483 mm

60. The base of the column is not welded to the tank floor, but is held in position with four angle iron supports.
    - ❏ true
    - ❏ false

SECTION FOUR

HEAT EXCHANGERS

Tubular Heat Exchanger Definition

A tubular style heat exchanger consists of a pressurized cylindrical steel shell with closures on each end, one or two tube sheet(s), and a tube bundle. At least one of the heads would be removable. See illustration #4-1. The tube bundle inside the shell will be one of two basic designs:

• A single tubesheet with a U-tube bundle
• Two tubesheets with straight tubes joining them together.

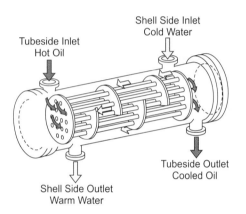

Illustration #4-1 - Typical Heat Exchanger

The tube sizes vary in diameter and thickness from one exchanger to another, but most are 5/8 to 3/4 inches (16 - 19 mm) in outside diameter (OD). The design of each tubular heat exchanger will depend on the end use. For instance, if the tube bundle of an exchanger will require frequent cleaning, the design will permit the tube bundle to be pulled out of the shell. Access from one or both ends also will affect the design. Another term used to refer to tubular exchangers is "shell and tube heat exchangers".

TEMA Designation System: TEMA is the abbreviation for the Tubular Exchanger Manufacturers Association.

This is the standard that is followed by designers, manufacturers, and users of heat exchangers. The TEMA standard is used in conjunction with ASME Section VIII, Division 1 and other related ASME codes. Such design criteria as material specifications, welding requirements, shell and nozzle design, and any other criteria related to the pressure components of heat exchangers meet the ASME code requirements.

A section of the TEMA standard designates heat exchangers as to their size and type. The designation, by letters and numbers, includes such items as: the shell diameter, type of shell, tube length, type of front head, and type of rear head. This information will be identified on the manufacturers drawings and on the nameplate of the completed exchanger. A description of this system of designating various types of tubular heat exchangers can be found in IPT's Metal Trades Handbook, or in the actual TEMA standard if further information is required on this topic.

Operating Principle

The function of a heat exchanger is to remove the heat from one medium and pass it over to another. This is usually accomplished through the heat transfer from one liquid to another, for example cooling hot oil by using cold water. In a reverse process, the exchange purpose could be for heating.

Often in the operation of an industrial plant, a product is heated by an operation process, and later the product will require cooling. If the heat can be recovered from one process and used for another process, there is less waste heat, and therefore greater plant efficiency. Shell and tube heat exchangers do this very efficiently.

The heat transfer method is a result of one liquid passing through the inside of the tubes, while another liquid passes over the outside surface of the same tubes, and heat is transferred from one to the other. The greater the number of tubes for the liquid to come in contact with, the greater the heat exchange surface, and therefore more efficient heat transfer.

In the basic heat exchanger design shown in illustration #4-1, hot oil enters the top of the head on one end, passes through all the tubes, and exits out the other head. Cold water enters the top of the shell, circulates around the outside of the tubes, and exits out the bottom. In this process, the hot oil is cooled, and the water is heated.

The two common terms used to define the passes the liquids make in a heat exchanger are shellside and tubeside. The liquid passing over the outside of the heat exchanger tubing is called the shell side flow. The liquid passing through the inside of the tubes is called the tubeside flow.

To better understand the operating principle, compare the operation of a tubular heat exchanger to a typical gas fired hot water heater in a house. On most low efficiency hot water heaters there is only one tube, which is enclosed inside the shell. The water is on the outside of the tube and hot flue gas is inside the tube. This tube runs from bottom to top on the inside of the hot water tank. The water inside the tank makes contact with the heated tube and the heat from the flue gas is exchanged or transferred to the water. This single, large diameter tube is not as efficient as a larger number of smaller diameter tubes, however the operating principle is similar.

Components

Shell: The most common design of heat exchanger is the shell and tube type. The purpose of the shell is to house the tube bundle. The shell is commonly made of carbon steel, pressure vessel quality plate. Due to the need to clean the outside of the tube bundle, the unit is normally designed to allow the bundle to be removed. See illustration #4-2.

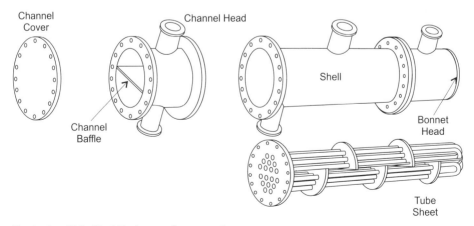

Illustration #4-2 - Heat Exchanger Components

Heads and Covers: Two common designs for heat exchangers are:
- Removable heads on each end.
- Fixed head on one end and a removable head on the other end.

A removable head is fastened to the shell with a flanged, gasketed and bolted joint to make a leak tight seal. Two common head designs are, bonnet heads, and channel heads. A channel head is shown in illustration #4-2. Channel heads can vary in design. A common design consists of a baffle (or baffles) to split the tube side flow. With one baffle, the liquid flows one way through half the tubes, and the other way through the other half. Two common types of heads with two pass baffles are shown in illustration #4-3. The channel head will bolt directly to the shell on one end of the head and have a removable end cover on the other. A bonnet type head is also shown.

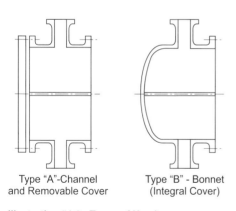

Type "A"-Channel and Removable Cover

Type "B" - Bonnet (Integral Cover)

Illustration #4-3 - Types of Heads

Tubesheets: Heat exchanger tubesheets consist of a flat, circular plate with holes drilled in a specific pattern. There are four specific designs used for the hole pattern, they are: triangular, rotated triangular, square and rotated square.

The triangular has a pitch angle of 30 degrees, the rotated triangular has a pitch angle of 60 degrees, the square has a pitch angle of 90 degrees, and the rotated square has a pitch angle of 45 degrees. See illustration #4-4 for an example of each of these patterns. The tubesheet patterns vary to allow for different cleaning methods and flow characteristics of the shellside (outside) of the tube bundle. On exchanger drawings, this hole pattern will determine the layout of the tubesheet.

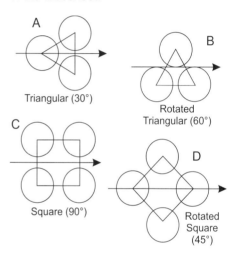

Illustration #4-4 - Tubesheet Layout Patterns

The term "pitch" refers to the center-to-center distance between each hole in the tubesheet. On heat exchanger drawings the tube hole pitch is either shown as a dimension on the tubesheet layout drawing, or as a note specifying the center-to-center distance. See illustration #4-5.

Tierods and Spacers: Two other terms that are encountered when reading heat exchanger drawings are tierods and spacers. The tube bundle is made up of the tubesheet, tubes, baffles, tierods, and spacers.

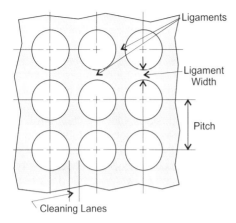

Illustration #4-5 - Tube Sheet Pitch

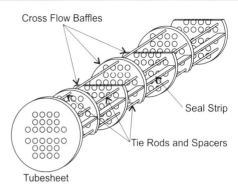

Illustration #4-6A - Tube Bundle Assembly

The bundle is assembled first as a cage made up of the tubesheets (or tubesheet depending on the design), the tierods, baffles and spacers. See illustration #4-6A.

The tierods fasten the tubesheets together along with the baffles. Each tubesheet will have drilled and tapped holes. These tapped holes only go partially through the tubesheet from the back side, thereby allowing the tierods to be threaded into the tubesheet. The baffles also have holes drilled in them for the tierods, however these holes are larger to allow the baffles to slide over the tierods. The spacers, which are made of small diameter pipe or tubing, slide over the tierods and are designed to keep the correct center-to-center spacing of the baffles in the bundle cage. See illustration #4-6B for location of the tierods, spacers and baffles. Note that in this example there is only one tubesheet, which would mean this exchanger is a U-tube bundle design. A U-tube bundle is shown in illustration #4-2. Another common bundle design has two tubesheets, one on each end.

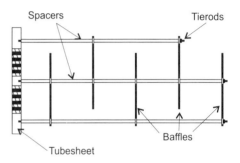

Illustration #4-6B - Tierods and Spacers

Baffles: The baffles in a heat exchanger are primarily used to direct the flow of the shell side liquid in a particular pattern over the outside of the tubes. The more the liquid makes contact with the tube surface, the more efficient the heat exchanger will be. Therefore arranging the baffles so the liquid must pass back and forth over the tubes allows for more heat transfer. The baffles are also arranged in certain patterns to help keep the heat exchanger from fouling or plugging up during operation. In addition, the baffles support the tubes inside the heat exchanger shell and they also help to keep the tubes straight. See illustration #4-7.

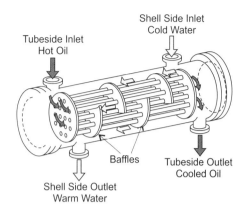

Illustration #4-7 - Heat Exchanger Baffles

Heat exchangers are designed with a head or heads that can be removed periodically so the tube bundle can be cleaned. The channel type heads shown in illustration #4-8 have a baffle (or baffles) to direct the flow of the tube side liquid.

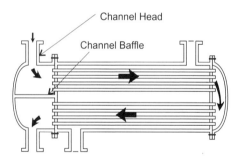

Illustration #4-8A - Two Pass Exchanger

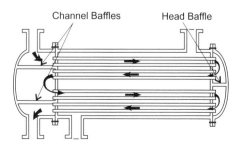

Illustration #4-8B - Four Pass Exchanger

A two pass heat exchanger has one baffle in the channel head that splits the channel head in half. This allows the liquid to enter one half of the tube bundle, pass through the tubes, make a turn at the other end and pass back through the other half of the tube bundle. Other channel head designs allow for two, three or four passes through the tube bundle. This greatly increases the efficiency of the heat exchanger. See illustration #4-8 for examples of two and four pass heat exchangers.

A kettle type reboiler is one type of heat exchanger commonly used in gas processing plants. It is often used to reheat or reboil a product that will be sent to a distillation tower for further refining. The space above the tube bundle allows the vapors being produced from the boiling liquid to be vented off and sent into the tower. See illustration #4-9 for a typical example of a kettle type reboiler.

This reboiler is similar to the kettle type shown in drawing 4-10.

Heat Exchanger General Questions

1. The two basic types of heat exchangers are the single tubesheet with a U tube bundle, and two tubesheets with joining straight tubes.
   ❏ true
   ❏ false

2. What does the abbreviation TEMA mean in regard to heat exchangers?

Answer: _____

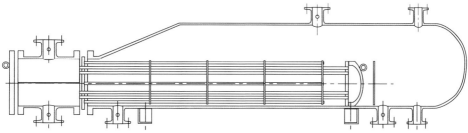

Illustration #4-9 - Kettle Type Reboiler

3. The basic function of a heat exchanger is to transfer the heat of one medium over to another.
   - ❏ true
   - ❏ false

4. Under normal conditions, which of the following heat exchangers would be the most efficient?
   - ❏ 1 - 4 inch tube
   - ❏ 2 - 3 inch tubes
   - ❏ 4 - ¾ inch tubes
   - ❏ 40 - ¾ inch tubes

5. A liquid passing over the outside of the heat exchanger tubes is referred to as:
   - ❏ tube side flow
   - ❏ shell side flow
   - ❏ end to end flow
   - ❏ circulation flow

6. A liquid passing through the inside of the heat exchanger tubes is referred to as:
   - ❏ tube side flow
   - ❏ shell side flow
   - ❏ warming flow
   - ❏ circulation flow

7. What is the primary reason for designing a tube bundle that is removable?

Answer: _____

8. All exchangers are designed with two heads.
   - ❏ true
   - ❏ false

9. What is the purpose of a baffle plate in the center of a heat exchanger head?

Answer: _____

10. What word describes the center-to-center distance between tubesheet holes?

Answer: _____

11. In a heat exchanger with two heads, what is used to hold the tubesheets and baffles in place before the tubes are installed?
   - ❏ gaskets
   - ❏ studs
   - ❏ flanges
   - ❏ tierods

12. What is the purpose of tapped holes in the backside of tubesheets?

Answer: _____

13. Which heat exchanger would be more efficient?
   - ❏ no head baffle or shell baffles
   - ❏ no head baffle and one shell baffle
   - ❏ one head baffle and two shell baffles
   - ❏ one head baffle and three shell baffles

14. A kettle reboiler heat exchanger has a space above the tube bundle for venting off vapors.
   - ❏ true
   - ❏ false

The following questions refer to drawing 4-10A, the Kettle Type Shell Reboiler, sheet 1 of 4

15. What is the outside diameter of the channel head?
   - ❏ 16 inches
   - ❏ 20-3/8 inches
   - ❏ 41 inches
   - ❏ 48 inches

16. Calculate the distance from the outside of the channel head to the center of gravity.

Answer: _____

17. What is the pressure rating of the shell outlet flange?
   - ❏ 150#
   - ❏ 300#
   - ❏ 600#
   - ❏ 900#

18. Calculate the center to center distance between the two ¾ inch full couplings used for the level gage.

Answer: _____

19. What are the dimensions of the slotted anchor bolt holes in the saddles?

Answer: _____

20. How much does this vessel weigh, including the tube bundle?
   - ❏ 2,400 lbs.
   - ❏ 9,000 lbs.
   - ❏ 11,400 lbs.
   - ❏ 19,000 lbs.

21. The inlet nozzle for the channel head is larger than the outlet nozzle.
   - ❏ true
   - ❏ false

22. What is the total weight of the vessel when full of water for hydro-testing?
   - ❏ 2,400 lbs.
   - ❏ 9,000 lbs.
   - ❏ 11,400 lbs.
   - ❏ 19,000 lbs.

23. What is the distance from the underside of the channel outlet nozzle to the top of the channel inlet nozzle.

Answer: _____

24. What is the minimum clearance needed to remove the bundle from this heat exchanger?

Answer: _____

25. Determine the measurement from the underside of the saddle baseplate to the top of the 10 inch shell inlet flange.

Answer: _____

26. What does the tube bundle for this vessel weigh?
    - ❏ 2,400 lbs.
    - ❏ 9,000 lbs.
    - ❏ 11,400 lbs.
    - ❏ 19,000 lbs.

27. The shell side hydro-test pressure for this vessel is 325 psi.
    - ❏ true
    - ❏ false

28. The tubeside fluid will make two passes through the bundle.
    - ❏ true
    - ❏ false

29. If the plate thickness of the shell was ½ inch when new, how thick will the shell be after it has corroded to its maximum allowable corrosion allowance?
    - ❏ ¼ inch
    - ❏ 3/8 inch
    - ❏ ½ inch
    - ❏ 5/8 inch

The following questions refer to drawing 4-10B, the Kettle Type Reboiler Shell, Channel and Tubesheet detail, sheet 2 of 4

30. From the tubesheet detail, determine the overall thickness of the tubesheet.

Answer: _____

31. What is the bolt circle (BC) diameter for the bolt holes drilled in the tubesheet?

Answer: _____

32. What is the height of the weir that controls the liquid level on the shell side of this exchanger?

Answer: _____

33. Determine the distance from the channel side face of the tube sheet to the outside of the tube bends for the tube bundle (bundle length).

Answer: _____

34. Calculate the distance from the back of the weir to the outside of the shell head on the left end of the exchanger.

Answer: _____

35. What is the thickness of the partition plate in the channel head?

Answer: _____

36. There are two lifting lugs used to install or remove the channel head.
    - ❏ true
    - ❏ false

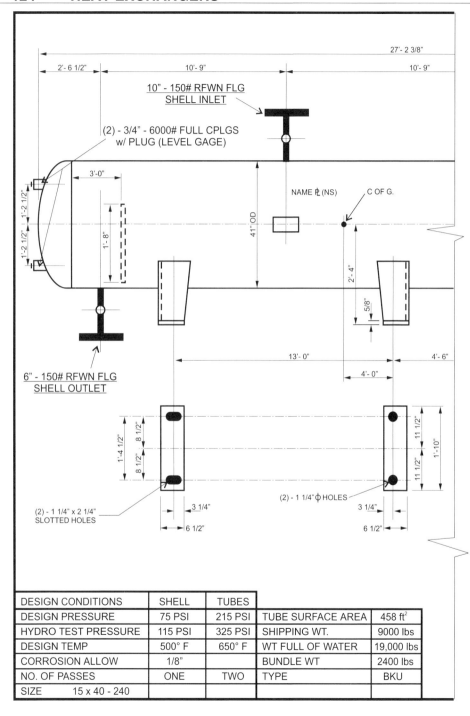

27'- 2 3/8"

2'- 6 1/2"   10'- 9"   10'- 9"

10" - 150# RFWN FLG
SHELL INLET

(2) - 3/4" - 6000# FULL CPLGS
w/ PLUG (LEVEL GAGE)

3'-0"

NAME ℄ (NS)   C OF G.

41" OD

1'- 2 1/2"
1'- 2 1/2"
1'- 2 1/2"

1'- 8"

2'- 4"

5/8"

6" - 150# RFWN FLG
SHELL OUTLET

13'- 0"   4'- 6"

4'- 0"

8 1/2"
8 1/2"
1'-4 1/2"

11 1/2"
11 1/2"
1'-10"

(2) - 1 1/4" ⌀ HOLES

(2) - 1 1/4" x 2 1/4"
SLOTTED HOLES

3 1/4"   3 1/4"

6 1/2"   6 1/2"

DESIGN CONDITIONS	SHELL	TUBES		
DESIGN PRESSURE	75 PSI	215 PSI	TUBE SURFACE AREA	458 ft^2
HYDRO TEST PRESSURE	115 PSI	325 PSI	SHIPPING WT.	9000 lbs
DESIGN TEMP	500° F	650° F	WT FULL OF WATER	19,000 lbs
CORROSION ALLOW	1/8"		BUNDLE WT	2400 lbs
NO. OF PASSES	ONE	TWO	TYPE	BKU
SIZE 15 x 40 - 240				

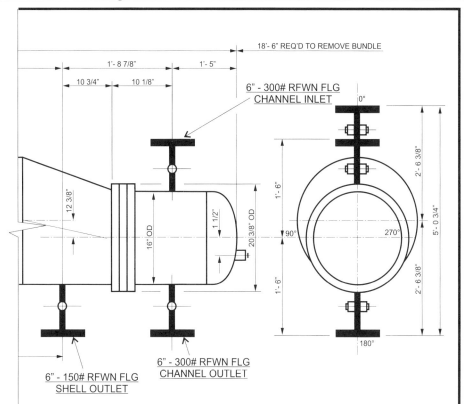

18'- 6" REQ'D TO REMOVE BUNDLE

1'- 8 7/8"   1'- 5"

10 3/4"   10 1/8"

6" - 300# RFWN FLG
CHANNEL INLET

0°

2'- 6 3/8"

5'- 0 3/4"

1'- 6"

12 3/8"

16" OD

1 1/2"

20 3/8" OD

90°   270°

1'- 6"

2'- 6 3/8"

180°

6" - 300# RFWN FLG
CHANNEL OUTLET

6" - 150# RFWN FLG
SHELL OUTLET

GENERAL NOTES:

CONSTRUCTION TO BE PER ASME CODE, SECTION VIII LATEST REVISION, TEMA

CLASS "R" & CUST. SPEC.

ALL BOLT HOLES TO STRADDLE C's, UNLESS OTHERWISE NOTED

EACH NOZZLE TO HAVE (1) 1" & (1) 3/4" - 6000 IPS CONNECTIONS AS SHOWN, WITH PLUGS

CODE STAMP REQ'D - YES

STRESS RELIEVE CHAN. & "U" BENDS

X-RAY SPOT (CHANNEL & SHELL)

IPT FABRICATING

Kettle Type Reboiler

DRAWING 4-10A - 1 OF 4   DATE: JAN. 2001

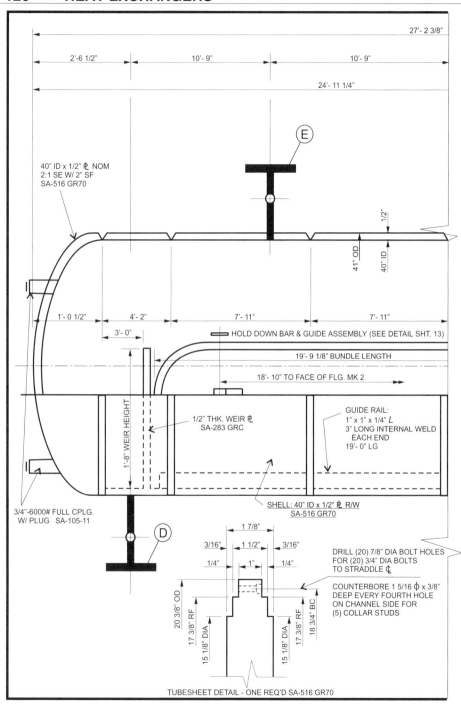

27'- 2 3/8"

2'-6 1/2"   10'- 9"   10'- 9"

24'- 11 1/4"

E

40" ID x 1/2" ℄ NOM
2:1 SE W/ 2" SF
SA-516 GR70

1/2"

41" OD   40" ID

1'- 0 1/2"   4'- 2"   7'- 11"   7'- 11"

3'- 0"

HOLD DOWN BAR & GUIDE ASSEMBLY (SEE DETAIL SHT. 13)

19'- 9 1/8" BUNDLE LENGTH

18'- 10" TO FACE OF FLG. MK 2

1"-8" WEIR HEIGHT

1/2" THK. WEIR ℄
SA-283 GRC

GUIDE RAIL:
1" x 1" x 1/4" L
3" LONG INTERNAL WELD
EACH END
19'- 0" LG

3/4"-6000# FULL CPLG.
W/ PLUG SA-105-11

SHELL: 40" ID x 1/2" ℄ R/W
SA-516 GR70

D

1 7/8"

3/16"   1 1/2"   3/16"

1/4"   1"   1/4"

DRILL (20) 7/8" DIA BOLT HOLES
FOR (20) 3/4" DIA BOLTS
TO STRADDLE ℄

COUNTERBORE 1 5/16 φ x 3/8"
DEEP EVERY FOURTH HOLE
ON CHANNEL SIDE FOR
(5) COLLAR STUDS

20 3/8" OD

17 3/8" RF   17 3/8" RF

15 1/8" DIA   15 1/8" DIA

18 3/4" BC

TUBESHEET DETAIL - ONE REQ'D SA-516 GR70

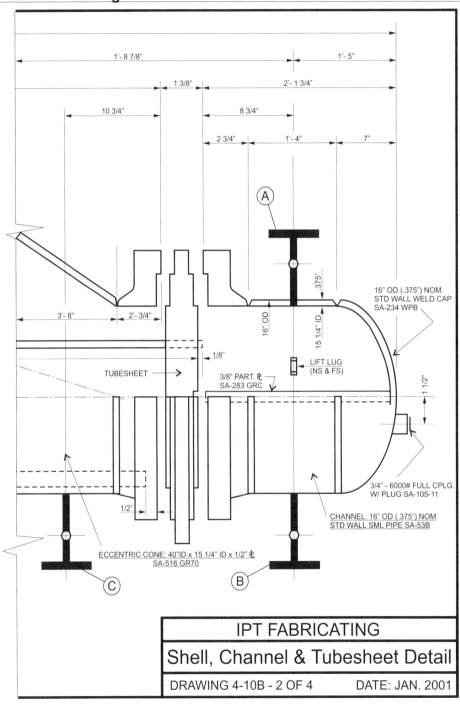

1'- 8 7/8"

1'- 5"

1 3/8"

2'- 1 3/4"

10 3/4"

8 3/4"

2 3/4"

1'- 4"

7"

(A)

.375"

16" OD (.375") NOM.
STD WALL WELD CAP
SA-234 WPB

16" OD

15 1/4" ID

3'- 8"

2'- 3/4"

1/8"

LIFT LUG
(NS & FS)

TUBESHEET →

3/8" PART. ℄
SA-283 GRC

1 1/2"

1/2"

3/4" - 6000# FULL CPLG.
W/ PLUG SA-105-11

CHANNEL: 16" OD (.375") NOM
STD WALL SML PIPE SA-53B

ECCENTRIC CONE: 40"ID x 15 1/4" ID x 1/2" ℄
SA-516 GR70

(C)

(B)

IPT FABRICATING

Shell, Channel & Tubesheet Detail

DRAWING 4-10B - 2 OF 4   DATE: JAN. 2001

37. State the amount the tube end protrudes past the face of the tubesheet on the channel head side?

Answer: _____

38. What is the leg size and thickness of the angle iron used as the guide rail for installing or removing the bundle?

Answer: _____

The following questions refer to drawing 4-10C, the Kettle Type Reboiler Tube Hole Layout drawing, sheet 3 of 4

39. The maximum diameter that the tube holes can measure after completion of drilling and reaming is:
   ❏ .750 in.
   ❏ .752 in.
   ❏ .758 in.
   ❏ .760 in.

40. What is the width of the grooves for the tube hole grooving detail?
   ❏ .010 of an inch
   ❏ 1/64 of an inch
   ❏ .125 of an inch
   ❏ .375 of an inch

41. What is the distance from the channel head side of the tubesheet face to the center of the second groove in any of the tube holes?
   ❏ 3/8 of an inch
   ❏ ½ of an inch
   ❏ 7/8 of an inch
   ❏ 15/16 of an inch

42. How many tube holes will be drilled and reamed in the tubesheet.
   ❏ 32 holes
   ❏ 62 holes
   ❏ 124 holes
   ❏ 128 holes

43. How many holes will be drilled in the tubesheet to accommodate the tierods.
   ❏ 2
   ❏ 4
   ❏ 6
   ❏ 8

44. The distance from the center of the tubesheet to the center of each of the tierod holes, both horizontal and vertical, is 7 inches.
   ❏ true
   ❏ false

45. The center to center distance between horizontal rows 2 and 3 for this tubesheet is 1-1/8 inches.
   ❏ true
   ❏ false

46. State the outside diameter of the tubes.

Answer: _____

47. The tube pitch for this tubesheet is 1 inch square.
   ❏ true
   ❏ false

48. State the number of passes that this exchanger is categorized as:

Answer: _____

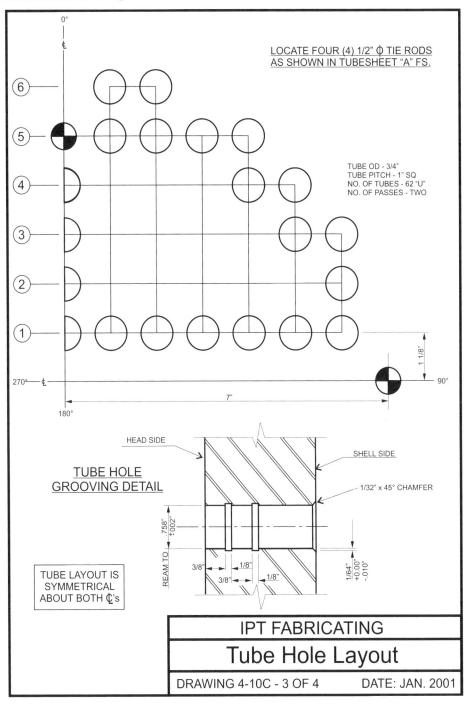

LOCATE FOUR (4) 1/2" ⌀ TIE RODS
AS SHOWN IN TUBESHEET "A" FS.

TUBE OD - 3/4"
TUBE PITCH - 1" SQ
NO. OF TUBES - 62 "U"
NO. OF PASSES - TWO

1 1/8"

7"

TUBE HOLE
GROOVING DETAIL

HEAD SIDE

SHELL SIDE

1/32" x 45° CHAMFER

REAM TO .758" +.002"

3/8"

1/8"

3/8"

1/8"

1/64" +0.00" -.010"

TUBE LAYOUT IS
SYMMETRICAL
ABOUT BOTH ₵'s

IPT FABRICATING

Tube Hole Layout

DRAWING 4-10C - 3 OF 4   DATE: JAN. 2001

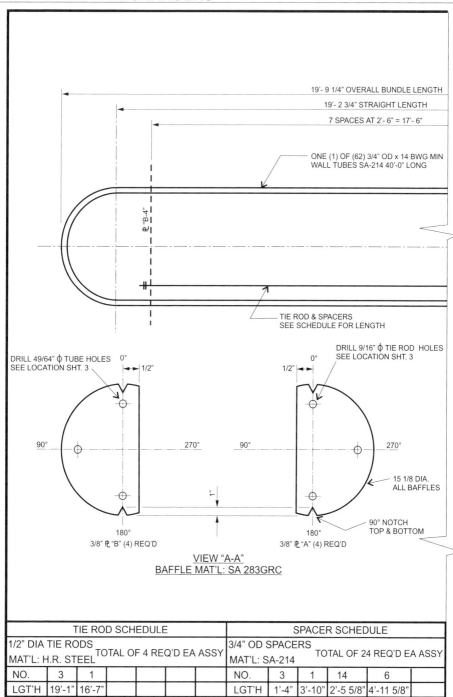

19'- 9 1/4" OVERALL BUNDLE LENGTH

19'- 2 3/4" STRAIGHT LENGTH

7 SPACES AT 2'- 6" = 17'- 6"

ONE (1) OF (62) 3/4" OD x 14 BWG MIN WALL TUBES SA-214 40'-0" LONG

℄ "B-4"

TIE ROD & SPACERS
SEE SCHEDULE FOR LENGTH

DRILL 49/64" φ TUBE HOLES
SEE LOCATION SHT. 3

DRILL 9/16" φ TIE ROD HOLES
SEE LOCATION SHT. 3

0°   1/2"

1/2"   0°

90°   270°   90°   270°

15 1/8 DIA.
ALL BAFFLES

1"

90° NOTCH
TOP & BOTTOM

180°
3/8" ℄ "B" (4) REQ'D

180°
3/8" ℄ "A" (4) REQ'D

VIEW "A-A"
BAFFLE MAT'L: SA 283GRC

TIE ROD SCHEDULE								SPACER SCHEDULE					
1/2" DIA TIE RODS MAT'L: H.R. STEEL			TOTAL OF 4 REQ'D EA ASSY					3/4" OD SPACERS MAT'L: SA-214			TOTAL OF 24 REQ'D EA ASSY		
NO.	3	1						NO.	3	1	14	6	
LGT'H	19'-1"	16'-7"						LGT'H	1'-4"	3'-10"	2'-5 5/8"	4'-11 5/8"	

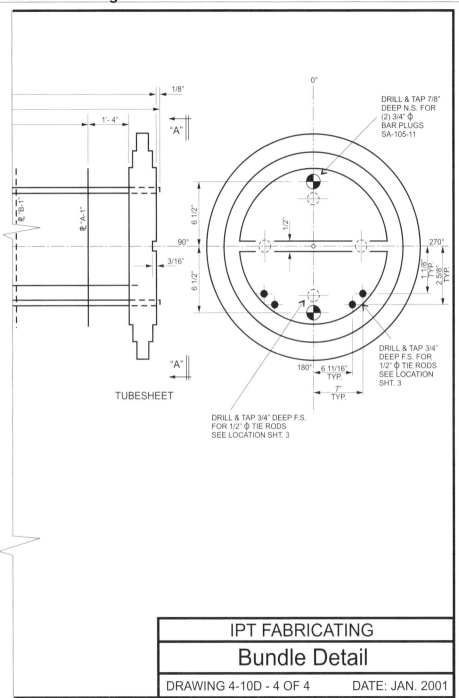

1/8"

1'- 4"

"A"

"A"

℄ "B-1"

℄ "A-1"

3/16"

TUBESHEET

0°

DRILL & TAP 7/8"
DEEP N.S. FOR
(2) 3/4" φ
BAR PLUGS
SA-105-11

6 1/2"

6 1/2"

1/2"

90°

270°

1 1/8"
TYP.

2 5/8"
TYP.

180°

6 11/16"
TYP.

7"
TYP.

DRILL & TAP 3/4"
DEEP F.S. FOR
1/2" φ TIE RODS
SEE LOCATION
SHT. 3

DRILL & TAP 3/4" DEEP F.S.
FOR 1/2" φ TIE RODS
SEE LOCATION SHT. 3

IPT FABRICATING

Bundle Detail

DRAWING 4-10D - 4 OF 4   DATE: JAN. 2001

The following questions refer to drawing 4-10D, the Kettle Type Reboiler Bundle Detail Drawing, sheet 4 of 4

49. Calculate the difference between the overall bundle length and the straight length of the tubes.

Answer: _____

50. What is the minimum gage thickness of the tubes in the bundle?
  - ❏ 75 gage
  - ❏ 62 gage
  - ❏ 16 gage
  - ❏ 14 gage

51. What is the depth of the holes drilled in the tubesheet for the tierods?

Answer: _____

52. What is the diameter of the tierod holes drilled in the baffles?
  - ❏ 1/2 inch
  - ❏ 9/16 inch
  - ❏ 5/8 inch
  - ❏ 3/4 inch

53. What is the diameter of the tube holes drilled in the baffles?
  - ❏ 49/64 inch
  - ❏ .758 inch
  - ❏ 3/4 inch
  - ❏ 5/8 inch

54. What is the diameter of all of the baffles, as stated in the drawing?

Answer: _____

55. How many half baffles will be required for this tube bundle?
  - ❏ 4
  - ❏ 8
  - ❏ 12
  - ❏ 16

56. The height of the 90 degree notches cut in the baffle plates is 1 inch.
  - ❏ true
  - ❏ false

57. What is the straight length of the tubes prior to their being bent for the U shape bundle?
  - ❏ 20 feet
  - ❏ 30 feet
  - ❏ 40 feet
  - ❏ 80 feet

58. What is the center to center spacing between baffles spaced along the length of the tube sheet?

Answer: _____

Oil Cooler Drawing

Drawing 4-12 is an oil cooler heat exchanger. This oil cooler is a common heat exchanger design. It has a removable channel head on one end, and a removable rear cover on the other end, called the bonnet. Refer to illustration #4-11 to locate the following main components of an oil cooler exchanger:

- Item number 1 is the channel head cover
- Item number 2 is the channel head
- Item number 3 is the tubesheet
- Item number 4 is the shell
- Item number 5 is the removable rear cover or bonnet
- Item number 6 are the lifting lugs
- Item number 7 are the saddles

Again referring to illustration #4-11A, there are two nozzles on the channel cover. These are the inlet and outlet nozzles for the fluid that travels through the inside of the tubes. The two nozzles located on the shell of the oil cooler are the inlet and outlet nozzles for the fluid that flows across the outside of the tubes.

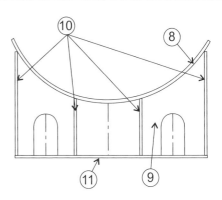

Illustration #4-11B - Parts of the Saddle

Illustration #4-11B is a view of the saddles used to support the oil cooler. The terminology used to name the parts that make up the saddles is as follows:

- Item number 8 is the wear plate
- Item number 9 is the web plate
- Item number 10 are the inner and outer rib stiffeners
- Item number 11 is the base plate

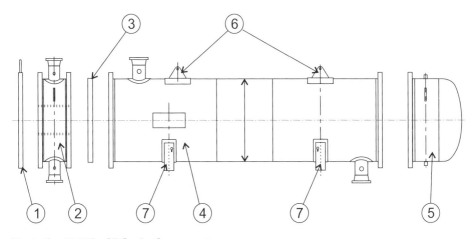

Illustration #4-11A - Oil Cooler Components

The following questions refer to drawing 4-12A, Oil Cooler, sheet 1 of 3

59. View A-A is an end view of the channel head showing the general arrangement of the channel head baffles, orientation of lifting lugs and nozzles.
   ❏ true
   ❏ false

60. The outside diameter of the shell is:
   ❏ 64 inches
   ❏ 59¾ inches
   ❏ 59¼ inches
   ❏ does not specifiy

61. State the overall length of this heat exchanger in millimeters.

Answer: _____

62. The location of the longitudinal seam for the channel head is on the:
   ❏ 90 degree centerline
   ❏ 180 degree centerline
   ❏ 270 degree centerline
   ❏ 360 degree centerline

63. How many individual courses will be needed to make up the shell of the main heat exchanger body (not including the channel cover or rear cover)
   ❏ one course
   ❏ two courses
   ❏ three courses
   ❏ four courses

64. After the channel head is bolted to the shell of the heat exchanger, the distance between the two flanges to accommodate the tubesheet is how many inches?

Answer: _____

65. What is the distance from the left 0 (zero) reference line to the centerline of the fixed end saddle?

Answer: _____

66. Which answer indicates the center to center distance between the fixed end saddle and the sliding end saddle in millimeters.
   ❏ 816 mm
   ❏ 3816 mm
   ❏ 4632 mm
   ❏ 5448 mm

67. The distance from the left 0 (zero) reference line to the centerline of nozzle D on the channel head is:
   ❏ 18 inches
   ❏ 20 inches
   ❏ 24 inches
   ❏ 28 inches

68. How many lifting lugs (item # 9) will be installed on the channel head?
   ❏ one
   ❏ two
   ❏ three
   ❏ four

69. The inside radius of the saddle wear plate will be:

Answer: _____

70. State the width and length dimensions (in inches) of the saddle base plate.

Answer: _____

71. What is the leg size of the fillet welds on the saddle?

Answer: _____

72. State the dimensions of the slotted holes (in millimeters) in the sliding saddle.

Answer: _____

73. Referring to the Nozzle Schedule for the oil cooler, what is the nominal pipe size of nozzle C?
   - ❏ 8 inch NPS
   - ❏ 10 inch NPS
   - ❏ 12 inch NPS
   - ❏ 14 inch NPS

Drawing 4-12B, Oil Cooler, sheet 2 of 3

Drawing 4-12B depicts the tube bundle, tube sheet layout, and baffle plate details. This tube bundle consists of a tube sheet on each end, baffles, tie rods and spacers. The design of tube bundles vary but generally they are similar in their make up. The baffles are used to support the tubes and keep them from bowing, and direct the path of the shell side fluid. Most heat exchangers will have the shell side fluid pass through the exchanger a minimum of two times before it exits the unit.

The following questions refer to the Oil Cooler, drawing 4-12B, sheet 2 of 3

74. Determine how many baffle plates and support plates are needed for one tube bundle.
   - ❏ 10
   - ❏ 12
   - ❏ 14
   - ❏ 17

75. State the material thickness of the baffle plates in inches.

Answer: _____

76. What is the center to center spacing between any two baffle plates marked number 113 and 114?
   - ❏ 10 inches
   - ❏ 12 inches
   - ❏ 12½ inches
   - ❏ 14 inches

77. How many tubes in total will be installed in this heat exchanger?

Answer: _____

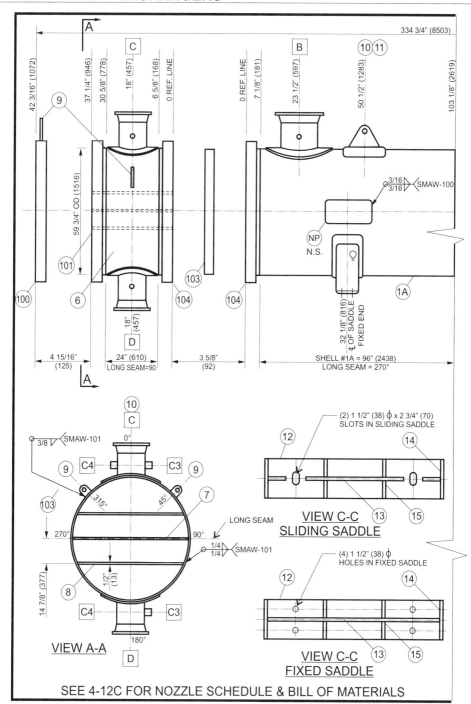

334 3/4" (8503)

42 3/16" (1072)

A

C

37 1/4" (946)
30 5/8" (778)
18" (457)
6 5/8" (168)
0 REF. LINE

0 REF. LINE
7 1/8" (181)

B

23 1/2" (597)

10 11

50 1/2" (1283)

103 1/8" (2619)

9

59 3/4" OD (1516)

101

6

18" (457)

D

3/16
3/16 SMAW-100

NP
N.S.

32 1/8" (816)
℄ OF SADDLE
FIXED END

1A

100

103

104

104

4 15/16"
(125)

24" (610)
LONG SEAM=90

3 5/8"
(92)

SHELL #1A = 96" (2438)
LONG SEAM = 270°

A

10
C

3/8 SMAW-101

0°

9 C4   C3 9

103

315°   45°

7

LONG SEAM

270°

90°

1/4
1/4 SMAW-101

14 7/8" (377)

1/2"
(13)

8

C4   C3

VIEW A-A

180°

D

(2) 1 1/2" (38) φ x 2 3/4" (70)
SLOTS IN SLIDING SADDLE

12   14

13   15

VIEW C-C
SLIDING SADDLE

(4) 1 1/2" (38) φ
HOLES IN FIXED SADDLE

12   14

13   15

VIEW C-C
FIXED SADDLE

SEE 4-12C FOR NOZZLE SCHEDULE & BILL OF MATERIALS

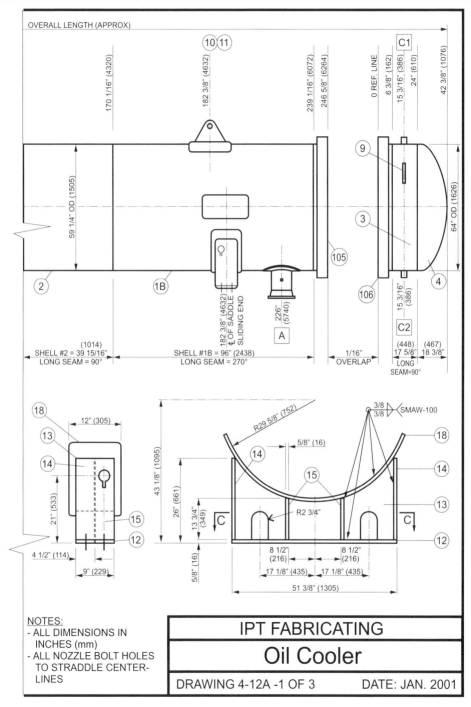

OVERALL LENGTH (APPROX)

170 1/16" (4320)

182 3/8" (4632)

239 1/16" (6072)

246 5/8" (6264)

10 11

C1

0 REF. LINE

6 3/8" (162)

15 3/16" (386)

24" (610)

42 3/8" (1076)

59 1/4" OD (1505)

64" OD (1626)

9

3

4

105

106

2

1B

182 3/8" (4632)
₵ OF SADDLE
SLIDING END

226"
(5740)

A

C2

(448)   (467)

17 5/8"   18 3/8"

(1014)
SHELL #2 = 39 15/16"
LONG SEAM = 90°

SHELL #1B = 96" (2438)
LONG SEAM = 270°

1/16"
OVERLAP

LONG
SEAM=90°

18

12" (305)

13

14

43 1/8" (1095)

R29 5/8" (752)

5/8" (16)

3/8
3/8

SMAW-100

18

14

15

14

26" (661)

13 3/4"
(349)

C

C

13

21" (533)

15

12

5/8" (16)

8 1/2"
(216)

8 1/2"
(216)

12

4 1/2" (114)

9" (229)

R2 3/4"

17 1/8" (435)   17 1/8" (435)

51 3/8" (1305)

NOTES:
- ALL DIMENSIONS IN
  INCHES (mm)
- ALL NOZZLE BOLT HOLES
  TO STRADDLE CENTER-
  LINES

IPT FABRICATING

Oil Cooler

DRAWING 4-12A -1 OF 3   DATE: JAN. 2001

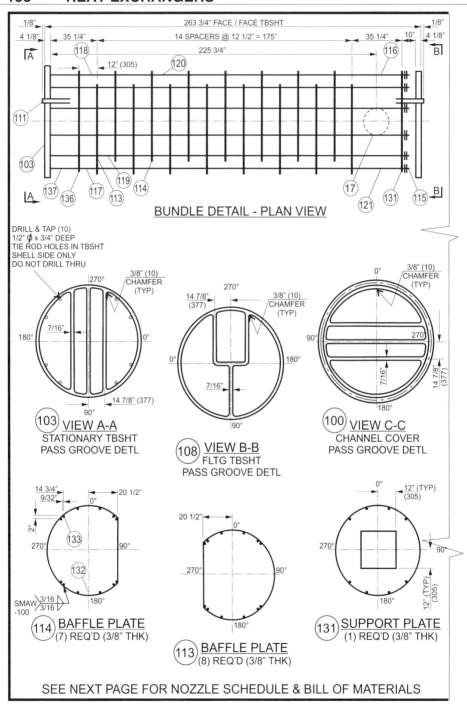

BUNDLE DETAIL - PLAN VIEW

263 3/4" FACE / FACE TBSHT

14 SPACERS @ 12 1/2" = 175"

225 3/4"

12" (305)

DRILL & TAP (10)
1/2" ⌀ x 3/4" DEEP
TIE ROD HOLES IN TBSHT
SHELL SIDE ONLY
DO NOT DRILL THRU

(103) VIEW A-A
STATIONARY TBSHT
PASS GROOVE DETL

(108) VIEW B-B
FLTG TBSHT
PASS GROOVE DETL

(100) VIEW C-C
CHANNEL COVER
PASS GROOVE DETL

(114) BAFFLE PLATE
(7) REQ'D (3/8" THK)

(113) BAFFLE PLATE
(8) REQ'D (3/8" THK)

(131) SUPPORT PLATE
(1) REQ'D (3/8" THK)

SEE NEXT PAGE FOR NOZZLE SCHEDULE & BILL OF MATERIALS

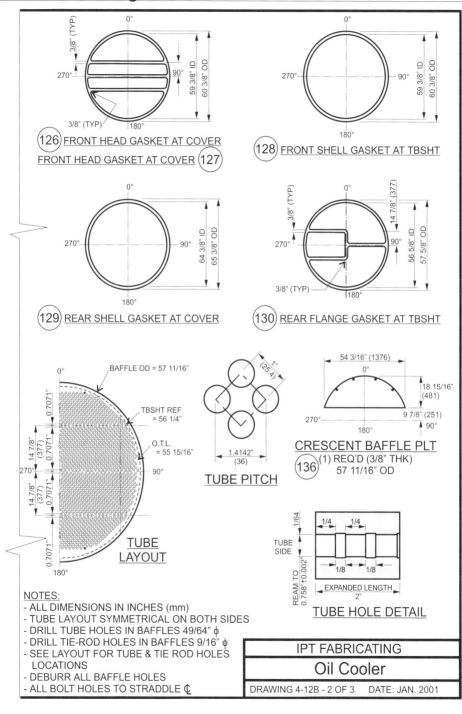

(126) FRONT HEAD GASKET AT COVER

FRONT HEAD GASKET AT COVER (127)

(128) FRONT SHELL GASKET AT TBSHT

(129) REAR SHELL GASKET AT COVER

(130) REAR FLANGE GASKET AT TBSHT

BAFFLE OD = 57 11/16"

TBSHT REF = 56 1/4"

O.T.L. = 55 15/16"

TUBE LAYOUT

TUBE PITCH

CRESCENT BAFFLE PLT
(136) (1) REQ'D (3/8" THK)
57 11/16" OD

TUBE HOLE DETAIL

NOTES:
- ALL DIMENSIONS IN INCHES (mm)
- TUBE LAYOUT SYMMETRICAL ON BOTH SIDES
- DRILL TUBE HOLES IN BAFFLES 49/64" φ
- DRILL TIE-ROD HOLES IN BAFFLES 9/16" φ
- SEE LAYOUT FOR TUBE & TIE ROD HOLES
  LOCATIONS
- DEBURR ALL BAFFLE HOLES
- ALL BOLT HOLES TO STRADDLE ₵

IPT FABRICATING

Oil Cooler

DRAWING 4-12B - 2 OF 3   DATE: JAN. 2001

NOZZLE SCHEDULE

MARK	SIZE	RATING	TYPE	SERVICE	NOZ-ZLE BORE	REPAD	Pro-jec-tion o/s	Wel d de-tail	WLED SIZE		ra-dius	Item no.'s
									A	C		
A	8"	300#	RFWIN	SHELL INLET	SCH XH	15"OD x 3/8"THK	11 3/8"	24, 27	3/8	3/8	1/8	19, 20, 21
B	16"	300#	RFWIN	SHELL OUTLET	SCH 60	29"OD x 3/8"	11 3/8"	24, 27	3/8	3/8	1/8	23, 24, 25
C	10"	300#	RFWIN	CHANNEL INLET	SCH 80	20"OD x 3/8" THK	11 1/8"	24, 27	3/8	3/8	1/8	26, 27, 28
D	10"	300#	RFWIN	CHANNEL OUTLET	SCH 80	20"OD x 3/8" THK	11 1/8"	24, 27	3/8	3/8	1/8	26, 27, 28
C1	1"	6000#	CPLG	VENT c/w PLUG				29	3/8		1/8	31
C2	1"	6000#	CPLG	DRAIN c/w PLUG				29	3/8		1/8	31
C3	1"	6000#	CPLG	TI c/w PLUG				29	3/8		1/8	30

BILL OF MATERIALS - FOR DRAWING 4-12A

ITEM	QTY	PART	DESCRIPTION
1A,B	2	SHELL CYL.	58" ID x 5/8" THK x 96" LG
2	1	SHELL CYL.	58" ID x 5/8" THK x 39 15/16" LG
3	1	SHELL AUX.	62 3/4" ID x 5/8" THK x 17 5/8" LG
4	1	SHELL CVR.	62 3/4" ID X 11/16" NOM (5/8" min) 2:1 SE HEAD c/w 2" SF
6	1	CHAN CYL.	58" ID x 7/8" THK x 24" LG
7	1	PASS PL	1/2" THK x 37 1/4" x 58" LG
8	2	PASS PL	1/2" THK x 37 1/4" x 49 13/16" LG
9	5	LIFT LUG	3/4" THK x 10" x 5" LG
10	2	LIFT LUG	1 1/2" THK x 10" x 14" LG
11	2	REPAD	1" x 12" x 21" LG (ROLLED TO 59 1/4" ID)
12	2	BASE PLT	5/8" THK x 9" x 51 3/8" LG
13	2	WEB PLT	5/8" THK x 26" x 50 1/8" LG
14	4	OUTER RIB	5/8" THK x 9" x 26" LG
15	8	INNER RIB	5/8" THK x 4 3/16" x 13 3/4" LG

BILL OF MATERIALS - DRAWING 4-12B			
ITEM	QTY	PART	DESCRIPTION
100	1	COVER	64 15/16" OD x 5 1/4" THK
101	1	FLANGE	64 15/16" OD x 58" ID x 6 5/8" THK
102	1	FLANGE	64 15/16" OD x 58" ID x 6 5/8" THK
103	1	TUBESHEET	60 3/8" OD x 4 1/8" THK
104	1	FLANGE	64 15/16" OD x 58" ID x 7 1/8" THK
105	1	FLANGE	68 5/8" OD X 58" ID x 7 9/16" THK
106	1	FLANGE	68 5/8" OD x 62 3/4" ID x 6 3/8" THK
107	1	SPLIT RING	61 5/8" OD x 56 3/8" ID x 8 1/2" THK
108	1	TUBESHEET	57 5/8" OD x 4 1/8" THK
109	1	FLANGE	61 5/8" OD x 56 3/8" ID x 6 1/4" THK
110	1	DISHED HD	56 3/8" OD x 1 1/2" THK (1 7/16" min) (45" DISH R)
111	2216	TUBES	3/4" OD x 14 BWG x 264" LG
112	1	PASS PLATE	1/2" THK x 13 3/16" x 28 3/16" LG
113	8	BAFFLE PLT	57 11/16" OD x 3/8" THK
114	7	BAFFLE PLT	57 11/16" OD x 3/8" THK
115	10	TIE ROD	1/2" O x 249" LG (TBE) c/w 2-NUTS EA
116	1	SPACER	3/4" OD x 14 BWG x 47 3/8" LG
117	9	SPACER	3/4" OD x 14 BWG x 11 5/8" LG
118	1	SPACER	3/4" OD x 14 BWG x 24 1/8" LG
119	112	SPACER	3/4" OD x 14 BWG x 12 1/8" LG
120	13	SPACER	3/4" OD x 14 BWG x 24 5/8" LG
121	9	SPACER	3/4" OD x 14 BWG x 34 7/8" LG
122	84	STUD	1" O x 13" LG c/w 2-NUTS EA
123	84	STUD	1" O x 17 3/4" LG c/w 2-NUTS EA
124	92	STUD	7/8" O x 14 1/4" LG c/w 2-NUTS EA
125	64	STUD	1 1/8" O x 21 1/4" LG c/w 2-NUTS EA
126	2	GASKET	60 3/8" OD x 59 3/8" ID x 1/8" THK (c/w 3-RIBS)
127	2	GASKET	60 3/8" OD x 59 3/8" ID x 1/8" THK (c/w 3-RIBS)
128	2	GASKET	60 3/8" OD x 59 3/8" ID x 1/8" THK (w/o RIBS)
129	2	GASKET	65 3/8" OD x 64 3/8" ID x 1/8" THK (w/o RIBS)
130	2	GASKET	57 5/8" OD x 56 5/8" ID x 1/8" THK (c/w 3-RIBS)
131	1	SUPT PLT	57 11/16" OD x 3/8" THK
132	2	SEAL STRIP	1/4" THK x 2" x 176 1/2" LG
133	4	SEAL STRIP	1/4" THK x 2" x 176 1/2" LG
134	1	PASS PLATE	29 1/4" x 13 3/16" x 1/2" THK
135	2	PASS PLATE	24" x 10 5/8" x 1/2" THK
136	1	BAFFLE PLT	57 11/16" OD x 3/8" THK
137	10	SPACER	3/4" OD x 14 BWG x 23 1/16" LG

IPT FABRICATING

Oil Cooler

DRAWING 4-12C -3 OF 3   DATE: JAN. 2001

78. What is the outside diameter of the 14 gage tubes?
    - ❏ ¼ inch
    - ❏ ½ inch
    - ❏ ¾ inch
    - ❏ 1 inch

79. What is the diameter of the tie rod holes to be drilled and tapped in the stationary tubesheet.
    - ❏ 1 inch
    - ❏ ¾ inch
    - ❏ ½ inch
    - ❏ ¼ inch

80. To what depth will the tierod holes be drilled and tapped into the stationary tubesheet,?
    - ❏ ¼ inch
    - ❏ ½ inch
    - ❏ ¾ inch
    - ❏ 1 inch

81. What will be the diameter of the tube holes drilled in the baffles?

Answer: _____

82. What is the plus/minus tolerance allowed for the drilling and reaming of the tubesheet holes as indicated in the tube hole detail?

Answer: _____

83. What is the face to face distance between the tubesheets?
    - ❏ 264 inches
    - ❏ 263 3/4 inches
    - ❏ 225 3/4 inches
    - ❏ 4 1/8 inches

84. The tie rod holes drilled into the baffles will be 1/2 inch in diameter.
    - ❏ true
    - ❏ false

SECTION FIVE

STRUCTURAL STEEL

Structural Drawings

Introduction

Structural steel is manufactured by forming billets and blooms into various shapes. Some of these include channels, angles, and beams. This method is called hot rolling and results in a single piece of steel being formed into the desired shape. Hot rolling steel produces a much stronger uniform shape than welding individual pieces together to make the same form. Carbon steel is the usual grade of material used for building steel and other structures, although high strength, low alloy steels may be used if the end use requires it.

The standard views used to illustrate steel structures on drawings are plan views, elevation views and section views.

On a steel structure, such as the skeleton frame of a building, the plan view is a view looking down onto the top of the structure. If the building is a one story structure then only one plan view would be required. See illustration #5-1 for an example of a plan view. Plan view drawings of steel structures are usually single line drawings showing the location of columns, beams and other building parts.

The elevation view is a view looking from one side or elevation of the building. Elevation views show the height or vertical dimensions of the structure and building parts, such as columns, beams and cross bracing. See illustration #5-2.

Section views give a close up detail of a part or section of the building. See illustration #5-3 for a section view of a column and roof support system.

For the fabrication of structural steel that will make up the building, designers use detail drawings. These detail drawings show the location of holes, clips, base plates and other parts that attach to the main steel member. If a wide flange shape is being used to make a beam, then the detail drawing will include all of the information needed to get the correct size of beam and any detail pieces and other information needed to layout and fabricate the beam. These detail drawings are often referred to as fabrication drawings, working drawings, or shop drawings. It is common practice for structural steel shops to develop one shop drawing for each structural member in a building. All detail pieces including clips, gussets or base plates that would attach to the member would be included on the drawing.

Illustration #5-4 shows a horizontal beam with a double angle iron connection on each end. This beam is coped out (cut out) on one end. There is enough information, using only two views, for the fabricator to manufacture this beam. In this case the two views drawn are the elevation and end view. This is typical of structural steel drawings and will be discussed later in greater detail.

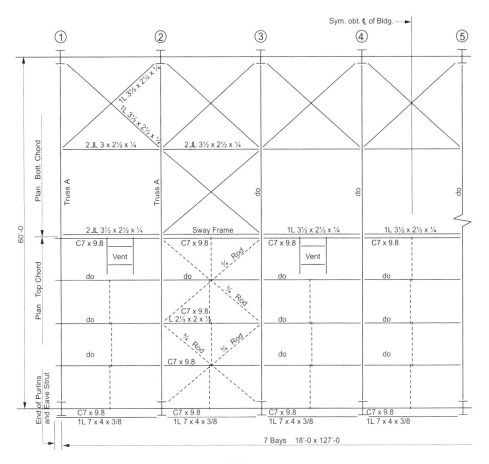

PLAN

Illustration #5-1 - Typical Plan View of a Building

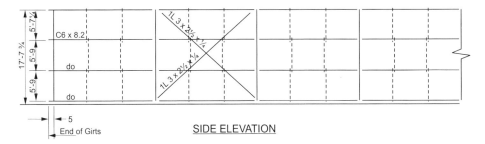

SIDE ELEVATION

Illustration #5-2 - Typical Elevation View of a Building

CROSS SECTION

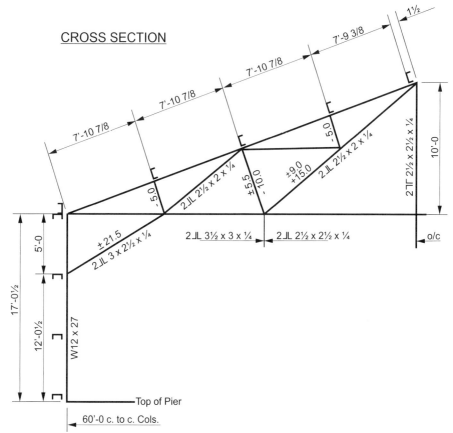

Illustration #5-3 - Cross Section

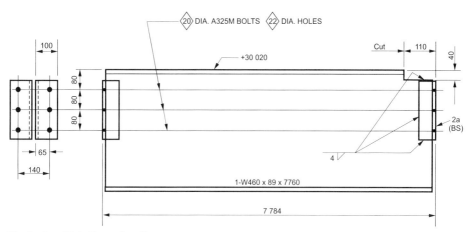

Illustration #5-4 - Beam Detail

Structural Shapes Nomenclature

Illustration #5-5 shows several of the more common steel shapes, including channel iron, angle iron, wide flange beam, and standard I beam. These shapes are frequently used as the building material for steel structures. Each of these shapes have specific names to define their parts. The term leg is used to define the sides of angles, and flange and web define the parts of beams and channels.

Designation of Structural Shapes

A standard method of designating steel shapes is shown in illustration #5-5. Each shape is given a letter designation, such as W for wide flange, L for angle iron, or C for channel. The letter is then followed by a number which specifies the depth of the shape. In the case of the wide flange example it is 14, which means the nominal depth of the beam is 14 inches. The number 53 that follows the W14 is the weight of the beam. In this case it is 53 pounds per foot. For steel specified in metric the weight is quoted as kilograms per meter of length. The designation when put in sequential form is W14 x 53. The same designation for metric would be W360 x 79. In this case the 360 is the nominal depth in millimeters and the 79 is the kilograms per meter of beam (one kilogram = 2.2 lbs.).

Also shown in illustration #5-5 is a structural tee cut from a full sized steel shape. Steel mills do not produce structural tees. They are fabricated by cutting full sized structural shapes in half through the web. In the case of the tee cut from a wide flange beam, its size is stated as one half the member it was cut from, and the letter T is included in the designation.

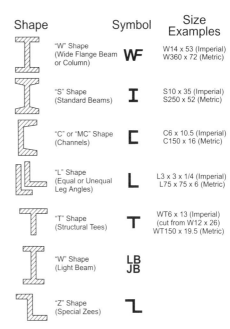

Shape	Symbol	Size Examples
"W" Shape (Wide Flange Beam or Column)	**WF**	W14 x 53 (Imperial) W360 x 72 (Metric)
"S" Shape (Standard Beams)	**I**	S10 x 35 (Imperial) S250 x 52 (Metric)
"C" or "MC" Shape (Channels)	**C**	C6 x 10.5 (Imperial) C150 x 16 (Metric)
"L" Shape (Equal or Unequal Leg Angles)	**L**	L3 x 3 x 1/4 (Imperial) L75 x 75 x 6 (Metric)
"T" Shape (Structural Tees)	**T**	WT6 x 13 (Imperial) (cut from W12 x 26) WT150 x 19.5 (Metric)
"W" Shape (Light Beam)	**LB JB**	
"Z" Shape (Special Zees)	**⌐Ⅼ**	

Illustration #5-5 - Structural Steel Shapes

Therefore a wide flange beam designated as W24 x 76 cut in half would result in two WT12 x 38 structural tees.

Building Steel Nomenclature

In most steel structures a variety of steel shapes are joined together, which when assembled, complete the structure. Welding and bolting are the two most common methods of joining these shapes together. In a building the steel structure appears as a rigid steel frame with the members and their connections designed to withstand the dead and live loads imposed upon them. These loads are transferred from the roof and floors of the building to the horizontal beams and girders, and then to the vertical columns. From the columns, the loads are transferred to the base plates, and finally to the footings or pilings.

This type of structure allows the weight of the building to be carried by the steel frame and therefore does not require massive load bearing walls to carry the compressive forces.

Specific terminology or nomenclature is used to describe the parts of a building. Some of the more typical ones are columns, beams, girders, trusses and open web steel joists.

The columns are the vertical supports that run from the ground floor to the roof of the building.

The girders are the main support members that connect to the columns.

Beams are the intermediate horizontal supports for the roof or floor system and connect to the girders.

Trusses are often used to support roof and floor systems and are sometimes used in place of girders. Open web steel joists perform a similar function to beams, and like trusses often are used instead of beams.

Trusses and open web steel joists, although deeper in section than beams and girders are used because they can support similar loads but weigh less than beams and girders.

Illustration #5-6 depicts the various components that can be part of a steel structure. Not every one of the components noted will be used in a single structure.

The terms listed below match the numbers in illustration #5-6.

1. Anchors or hangers for open web steel joints.
2. Anchors for structural steel.
3. Base for steel columns.
4. Beams, purlins, girts.
5. Bearing plates for structural steel.
6. Bracing for steel members or frames.
7. Brackets attached to the steel frame.
8. Column.
9. Conveyor frame work.

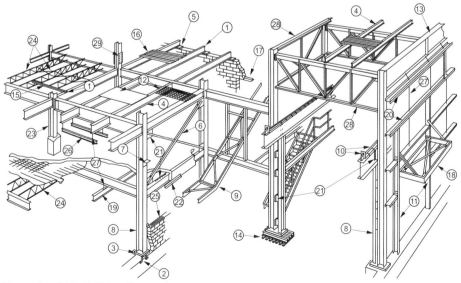

Illustration #5-6 - Building Nomenclature

10. Crane rail beams and stops if size and connections are shown.
11. Door frames constituting part of and connected to the steel frame.
12. Floor and roof plates, grating, connecting to steel frame.
13. Girders.
14. Grillage beams of steel.
15. Headers or trimmers for support of open-web steel joists where such headers or trimmers frame into structural steel members.
16. Light-gage cold formed steel used to support floor and roofs.
17. Lintels used over window openings.
18. Marquees (structural frame only) when forming an integral part of the steel frame.
19. Monorail beams of standard structural shapes.
20. Sash angles connected to the steel frame.
21. Separators, angles, tees, clips and other detail fitting to the steel frame.
22. Shelf angles.
23. Steel core for composite columns.
24. Steel joists (standardized trusses) open-web steel joists, bracing, and accessories when supplied with the steel joists.
25. Steel window sills attached to the steel frame and forming part thereof.
26. Suspended ceiling supports of structural steel shapes 3 inches (75 mm.) or greater in depth.
27. Ties, hangers and sag rods forming part of the structural frame.
28. Trusses and brace frames.

Terms Common to Structural Drawings

There are several terms common to structural steel drawings. These terms are normally abbreviated on the drawing. Their meaning and abbreviated form (where applicable) are noted in the following text and illustrations.

Columns (abbreviated col) are vertical support members in a structural steel frame. An example would be a building. Columns are most commonly made from wide flange beams, pipe, round tubing or square tubing.

Beams (abbreviated bm) are horizontal support members in a structural steel frame building. Beams are commonly made from wide flange shapes or other rolled structural steel.

Girders (abbreviated gird) are horizontal support members in a structural steel frame. They are used to span between columns in a building or between supports in structures like bridges. Girders are heavy duty beams that have intermediate beams attached to them to complete the structure.

Girders can be made from heavy beams produced by steel mills or fabricated from plate steel. Heavy duty girders are commonly fabricated by welding steel plates into the shape of a beam.

Trusses are built-up shapes that support floors and roof systems. They are used in place of girders when long spans are desired but overall weight is a consideration. They are generally deeper in section than a girder used to support the same weight and span, but weigh less.

Open Web Steel Joists (abbreviated OWSJ) are manufactured horizontal support members. They serve a similar purpose as beams. OWSJ's are built-up members similar to trusses but lighter in design. OWSJ's are used in place of beams because they can support similar loads but weigh less.

Gage (abbreviated Ga) - Bolt holes required in structural members such as angles, channels and beams are layed out on gage lines. Gage is the distance measured from the heel of an angle iron or channel to the center of the bolt hole. The term gage, when referring to holes in the flanges of structural beams, like standard I beams or wide flange beams, is measured from the center of the beam web to the center of the hole or holes. See illustration #5-7A.

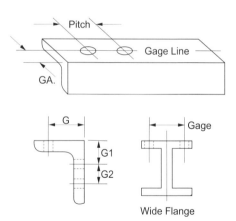

Illustration #5-7A - Gage and Pitch Lines

The gage distance varies depending on the size of the steel member. Standard gage distances are specified in engineering manuals such as the Canadian Institute for Steel Construction's Steel Handbook.

The gage distance is designed to allow enough edge distance from the edge of the hole to the outside of the structural member so the material does not shear under load, and also to allow sufficient clearance for impact sockets and wrenches used for tightening fasteners.

Pitch is the center to center distance between holes along the same row. Similar to the gage distance, the correct pitch allows enough clearance for wrenches to fit in between the bolt heads or the nuts when installing and tightening the fasteners. See illustration #5-7A.

Edge Distance is a term used to describe the distance measured from the center of a hole to the outside edge of the material. See illustration #5-7B. An example would be bolt holes in the flange of a beam. If the hole is too close to the outside edge of the beam there is a possibility the material could fail at that location. Engineering handbooks specify the minimum edge distance for various hole diameters.

Essentially, as the hole diameter increases so does the distance from the edge of the material to the center of the hole. See illustration #5-7C for an example of an edge distance chart.

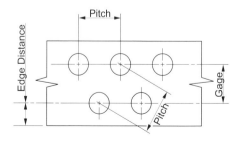

Illustration #5-7B - Gage and Pitch Layout

Terms Common to Structural Drawings   151

Minimum Edge Distance for Bolt Holes		
Bolt Diameter	At Sheared Edge	At Rolled or Gas Cut Edge
5/8 (16)	1 1/8 (28)	7/8 (22)
3/4 (20)	1 11/32 (34)	1 (26)
7/8 (22)	1 1/2 (38)	1 1/8 (28)
15/16 (24)	1 5/8 (42)	1 3/16 (30)
1 (26)	1 7/8 (48)	1 11/32 (34)
1 1/8 (30)	2 (52)	1 1/2 (38)
1 1/2 (38)	2 1/2 (64)	1 13/16 (46)
> 1 1/2 (38)	1¾ x Diameter	1¼ x Diameter
Gas cut edges shall be smooth and free from notches.		
Example Chart Only		

Illustration #5-7C - Minimum Edge Distance

Gage Outstanding Leg - Angles are often used as part of a connection for structural steel. This requires one leg of the angle to be welded or bolted to the flanges or web of the beam while the other leg protrudes away from the beam. This protruding leg is referred to as the outstanding leg. It is common for the outstanding leg to have connection holes in it. The gage distance for these holes is measured from the heel of the protruding leg to the center of the holes. This distance is referred to on the drawing as gage outstanding leg and is abbreviated as GOSL. See the beam detail in illustration #5-4 and illustration #5-7D for examples.

Gage Outstanding Leg

Illustration #5-7D

Cope or Block) - When structural members are required to fit into each other the intersecting shape may have to be cut to the profile of that member. This is referred to as coping or blocking.

For detailing purposes the drawing normally specifies dimensions of the cut to be made. See illustration #5-8

Block - Blocking a beam will usually remove only a portion of the flange and no material from the web. See illustration #5-8.

Cope - Coping a beam will usually remove material from both the flange and the web. For an example, see page 154, beam drawing #5-B13

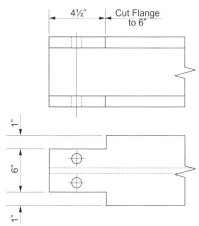
4½"   Cut Flange to 6"
1"
6"
1"

Illustration #5-8 - Blocking a Beam

Mill Tolerance - Structural shapes are produced by feeding hot billets or blooms (bars of steel) through rolling mills, which consecutively squeeze the hot bars into the desired shape. See illustration #5-9 for an example of a billet of steel being shaped into a channel.

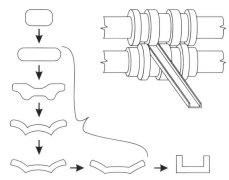

Illustration #5-9 - The Making of a C Shape

Due to changing conditions, for instance roll wear, unequal cooling and other factors, rolling variations take place. This means that steel shapes are not consistent in their dimensions, which presents problems for designers and fabricators. This is called mill tolerance and is the allowable variations or differences between shapes. Illustration #5-10 shows an exaggerated view of mill tolerance when splicing two beams together.

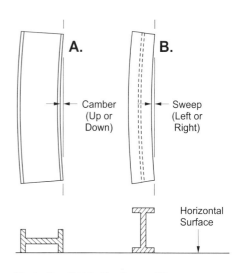

Illustration #5-11 - Camber and Sweep

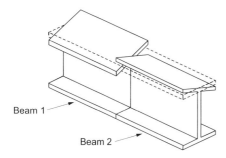

Illustration #5-10 - Error Between Mating Shapes

Camber is an up or down roll or curve in a structural beam or channel that runs parallel with the flanges. Camber can be built into a steel beam or can be a result of unequal cooling of the steel. See illustration #5-11A.

Sweep is a left or right roll or curve in a structural beam or channel that runs parallel with the web. It is a result of unequal cooling of the steel. See illustration #5-11B. The maximum camber and sweep permitted for structural shapes is specified in engineering standards.

Piece Marks - The steel members in a building and other structures are coordinated by means of piece marks. See illustration #5-12 for an example of the piece mark symbol. There is no standard system used for piece marks, as different shop fabricators use different piece marks to represent the items on the drawing. For example, C15 could mean column number 15 in one shop and connector plate number 15 in another.

Computer produced drawings are more standardized than drawings produced by hand and therefore piece mark numbers are also becoming more standardized. It is generally excepted that C is the letter designation for column, B is the letter designation for beam, and P is the letter designation for connector plates or clips.

Symbols Common to Structural Drawings

In many cases symbols are used on drawings to reduce the length of notes and other information that the designer is conveying to the drawing reader. Structural drawings are no exception. Illustration #5-12 shows a list of some of the more common symbols, however some companies will develop their own symbols to meet their particular requirements.

Symbol	Meaning	Meaning	Symbol
₡	And	Channels	[⊔
@	At	Angle or Angles	L or ∟s
₵	Centerline	Back-to-back Angles	⊐L
⊥	Perpendicular	Round or Diameter	⌀
MK	Mark Number	Square	▱
=	Equal	Structural Tee	T
⟨R⟩or⟨A⟩ Revision	Revision	Feet and Inches	' "
ℙ	Plate	Degree of Finish	65⟋
◺2 / 12 Pitch	Pitch	Plus or Minus	±
WF or W Wide Flange	Wide Flange	Parallel	‖

Illustration #5-12 - Structural Symbols

Structural Drawing (Beam 5-B13)

This fabrication drawing is of a basic beam consisting of a side elevation view. All information needed to fabricate the beam is shown on this view. This beam is made from a wide flange shape. The top and bottom flange and the web on each end of the beam are coped so that they will intersect into another beam of the same size without interference. This type of cope allows clearance between the flanges of the intersecting beams.

The holes on each end of the beam are called connecting holes, this allows the use of bolts to secure the beam into the designed connection.

Structural steel fabrication drawings or shop drawings commonly use one view with notes to give the detail information needed. For instance on this drawing the abbreviation N/S is used. This stands for near side. The fabricator knows that the top flange of this beam is to be cut flush to the web. The other side of the flange (far side or F/S) will not be cut. By using this note the draftsperson does not have to show another view of the beam to relate this information. The other abbreviations used are T&B and (B/E). These mean *top and bottom*, and *both ends* of the beam. In other words the coping is to be done to the top and bottom flanges and the web on both ends (B/E) of the beam on the near side only.

The center of the first hole on the end of the beam is measured from the top flange (3 inches). The other holes have a center to center distance (c/c) or gage between them of 3 inches.

Structural drawings of beams are dimensioned from the left end. The dimensions run from left to right, as can be noted with the location of the holes on each end of 5-B13. All dimensions along the length of the beam originate from the left side reference line marked R.D., which is the abbreviation for *running dimensions*. The overall length of the beam is noted along with the beam size and weight on the dimension line at the bottom of beam one. This is also typical of structural drawings.

The hole size is noted as a general note and therefore does not appear on the drawing itself. In the case of 5-B13, the bill of materials describes only the beam, as there is no other material required for fabrication.

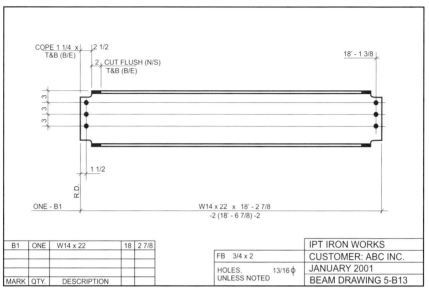

MARK	QTY.	DESCRIPTION		
B1	ONE	W14 x 22	18	2 7/8

FB 3/4 x 2	
HOLES, UNLESS NOTED	13/16 φ

IPT IRON WORKS
CUSTOMER: ABC INC.
JANUARY 2001
BEAM DRAWING 5-B13

The following questions refer to beam drawing 5-B13

1. To what depth is the cope made into the beam web?

Answer: _____

2. How far back will the fabricator measure from the end of the beam for the cope?

Answer: _____

3. The flanges of this beam are cut flush on both sides of the beam and on both ends, top and bottom.
   ❏ true
   ❏ false

4. Measured from the end of the beam, how far will the flanges be cut for clearance purposes?

Answer: _____

5. What is the distance from the center of the right end holes to the right end of the beam?
   ❏ 1 inch
   ❏ 1¼ inches
   ❏ 1½ inches
   ❏ 2 inches

6. What is the diameter of the field bolts used to secure this beam to the connection?
   ❏ ½ inch
   ❏ ¾ inch
   ❏ 1 inch
   ❏ 1¼ inch

7. What is the overall length of this beam?

Answer: _____

8. The nominal depth of this beam is 14 inches and it weighs 22 lbs. per foot.
   ❏ true
   ❏ false

9. State the diameter of the holes in each end of this beam.

Answer: _____

10 How many beams will be fabricated from this drawing?
   - ❏ 1
   - ❏ 2
   - ❏ 3
   - ❏ 4

Structural Drawing (Beam 5-B14)

Drawing 5-B14 is a beam with two connector plates labeled Pa. As discussed earlier in this text, it is common for fabricating companies to assign piece mark numbers that relate to the item; for example Pa would mean plate A. This beam also has several angle irons welded to both the top and the bottom flange. As indicated before, most structural drawings are dimensioned from left to right, and a system called datum (baseline) dimensioning is used to locate holes, clips and other items on the drawing. Structural drawings dimensioned using the baseline system use a common reference point to start all dimensions.

In this drawing, the reference point is the left end of the beam. The first hole location on the bottom flange is dimensioned using the baseline system. The dimension to this first hole is shown as 15 ft- 3 in, with only the terminal point of the dimension line shown. The drawing reader must know where the dimension originated from, and again in the case of this beam, it originated from the left end.

There are holes in the bottom flange of this beam, and the abbreviation GA is used to indicate that holes in the flanges located across from each other are spaced 3 inches apart, center to center. This eliminates the need for a second detail drawing to illustrate these holes.

The gage distance of 3 inches is laid out from the center of the web of the beam, 1½ inches on each side of the web centerline. In some cases flange holes may only be required on one side of the flange. The draftsperson would indicate this by displaying the gage distance of 3 inches but noting in abbreviated form that the holes are on the near side (N/S) of the beam or the far side (F/S) of the beam. See illustration #5-15 for an example of an angle clip noted near side only.

The following questions refer to beam drawing 5-B14

11. Write out the required beam descriptions.

Answer: _____

12. What is the gage distance for all holes in the bottom flange of the beam?

Answer: _____

13. What is the leg size of the fillet welds that join 'aa' to the beam flanges?

Answer: _____

14. How many 'Pa's are required for beam B2B?

Answer: _____

15. What is the cut length of items 'Pa'?

Answer: _____

16. What is the overall length of beam B2C?

Answer: _____

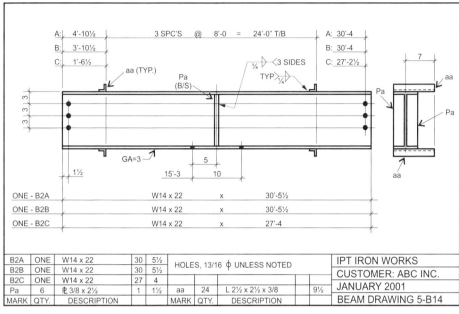

B2A	ONE	W14 x 22	30	5½	HOLES, 13/16 φ UNLESS NOTED				IPT IRON WORKS
B2B	ONE	W14 x 22	30	5½					CUSTOMER: ABC INC.
B2C	ONE	W14 x 22	27	4					JANUARY 2001
Pa	6	℞ 3/8 x 2½	1	1½	aa	24	L 2½ x 2½ x 3/8	9½	BEAM DRAWING 5-B14
MARK	QTY.	DESCRIPTION			MARK	QTY.	DESCRIPTION		

17. Calculate the distance from the left end of beam B2 to the center of plate 'Pa'.

Answer: _____

18. Describe fully the welding required for all plates marked 'Pa'.

Answer: _____

19. How many angles marked 'aa' are required for beam B2A?

Answer: _____

20. What is the heel to heel distance between each angle marked 'aa'?
    - ❑ 3 feet
    - ❑ 8 feet
    - ❑ 16 feet
    - ❑ 24 feet

21. The distance laid out for the first angle 'aa' on the left end of beam B2B is:
    - ❑ 4'-10½"
    - ❑ 3'-10½"
    - ❑ 2'-8½"
    - ❑ 1'-6½"

22. Describe fully the leg size, thickness and cut length of angles 'aa'.

Answer: _____

23. How many holes will be drilled in one beam?
    - ❑ 6
    - ❑ 8
    - ❑ 10
    - ❑ 12

24. What is the thickness of item number 'Pa'?

Answer: _____

25. Referring to angles 'aa', how far do they protrude from the center of the beam web as shown in the right side view?

Answer: _____

26. Angles 'aa' protrude past the flange on the near side only.
    ❏ true
    ❏ false

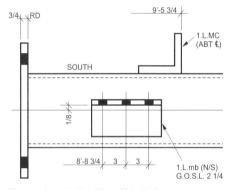

3/4   RD   9'-5 3/4

                                            1.L.MC
                                            (ABT ℄)
        SOUTH

    1/8

    8'-8 3/4   3   3
                                  1.L.mb (N/S)
                                  G.O.S.L. 2 1/4

Illustration #5-15 - Near Side Holes

Structural Drawing (Beam 5-B16)

Drawing 5-B16 is a beam that will connect between two columns. The end of the beam is not coped to fit into another structural member, but instead it has two end plate connections. As well, the end plates on each end of this beam have gusset plates that allow diagonal bracing or cross bracing to be connected to them. This is a common type of beam used in steel buildings.

It should be noted that there is not enough detail given on this drawing to make the end plates or the gusset plates. These would be detailed on a separate drawing.

This drawing varies from the previous beam drawings of 5-B13 and 5-B14 as there is a top view of the beam, two end views and a section view.

View A-A and View B-B, correspond to the two directional viewing lines on the elevation view of the beam (two end views). It is common practice to coordinate the viewing line and the actual view drawn by using corresponding capital letters. The same is true for section C-C. In this case the line used is the same, but is referred to as a cutting plane line.

The dimensioning system used for locating holes and other items on the beam is referred to as datum or baseline dimensioning. This means that all the dimensions originate from a common reference point, which is the left end of the actual beam, not including the plate P72.

The following questions refer to beam drawing 5-B16

27. What is the overall length of each beam marked B3?

Answer: _____

28. What is the plate thickness of P17?

Answer: _____

29. Describe the location of the erection mark to be included on the beam.

Answer: _____

30. Which of the following piece marks refer to the end plate connections?
    ❏ P73 and P17
    ❏ P14 and P72
    ❏ P14 and P17
    ❏ P73 and P17

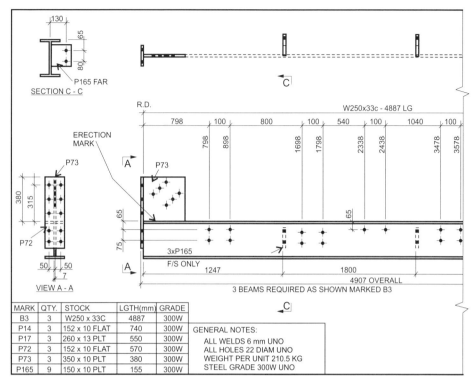

SECTION C - C

P165 FAR

W250x33c - 4887 LG

R.D.

ERECTION MARK

P73

A

P73

P72

3xP165

F/S ONLY

VIEW A - A

3 BEAMS REQUIRED AS SHOWN MARKED B3

4907 OVERALL

MARK	QTY.	STOCK	LGTH(mm)	GRADE
B3	3	W250 x 33C	4887	300W
P14	3	152 x 10 FLAT	740	300W
P17	3	260 x 13 PLT	550	300W
P72	3	152 x 10 FLAT	570	300W
P73	3	350 x 10 PLT	380	300W
P165	9	150 x 10 PLT	155	300W

GENERAL NOTES:
ALL WELDS 6 mm UNO
ALL HOLES 22 DIAM UNO
WEIGHT PER UNIT 210.5 KG
STEEL GRADE 300W UNO

31. What is the gage distance between web holes located at dimension 4153?
- ❏ 65 mm
- ❏ 75 mm
- ❏ 80 mm
- ❏ 90 mm

32. How many holes will be made in P73?

Answer: _____

33. What is the gage distance of the holes in end connection P72?
- ❏ 65 mm
- ❏ 75 mm
- ❏ 80 mm
- ❏ 100 mm

34. How many holes will be made in the web of beam B3?
- ❏ 8 holes
- ❏ 12 holes
- ❏ 14 holes
- ❏ 16 holes

35. All dimensions for hole locations in the web of the beam originate from the left side of P72.
- ❏ true
- ❏ false

36. Referring to the front and top view of the beam, on which side of the beam will all P165's be installed?
- ❏ near side
- ❏ far side
- ❏ both sides
- ❏ top flange

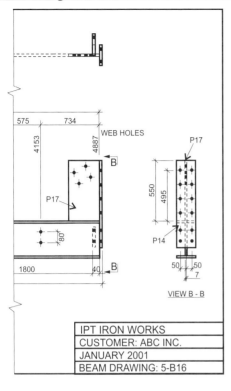

IPT IRON WORKS
CUSTOMER: ABC INC.
JANUARY 2001
BEAM DRAWING: 5-B16

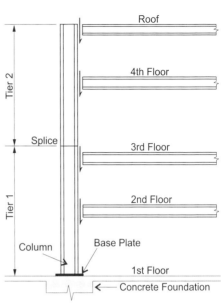

Illustration #5-17 - Spliced Column

37. The pitch of the web holes at 898 and 4153 is 80 mm.
❏ true
❏ false

38. What is the weight of each completed B3?

Answer: _____

Columns

Columns are used in buildings as compression members and are positioned vertically in the building structure. They are designed to support loads parallel to the longitudinal axis of the member. See illustration #5-17. Columns are commonly fabricated using W shapes especially in the 8, 10, 12 and 14 inch (W200, W250, W310 and W360) sizes. For light industrial applications, small commercial buildings, schools, and similar structures, columns are frequently fabricated from tubular sections that are either round, square or rectangular in shape.

To handle very heavy applications, engineers will custom design columns. This is accomplished by adding cover plates to the flanges, by combining two W shapes together by lacing, by boxing them in, or by using other methods.

The height of a building will affect the length of columns. It is often not practical or possible to make the column length equal to the height of the building. In most structures the columns are designed to be about two stories in length, plus a specified distance above the floor level for connecting purposes.

For buildings with more than two stories or floors, the columns will be designed to stack on top of each other. This makes it necessary to design a splice into the column. See illustration #5-17. As the building is erected, the column splices will be made by either bolting or welding.

Understandably, the greatest weight on the columns will be those on the bottom, and therefore they will be the heaviest in design. Often the size of the column decreases the higher up it is located in the building. The weight problem is why engineers design buildings from the top down. As the weight on the columns increases the design of the columns must change to support greater loads.

The loads supported by the columns in a building will be transferred to a concrete foundation. The load bearing surface on the concrete pilings must be spread out.

This is accomplished by welding a steel base plate to the end of the column. See illustration #5-17. Base plates ensure that the load imposed on the concrete foundation is spread out over a larger surface area than the end of the column to avoid crushing the concrete. The heavier the load on the column the thicker the base plate, and the more surface area the plate will cover.

Connection points for floor beams and lateral bracing are designed into the column by using various styles of connections. Some require only holes drilled in the web or the flanges of the column, while other connection designs use steel connector plates or angle iron. These types of connections are welded or bolted directly to the column.

Column Drawings (Column 5-C18)

This column would be used in a commercial building and is designed to support lighter loads.

It is made of HSS square tubing and has a base plate on the bottom and a cap plate on top. It has two connection angle irons along its length, one of which will possibly support an intermediate floor or mezzanine. The other is at the top of the column for roof beams or trusses.

The drawing note indicates the direction WEST. It is common practice to mark the direction the column will face when it is erected. The fabricator will mark or tag the column with the piece mark number of the beam in this location as noted on the drawing. When the column is raised into position, it will be oriented so that the piece mark number or tag faces WEST.

This drawing is also dimensioned using the baseline dimensioning system. Location dimensions for the angle clips originate from the left end of the beam. This is noted on the drawing as RD and is the abbreviation for running dimensions. It is important to note where these originate. For this column it is from the end of the member, not the underside of the base plate. Each item on the column dimensioned from the RD will be located using only a single dimension line with the dimension placed on that line.

The following questions refer to column 5-C18.

39. How many columns will be fabricated?

Answer: _____

40. What is the difference between columns C1A and C1B?

Answer: _____

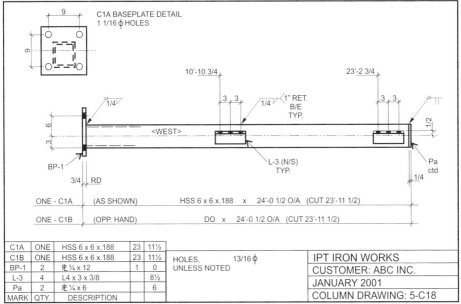

C1A BASEPLATE DETAIL
1 1/16 ϕ HOLES

9

9

10'-10 3/4

23'-2 3/4

3 3

1/4

1" RET.
B/E
TYP.

3 3

1/4

6

3

<WEST>

1/2

BP-1

L-3 (N/S)
TYP.

Pa
ctd

3/4 RD

1/4

ONE - C1A   (AS SHOWN)   HSS 6 x 6 x.188   x   24'-0 1/2 O/A   (CUT 23'-11 1/2)

ONE - C1B   (OPP. HAND)   DO   x   24'-0 1/2 O/A   (CUT 23'-11 1/2)

MARK	QTY.	DESCRIPTION		
C1A	ONE	HSS 6 x 6 x.188	23	11½
C1B	ONE	HSS 6 x 6 x.188	23	11½
BP-1	2	₧ ¾ x 12	1	0
L-3	4	L4 x 3 x 3/8		8½
Pa	2	₧ ¼ x 6		6

HOLES,   13/16 ϕ
UNLESS NOTED

IPT IRON WORKS
CUSTOMER: ABC INC.
JANUARY 2001
COLUMN DRAWING: 5-C18

41. What is the cut length of the 6 inch square tubing?

Answer: _____

42. How thick is the base plate?

Answer: _____

43. Describe the size of the angle iron used as a connection.

Answer: _____

44. What is the distance from the bottom of the base plate to the center hole of the first angle clip?
   ❏ 10'-10 3/4
   ❏ 10'-11 1/2
   ❏ 11'-1 3/4
   ❏ 11'-2 1/2

45. Name the size and type of weld used to join the base plate to the square tubing.

Answer: _____

46. Approximately how many inches of weld are required to join the base plate to the column?
   ❏ 6 inches
   ❏ 12 inches
   ❏ 18 inches
   ❏ 24 inches

47. Referring to the tail of the welding symbol of the angle iron clips, write out in full the drawing note.

Answer: _____

48. What is the length of the column including the base plate and the cap plate?

Answer: _____

49. Referring to the dimensions of the column what does the abbreviation O/A stand for?

Answer: _____

50. State the running dimension needed for locating the angle iron clip closest to the top of the column.

Answer: _____

51. What is the diameter of the holes in the base plate?

Answer: _____

52. Describe the type of weld used to join the cap plate to the top of the column.

Answer: _____

53. How many holes will be required in the base plate of the column?
   - ❏ 1 hole
   - ❏ 2 holes
   - ❏ 3 holes
   - ❏ 4 holes

Column Drawing 5-C19

Column 5-C19 is made from a wide flange beam. The roof rafter beams will sit on the top plate of this column. The top plate does not sit squarely on the column but is angled slightly to meet the slope of the building roof. It is a typical column in that it has a base plate on the bottom, a cap plate on top, and various connection holes in the web and flanges. It also has angle iron clips on one side. The location dimensions for the holes in the flanges and web originate from the RD location noted on the drawing. This reference point is the left hand end of the wide flange. The actual layout for the holes and clips of the beam will be done prior to the base plate being installed.

In this manner the tradesperson simply has to clip the tape measure onto the end of the beam and read the dimensions noted on the drawing to correctly layout these locations.

As mentioned previously, it is standard practice to draft structural drawings using one elevation view and then detail views as necessary. Much of the information that is needed to fabricate the column is given in the form of notes. This saves drafting time and allows the use of standard size paper (11 x 17 inch) to be used as the drawing format. An example of these notes can be seen in reference to the base plate layout. In this example the only view of the base plate is the one at the end of the column. The size of the base plate can be determined from the bill of materials. The location for the holes in the base plate is shown on the drawing as dimensions and notes.

The terminology near side (N/S) and far side (F/S) is used to note copes, clips, and holes that may be on one side only of the beam. Near side is always the side facing the drawing reader, far side is always the opposite side to the drawing reader. Of course the term both sides means just that.

The term '3 inch GA' noted on the top flange of this column means at all hole locations along the top flange of this beam, there will be two holes 3 inches apart, centered on the web of the beam. If the design were to call for only one hole at any of these locations they would be noted as either near side or far side. All other holes would be at 3 inch gage unless noted otherwise. The hole diameter is given as a general note at the bottom of the drawing. No size of hole dimension is put on the drawing unless the diameter is different than the general note. If a hole diameter is different it will be noted on the drawing.

The following questions refer to Column drawing 5-C19.

54. Write out the beam size, weight per foot and length of A3.

Answer: _____

55. What is the overall length of this column?

Answer: _____

56. What are the overall dimensions of plate 'Pa'?

Answer: _____

57. How many columns A3 will be fabricated from this drawing?
- ❏ 1
- ❏ 2
- ❏ 3
- ❏ 4

58. State the diameter of the holes drilled in the web of this column.

Answer: _____

59. What is the gage outstanding leg for the holes in part 'Ma'.

Answer: _____

60. State the two running dimensions of plates 'Pc'.

Answer: _____

61. Which direction will plate Pc face after the column is erected?
- ❏ north
- ❏ south
- ❏ east
- ❏ west

62. Calculate the number of holes that will be drilled or punched in the top flange of A3.

Answer: _____

63. What is the diameter of the hole located in plate 'Pc' at location 29'-9"?

Answer: _____

64. Determine the number of holes required in plate 'Pb'.

Answer: _____

65. Write out the general note referring to the paint specifications.

Answer: _____

66. Calculate the heel to heel spacing between the third and fourth angles 'Ma' counting from the bottom of the column.

Answer: _____

67. How many holes are required in base plate 'Pa'?
- ❏ 1
- ❏ 2
- ❏ 3
- ❏ 4

68. What is the diameter of the holes in plate 'Pa'?

Answer: _____

69. What is the shortest length of bolt required for field connections?
- ❏ ¾"
- ❏ 1½"
- ❏ 1¾"
- ❏ 2¼"

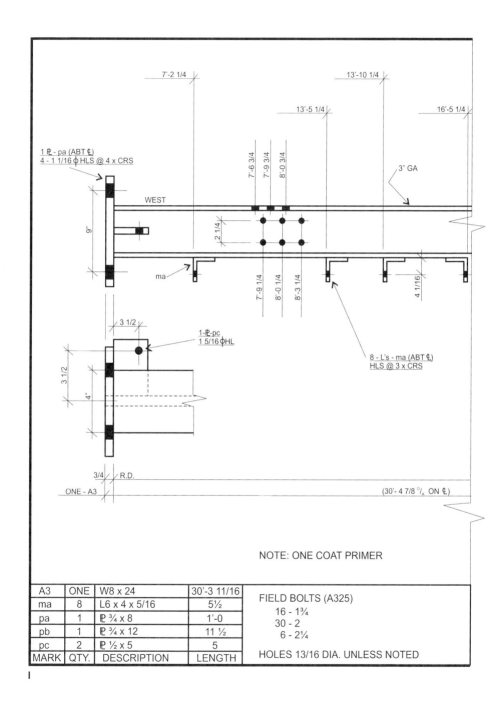

NOTE: ONE COAT PRIMER

MARK	QTY.	DESCRIPTION	LENGTH
A3	ONE	W8 x 24	30'-3 11/16
ma	8	L6 x 4 x 5/16	5½
pa	1	ℙ ¾ x 8	1'-0
pb	1	ℙ ¾ x 12	11 ½
pc	2	ℙ ½ x 5	5

FIELD BOLTS (A325)
   16 - 1¾
   30 - 2
   6 - 2¼

HOLES 13/16 DIA. UNLESS NOTED

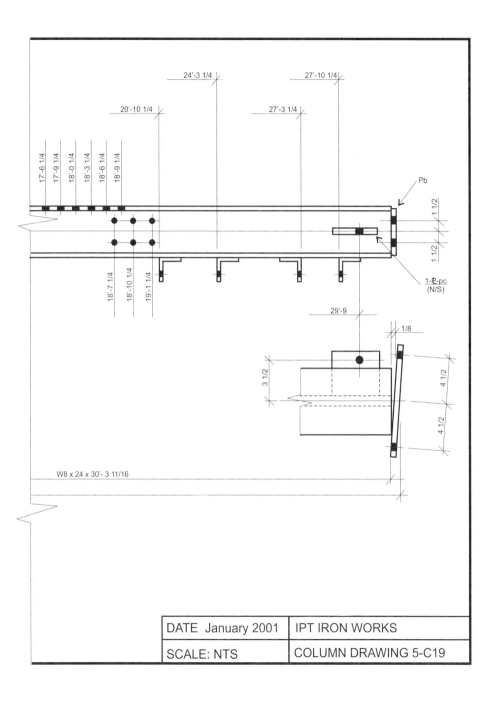

DATE January 2001	IPT IRON WORKS
SCALE: NTS	COLUMN DRAWING 5-C19

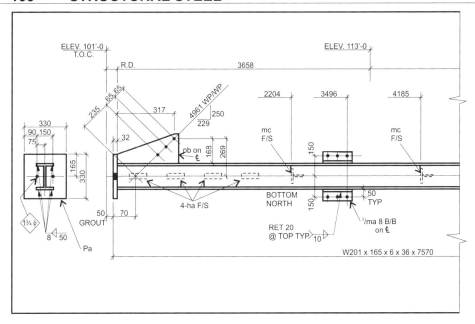

70. If the hole size is 1/16 inch larger than the diameter of bolt, what is the diameter of the field bolts required for the web hole connections?
    - ❏ 1"
    - ❏ ¾"
    - ❏ ½"
    - ❏ ¼"

71. How many field bolts in total are required as stated on the drawing?
    - ❏ 6 bolts
    - ❏ 16 bolts
    - ❏ 30 bolts
    - ❏ 52 bolts

72. Determine if this statement is true or false. Plate 'Pb' sits flat on the end of the W8 beam.
    - ❏ true
    - ❏ false

73. Calculate the distance from the underside of the base plate to the heel of the last angle 'Ma'.

Answer: _____

Column Drawing 5-C20

Column drawing 5-C20 is more typical of columns for multi-story buildings. It is designed to accommodate a splice at the top allowing another column to be positioned above it. A connector plate at the base of the column allows diagonal bracing to be attached at that location. The diagonal bracing that attaches to this column will attach at the top of the column adjacent to it.

The overall dimension shown at the bottom of the column drawing lists a series of numbers. They are W201 x 165 x 6 x 36 x 7570. These numbers represent the various dimensions of the actual beam in millimeters.

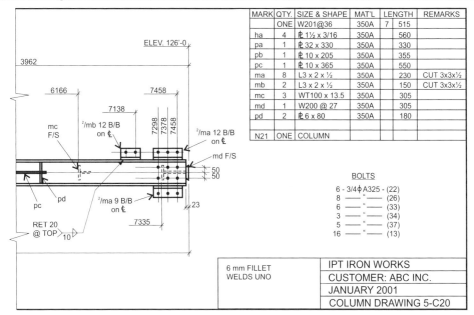

MARK	QTY.	SIZE & SHAPE	MAT'L	LENGTH		REMARKS
	ONE	W201@36	350A	7	515	
ha	4	℄ 1½ x 3/16	350A		560	
pa	1	℄ 32 x 330	350A		330	
pb	1	℄ 10 x 205	350A		355	
pc	1	℄ 10 x 365	350A		550	
ma	8	L3 x 2 x ½	350A		230	CUT 3x3x½
mb	2	L3 x 2 x ½	350A		150	CUT 3x3x½
mc	3	WT100 x 13.5	350A		305	
md	1	W200 @ 27	350A		305	
pd	2	℄ 6 x 80	350A		180	
N21	ONE	COLUMN				

BOLTS

6 - 3/4 φ A325 - (22)
8 ——— " ——— (26)
6 ——— " ——— (33)
3 ——— " ——— (34)
5 ——— " ——— (37)
16 ——— " ——— (13)

6 mm FILLET WELDS UNO

IPT IRON WORKS
CUSTOMER: ABC INC.
JANUARY 2001
COLUMN DRAWING 5-C20

The W201 is the exact depth as measured from flange surface to flange surface, the 165 is the width of the flanges, the 6 indicates the web thickness, the 36 is the weight of the beam in kilograms per meter of beam length. The 7570 is the overall length of the column including base plate. Fabrication shops add this information to drawings so that the tradesperson fabricating the column can check the dimensions of the beam before any work is performed to ensure the correct size is used.

The following questions refer to column drawing 5-C20

74. Determine the cut length of beam W201.

Answer: _____

75. What is the thickness of the base plate?

Answer: _____

76. Referring to the angle clips 'ma', what is the distance from the heel of the angle to the center of the holes in the angle?

Answer: _____

77. Write in full the abbreviation B/B as it refers to angles 'ma'.

Answer: _____

78. Write out the rise over run slope for the holes in connector plate 'pb'.

Answer: _____

79. Calculate the distance from the underside of the base plate to the center of the top hole in connector plate 'pb'.

Answer: _____

80. Which two dimensions would be used to locate the center of the top hole in plate 'pb'?

Answer: _____

81. What is the center to center distance between holes as layed out on the workline for 'pb'?

Answer: _____

82. There are three detail pieces 'mc' required for this column. What is the distance from the center 'mc' to the left end of the beam?

Answer: _____

83. What type of weld is required to attach plate 'pc' to the beam web?

Answer: _____

84. What is the leg size of the fillet weld required to attach all 'ma's?

Answer: _____

85. What will be the length of the return weld for item 'ma'?

Answer: _____

86. Calculate the running dimension center to center distance between the column web holes located at the top of the column.

Answer: _____

87. The hole gage for the holes noted in the above question is 100 mm center to center.
    ❏ true
    ❏ false

88. What grade of material is used to fabricate all of the pieces necessary for the column?

Answer: _____

Steel Trusses

Definition and Purpose of Trusses

Beams are used to support horizontal loads, and girders are large beams also used to support horizontal loads. Girders are often used in bridge construction as the horizontal members that support the road surface. Girders and beams are made stronger by increasing the thickness of their flanges and web, and by increasing their depth. Or in other words, the deeper the beam the stronger it becomes. However, this increased depth also increases the weight of the beam, and works against it concerning its ability as a load carrying member. The heavier and the longer the beam, the less load it can support because of its own weight.

This is where trusses come into the structural steel picture. A truss is nothing more than a beam with material removed from the center making it lighter in design. The truss strength is in the fact that it is deeper than a beam used to support an identical load over the same span. Therefore, the truss will be lighter in weight but greater in depth than a beam or a girder. However, there are two main reasons why trusses are not used in all applications:
• A truss is deeper, which means that head room could be a consideration.
• A truss is manufactured piece by piece and could cost more to fabricate than a beam of equal load carrying ability.

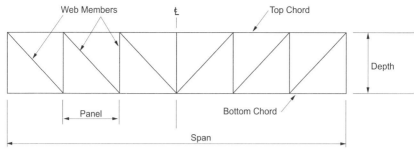

Illustration #5-21 - Typical Truss

Truss Nomenclature

The following definitions can be compared to the truss diagram shown in illustration #5-21.

Chords: The chords are the two horizontal members that run the length of the truss. This means there is a top and bottom chord for each truss. The web members connect to the chords.

Chord members are made of various structural shapes depending on the design of the truss. Common shapes are angle iron for light duty trusses, wide flange beams for heavier designs and closed shapes (square tubing) for a better esthetic appearance when the truss is exposed in public buildings.

Web Members: The web members make up the middle of the truss between the top and bottom chords. Most truss web members are diagonal, however in certain engineering applications both diagonal and vertical web members are used. Common structural shapes used for web members are angle iron, hollow structural tubing, and pipe.

Panels: Truss panels are symmetrical sections of the truss. As shown in illustration #5-21, they are the symmetrical sections between vertical web members. The panel points are dimensioned on the drawing and establish the work points for designing the truss and laying out the truss for fabrication purposes.

Span: The span of a truss is the center to center distance between the bearing points or connection points of the truss.

Depth: The depth of the truss is the dimension from the top of the top chord to the bottom of the bottom chord. This definition can vary depending on the type of structural shape used for the chords and their orientation in the truss.

Open Web Steel Joists: Open web steel joists, commonly abbreviated 'OWSJ' on drawings, are a type of truss because their design is similar. They are often called joists instead of the full term, open web steel joists. Steel joists are used to span between beams or trusses to make up floor and roof systems. Open web steel joists look like a truss but are lighter in design. They are often made using roll formed channel or angle iron for the top and bottom chords and round bar for the web members.

Truss Drawing 5-T22

Truss drawing 5-T22 is foreshortened by using break lines. The reason is that the truss is continuous in design along its length. This truss section connects into the opposite hand truss section on the right side.

Only one half of the truss is shown on this drawing and the other half is detailed on another drawing.

The reason for this is that the other half is not an exact opposite. It will be drawn as a separate truss with its own mark number. However, it is likely that the only difference would be the location of the clips connecting the two. The ends of this truss will sit on columns. To complete the roof framing, open web steel joists will span between the trusses for this building. The ends of the open web steel joists will sit on the top chord of the truss right over top of each vertical web member. The top and bottom chords are made of wide flange beam and the web members are made of square hollow structural tubing. Notice the panel points as indicated on the drawing, and also the diagonal web members. The dimensioning of this drawing is very similar to most structural drawings as it is dimensioned from left to right.

The following questions refer to truss drawing 5-T22.

89. What is the overall length of this truss?

Answer: _____

90. The length of each piece 'ma' as stated in the bill of materials is?

Answer: _____

91. Describe the type, nominal size and weight description of the material used to make the chords.

Answer: _____

92. What is the size of the square tubing used to make the web members?

Answer: _____

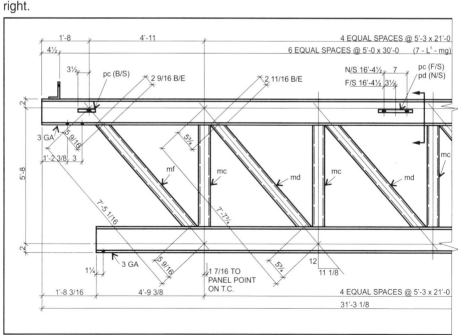

93. What is the wall thickness of the tubing used for the web members?

Answer: _____

94. Determine the overall depth of the truss.

Answer: _____

95. Write out the piece mark assigned to the vertical web members.

Answer: _____

96. How many pieces 'mc' are required for **one** complete truss?

Answer: _____

97. What is the approximate angle the ends of 'md' will be cut at?

Answer: _____

98. What is the panel point dimension between vertical web members?

Answer: _____

99. What is the center to center dimensions between pieces 'mg'?

Answer: _____

100. How many holes are in the bottom chord of the truss?

Answer: _____

101. What is the hole gage for the bottom flange of the top chord.

Answer: _____

102. What is the center to center dimension between work points for the diagonal web member 'md'?

Answer: _____

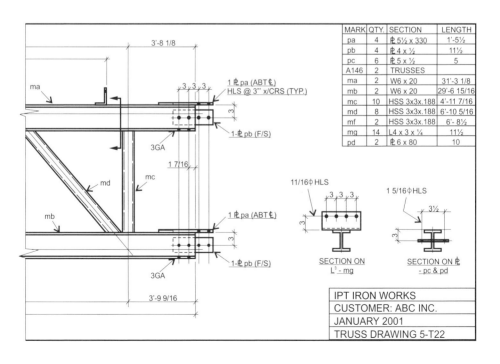

MARK	QTY.	SECTION	LENGTH
pa	4	℄ 5½ x 330	1'-5½
pb	4	℄ 4 x ½	11½
pc	6	℄ 5 x ½	5
A146	2	TRUSSES	
ma	2	W6 x 20	31'-3 1/8
mb	2	W6 x 20	29'-6 15/16
mc	10	HSS 3x3x.188	4'-11 7/16
md	8	HSS 3x3x.188	6'-10 5/16
mf	2	HSS 3x3x.188	6'- 8½
mg	14	L4 x 3 x ¼	11½
pd	2	℄ 6 x 80	10

SECTION ON
L⁵ - mg

SECTION ON ℄
- pc & pd

IPT IRON WORKS
CUSTOMER: ABC INC.
JANUARY 2001
TRUSS DRAWING 5-T22

103. What is the distance measured from the left end of the bottom chord to locate the first hole in the bottom flange?

Answer: _____

104. Which of these plates will be installed on the near side only of the top chord web?

      ❏ pc
      ❏ pd
      ❏ ma
      ❏ pa

105. Calculate the measurement from the left hand end of the top chord to the heel of the last angle clip 'mg' on the right hand end of the truss.

Answer: _____

106. How far is the center of the holes in plate 'pb' from the top flange of 'ma'?

Answer: _____

107. What would be the measurement from the left hand end to the second hole center to locate plate 'pd' on the near side of the top chord web ?

Answer: _____

108. What is the diameter of the holes in plates 'pc and pd'?

Answer: _____

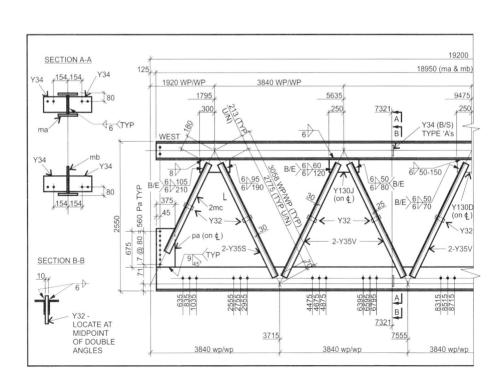

Truss Drawing 5-T23

Truss drawing 5-T23 is typical of a large span truss for a floor system in a public building.

It is fabricated using a wide flange beam for the top chord and a wide flange tee for the bottom chord. Back to back angles are used for the web members. This truss will be supported at the ends by bolting directly to the columns. Each truss that will make up the floor system will be interconnected by bridging pieces and cross bracing. Truss 5-T23 requires only bridging while other trusses in the floor system will be cross-braced to each other.

Bracing of the trusses helps to stabilize them from lateral movement as well as distributing the floor loads over the entire area. Details for the bridging and cross bracing are not shown on this drawing, only the required connector plates.

The following questions refer to truss drawing T23

109. What are the piece mark numbers for the top chord and the bottom chord members?

Answer: _____

110. What is the cut length of the top and bottom chords?

Answer: _____

111. What is the center to center distance between panel points?

Answer: _____

112. Referring to the note for direction marks on the top chord, what is to be marked on the truss?

Answer: _____

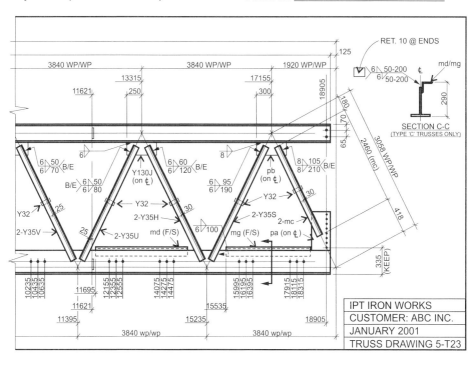

113. What is the overall depth of this truss?

Answer: _____

114. Referring to Section B-B, where will pieces Y32 be located?

Answer: _____

115. Referring to Section A-A, what is the dimension from the flange of the top chord to the center of the holes on all pieces Y34?

Answer: _____

116. Describe how the web members are attached to the bottom flange of the top chord.

Answer: _____

117. Write out the leg size of the fillet welds required to secure the web members to the chords.

Answer: _____

118. The length of the fillet welds noted in question #117 are all the same length.
    ❏ true
    ❏ false

119. Referring to Section C-C, describe the requirements for welding at the ends of 'md' and 'mg'.

Answer: _____

120. Referring to Section C-C, what is the term most commonly used to describe the fillet welds required to attach 'md and mg' to the bottom chord?

Answer: _____

121. What is the running dimension from the left hand end of the truss used to locate 'md' on the bottom chord?

Answer: _____

122. On which side of the chord will 'md' and 'mg' be located?

Answer: _____

123. How many holes are in each plate 'Pa'?

Answer: _____

124. Determine how many holes are required in the top chord of the truss.

Answer: _____

125. What is the distance from the flange of the top chord to the center of the first hole in the web?

Answer: _____

126. What is the center to center distance of the web holes in the top chord?

Answer: _____

127. How many full length panel points are required to be layed out on the bottom chord?

Answer: _____

128. What is the typical dimension from the work point in the web of the top chord needed to locate all web members on the connector plate?

Answer: _____

Truss Drawing 5-T24

Truss drawing 5-T24 represents a roof truss, also referred to as a rafter truss. This type of truss has a sloping top chord and a horizontal bottom chord. The slope of the top chord can vary with the desired roof pitch depending on the climate. In areas where there is little or no chance of snow accumulation on the roof, the pitch can be shallow. If the truss is used in an area where a large snow load accumulation is anticipated, then the pitch will be steeper. As noted on the drawing, the roof pitch of this truss is given as a rise over run relationship called a slope triangle. It is common to base the longest leg of the slope triangle on a standard dimension, such as 12 inches, or 250 millimeters in the case of metric measurement. Using this method of giving the slope or angle allows the fabricator to make the required miter cuts without having to determine how to layout the required angle in degrees.

Truss 5-T24 uses a wide flange tee for the top and bottom chords, and angle iron for web members. The back to back angle design is quite common and relatively inexpensive to manufacture.

The following questions refer to truss drawing 5-T24

129. State the roof pitch for the truss.
Answer: _____

130. Write out the depth and the weight per foot of the WT used for the bottom chord.
Answer: _____

131. Approximately how much WT 8 x 20 is required to make up the entire top chord?
Answer: _____

132. Which of the dimensions shown below relate to the overall span of the truss?
    ❏ 20 feet
    ❏ 20 feet 5 inches
    ❏ 40 feet
    ❏ 40 feet 10 inches

133. What is the actual out to out dimension of the fabricated truss?
    ❏ 20 feet
    ❏ 20 feet 5 inches
    ❏ 40 feet
    ❏ 40 feet 10 inches

134. Referring to the welding symbol located at the top of the truss, determine how much gap is required when fitting the two chord halves together.
Answer: _____

135. Name the type of weld required that is needed to attach the web angles to the top and bottom chords.
Answer: _____

136. Which side, "arrow side" or "other side", has the largest weld by size for the web angles to the top chord member joint?
Answer: _____

MARK	NO.	DESCRIPTION	LGTH
T24	ONE	TRUSS	
ma	2	WT 8 x 20	21'-10 1/2"
mb	1	WT 5 x 8.5	40'-10"
wa	2	L 2 1/2 x 2 x 1/4	3'-9 1/2"
wb	2	L 2 1/2 x 2 x 1/4	7'-11 1/2"
wc RL	4	L 3 1/2 x 3 1/2 x 5/16	7'-6 1/4"
wd RL	1	L 2 1/2 x 2 x 1/4	9'-11 1/4"
pa	4	BAR 2 1/2 x 3/8	11"
aa	12	L 4 x 3 x 3/8	11 1/2"
ab RL	4	L 6 x 4 x 1/2	4"
fa	2	BAR 1 1/2 x 5/16	4 1/2"
pb	2	BAR 3 1/4	1'-4"
pc	2	P 1/2 x 10	10 1/2"
pd	2	P 3/8 x 12	1'-4"
ac	6	L 3 x 3 x 3/8	4"

NOTE A:
GOUGE SINGLE U-GROOVE
AFTER FITTING

NOTE B:
GRIND WELDS ONLY IN WAY
OF FITTING ANGLES.
NO CAMBER.

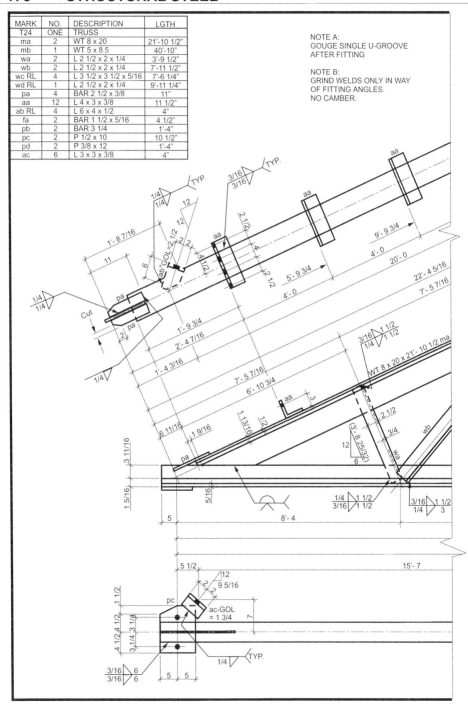

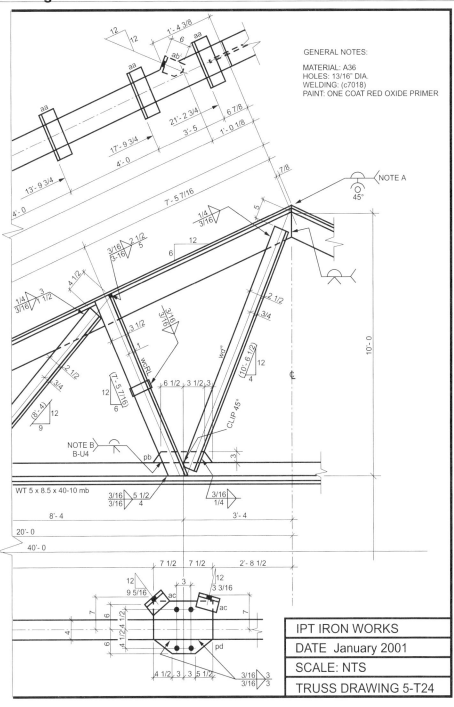

GENERAL NOTES:

MATERIAL: A36
HOLES: 13/16" DIA.
WELDING: (c7018)
PAINT: ONE COAT RED OXIDE PRIMER

NOTE A
45°

NOTE B
B-U4

WT 5 x 8.5 x 40-10 mb

IPT IRON WORKS

DATE January 2001

SCALE: NTS

TRUSS DRAWING 5-T24

137. Name the joint preparation required for welding of the two web sections of the WT8's at the peak of the truss.
- ❏ fillet weld
- ❏ vee groove preparation
- ❏ bevel groove preparation
- ❏ double bevel groove preparation

138. What is the name of the weld that is used on the other side of the joint when referring to the weld noted in question number 137?
- ❏ fillet weld
- ❏ full penetration weld
- ❏ back weld
- ❏ butt weld

Plan View Drawings

The term plan view drawing refers to a view looking at an object from the top. Structural steel plan view drawings are used to show the location of columns, beams, trusses and other structural members as viewed from the top of a floor, the roof, or any required elevation height. Roof framing plan drawing 5-P25A shows a view of the location of columns, beams and joists that make up the frame of a building roof. A grid system is used as a legend to identify quadrants of the building. As shown in drawing 5-P25A, it is a common practice to use letters of the alphabet on one side of the grid and numbers on the other. Other types of views can be incorporated into the plan view drawing for erection purposes, such as section views and detail views.

In plan view drawing 5-P25A, a numbered cutting plane line identifies the location where the section view was taken from. In this case, the corresponding section view is shown on another drawing using the same number. Detail views and other views would be shown in a similar way.

The detailing of the plan view is drawn using single lines that depict the center of the beams, trusses and columns. The dimensions shown are the center to center dimensions between these members.

Plan view drawings normally include a direction symbol to indicate North. The piece marks that are used to identify the various steel components, like columns and beams will appear on the plan view drawing.

Drawing 5-P25A shows the framing plan for a single story building. The grid system uses letters A, B, C, D on one side and numbers 1, 2, 3, 4, 5 on the other. This represents the center of the beams and columns that will make up the main support structure for the roof. This drawing shows two beam lines running on grid lines B and C. The columns and beams, along with the outside walls, are required to support the roof. Open web steel joists are used as intermediate supports for the roofing material. As with the beam line, the single lines used to indicate the open web steel joists represent their centers.

The various section views shown on drawing 5-P25B and C are used to give detail of the building at the locations identified by the numbered symbol.

The following questions refer to the Roof Framing Plan drawing 5-P25

139. According to this drawing how many steel columns are needed to support beam line C.
   - ❏ 2
   - ❏ 3
   - ❏ 4
   - ❏ 6

140. Referring to the two center spans of the roof framing plan, write out the complete description of the wide flange beams.

Answer: _____

141. What size are the columns supporting the wide flange beams?

Answer: _____

142. Are the columns square, rectangular or round?

Answer: _____

143. State the dimensions of the base plates used on the columns.

Answer: _____

144. Referring to the column base plates, how many anchor bolts are required for each one, and what is their diameter?

Answer: _____

145. Approximately how many millimeters will beam B10 extend past the center of column C5, for splicing purposes, after it is erected into place?

Answer: _____

146. Referring to the two beam lines, what is the piece mark number of the beams that will span between grid lines 2 and 3?

Answer: _____

147. What is the depth of the open web steel joists that will span between grid lines C and D?

Answer: _____

148. State the leg size and thickness of the angle iron used on the store front fascia found on grid line 5.

Answer: _____

149. Referring to section view 6, what is the clearance allowed for grout between the column base plate and the concrete piling?

Answer: _____

150. Will the roof slope down towards the center of the building or slope down towards the outer walls?

Answer: _____

151. Determine from section 2 what the thickness of the concrete floor will be.

Answer: _____

152. Referring to section 5, what will be the depth of the front fascia?

Answer: _____

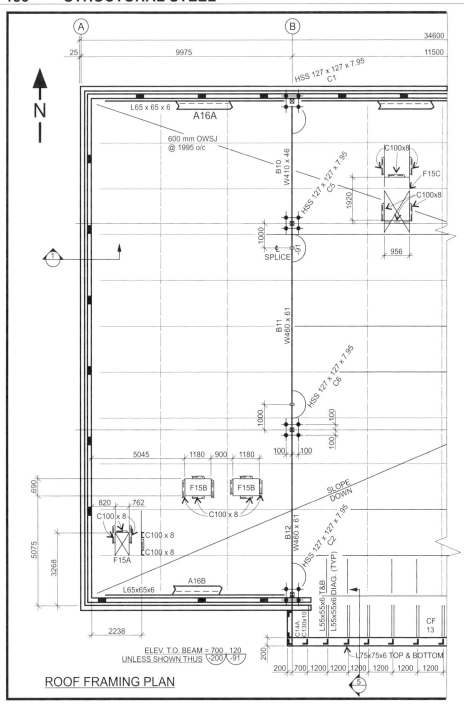

ROOF FRAMING PLAN

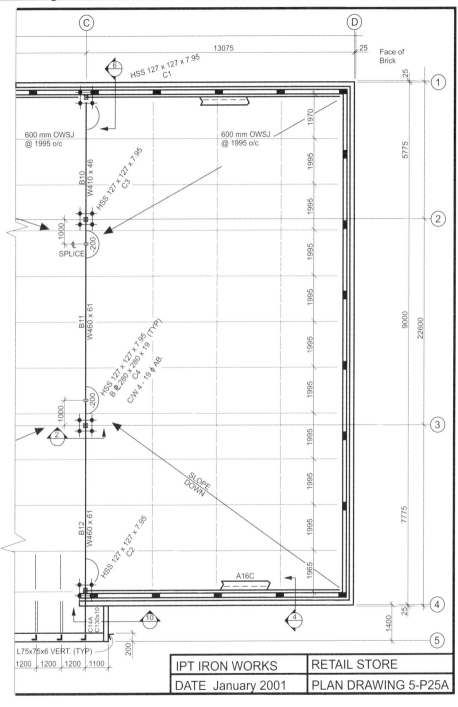

IPT IRON WORKS	RETAIL STORE
DATE January 2001	PLAN DRAWING 5-P25A

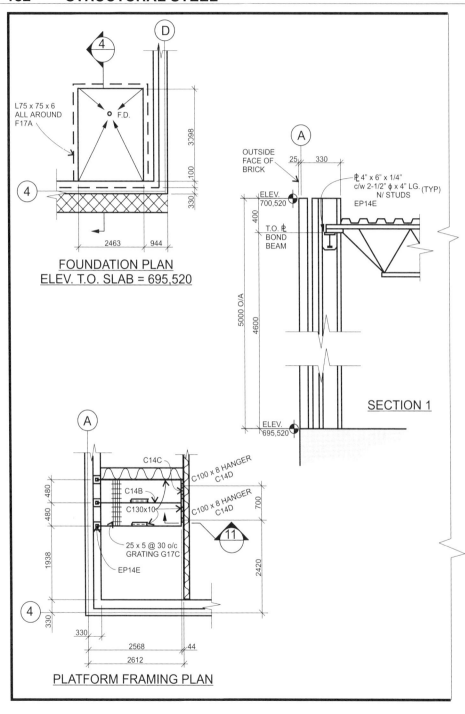

L75 x 75 x 6
ALL AROUND
F17A

F.D.

3398

100

330

2463   944

FOUNDATION PLAN
ELEV. T.O. SLAB = 695,520

OUTSIDE
FACE OF
BRICK

25   330

℄ 4" x 6" x 1/4"
c/w 2-1/2" φ x 4" LG. (TYP)
N/ STUDS
EP14E

ELEV.
700,520

400

T.O. ℄
BOND
BEAM

5000 O/A

4600

ELEV.
695,520

SECTION 1

A

C14C

C100 x 8 HANGER
C14D

480

480

C14B

C130x10

C100 x 8 HANGER
C14D

700

11

1938

25 x 5 @ 30 o/c
GRATING G17C

2420

EP14E

330

330

2568   44

2612

PLATFORM FRAMING PLAN

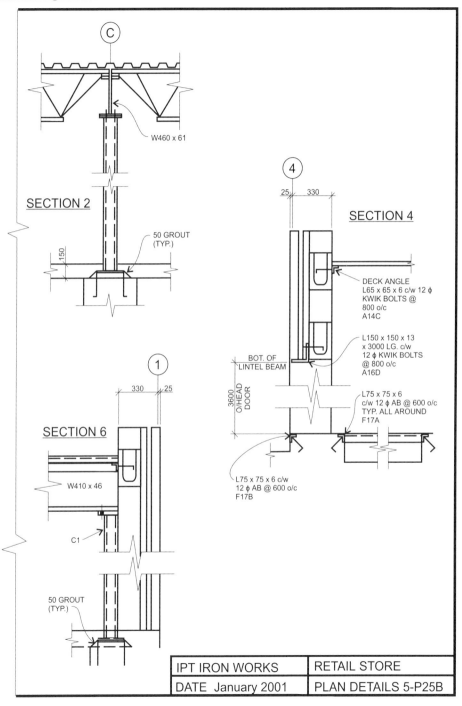

C

SECTION 2

W460 x 61

50 GROUT
(TYP.)

150

4

25 | 330

SECTION 4

DECK ANGLE
L65 x 65 x 6 c/w 12 φ
KWIK BOLTS @
800 o/c
A14C

L150 x 150 x 13
x 3000 LG. c/w
12 φ KWIK BOLTS
@ 800 o/c
A16D

1

330 | 25

SECTION 6

W410 x 46

C1

BOT. OF
LINTEL BEAM

3600
O/HEAD
DOOR

L75 x 75 x 6
c/w 12 φ AB @ 600 o/c
TYP. ALL AROUND
F17A

L75 x 75 x 6 c/w
12 φ AB @ 600 o/c
F17B

50 GROUT
(TYP.)

IPT IRON WORKS	RETAIL STORE
DATE January 2001	PLAN DETAILS 5-P25B

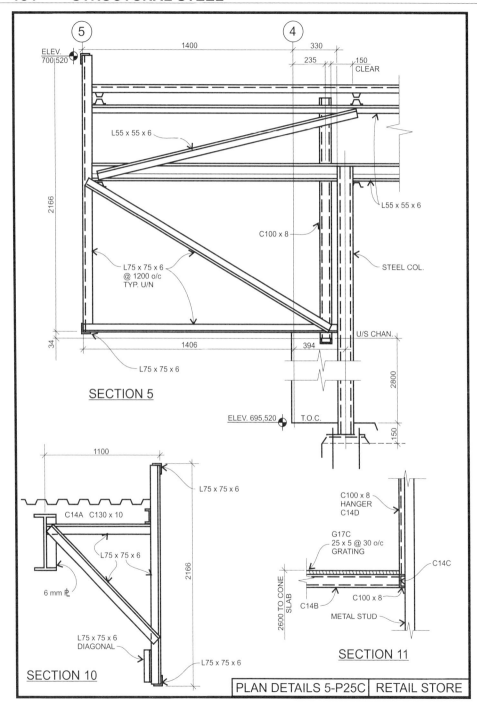

ELEV.
700,520

5

1400

4

330

235

150
CLEAR

L55 x 55 x 6

2166

L55 x 55 x 6

C100 x 8

L75 x 75 x 6
@ 1200 o/c
TYP. U/N

STEEL COL.

U/S CHAN.

34

1406

394

2800

L75 x 75 x 6

SECTION 5

ELEV. 695,520

T.O.C.

150

1100

L75 x 75 x 6

C14A C130 x 10

2166

L75 x 75 x 6

6 mm ℄

L75 x 75 x 6
DIAGONAL

L75 x 75 x 6

SECTION 10

C100 x 8
HANGER
C14D

G17C
25 x 5 @ 30 o/c
GRATING

C14C

2600 TO CONC
SLAB

C14B

C100 x 8

METAL STUD

SECTION 11

| PLAN DETAILS 5-P25C | RETAIL STORE |

Stairs

Steel stair construction varies considerably from that of wooden stairs. In most cases steel stairs consist of two stringers made of channel iron, and steel steps made from grating, or pans filled with concrete. Straight steel stairs (illustration #5-26) are common for most commercial and industrial applications, while steel spiral stairs (illustration #5-27) are used for more architecturally pleasing requirements.

Illustration #5-26 - Straight Steel Stair

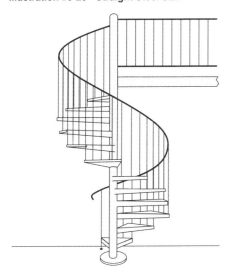

Illustration #5-27 - Spiral Steel Stair

Stair Nomenclature

Stringer: Stringers are the main support members for the stair. The treads will bolt or weld directly to a steel stair stringer. The stringer normally sits on the floor or landing and is attached to the upper landing by bolting or welding. Common steel stringer material is ten inch (250 millimeter) channel for straight stairs.

Tread: The treads, or steps are the horizontal members of a stair. Steel stair treads are often made from grating with a checker plate nosing piece attached to the grating. The treads have flat bars for bolting purpose. The flat bars are welded to the ends of the grating. See illustration #5-28A. Some steel stair treads for outside use have a special slip resistant nosing for extra safety in wet or snowy conditions. See illustration #5-28B.

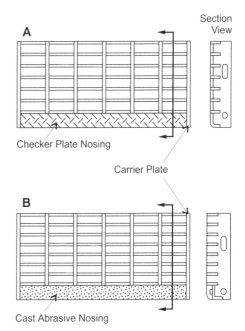

Illustration #5-28 - Stair Treads

Handrail: Handrails for steel stairs are usually made from small diameter pipe. Building codes specify the minimum handrail height for the top rail, the mid rail, and the maximum distance between vertical support posts. The handrails are usually welded to the posts, which are welded directly to the steel stair stringer, although in some applications the post may be attached to the stringer with bolts. See illustration #5-29 for an example of a typical steel handrail.

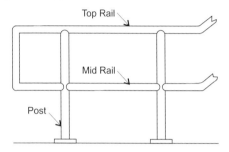

Illustration #5-29 - Steel Handrail

Landing: The landing is the platform between flights of stairs. The top of the stair stringer usually butts up to the front of the landing and will be either bolted or welded directly to the landing. The stair handrail and the landing handrail will be joined together to provide a continuous rail. It is common for a landing to be used when a turn is required in the stair design. This type of design is easier and safer than a spiral or winder type stair.

Nosing: The nosing is the front part of the stair tread. The nosing for steel stair treads is often made of checker plate or a slip resistant material for extra grip on outside stairs (see illustration #5-28).

Nosing Line: Stair drawings detail the location of the stair tread by showing the location of the nosing of the tread. When the stringer is laid out, the nosing line on the stringer is established.

The nose of the tread will line up with the nosing line marked on the stringer as they are being fit into position.

Total Rise: This is the term used to describe the vertical distance the stair will gain. Comparing a stair to a right angled triangle, the vertical leg is the rise.

Total Run: This is the term used to describe the horizontal distance the stair will cover. In a right triangle, the horizontal leg is the run.

Unit Rise: This is the term used to describe the height of one riser of the stair or the distance from the top of one tread to the top of the next tread.

Unit Run: This is the term used to describe the horizontal distance from the face of one tread to the face of the next tread.

In summary, the total rise and total run are used to determine the number of steps required for the stair, and also the unit rise and unit run of the stair. The unit rise, and the unit run dimensions are used to layout the stair stringer.

Step Length: This is the term used to describe the diagonal distance created when the unit rise and the unit run dimensions of a stair are used to make the hypotenuse of a right triangle. The step length is a useful dimension to know when laying out the stair.

See illustration #5-30 for an explanation of unit rise, unit run and step length.

Stair Drawing 5-S31

Stair drawing 5-S31 is an example of a simple straight steel stair designed with a pan style tread. This pan type of tread will be filled with concrete to complete the tread to the designed height. These types of stair treads are commonly used in public buildings like hospitals and apartment buildings as they offer a safer grip than conventional steel treads.

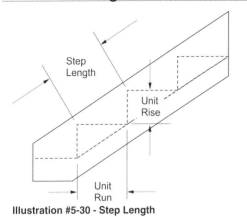

Illustration #5-30 - Step Length

MARK	QTY.	DESCRIPTION	LGTH	REMK
A16	ONE	STAIR		
ma R/L	2	C3'0 x 31	4590	1R/1L
pa	12	BENT ℔ 348 x 5	1050	
pb	ONE	BENT ℔ 348 x 5	1050	
pf	ONE	℔ 50 x 35	1050	
pg	2	℔ 67 x 5	183	
pk	ONE	℔ 67 x 5	115	
pm	ONE	℔ 67 x 5	161	
B16	TWO	STAIRS		
ma R/L	4			2R/2L
pc	24	BENT ℔ 348 x 5	900	
pd	2	BENT ℔ 365 x 5	900	
pg	4			
ph	2	℔ 50 x 35	900	
pk	2			
pm	2			

Bill of Materials 5-S31

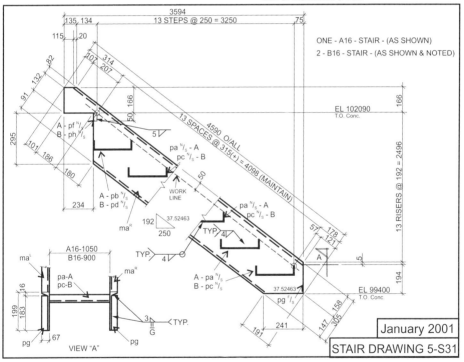

January 2001

STAIR DRAWING 5-S31

The stair stringers are cut out to fit into the landing and will be welded directly to the landing. Three sets of stairs will be fabricated from this drawing. The three stairs will be marked stair A or stair B.

The difference between stair A and stair B is the width. The bottom of the stringer channel is cut to sit flat on the concrete landing. The fabricator will build both the left hand and right hand stringer from the one view shown on the drawing.

The following questions refer to stair drawing 5-S31.

153. What is the total rise for this stair?
   ❑ 192 mm
   ❑ 250 mm
   ❑ 2496 mm
   ❑ 2690 mm

154. What is the total run for this stair?
   ❑ 192 mm
   ❑ 250 mm
   ❑ 3250 mm
   ❑ 4098 mm

155. What is the unit rise for this stair?
   ❑ 192 mm
   ❑ 250 mm
   ❑ 2496 mm
   ❑ 4098 mm

156. What is the unit run for this stair?
   ❑ 192 mm
   ❑ 250 mm
   ❑ 3250 mm
   ❑ 4098 mm

157. How many stair treads (pans) will be required for one stair?
   ❑ 11
   ❑ 12
   ❑ 13
   ❑ 14

158. What is the step length for the rise/run shown for this stair?
   ❑ 178
   ❑ 192
   ❑ 207
   ❑ 315

159. A note appears at both the bottom and top of the stair stringer and is abbreviated T.O. Conc.. Write out this abbreviation in full.

Answer: _____

160. Name the size of and type of weld used to attach the stair pans to the stringers.

Answer: _____

161. Which of the dimensions listed below refers to the distance the nosing line is measured from the heel of the stringer?
   ❑ 50 mm
   ❑ 71 mm
   ❑ 147 mm
   ❑ 158 mm

162. What is the vertical height from the floor to the top of the first stair pan?

Answer: _____

163. List the vertical and horizontal dimension used to layout the cut line for the bottom end of the stair stringers.

Answer: _____

164. What is the work point to work point dimension on the nosing line (work line) when referring to the distance from the nosing of the first tread to the nosing of the last tread?
   ❑ 2496 mm
   ❑ 3250 mm
   ❑ 4098 mm
   ❑ 4590 mm

165. What is the overall length of the treads for stair A?

Answer: _____

166. What is the overall length of the treads for stair B?

Answer: _____

167. Including the step to reach the first tread, how many risers are there in total?

Answer: _____

The following information refers to stair drawing 5-S32.

Stair drawing 5-S32 is similar to stair drawing 5-S31, however, instead of using a pan type tread the treads are made from steel grating with a checker plate nosing. The bottom of the stair stringers for this stair will be fastened directly to the floor while the top of the stair and platform will be supported on a separate structure. The fabricator will build both the left hand and right hand stringer from the one view shown on the drawing. Notice that there is a running dimension (abbreviated RD) table included on this drawing. This table is used to layout the locations of the stair treads on the nosing line without the fabricator having to calculate them. The handrail details are also shown.

The following questions refer to stair drawing 5-S32.

168. What is the total rise of this stair from the floor to the top of the landing?
   ❏ 151 mm
   ❏ 250 mm
   ❏ 2768 mm
   ❏ 3070 mm

169. What is the total run of this stair from the front of the stringer to the front of the landing?
   ❏ 4480 mm
   ❏ 4556 mm
   ❏ 4590 mm
   ❏ 7206 mm

170. What is the work point to work point dimension of the nosing line?
   ❏ 5360 mm
   ❏ 5231 mm
   ❏ 5305 mm
   ❏ 4480 mm

171. What is the rise between any two steps.

Answer: _____

172. What is the gage outstanding leg for the hole in piece 'ac'?

Answer: _____

173. Determine which of the distances listed below indicates the individual step length dimension.
   ❏ 151
   ❏ 250
   ❏ 327
   ❏ 401

174. Using the RD table determine the location dimension for the number 6 tread on the nosing line.

Answer: _____

175. From the bill of materials, what is the size and length of the channel iron used to make up piece 'mf'?

Answer: _____

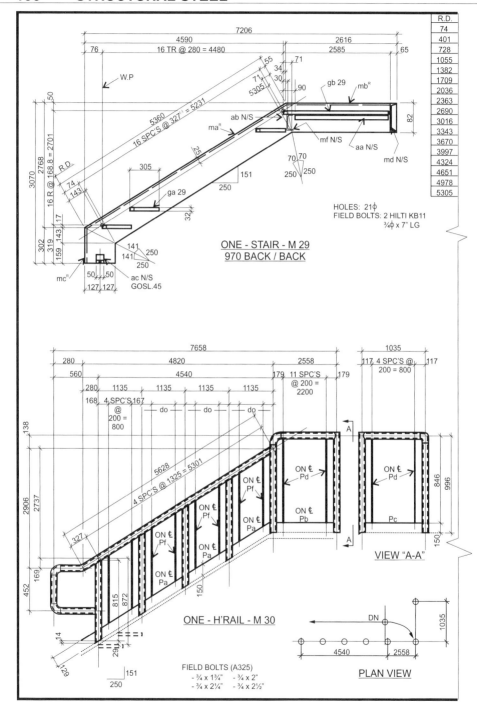

R.D.
74
401
728
1055
1382
1709
2036
2363
2690
3016
3343
3670
3997
4324
4651
4978
5305

HOLES: 21φ
FIELD BOLTS: 2 HILTI KB11
¾φ x 7" LG

ONE - STAIR - M 29
970 BACK / BACK

ONE - H'RAIL - M 30

VIEW "A-A"

PLAN VIEW

FIELD BOLTS (A325)
- ¾ x 1¾"   - ¾ x 2"
- ¾ x 2¼"   - ¾ x 2½"

MARK	NO.	DESCRIPTION	LGTH	WT.	MARK	NO.	DESCRIPTION	LGTH	WT.
M29	ONE	STAIR			Pc	1	---do---	1007	
ma R/L	2	C250 x 23	5360		Pd	17	FB 13 x 13	816	31
mb R/L	2	---do---	2616		Pf	20	---do---	637	
mc R/L	2	---do---	302						
md	1	---do---	970		M31	ONE	STAIR SUPPORT		
mf	1	C150 x 12	970		ma	2	HSS 102 x 102 x 6	2765	101
aa	2	L51 x 51 x 6	2480		Pa	2	₽ 16 x 300	300	22
ac	2	L102 x 102 x 10	102		Pb	2	FB 10 x 76	76	1
ga 29	16	STAIR TREADS			aa	1	L76 x 76 x 6	2690	37
	GRTG	305 x 32 x 5 BB	960		ab	1	---do---	1430	
					ac	1	---do---	1330	
gb 29	1	STAIR LANDING							
	GRTG	2551 x32 x 5 BB			ga 29	16	STAIR TREADS		
					ma	16	GRATING	30-102	
M30	ONE	H'RAIL					276 x 32 x 5 BB	960	
ma	1	HSS 42.3 φ x 2.79	18000	52	pa	32	FB 5 x 32	305	
Pa	4	FB 6 x38	1350	15	pb	16	CK ₽ 3 x 55	960	
Pb	1	---do---	2530		pc	48	₽ 6 x 26	29	

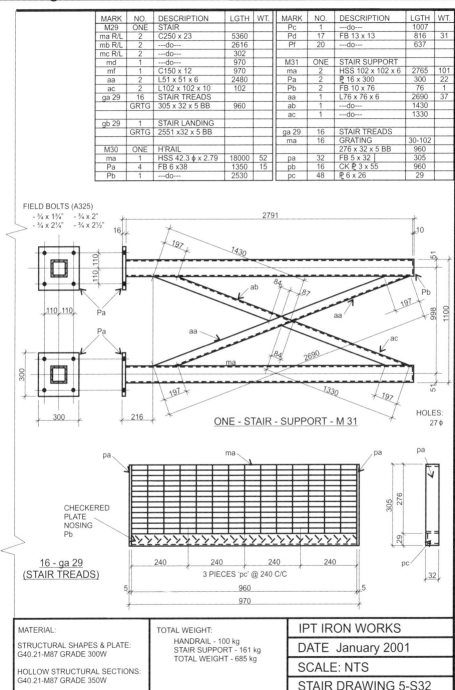

FIELD BOLTS (A325)
- ¾ x 1¾"   - ¾ x 2"
- ¾ x 2¼"   - ¾ x 2½"

ab
aa
ac
Pb
ma
Pa
Pa

ONE - STAIR - SUPPORT - M 31

HOLES:
27 φ

pa
ma
pa
pa

CHECKERED
PLATE
NOSING
Pb

16 - ga 29
(STAIR TREADS)

3 PIECES 'pc' @ 240 C/C

pc

MATERIAL:	TOTAL WEIGHT:	IPT IRON WORKS
STRUCTURAL SHAPES & PLATE: G40.21-M87 GRADE 300W	HANDRAIL - 100 kg STAIR SUPPORT - 161 kg TOTAL WEIGHT - 685 kg	DATE January 2001
		SCALE: NTS
HOLLOW STRUCTURAL SECTIONS: G40.21-M87 GRADE 350W		STAIR DRAWING 5-S32

176. Using the rise over run ratio shown on the drawing, write out the bevel dimensions of the miter cut for piece number 'MC'.

Answer: _____

177. What is the piece mark number of the stair treads?

Answer: _____

Questions 178 to 180 refer to the stair tread shown on drawing 5-S32

178. What is the overall width including piece 'pb' of the stair treads.

Answer: _____

179. How many pieces 'pa' in total are fabricated?

Answer: _____

180. What is the purpose of pieces 'pc'?

Answer: _____

Questions 181 to 184 refer to the stair support on drawing 5-S32

181. What structural shape is used to fabricate pieces 'ma'?

Answer: _____

182. Determine which of the angle irons used for cross bracing between the columns is not full length, and will be cut or coped?

Answer: _____

183. Calculate the edge distance from the center of any of the base plate holes to the outside edge of the base plate.
   - ❏ 40 mm
   - ❏ 80 mm
   - ❏ 110 mm
   - ❏ 220 mm

184. What does the symbol "do" refer to with reference to pieces 'ab' and 'ac'.

Answer: _____

Questions 185 to 192 refer to the stair handrail on drawing 5-S32

185. Is the HSS used to make piece 'ma' square, round or rectanglar?

Answer: _____

186. Referring to the plan view shown on this drawing how many vertical support posts will be required for this stair?

Answer: _____

187. How many pieces 'pf' will be installed between any two vertical supports posts for the steps?

Answer: _____

188. Calculate the total length of round HSS needed to fabricate one vertical support post.

Answer: _____

189. Determine how many pieces 'pd' will be installed into the front side platform handrail.

Answer: _____

190. What is the horizontal center to center distance between each vertical post on the stair?

Answer: _____

191. What will be the total weight in kilograms of the handrail when completed?

Answer: _____

192. What is the center to center distance between each vertical post as layed out along the slope of the stair?

Answer: _____

Ladders

Steel ladders are used to gain access to platforms in buildings, working areas of industrial plants, vessels and process towers, as well as a number of other applications. Building codes specify the guidelines regarding the design of steel ladders. The design criteria specifies the minimum width between the side rails, spacing of the ladder rungs, the maximum height above ground level for the use of a protective cage, and the design of the cage. The ladder rungs are usually made of ¾ in. (19 mm) diameter round bar spaced on average 12 inches (300 mm) apart and welded into holes in the side rails. The side rails can be made from a variety of materials like flat bar, square or rectangular tubing, or angle iron. When used, the cage is fabricated using several sizes of flat bar and is generally welded directly to the side rails.

There are no specific length or height restrictions regarding ladders, however, building codes do specify the use and location of platforms. For ladders that are used for high towers and smoke stacks, a safety rail system is included with the ladder. This allows the use of rail locks and a body harness as a safety measure in the event of a slip or fall while ascending or descending the ladder.

The following questions refer to ladder drawing 5-L33.

193. Name the type of material the ladder side rails are made from.

Answer: _____

194. What is the center to center spacing of the side rails?

Answer: _____

195. State the overall length of the ladder.

Answer: _____

196. How many pieces 'mb' are required and what is the center to center spacing between them?

Answer: _____

197. What is the bevel at the intersection of pieces 'ma and mc'?

Answer: _____

198. How many pieces 'ra' are required and what is the center to center spacing between them?

Answer: _____

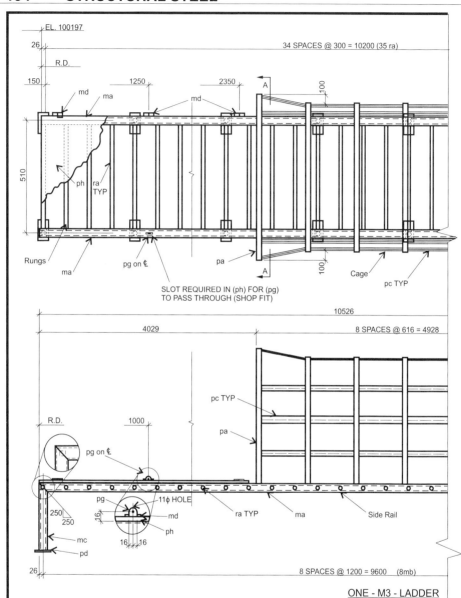

EL. 100197

26

R.D.

150

34 SPACES @ 300 = 10200 (35 ra)

1250

2350

A

100

md

ma

md

510

ph ra TYP

Rungs

ma

pg on ₵

pa

A

100

Cage

pc TYP

SLOT REQUIRED IN (ph) FOR (pg)
TO PASS THROUGH (SHOP FIT)

10526

4029

8 SPACES @ 616 = 4928

pc TYP

R.D.

1000

pa

pg on ₵

250
250

pg

11φ HOLE

16

md

ph

ra TYP

ma

Side Rail

16   16

mc

pd

26

8 SPACES @ 1200 = 9600   (8mb)

ONE - M3 - LADDER

MARK	QTY.	MATERIAL	LENGTH	WT.	MARK	QTY.	MATERIAL	LENGTH	WT.
M3	ONE	LADDER			md	3	BULLET HINGE	100	
ma	2	HSS 51x51x2.54	10526		mc	4	HSS 51x51x2.54	398	
mb	16	HSS 51x51x2.54	347		pg	1	Ꝓ 6 x 32	32	
pa	1	Ꝓ 50 x 6	2420±		ph	1	Ꝓ 6 x 560	2500	
pb	8	Ꝓ 50 x 6	2140±						
pc	7	Ꝓ 38 x 5	4985						
pd	20	Ꝓ 10 x 76	85		ra	35	BAR 19 x 19	459	

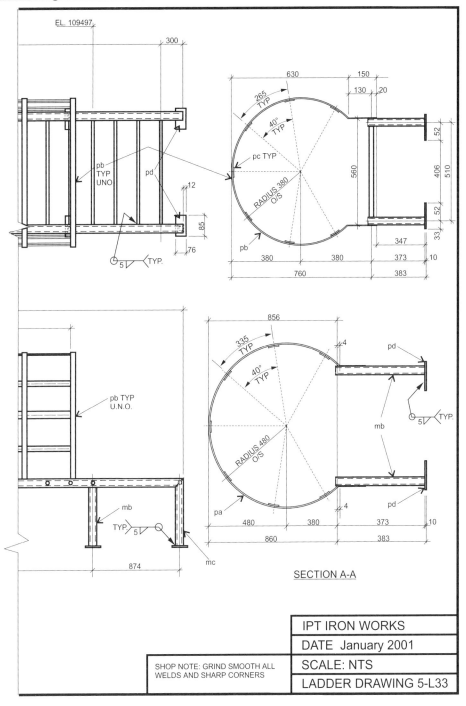

EL. 109497

300

630

150

130   20

265 TYP

40° TYP

pc TYP

pb TYP UNO

pd

RADIUS 380 O/S

560

510

406

52

52

33

12

85

76

5   TYP.

pb

380   380   347

760   373   10

383

856

335 TYP

40° TYP

pd

RADIUS 480 O/S

mb

5   TYP.

4

pb TYP U.N.O.

pa

pd

4

mb

TYP. 5

480   380   373   10

860   383

mc

874

SECTION A-A

| IPT IRON WORKS |
| DATE January 2001 |
| SCALE: NTS |
| LADDER DRAWING 5-L33 |

SHOP NOTE: GRIND SMOOTH ALL WELDS AND SHARP CORNERS

199. Calculate the difference in diameter between piece's 'pa' and 'pb'.

Answer: _____

200. What is the center to center distance between pieces 'pc' that will be welded to piece 'pb'?

Answer: _____

201. Referring to pieces 'pc', what is the typical angle formed between each piece?

Answer: _____

202. What size and type of weld is required to attach plate 'pd' to all pieces 'mc?

Answer: _____

203. Is plate 'pd' welded to all pieces 'mb' using a 5 mm fillet weld?

    ❏ yes
    ❏ no

204. What size and type of weld is used to attach all pieces 'ra' to the side rails?

Answer: _____

205. Referring to the radius noted for the cage hoops, what does the abbreviation O/S mean?

Answer: _____

206. Describe the purpose for Section A-A.

Answer: _____

207. State the diameter of the hole required in piece 'pg'.

Answer: _____

SECTION
SIX

REINFORCED CONCRETE

Reinforced Concrete

Introduction

A reinforced concrete drawing is classified as a type of structural drawing. It is best defined by its purpose, which is to accurately describe in sufficient detail the features of a concrete structure and to indicate the size and location of the reinforcing steel within the structure. There are many applications for reinforced concrete drawings, as anything that can be built out of reinforced concrete can have a drawing associated with it. Generally the applications can be broken down into the following areas; buildings, foundations, tanks, bridges, and hydraulic structures. Many of these structures are somewhat similar as they are made up of the same structural elements, which are beams, columns, and slabs.

Reinforced Concrete Views

To be able to properly interpret this information requires a basic understanding of engineering drafting theory. Without going into too much detail, it is sufficient to say that as in most structural drawings, reinforced concrete drawings borrow many of their ideas from the theory of orthographic projection. The idea is to describe an object, or a structure, by showing an arrangement of the top, front, and side so that someone reading the drawing can put these views together as a three dimensional view. However, for anything other than a very simple object, trying to show detailed information and dimensions on one three-dimensional view is confusing and inaccurate, although attempts are made with the use of computer drawings.

Reinforced concrete drawings consist of plan views, which are similar to top views and elevation views, which resemble front or side views.

In addition, there are usually section views, details and schedules. The views will be described in the following text as well as the method of tying all this information together by cross-referencing.

Title Block

The first item to look for on a drawing is the title block. It is always located in the lower right hand corner of the drawing. Within the title block will be the drawing title, indicating in general terms what the drawing is about. For example on larger detailed projects it is not possible to show all the information on one drawing, therefore some drawings are concerned with the plan view only, or the elevation of a building only. When this has been established it is possible to determine what part of the structure you are looking at and its orientation. The title block may also indicate the scale. Most structural drawings will be referred to as a scale drawing, which means that all the dimensions are drawn at a constant ratio. This allows all the features of a structure to appear proportional.

Other information perhaps appearing in the title block will be the name of the draftsperson who prepared the drawing, the designer, the project name, and the design company responsible for the drawing. Two other important pieces of information are the drawing number and any revision numbers. The drawing number is used as a way of referencing the drawing when information is shared between two or more drawings. The revision number, which usually appears to the right of the drawing number, refers to a particular version of the drawing. Different versions of the drawing may exist as a result of design changes that required modification of the drawing.

Always pay attention to the revision date on the drawing you are using.

Drawing Notes

Another method of conveying information other than by drawing or using schedules is with a note. A note is used when it is more convenient than drawing a view. A general note, which usually appears above or near the title block, is information that pertains to the entire drawing, such as the design code, or design loads used for the structure. However a project of any significant size will have a set of specifications that provide more complete information and take precedence over a general note.

Floor Plan Drawings

To get a general understanding of a blue print, or a set of blue prints for a project, it is always best to start with a type of drawing that reveals the most information about the structure and makes other drawings easier to understand. This is usually the plan view drawing, and most of the other drawings will refer back to it. As with any drawing, it is possible to have different views on the same drawing and with different scales. All these views will be identified with a title describing the view.

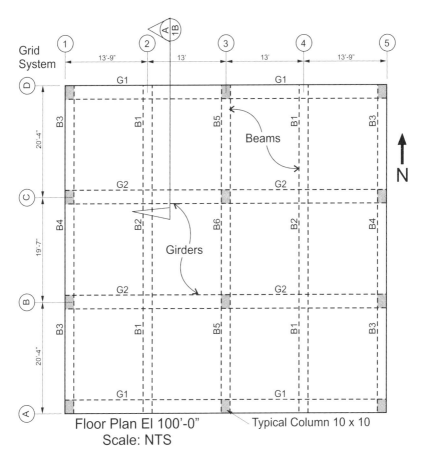

Floor Plan El 100'-0"
Scale: NTS

Illustration #6-1A - Floor Framing Plan

The title is always below the view that it is describing, along with the scale if it is different from other views on the drawing.

The floor plan view in illustration #6-1A gives the overall size of the building and describes the arrangement or layout of all the beams and slabs within the floor system. It is common practice to have the layout based on a grid system. In the grid system for this print the beam lines are numbered and are vertical, while the girders are lettered and are horizontal. The necessary dimensions are given, and the beams and slabs are identified by a symbol known as a mark.

The mark is used as a way to reference the beam in a table or schedule, which is shown in illustration #6-1D. Referring to illustration #6-1A, the beams are lettered with a B, the girders with a G, and their supporting columns are shaded. The clear span distance is the unsupported distance between the faces of the columns. The plan view will also show the orientation of the building in relation to north, which is shown by the north arrow symbol.

Detail and Section Views

Other drawings will show detail and section views. An important requirement of a detail or section view is to specify what part of the structure it is describing.

For a detail this can be stated in the title, such as Beam B1 detail, as shown in illustration #6-1B. For a section view, the section must be cross-referenced to a cutting plane line located on the drawing where the section was taken from.

The cutting plane line is, as the name suggests, a line showing where the imaginary slice through the structure would have to be made to reveal the desired section view. It will also have an arrow to indicate the direction of view so that it is properly orientated to the section view.

The cutting plane line and the section view are cross-referenced to each other by identifying both of them with the same symbol such as A, B (or A-A, B-B), etc. as shown in illustration #6-1A. The cutting plane line and the section view may be found on different drawings. When this happens, the cutting line and the section view refer to each other by way of their drawing number where they are located. For example section A, with the beam detail is on illustration #6-1B, while the cutting line is on illustration #6-1A. Anyone looking at illustration #6-1A would see cutting line A and a reference to illustration #6-1B. This instructs them to go to illustration #6-1B to get a detail view of section A. Section A on illustration #6-1B would specify illustration #6-1A to complete this cross-reference.

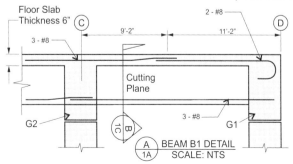

Illustration #6-1B - Beam Detail

Illustration #6-1C - Beam Section

Beam and Girder Schedule Illustration #6-1						
MARK	**QNTY.**	**SIZE**		**REINFORCEMENT**			
		W	**D**	**BOTTOM**	**TOP**	**REMARKS**	**STIRRUPS**
G1	4	10"	32"	2 - #10	2 - #10		#4 @ 12"
G2	4	10"	32"	3 - #10	3 - #10		#4 @ 12"
B1	4	8"	24"	3 - #8	2 - #8	NON CONT. END	#4 @ 12"
					3 - #8	CONT.END	
B2	2	8"	24"	3 - #8	3 - #8	BOTH ENDS	#4 @ 12"
B3	4	8"	24"	2 - #9	2 - #9	NON CONT. END	#4 @ 12"
					3 - #9	CONT.END	
B4	2	8"	24"	2 - #9	3 - #9	BOTH ENDS	#4 @ 12"
B5	2	8"	24"	3 - #7	2 - #7	NON CONT. END	#4 @ 12"
					3 - #7	CONT. END	
B6	1	8"	24"	3 - #7	3 - #7	BOTH ENDS	#4 @ 12"

Illustration #6-1D - Schedule of Materials

To further the cross-reference, illustration #6-1B shows cutting plane line B and a reference to illustration #6-1C. The view shown in illustration #6-1C is an end or cut off view of beam B1 and a cross reference back to illustration #6-1B.

Note: The structure shown in the plan view, illustration #6-1A, is not made up of a number of separate pieces as it would appear, but, other than the columns, is in fact one complete integral component. The girders, beams, and floor are all done as a continuous pour into a single unit 60 ft. 3 in. x 53 ft. 6 in.. The same applies to drawing 6-4A, as it is one unit 18.4 meters x 16.4 meters.

Beam and Slab Schedules

A beam or slab schedule is an efficient method of presenting repetitive information in a table format. Drawing the same detail for all the identical or nearly identical beams and slabs in a building would be time consuming and unnecessary. It would not necessarily make the drawing any easier to understand, and in fact, could well have the reverse effect by cluttering up the drawing.

A more practical way is to identify all the beams that are the same with a mark or number. In illustration #6-1A, all the beams are identical if they are the same size and have the same reinforcement. For example girder G1 is 10 in. wide and 32 in. deep.

Due to the repetitive nature of structural design, schedules are used extensively to keep the drawings from becoming too complicated. Schedules also provide a means of material take off (calculating the amount of material). When the number of beams is specified, the volume of concrete and the amount of each type of reinforcing can be determined. It is not practical to discuss all the different schedules that may occur, however with a basic understanding of structural drawings and a little perseverance it should be possible to understand any type of schedule if it is set up properly. A typical beam and slab schedule is shown in illustration #6-1D. The mark numbers correspond to those found in illustration #6-1A.

In order to understand the contents of these schedules and the drawing in general it is necessary to explain how steel reinforcing is used in a reinforced concrete structure.

Steel Reinforcing Bars

Without going into the details of structural theory, it is sufficient to say that steel reinforcing is used in concrete structures to provide extra strength in places where the concrete by itself would be inadequate. The steel reinforcing is in the form of steel tendons, referred to as rebar, which has a rough or deformed surface. The deformations are in the form of ribs that provide a good grip between the steel rebar and the concrete, as shown in illustration #6-2.

Fractions of an inch are commonly used for bar identification in the United States. This method identifies a bar by its diameter as a multiple of one-eighth of an inch. For example, a number 3 bar has a diameter of three-eighths of an inch.

In Canada, rebar is usually identified by a metric designation such as 10M, 20M; or merely as a number 10, or 20, etc.

The number refers to the nominal or rounded off value of the bar diameter in millimetres. A comparison of the two identification systems is shown in illustration #6-3.

The steel rebar can be in the form of a long steel tendon, or it can be bent into a variety of shapes as required by design. One common shape used to reinforce beams is called a stirrup. It is shown in section B, illustration #6-1C. Straight rebars are placed in the longitudinal direction of a beam, either on the top, bottom, or both. A stirrup is placed in a transverse direction so that it wraps around the longitudinal bars. The size and spacing of stirrups to correspond with illustration #6-1C is shown in illustration #6-1D. The stirrups and straight rebar pieces are fastened together with wire to create a steel arrangement that looks like a long cage.

An item similar in shape to a stirrup that serves a similar purpose in a column is referred to as a tie. Stirrups and ties are not used in slabs.

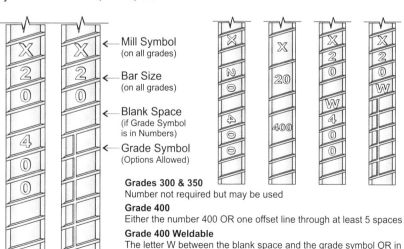

← Mill Symbol
(on all grades)

← Bar Size
(on all grades)

← Blank Space
(if Grade Symbol
is in Numbers)

← Grade Symbol
(Options Allowed)

Grades 300 & 350
Number not required but may be used
Grade 400
Either the number 400 OR one offset line through at least 5 spaces
Grade 400 Weldable
The letter W between the blank space and the grade symbol OR in the blank space

Illustration #6-2 - Identification of Deformed Concrete Reinforcing Bars

Comparison of Inch and Metric Rebar Sizes**						
Imperial			**Metric**			Metric bar is (+,-)
Size	Area in²	Area mm²	Size	Area in²	Area mm²	
#3	0.11	71	10M	0.16	100	+45%
#4	0.20	129	10M	0.16	100	-20%
#4	0.20	129	15M	0.31	200	+55%
#5	0.31	200	15M	0.31	200	SAME
#6	0.44	284	20M	0.47	300	+6.8%
#7	0.60	387	20M	0.47	300	-22%
#7	0.60	387	25M	0.78	500	+30%
#8	0.79	510	25M	0.78	500	-1.3%
#9	1.00	645	30M	1.09	700	+9%
#10	1.27	819	30M	1.09	700	-14%
#10	1.27	819	35M	1.55	1000	+22%
#11	1.56	1006	35M	1.55	1000	-0.6%
#14	2.25	1452	45M	2.33	1500	+3.5%
#18	4.0	2581	55M	3.88	1500	-3%
** Note: % difference based on area of bars in in²						

Illustration #6-3 - Comparison of Inch and Metric Rebar Sizes

A slab is wide and is usually relatively thin compared to a beam or a column, which makes it impractical to design a slab using a stirrup or tie. The steel reinforcing bars in a slab will generally be straight pieces laid out in an overlapping grid pattern. *IPT's Metal Trades Handbook has a section on Concrete Reinforcing which has additional data on various types of reinforcement and placement.*

Reinforcing Bar Placement

The end purpose of the structure will determine the engineered design of the slab, beam, or girder concerning the size and amount of rebar, its position in the structure, and the amount of concrete coverage. If the member is a heavy load carrying girder, as found on a long span bridge, the design will be quite elaborate. After the general arrangement of the beams and slabs has been established, it is then necessary to determine the placement of the rebar within these structural elements.

The schedule will indicate the size and quantity of the rebar, but not the location in sufficient detail to insure proper construction. To do this will require enlarged views of representative beams and slabs in the form of detail or section views. A section view is the view of an internal part of the structure. It should be noted that many of the details on these types of drawings are really more like section views, but industry practice is to refer to them as a detail as they serve the same purpose.

The beam B1 detail, shown in illustration #6-1B, indicates two types of reinforcing. The reinforcing schedule in illustration #6-1D for beam B1 shows one end for the top reinforcing to be continuous, and the other end is non-continuous.

The bottom reinforcing is continuous. Continuous means the bars overlap from one beam into the next, while non-continuous stops at the building edge. The top reinforcing in beam B1 stops at girder G1 in a loop.

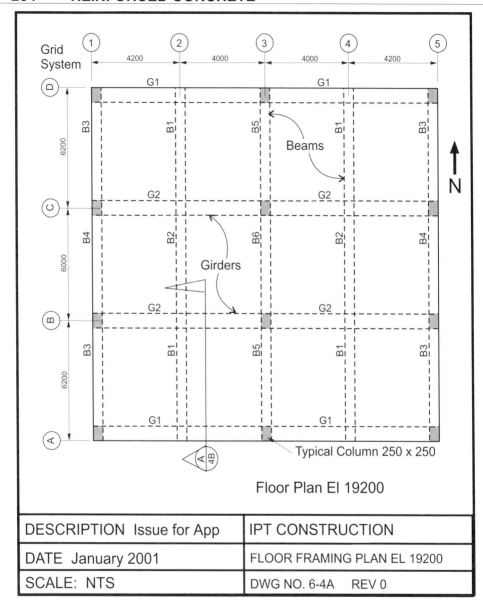

Grid System

4200   4000   4000   4200

G1   G1

B3   B1   B5   B1   B3

Beams

6200

G2   G2

B4   B2   B6   B2   B4

Girders

6000

G2   G2

B3   B1   B5   B1   B3

6200

G1   G1

Typical Column 250 x 250

Floor Plan El 19200

DESCRIPTION Issue for App	IPT CONSTRUCTION
DATE January 2001	FLOOR FRAMING PLAN EL 19200
SCALE: NTS	DWG NO. 6-4A REV 0

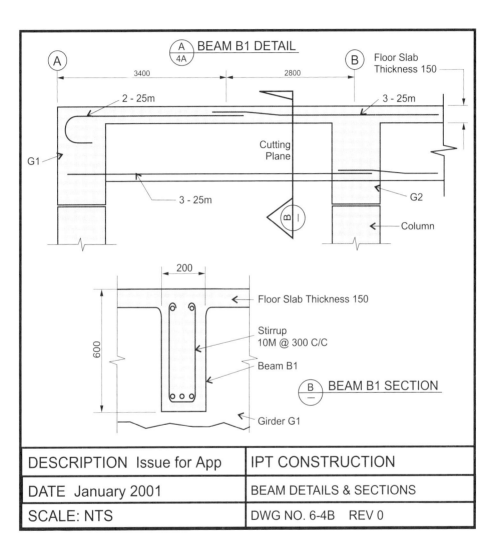

BEAM B1 DETAIL

Floor Slab Thickness 150

3400   2800

2 - 25m   3 - 25m

G1

Cutting Plane

3 - 25m

G2

Column

200

Floor Slab Thickness 150

Stirrup 10M @ 300 C/C

Beam B1

600

BEAM B1 SECTION

Girder G1

DESCRIPTION Issue for App	IPT CONSTRUCTION
DATE January 2001	BEAM DETAILS & SECTIONS
SCALE: NTS	DWG NO. 6-4B REV 0

Beam and Girder Schedule Illustration #6-1							
MARK	QNTY.	SIZE		REINFORCEMENT			
		W	D	BOTTOM	TOP	REMARKS	STIRRUPS
G1	4	250	800	2 - 35M	2 - 35M		10M @ 300
G2	4	250	800	3 - 35M	3 - 35M		10M @ 300
B1	4	200	600	3 - 25M	2 - 25M	NON CONT. END	10M @ 300
					3 -25M	CONT.END	
B2	2	200	600	3 - 25M	3 -25M	BOTH ENDS	10M @ 300
B3	4	200	600	2 -30M	2 - 30M	NON CONT. END	10M @ 300
					3 - 30M	CONT.END	
B4	2	200	600	2 - 30M	3 - 30M	BOTH ENDS	10M @ 300
B5	2	200	600	3 - 20M	2 - 20M	NON CONT. END	10M @ 300
					3 - 20M	CONT.END	
B6	1	200	600	3 - 20M	3 - 20M	BOTH ENDS	10M @ 300

DESCRIPTION Issue for App	IPT CONSTRUCTION
DATE January 2001	BEAM DETAILS & SECTIONS
SCALE: NTS	DWG NO. 6-4C REV 0

Floor Plan Elevation 19200

Drawings 6-4A, 6-4B, and 6-4C are similar to illustrations #6-1A, #6-1B, #6-1C and #6-1D except for the metric measurements. The following questions refer to these drawings.

1. How many times has drawing 6-4A been revised?
   - ❏ 0
   - ❏ 1
   - ❏ 2
   - ❏ 4

2. Drawing 6-4A indicates an elevation of 19200 mm or 19.2 meters.   If the first floor is at elevation 10 000 mm or 10.0 meters, then how high is floor elevation 19 200 above the first floor?
   - ❏ 10.2 m
   - ❏ 9.2 m
   - ❏ 8.2 m
   - ❏ 10.0 m

3. What is the overall length and width of the building in meters?
Answer: _____

4. How many columns in total are shown on grid lines 1, 3, and 5 on drawing 6-4A?
   - ❏ 4
   - ❏ 6
   - ❏ 8
   - ❏ 12

5. What is the width of girder G1 as indicated in the Beam and Girder Schedule for drawing 6-4A?
   - ❏ 200 mm
   - ❏ 250 mm
   - ❏ 600 mm
   - ❏ 800 mm

6. What is the center of column to center of column distance of girder G1?

Answer: _____

7. What is the clear span distance for girder G1 from drawing 6-4A?
   - ❏ 7825 mm
   - ❏ 8000 mm
   - ❏ 8100 mm
   - ❏ 8200 mm

8. What is the clear span distance for the following beams?
   - ❏ B1
   - ❏ B2
   - ❏ B3
   - ❏ B6

9. From the beam schedule for drawing 6-4A, how many of the following beams are required?
   - ❏ B2
   - ❏ B3
   - ❏ B4
   - ❏ B5

10. What is the rebar end connection for B1 from the beam schedule?
   - ❏ non-continuous both ends
   - ❏ continuous both ends
   - ❏ one end continuous, one end non-continuous
   - ❏ 10 M @ 300

11. From the beam schedule, what is the bottom reinforcement for the following beams?
   - ❏ B2 3
   - ❏ B3 2
   - ❏ B4 2
   - ❏ B5 3

12. What is the difference in depth between the beams and girders?

Answer: _____

13. How far apart are the girder stirrups?
   - ❏ 10 M
   - ❏ 250 mm
   - ❏ 300 mm
   - ❏ 600 mm

14. What size is a #7 rebar?
   - ❏ 1/8 inch
   - ❏ 3/8 inch
   - ❏ 5/8 inch
   - ❏ 7/8 inch

15. When comparing a #7 rebar to a 20 M bar, the 20 M bar will be:
   - ❏ larger
   - ❏ smaller
   - ❏ same size
   - ❏ will vary depending on manufacturer

Building Foundation Plan

Drawing 6-5A and 6-5B show the floor plan and part of the footing details for a warehouse. Note that the feet and inch symbols are not shown in this drawing. This structure uses two different types of foundations. One is referred to as a strip footing and is basically a strip of concrete wrapping around the perimeter of the building.

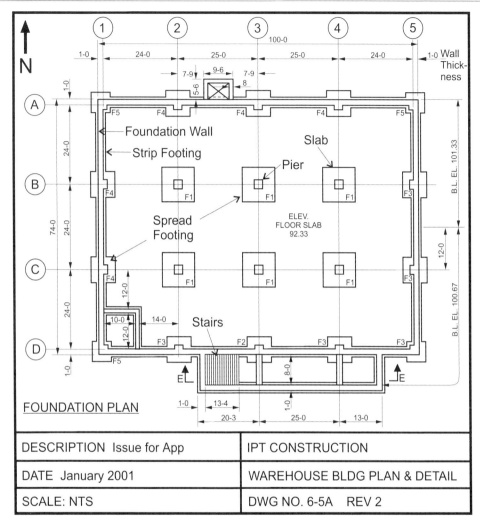

N

| 1 | 2 | 3 | 4 | 5 |

100-0

1-0   24-0   25-0   25-0   24-0   1-0 Wall Thickness

7-9   9-6   7-9

5-6   8

(A)   F5   F4   F4   F4   F5

Foundation Wall

Strip Footing

Slab

Pier

(B)   F4   F1   F1   F1   F3   B.L. EL. 101.33

Spread Footing   ELEV. FLOOR SLAB 92.33

74-0   24-0

(C)   F4   F1   F1   F1   F3   12-0

24-0   12-0

10-0   14-0   Stairs   B.L. EL. 100.67

12-0

(D)   F3   F2   F3   F3

F5

EL   8-0   E

FOUNDATION PLAN

1-0   13-4   1-0

20-3   25-0   13-0

DESCRIPTION Issue for App	IPT CONSTRUCTION
DATE January 2001	WAREHOUSE BLDG PLAN & DETAIL
SCALE: NTS	DWG NO. 6-5A REV 2

In northern climates it usually extends to a level below the frost line (this is the type of foundation that is commonly used in residential construction). The strip footing can be seen on the left side of drawing 6-5B, section view Elevation E-E. The width is specified as 1 ft. 8 in. (shown as 1-8). The strip footing supports the wall for the building. The wall is one foot thick, as indicated in the Foundation Plan.

The wall height is calculated by subtracting the bottom of the wall elevation from the top of the wall elevation (see Elevation E-E).

The other type of foundation shown in the Foundation Plan is referred to as a spread footing.

This type is often used in commercial and industrial type construction. A spread footing consists of a pier or short column supported by a rectangular slab, as shown in drawing 6-5B.

The purpose of the pier is to support the heavy load of the column.

As shown in the Foundation Plan, the spread footing has also been incorporated into the wall of the strip footing.

The piers, and the supporting slabs below, are shown at the grid points around the exterior wall. Locating the center of the columns and supporting piers is one of the major reasons for using a grid system.

The detail of the piers shows the vertical rebars that are enclosed in the ties that wrap around them.

Also shown is an L shaped reinforcing bar called a dowel. The purpose of this dowel is to provide connecting strength between the pier and the slab.

Elevation E-E is a view of a portion of the front wall of the building, showing a section view of the stairs. Detailed information for the stairs includes length, width, height, and reinforcing.

Another major feature in Elevation E-E are five large openings in the wall, recognized as large rectangles with a cross through the middle to indicate an opening. Four of these are for windows and one is a door opening.

The following questions refer to Building Plan drawings 6-5A and 6-5B.

16. What is the overall length and width of the building?

Answer: _____

17. How many type F3 footings are required?
- ❏ 20
- ❏ 14
- ❏ 6
- ❏ 5

18. All the plan view grid spacings are the same.
- ❏ true
- ❏ false

19. How many 9 ft. x 9 ft. footings are required?
- ❏ 20
- ❏ 14
- ❏ 6
- ❏ 5

20. What is the thickness for the following footings?
- ❏ F1
- ❏ F2
- ❏ F3
- ❏ F4
- ❏ F5

21. What is the width of the stairway?
Answer: _____

22. Which footing has the largest diameter rebar?
- ❏ F1
- ❏ F3
- ❏ F4
- ❏ All sized the same

23. The bottom of wall elevation is:
- ❏ 92.33 feet
- ❏ 91.33 feet
- ❏ 90.33 feet
- ❏ 89.33 feet

24. What is the size of the longitudinal reinforcement (parallel to steps) for the stairs on ELEVATION E-E?
- ❏ #5 @ 6 in.
- ❏ #4 @ 12 in.
- ❏ 1 1/2 C.L.
- ❏ none of the above

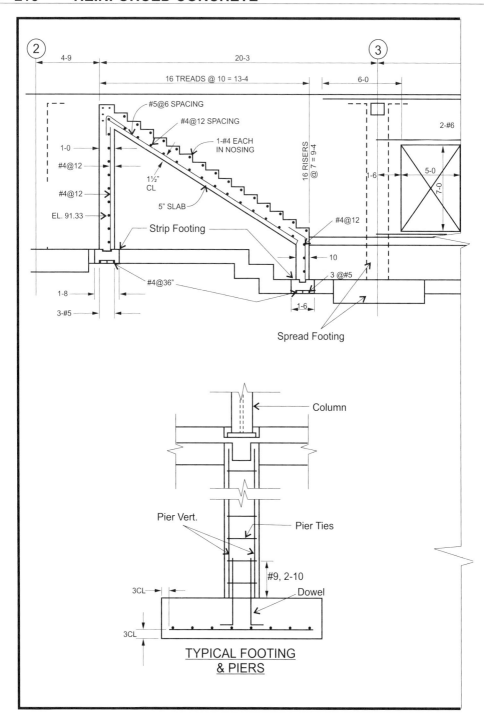

② ③

4-9 20-3

16 TREADS @ 10 = 13-4 6-0

#5@6 SPACING

#4@12 SPACING

1-#4 EACH IN NOSING

2-#6

1-0

#4@12

16 RISERS @ 7 = 9-4

5-0

1-6

7-0

#4@12

1½" CL

EL. 91.33

5" SLAB

#4@12

Strip Footing

10

3 @#5

#4@36"

1-8

3-#5

1-6

Spread Footing

Column

Pier Vert.

Pier Ties

#9, 2-10

3CL

Dowel

3CL

TYPICAL FOOTING
& PIERS

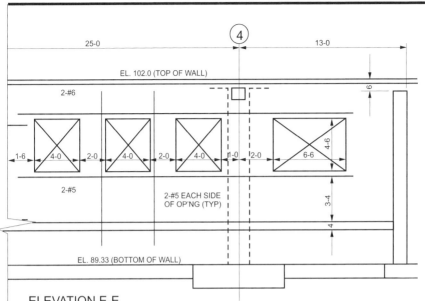

ELEVATION E-E

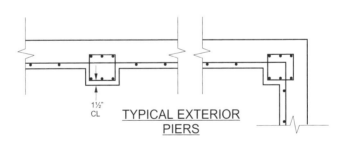

1½"
CL

TYPICAL EXTERIOR PIERS

FOOTING SCHEDULE		
MARK	SIZE	REINF.
F1	9-0 x 9-0 x 1-11	10-#8 E.W.
F2	8-0 x 8-0 x 1-10	10-#7 E.W.
F3	7-6 x 7-6 x 1-8	9-#7 E.W.
F4	7-0 x 7-0 x 1-7	8-#7 E.W.
F5	6-6 x 6-6 x 1-6	9-#6 E.W.

DESCRIPTION Issue for App	IPT CONSTRUCTION
DATE January 2001	BLDG ELEVATION & DETAILS
SCALE: NTS	DWG NO. 6-5B REV 2

25. What size bar is used for the nosing in each stair tread?

Answer: _____

26. What is the measurement of the rise and run for each step in the stairs?
    - ❏ 16 x 16
    - ❏ 7 x 10
    - ❏ 10 x 7
    - ❏ 9 ft 4 x 14 ft 4

27. The windows have a height of:
    - ❏ 4 ft.
    - ❏ 4 ft. 6 in.
    - ❏ 5 ft
    - ❏ 6 ft. 6 in.

28. ELEVATION E-E and the FOUNDA-TION PLAN are both drawn to the same scale?
    - ❏ true
    - ❏ false

29. The C.L. distance for the rebar at the bottom of the footings is
    - ❏ 1-1/2 in.
    - ❏ 3 in.
    - ❏ #5 @ 2 ft 6 in.
    - ❏ dowel size not shown

Curtain Walls and Windows

Curtain Wall Panels

A curtain wall is the exterior skin of a building that acts as the building envelope. It has two basic functions. First it must provide protection against the elements and the effects of wind, rain, heat and cold. To do this the curtain wall must prevent air infiltration, rain penetration, and heat loss or gain. It is designed to work with the heating, ventilating, and air conditioning systems, abbreviated HVAC, to control the internal environment of the building. That is one of the reasons why many buildings do not have windows that open, and why revolving doors are used to minimize uncontrolled air exchange.

The second function of a curtain wall is to act as a structural membrane to resist horizontal loads from the wind and transfer them to the structural frame of the building. To do this the wall panels must be designed to meet the structural requirements as specified by the local building code.

In order for the curtain wall to function both as a structural component, and as a barrier against the elements requires a high degree of precision in design, fabrication, and construction.

The actual wall is constructed using a variety of materials, depending on climate, end use, building height and size. Some of the methods include metal sheeting, brick, concrete blocks, precast concrete panels, insulated glass units, or combinations of several types.

Precast concrete panel size varies with the size and type of structure, ranging from a panel, weighing several tons for a single story strip mall or a high ceiling warehouse, to a multi-story apartment or office building. In some instances, the individual panels can exceed 40 ft. wide, 50 ft. high, be over a foot thick, and sometimes weigh 300,000 pounds, or more. The panels can be solid or have window and door openings.

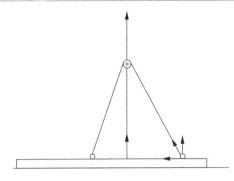

Illustration #6-6A - Hook Up Prior to Lifting

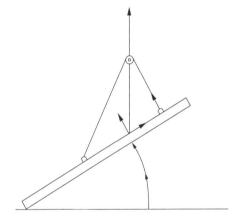

Illustration #6-6B - Sling Position During Lift

They hang off the building structure with brackets mounted at predetermined locations and have a seal between the abutting joints.

Hoisting the panels in place must be a carefully engineered process, especially with a multi-story building, due to the weight of concrete. Illustrations #6-6A,B and C show an example of a large precast panel and the hoisting apparatus used to lift it into place.

Curtain Wall Views

The first step when viewing a new drawing is to check the information in the title block.

Reinforcing Bars

Illustration #6-6C - Lift in Progress

This identifies the drawing by a title and number to correctly cross-reference the drawing to other related drawings. Although title blocks have been discussed in detail in other sections, there are always different variations of title blocks and their information.

As in most engineering drawings, the best starting point with a building project is the plan view. This provides an overview of the building, and most other drawings are referenced back to this main drawing.

Typically a plan view of a building will be set up on a grid system, as shown in drawing 6-7A. In this drawing the vertical rows are displayed with numbers and the horizontal rows with letters. Only a portion of the building is shown in this example. The grid system will provide a point of reference on other drawings where only isolated parts of the building are shown, such as elevation or detail views.

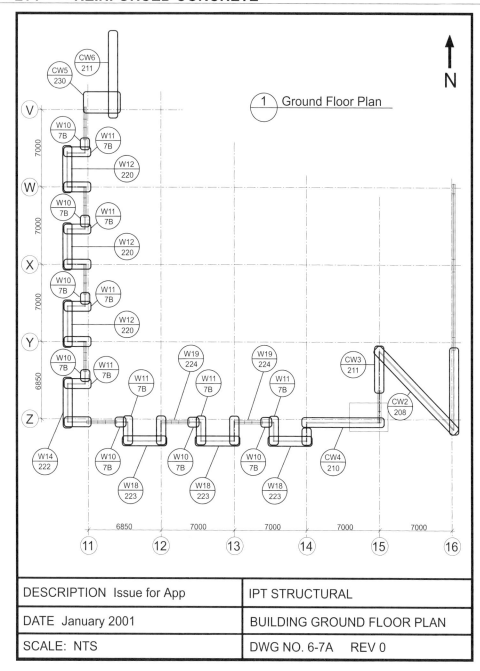

N

1 Ground Floor Plan

DESCRIPTION Issue for App	IPT STRUCTURAL
DATE January 2001	BUILDING GROUND FLOOR PLAN
SCALE: NTS	DWG NO. 6-7A REV 0

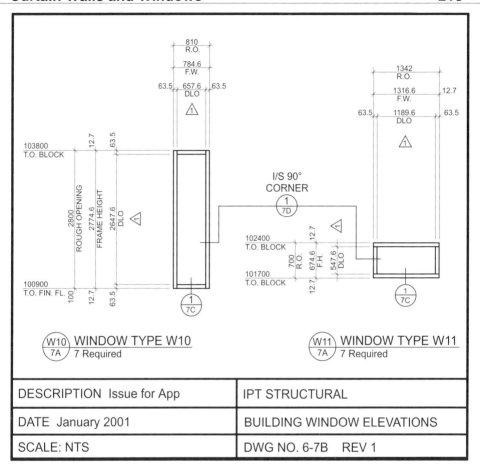

W10 WINDOW TYPE W10	**W11** WINDOW TYPE W11
7A / 7 Required	7A / 7 Required

DESCRIPTION Issue for App	IPT STRUCTURAL
DATE January 2001	BUILDING WINDOW ELEVATIONS
SCALE: NTS	DWG NO. 6-7B REV 1

From the floor plan view, it can be seen that much of the drawing is in bold or dark lines that stand out as the predominant feature of the drawing. This is done to highlight only the important information on the drawing. The remainder of the drawing is lighter and any other lines are for visual reference. As this drawing is only concerned with the curtain wall and windows around the exterior of the building, the drawing is reasonably uncomplicated and easy to understand. Each panel is cross-referenced to an elevation drawing.

For example window type W10 is indicated in a bubble or circle as W10 with the number 7B underneath or W10/7B. This instructs the user of the print to go to drawing 6-7B to see the detail for this particular window.

Window Detail Drawings

Drawing 6-7B is an elevation or front view of two types of windows for this building. Both W10 and W11 are shown in a bubble with a number 7A to cross-reference them back to the first drawing.

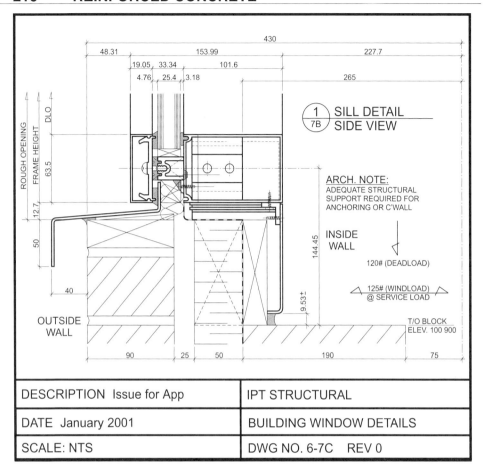

DESCRIPTION Issue for App	IPT STRUCTURAL
DATE January 2001	BUILDING WINDOW DETAILS
SCALE: NTS	DWG NO. 6-7C REV 0

This elevation drawing provides information about the size and shape of the window, including the rough opening size, the frame size, the DLO size (daylight opening or clear opening size). It also provides important information about the vertical location of the window. This is shown by a reference to a building elevation. In this print the bottom of window W10 is referenced as; T.O. FIN. FL. 100900, which is an abbreviation for, Top of Finished Floor 100900 mm or 100.9 meters above some previously established reference point.

This elevation is measured from a conveniently chosen reference point depending on the type of construction or the drafting standards of the design company. The starting reference elevation is often given an arbitrary value of 100.0 m for convenience, although some elevation views will use the actual distance above sea level as the starting point.

Elevation drawing 6-7B, also has bubbles to cross-reference this drawing to other curtain wall, window frame or detail drawings. Using window W10 as an example, there is a cross-reference to 7C and detail number 1.

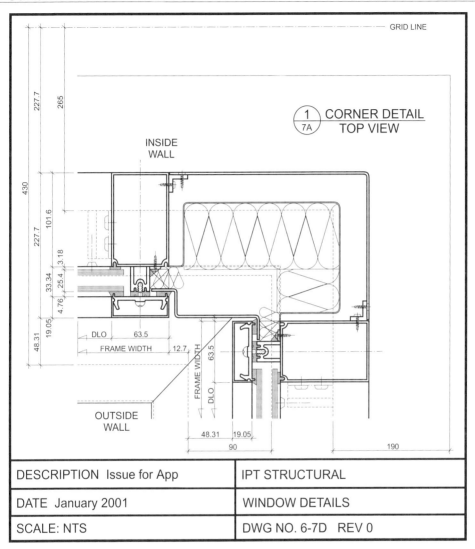

DESCRIPTION Issue for App	IPT STRUCTURAL
DATE January 2001	WINDOW DETAILS
SCALE: NTS	DWG NO. 6-7D REV 0

Drawing 6-7C shows a cross-section of a window sill detail and how it relates to the building structure. This would provide important information for the proper installation of the window, including the structural support, weather proofing, flashing and interior finish.

Another type of cross-reference on drawing 6-7B is a line connecting window W10 and window W11.

This line is called a match line and provides another type of visual reference to help relate different parts of the curtain wall system.

The match line with cross reference 1/7D, and a note that reads I/S 90 CORNER (which means an inside corner of 90 degrees) is located on the offset. To see this detail we would look at drawing 6-7D.

When looking at drawing 6-7D it is important to distinguish between the exterior and the interior parts of the building. A reference back to drawing 6-7A and the floor plan shows the relationship of the W10 and W11 windows.

As this type of window drawing can be somewhat detailed and confusing, a brief summary might help.

Drawing 6-7A shows a floor plan view of the wall and window layout. The windows are marked with a W number and the curtain walls with a CW number. Only the details for two types of windows are shown for this building.

Drawing 6-7B is a side or elevation view of two different sized windows. The measurements show the opening height location, opening size, and frame size.

Drawing 6-7C is a side view of the sill at the bottom of the two types of windows. It shows the inside and outside flashing, and the frame holding the glass.

Drawing 6-7D is a top detail view of a corner showing the glass and the frame for the two windows.

The following questions refer to drawings 6-7A to 6-7D.

30. Which of the following curtain wall units intersect at grid Y-15?
    ❏ CW1 and CW2
    ❏ CW2 and CW3
    ❏ CW3 and CW4
    ❏ W10 and W15

31. Identify the drawing numbers where the elevation view can be found for:
    ❏ window type W10
    ❏ window type W11
    ❏ curtain wall CW6
    ❏ curtain wall CW2

32. Windows W10, and W11 have the same top elevation.
    ❏ true
    ❏ false

33. What is the elevation for the top of window W11?
Answer: _____

34. How many windows are required for window types W10 and W11?
Answer: _____

35. What are the rough opening sizes for windows W10 and W11?
    ❏ W10
    ❏ W11

36. What is the frame height for windows W10 and W11?
    ❏ W10
    ❏ W11

37. What is the frame width for windows W10 and W11?
    ❏ W10
    ❏ W11

38. What is the clearance between the rough opening and the frame for windows W10, and W11?
Answer: _____

39. What window type is adjacent to window W10?
Answer: _____

40. If the daylight opening (DLO) dimension is the difference between the outside and inside frame measurements, what is the width of the frame for window W10?
Answer: _____

41. On drawing 6-7B, elevation W10, there are two details marked as no.1. On which drawings are these details found?

Answer: _____

42. W10 is based on an elevation of 100900. How far above this level does the rough opening start?
- ❏ 10 mm
- ❏ 100 mm
- ❏ 1000 mm
- ❏ 2800 mm

43. What is the overhang and projection from the outside wall for the flashing on window W10?

Answer: _____

44. On drawing 6-7C determine the exterior frame width and thickness:

Answer: _____

45. On drawing 6-7C determine the interior frame width and thickness:

Answer: _____

46. On drawing 6-7C determine the distance between the exterior and the interior frame:

Answer: _____

47. On drawing 6-7C determine the thickness of the glass:

Answer: _____

48. On drawing 6-7C determine the thickness of the exterior brick:

Answer: _____

49. On drawing 6-7D determine the exterior frame width and thickness:

Answer: _____

50. On drawing 6-7D determine the interior frame width and thickness:

Answer: _____

51. On drawing 6-7C determine the overall measurement from the outside to inside for the window frame unit:

Answer: _____

52. There are no revisions to drawings 6-7C and 6-7D.
- ❏ true
- ❏ false

SECTION SEVEN

BOILERS

Basic Boiler Design

The term boiler is used to describe a wide variety of heating devices that produce hot water and/or steam. A boiler in its simplest form is a pressurized heat exchanger using some type of fuel, for example, oil, gas, coal, or nuclear energy to heat water, usually to create steam. Two general classifications of boilers are:

• Firetube boiler
• Watertube boiler

The main difference between firetube and watertube boilers, other than their basic design, is in the efficiency and amount of pressure and steam each can produce.

Firetube Boiler: This boiler has the water outside the tube(s) and the heat source inside the tube(s). They are generally used for hot water heating systems and some low pressure steam production. A firetube boiler essentially consists of a water holding tank that has one, or a number of firetubes installed within the water tank. The firetubes are heated by direct contact with the heat source, by hot flue gases passing through them, or a combination of both. See illustration #7-1 for a simplified cross-section of a firetube boiler.

As shown in illustration #7-1, there is a furnace tube in which the actual combustion takes place. The flue gases produced in the furnace tube will then flow through the flue tubes and out the stack or chimney. This is called a two pass firetube boiler. The furnace tube and the flue tubes are surrounded by the water that is being heated.

Watertube Boiler: This type of boiler has the water contained inside a tube (or tubes) and is heated by a source outside the tube. Watertube boilers are used when large volumes of steam at high temperatures and pressures are required; for example, in electrical utility plants. They are more complex in design than firetube boilers, however, they are also more efficient and are capable of a wide range of operating conditions.

The water for this type of boiler is contained inside small diameter tubes. The tubes are heated by direct contact with the heat source, by the hot flue gases passing over the tubes, or a combination of both. In the case of a watertube boiler, the floor, the roof and the walls of the furnace area are made up of tubes containing water. These can be individual tubes or fabricated sections of tubes. See illlustration #7-2 for an example of a wall section.

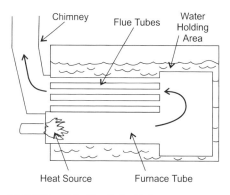

Illustration #7-1 - Fire Tube Boiler

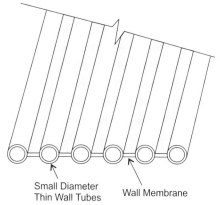

Illustration #7-2 - Wall Tubes

This design makes the boiler more efficient because of the large heating surface.

In addition to the furnace of the boiler being made of tubes, there may also be extra tube banks or elements containing steam inside the furnace in the path of the hot flue gases. These extra tube banks also increase the heating surface of the boiler and are used to increase the steam temperature.

Higher operating pressure and temperature is attainable with a watertube boiler because the water is contained inside tubes instead of a water tank. A tank would require very thick walls to safely contain the water and steam at a high pressure. To create high steam pressure it is also necessary to heat the water to extremely high temperatures before it is changed to steam. Modern steam boilers for electrical power generation average about 2450 psi. steam pressure. The temperature of the steam is around 1000°F (605°C). The water must be kept as a liquid until about 800°F (480°C), and to do this the boiler must operate at higher pressures.

Watertube boilers are designed very differently than firetube boilers. A simple watertube boiler design can be seen in illustration #7-3. It also has extra components that help produce large volumes of steam at high pressures and temperatures. One of these major components, and the one considered to be the heart of the boiler, is the steam drum. The steam drum is usually located at, or close to the top of the boiler. In illustration #7-3, the furnace of the boiler is made up of tubes that contain the water. As the water is heated it rises to the top of the boiler furnace walls and collects in the steam drum. The steam drum is never full of water, as there is always a space left for the steam to flash out of the heated water.

The steam that does not flash out cools slightly in the drum and reverts to the water stage. It then circulates back down to the lower part of the boiler through the downcomer tubes. This type of boiler is called a natural circulation boiler.

The internals of one type of steam drum are shown in illustration #7-4.

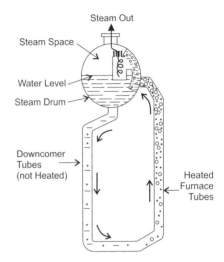

Illustration #7-3 - Natural Circulation

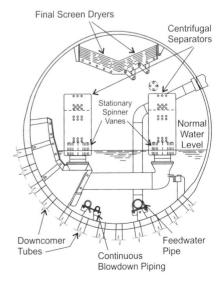

Illustration #7-4 - Steam Drum Internals

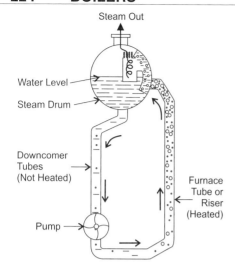

Illustration #7-5 - Forced Circulation

Steam Generator Component Parts

The term boiler is often used as a general term to describe every type of hot water boiler and steam boiler. However, the term boiler is too general for large industrial applications where the unit is only used to produce steam. It is more correct to refer to these types of units as steam generators. A steam generator contains a number of components that contribute to the efficiency of the unit and add more steam generating capability. Some of the names of these components are; economizer, air heater, superheater, and reheater, to mention a few. Illustration #7-6 shows a sectional view of a small industrial watertube boiler. This boiler would be fired on natural gas or oil. The only extra component it contains beside the boiler proper is a superheater.

Natural circulation boilers are satisfactory for lower demand production, but if the end use of the boiler requires the unit to be more responsive, then a forced circulation boiler is used. The forced circulation boiler shown in illustration #7-5 has pumps to move the water through the flow circuits. It is practical for large steam generating boilers to utilize as much of the heat being produced as possible. To obtain higher efficiency, extra components are needed. However, these extra components restrict the water flow and therefore pumps are required to move the water through the flow circuit.

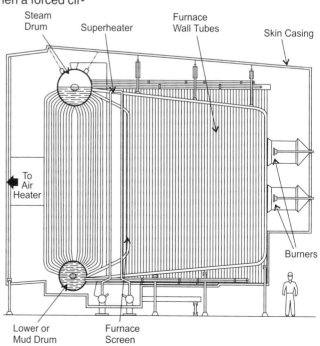

Illustration #7-6 - Industrial Watertube Boiler

The superheater will increase the temperature of the steam that is routed through it from the steam drum.

Steam Generator Construction

Illustration #7-7 shows the construction of one type of steam generator. The steam drum is suspended from two large U bolt type hangers. The tubes joining the two drums are being installed. Each tube end will protrude in through the shell of the drum and the tube diameter will be expanded to create a leak tight joint. See IPT's Metal Trades Handbook for more explanation of tube expansion.

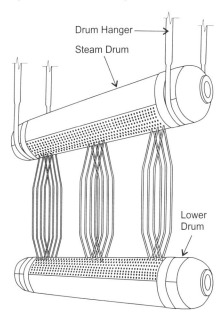

Drum Hanger

Steam Drum

Lower Drum

Illustration #7-7 - Boiler Under Construction

Definition of Steam Generator Components

Illustration #7-8 is a sectional view of one design of a large coal fired steam generator that is used for power production. This unit has additional components that contribute to the efficiency of the steam generator.

It should be noted that there is a very wide variety of boiler and steam generator designs to meet the demands of various industries. The steam generator unit illustrated shows the location of the component parts for this type of unit only. However, other than placement, the components are similar between this unit and most other steam generators.

The following lists a number of the primary components associated with boilers and steam generators, as shown and numbered in illustration #7-8. Only the components more commonly found in this and other types of generating units are referred to.

Steam Drum (item #1)

A steam drum is a thick walled horizontal pressure vessel, and is the heart of any watertube boiler. All water and steam contained in the boiler and the steam generating components will start from, or circulate back to the steam drum. The steam drum contains various internals. The function of the drum internals is for steam purification, steam drying and water treatment. Connected to the drum are tubes and pipes that are the links between the steam drum and other headers supplying or receiving water or steam. The internals used in a drum will vary according to the end use of the water or steam being produced by the boiler. The steam drum is usually located at or near the top of the boiler. However, in forced circulation boilers the steam drum location does not have to be the highest point in the boiler.

Lower Drum(s) (item #2)

The lower drum(s) serve as a collection point for the water before it is distributed into individual tubes that make up the furnace walls of a watertube boiler. At one time the lower drums were referred to as mud drums.

This term was used because the boiler water may not have been put through any water treatment process. This resulted in the mud drum being a collection point for sludge and sediment. With advanced systems for water purification and treatment there is very little if any accumulation of sludge or sediments in the lower drums of modern boilers. Due to the high operating pressure and high velocity of the steam in a modern boiler, any sediment in the water would quickly play havoc with the tubing and turbine components. There are internals in the lower drum, but their primary purpose is for flow control to the wall tubes.

Superheater and Reheater Elements (item #3)

These elements are made of steel tubes that are bent to form continuous heating elements inside of the furnace. The ends of each element will connect to an inlet header and an outlet header. In the steam generator shown in illustration #7-8, the superheater and reheater elements are suspended inside the furnace from the top by hanger rods that are attached to structural steel outside of the furnace. The function of the superheater elements is to increase the steam temperature and reduce the moisture content of the steam. After the steam has passed from the superheater and through the electrical generator turbine, it will cool somewhat and will then be routed back into the boiler and through the reheater tubes. The steam will then make one more pass from the reheater to the turbine, and then be condensed back into water by cooling the steam. This water will return to the boiler economizer and the circulation process will continue.

Economizer (item #4)

The function of the economizer is to increase the temperature of the boiler feedwater before it goes into the steam drum. The economizer is similar in design to the superheaters and reheaters, the exception being that the economizer elements are normally spaced closer together. The flue gases from the boiler's furnace pass over the surface of the economizer tubes to heat the feedwater inside the tubes. This process increases the efficiency of the boiler by making use of waste heat that would be lost to the atmosphere if not utilized. Economizers can be positioned outside the boiler furnace area, as shown in illustration #7-8, or inside the boiler furnace as part of the overall unit.

Air Heater (item #5)

The function of the air heater is to preheat the incoming air for the boiler furnace. The air heater is correctly called the air preheater. There are two basic types of air heaters. One uses small diameter tubes in which the incoming combustion air and out going flue gases pass by each other but are separated by the walls of the tubing. This allows the heat from the flue gases to be exchanged over to the combustion air. This also increases the efficiency of the unit in a similar manner as the economizer.

The other type of air heater design utilizes thin corrugated plates packed inside a rotating wheel. As this wheel rotates, the corrugated plates pass alternately through the flue gas stream that heats them, and then into the incoming air stream. As the heated plates pass through the air stream they give up their heat to the incoming combustion air.

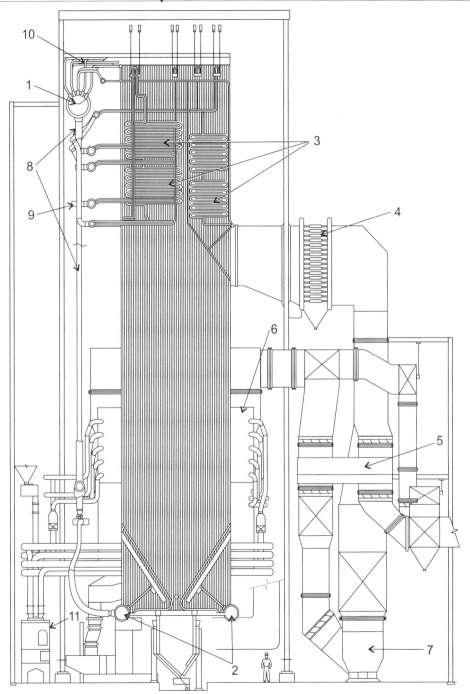

Illustration #7-8 - Sectional View of Steam Generator

Burners (item #6)

Burner is a general term describing the part of the boiler where the fuel and air combine to produce fire for the required heat. The type of fuel varies, with oil, gas and coal being the most common. Burner design also varies depending on the type of fuel burned in the boiler. The burners shown in illustration #7-8 are for a coal fired boiler.

Draft Fans (item #7)

Draft fans are used to force air into the furnace area of the boiler, and also to draw the flue gases out of the boiler. In complex boiler designs such as the unit in illustration #7-8, a natural draft would not be sufficient to move the huge volume of air needed in the furnace for combustion, and to remove the flue gases quickly out of the furnace. Therefore it is necessary to force the draft with fans at the rate needed to operate the boiler at peak efficiency.

Downcomers (item #8)

Downcomers are the pipes or tubes that link the steam drum to the lower drum(s).

Headers (item #9)

Headers are used to collect or distribute water and steam throughout the unit. They are made of heavy wall pipe that will have banks of tubing welded into them. In the case of low pressure boilers, the tubing ends may be expanded into the headers instead of welded. The number of different headers used depends on the complexity of the unit. This boiler requires numerous headers. There are waterwall headers, superheater and reheater headers, and economizer headers, to mention a few.

Riser Tubes (item #10)

The riser tubes are larger diameter tubes that are bent to the required shape to interconnect the steam drum and various headers, including the superheater, reheater and waterwall headers.

They carry the water from the waterwall headers into the steam drum, and steam from the drum into the superheater and reheater headers.

Coal Pulverizer (item #11)

The pulverizer receives coal from the coal hopper. The coal is then finely ground and blown into the burners by the combustion air.

Boiler Air Flow

Illustration #7-9 shows the air flow through a coal fired boiler. The outside air is pulled in through a forced draft (FD) fan(s). The air is pushed through the air heater and coal pulverizers to the burners. Combustion takes place. The air and burning fuel produces heat and hot flue gases. The flue gases pass through the furnace area over the superheater and reheater elements and then through the feedwater economizer. The last stages have the flue gas passing through the air heater, scrubber and precipitator to remove the fly ash. It is then pulled into the induced draft (ID) fan(s) and finally pushed out the stack. The induced draft fans create a vacuum effect on the boiler side, helping to move the air and flue gases through the boiler.

General Boiler Questions

1. A pressurized vessel used to produce hot water or steam is called a:

Answer: _____

2. A boiler has water circulating through the inside of the tubes and hot flue gases on the outside of the tube. Is this a watertube boiler or a firetube boiler?

Answer: _____

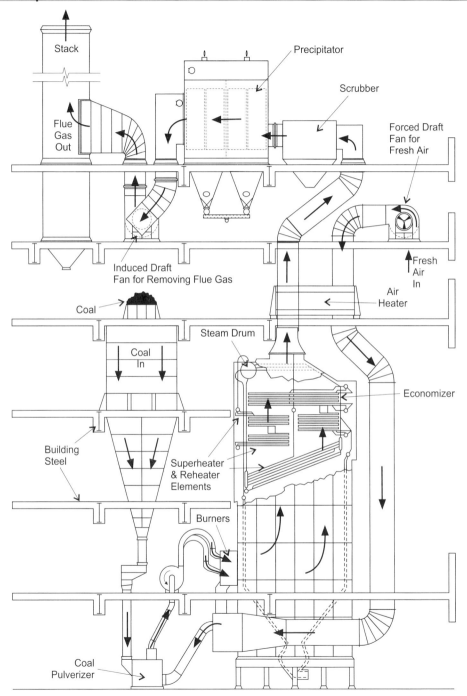

Stack

Precipitator

Scrubber

Flue
Gas
Out

Forced Draft
Fan for
Fresh Air

Induced Draft
Fan for Removing Flue Gas

Fresh
Air
In

Coal

Air
Heater

Steam Drum

Coal
In

Economizer

Building
Steel

Superheater
& Reheater
Elements

Burners

Coal
Pulverizer

Illustration #7-9 - Air Flow Though a Coal Fired Boiler

3. A firetube boiler is designed to operate at higher pressures and temperatures?
   - ❏ true
   - ❏ false

4. The pressure part of a watertube boiler in which all water and steam will pass through at least once is the:
   - ❏ steam drum
   - ❏ lower drum
   - ❏ economizer
   - ❏ superheater

5. The steam drum is never full of water. The reason for this is to allow a steam space above the water.
   - ❏ true
   - ❏ false

6. Is a natural circulation boiler or a forced circulation boiler best suited to meet frequent changes in operating requirements?

   Answer: _____

7. Determine if this statement is true or false. Economizers, superheaters, reheaters and airheaters are additional components that increase the efficiency of a steam generator and make steam.
   - ❏ true
   - ❏ false

8. Which of these drums serve as the main distribution point for feeding the individual furnace wall tubes of a water tube boiler?
   - ❏ steam drum
   - ❏ lower drum
   - ❏ superheater drum
   - ❏ economizer drum

9. The name of the steam generator component that is used to heat the steam to its highest temperature before it goes to the turbine is:
   - ❏ steam drum
   - ❏ superheater
   - ❏ reheater
   - ❏ economizer

10. After the steam has passed through the first stage of a turbine it is often sent back to the steam generator to be:
    - ❏ superheated
    - ❏ reheated
    - ❏ condensed
    - ❏ purified

11. This component is used to preheat the boiler feedwater before it enters the steam drum. It is called a/an:
    - ❏ superheater
    - ❏ reheater
    - ❏ airheater
    - ❏ economizer

12. What is the name of the device used to pre-heat the incoming combustion air?

    Answer: _____

13. The boiler draft fan that supplies the burners and the furnace with combustion air is called:

    Answer: _____

14. The boiler draft fan that is used on the exhaust side of the furnace is called:

    Answer: _____

15. Identify the boiler component that is NOT heated by flue gases passing over it as the gases travel out of the steam generator to the exhaust stack.
- ❏ reheater
- ❏ economizer
- ❏ airheater
- ❏ steam drum

Boiler Drawing 7-10

Boiler drawing 7-10 is a section view of the side elevation of a small industrial boiler. It is a watertube boiler that is fired by natural gas. This boiler is bottom supported but may have some of its components supported by structural steel from hanger rods. This particular section view of the boiler does not show all of the support details, therefore it is difficult to determine the exact method of support for the pressure parts. The method of support used for boilers is critical for two reasons, (1) the high operating temperature of the steel boiler parts, (2) the need for free movements of components due to expansion and contraction of the steel. Larger units are often top supported. This allows the boiler to expand downward. Steel is stronger in tension than in compression, which in the case of a large boiler means the unit will not collapse under its own weight when the steel heats to its operating temperature.

In boiler drawing 7-10, the boiler can support its own weight while operating. This makes the design simpler as there is no need for a separate steel structure to support the entire boiler. This boiler utilizes buckstays to add structural support to the furnace waterwalls. The buckstays are usually wide flange beams or channels (see item 1).

The buckstays reinforce the flat boiler walls during operation and help keep the walls from buckling outwards or collapsing inwards if the pressure inside of the furnace changes during operation. This particular unit has a superheater and an airheater as auxiliary components. It uses a forced draft fan to move the air and combustion gases through the boiler furnace and the air heater. This boiler is a forced circulation type concerning the movement of water and steam.

The following questions refer to boiler drawing 7-10.

16. Which one of the noted boiler pressure parts does this unit **not** have?
- ❏ steam drum
- ❏ superheaters
- ❏ lower drum
- ❏ downcomers

17. What is the inside diameter of the steam drum?

Answer: _____

18. Write out the roof beam description as noted on the drawing.

Answer: _____

19. Calculate the height to the center of the steam drum from the ground floor.

Answer: _____

20. The distance from the center of the steam drum to the low level alarm is:
- ❏ 6 inches
- ❏ 7 inches
- ❏ 13 inches
- ❏ 14 inches

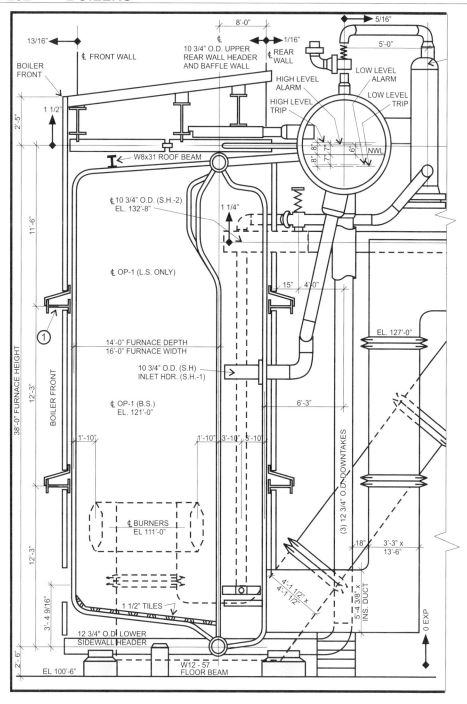

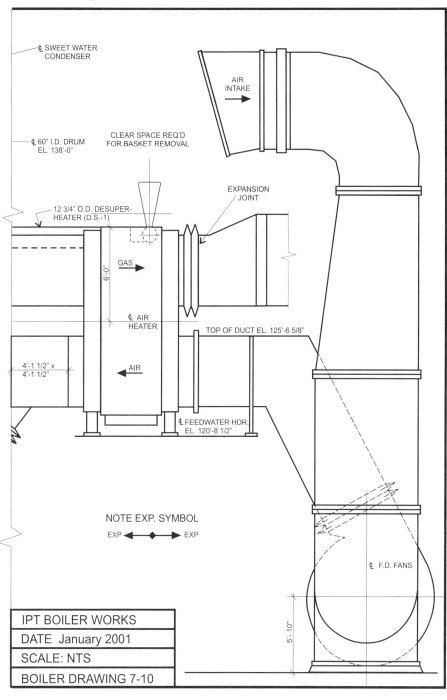

¢ SWEET WATER
CONDENSER

AIR
INTAKE

¢ 60" I.D. DRUM
EL. 138'-0"

CLEAR SPACE REQ'D
FOR BASKET REMOVAL

EXPANSION
JOINT

12 3/4" O.D. DESUPER-
HEATER (D.S.-1)

6'-0"

GAS

¢ AIR
HEATER

TOP OF DUCT EL. 125'-6 5/8"

4'-1 1/2" x
4'-1 1/2"

AIR

¢ FEEDWATER HDR.
EL. 120'-8 1/2"

NOTE EXP. SYMBOL

EXP ◆ EXP

¢ F.D. FANS

5'- 10"

| IPT BOILER WORKS |
| DATE January 2001 |
| SCALE: NTS |
| BOILER DRAWING 7-10 |

21. The distance from the center of the steam drum to the normal water level is six inches.
- ❏ true
- ❏ false

22. How far will the steam drum expand away (to the right) from the boiler, as noted on the drawing?
- ❏ 1/16 of and inch
- ❏ 5/16 of and inch
- ❏ 9/16 of and inch
- ❏ 5/8 of and inch

23. Which of these dimensions refers to the furnace depth, as noted on the drawing?
- ❏ 14'-0"
- ❏ 16'-0"
- ❏ 24'-0"
- ❏ 38'-0"

24. What is installed over top of the floor tubes to protect them?

Answer: _____

25. Which dimension represents the vertical distance from the center of the burners to the center of the steam drum?
- ❏ 10'-6"
- ❏ 27'-0"
- ❏ 39'-0"
- ❏ 42'-3"

26. What is the outside diameter of the upper rear wall header?

Answer: _____

27. At what elevation are the observation ports located on both sides of this unit?
- ❏ 100'-6"
- ❏ 117'-0"
- ❏ 121'-0"
- ❏ 134'-5"

28. If facing the front of the boiler, which statement listed is correct?
- ❏ this drawing is a right side section view of the boiler
- ❏ this drawing is a right side view of the boiler
- ❏ this drawing is a left side section view of the boiler
- ❏ this drawing is a left side view of the boiler

29. Referring to the air heater, is the gas flow through the upper or the lower half of the unit?

Answer: _____

30. How many expansion joints are shown on this drawing for both the air ducts and gas ducts?
- ❏ 3
- ❏ 4
- ❏ 5
- ❏ 7

Boiler Drawing 7-11

Boiler drawing 7-11 shows the front and side sectional elevation views of a boiler used to generate steam for heating and other utility purposes. This boiler is a two drum design with the furnace tubes bent to form a backwards "D". The unit has a superheater section built into it although there is little information on this drawing about it.

The following questions refer to the side elevation view Sect. A-A boiler drawing 7-11.

31. What is the inside diameter of the steam drum?

Answer: _____

32. What is the inside diameter of the lower drum?

Answer: _____

33. What is the wall thickness of the steam drum?

Answer: _____

34. What is the wall thickness of the lower drum in inches?

Answer: _____

35. Determine if this statement is true or false: "this is a top supported boiler".
    - ❏ true
    - ❏ false

36. Calculate the distance from the floor to the top outside surface of the bottom drum.

Answer: _____

37. What is the diameter and minimum wall thickness of the furnace tubes as noted in the tube schedule?

Answer: _____

38. Determine if this statement is true or false: "this unit has an economizer that is heated by the flue gases".
    - ❏ true
    - ❏ false

39. What is the diameter and minimum wall thickness of the superheater inlet header?

Answer: _____

40. What is the vertical center to center distance between the superheater headers?

Answer: _____

41. Calculate the horizontal distance from the drum centerline to the centerline of the superheater inlet header.

Answer: _____

The following questions refer to the front elevations views of boiler drawing 7-11.

42. What is the center to center distance between the steam drum and the lower drum?

Answer: _____

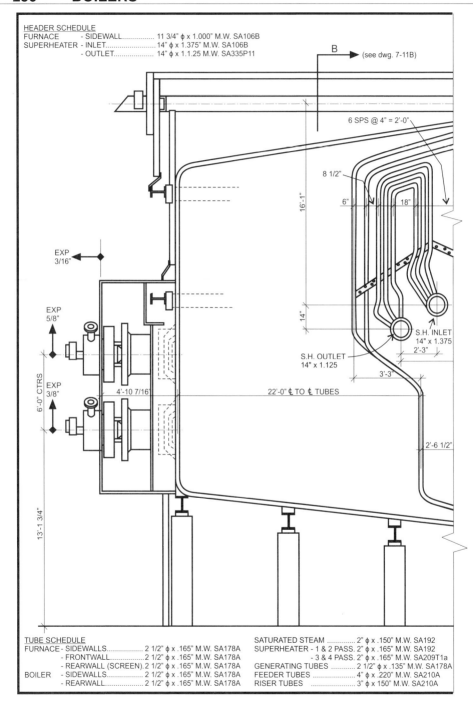

HEADER SCHEDULE
FURNACE   - SIDEWALL............... 11 3/4" φ x 1.000" M.W. SA106B
SUPERHEATER - INLET...................... 14" φ x 1.375" M.W. SA106B
            - OUTLET.................. 14" φ x 1.1.25 M.W. SA335P11

B (see dwg. 7-11B)

6 SPS @ 4" = 2'-0"

8 1/2"

16'-1"

6"   18"

EXP
3/16"

EXP
5/8"

14"

S.H. INLET
14" x 1.375
2'-3"

S.H. OUTLET
14" x 1.125

EXP
3/8"

4'-10 7/16"

3'-3"

6'-0" CTRS

22'-0" ₵ TO ₵ TUBES

2'-6 1/2"

13'-1 3/4"

TUBE SCHEDULE
FURNACE- SIDEWALLS................ 2 1/2" φ x .165" M.W. SA178A
       - FRONTWALL................ 2 1/2" φ x .165" M.W. SA178A
       - REARWALL (SCREEN).2 1/2" φ x .165" M.W. SA178A
BOILER - SIDEWALLS................ 2 1/2" φ x .165" M.W. SA178A
       - REARWALL................ 2 1/2" φ x .165" M.W. SA178A

SATURATED STEAM .... 2" φ x .150" M.W. SA192
SUPERHEATER - 1 & 2 PASS. 2" φ x .165" M.W. SA192
            - 3 & 4 PASS. 2" φ x .165" M.W. SA209T1a
GENERATING TUBES .... 2 1/2" φ x .135" M.W. SA178A
FEEDER TUBES .... 4" φ x .220" M.W. SA210A
RISER TUBES .... 3" φ x 150" M.W. SA210A

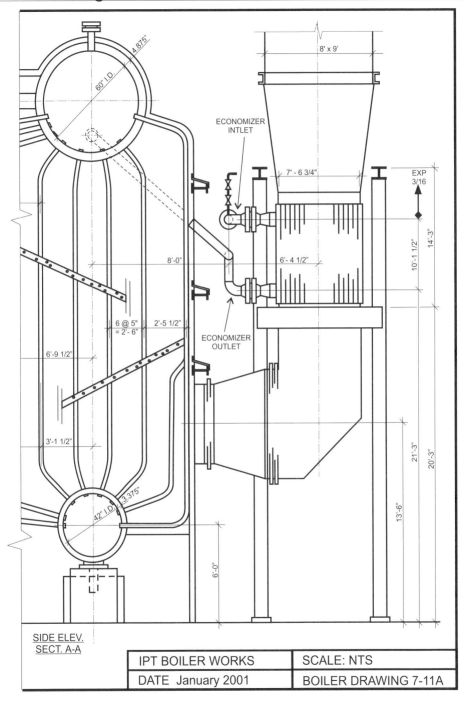

60" I.D.

4.875"

ECONOMIZER
INTLET

8' x 9'

EXP
3/16

7' - 6 3/4"

14'-3"

10'-1 1/2"

8'-0"

6'- 4 1/2"

6 @ 5"
= 2'- 6"

2'-5 1/2"

ECONOMIZER
OUTLET

6'-9 1/2"

3'-1 1/2"

42" I.D.

3.375"

21'-3"

20'-3"

13'-6"

6'-0"

SIDE ELEV.
SECT. A-A

IPT BOILER WORKS	SCALE: NTS
DATE January 2001	BOILER DRAWING 7-11A

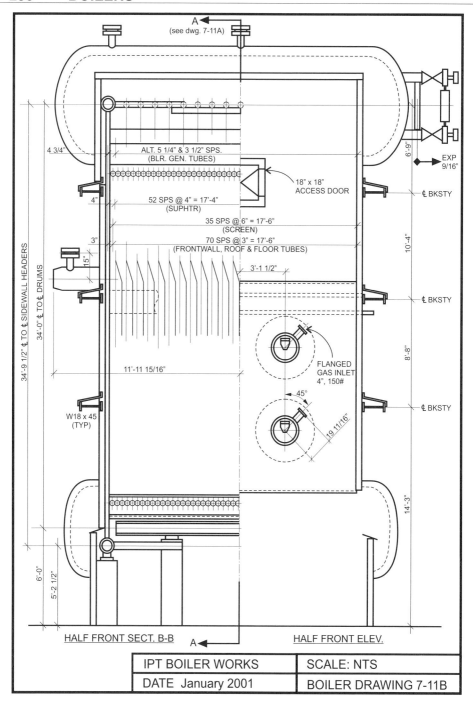

HALF FRONT SECT. B-B

HALF FRONT ELEV.

IPT BOILER WORKS	SCALE: NTS
DATE January 2001	BOILER DRAWING 7-11B

43. Determine the difference between the center to center distance of the side wall headers and the center to center distance of the drums.

Answer: _____

44. Calculate the distance from the floor to the center of the second buckstay on the right hand side of the boiler.

Answer: _____

45. State the size and weight description of the buckstays as noted on the drawing.

Answer: _____

46. Determine if this statement is true or false. Cutting plane line A-A as noted on this drawing refers to Sect. A-A of the side elevation drawing.

    ❏ true
    ❏ false

47. Which distance noted below refers to the spacing of the frontwall, roof and floor tubes?

    ❏ 2 inches
    ❏ 3 inches
    ❏ 4 inches
    ❏ 6 inches

48. What is the spacing of the superheater tubes?

    ❏ 2 inches
    ❏ 3 inches
    ❏ 4 inches
    ❏ 6 inches

49. At what degree or angle from vertical are the gas inlets for the burners installed?

Answer: _____

50. By observing the expansion symbol on the right hand side, how much side expansion is expected?

Answer: _____

SECTION EIGHT

PIPING

Introduction

Pipe is used extensively in virtually every industry for the movement of liquids and gases. Piping is a major component of refineries, petrochemical plants, steam generating plants, pulp and paper plants, food processing plants, and numerous other industries.

To help interpret pipe drawings and all the components that are interconnected by the piping systems, the drawing reader will have an advantage if they have an understanding of other project drawings, for example, structural and pressure vessel drawings.

The term "piping" in this text refers to the fittings, flanges, valves and other items that make up or form part of the overall piping system. Most plant piping is classed as ferrous and is primarily made from carbon steel.

Other piping systems may require the use of more exotic metals such as stainless steel. Products like fiberglass, aluminum, copper, clay, several types of plastic, or other materials may also be used for a specific end use.

Three terms used for piping systems include:

- Process Piping: Used to transport fluids between storage tanks and processing units in and around industrial plants.
- Service Piping: Used to convey steam, air, water and/or other liquids and gases for processing.
- Utility Piping: Used to define piping systems for conveying water, fuel gases and fuel oils. It also refers to piping systems in a plant on the utility side of the operation.

Pipe Sizing

Nominal pipe size (NPS) is a term used to indicate the diameter of pipe, ranging from ½ inch to 42 inches (12 to 1050 mm). For smaller sizes, up to and including 12 inch (300 mm), the term nominal does not refer to either the outside or inside diameter. However, for standard wall pipe the stated nominal size is close to the inside diameter. For example, a 3 inch (75 mm) pipe has an actual outside diameter of 3½ inches (88 mm), while the inside diameter with a standard wall thickness is approximately 3 inches (75 mm).

Regardless of the pipe wall thickness for any given size, the outside diameter of the pipe never changes, but as the wall thickness of pipe increases or decreases, the inside diameter will change. See illustration #8-1 which displays the various wall thickness' for 1 inch (25 mm) NPS pipe.

When working with pipe it is a good practice to memorize the outside diameters of the different sizes up to 12 inch (300 mm).

Two standards are used to classify pipe wall thickness. The American National Standards Institute (ANSI) assigns each wall thickness a schedule number, for example sch. 10, sch. 40, sch. 80, sch. 160, etc. The American Society for Testing Materials (ASTM) uses the designations of standard wall (std), extra strong (xs), and double extra strong (xxs).

Complicating the issue is the fact that pipe sizes ranging from ½ inch to 12 inches (12 to 300 mm) inclusive refer to the nominal inside diameter of the pipe, while pipe sizes starting at 14 inch (350 mm) and up refer to the actual outside diameter of the pipe. What does this mean?

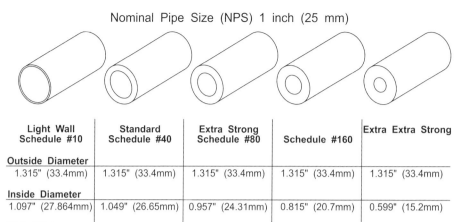

Nominal Pipe Size (NPS) 1 inch (25 mm)

	Light Wall Schedule #10	Standard Schedule #40	Extra Strong Schedule #80	Schedule #160	Extra Extra Strong
Outside Diameter	1.315" (33.4mm)	1.315" (33.4mm)	1.315" (33.4mm)	1.315" (33.4mm)	1.315" (33.4mm)
Inside Diameter	1.097" (27.864mm)	1.049" (26.65mm)	0.957" (24.31mm)	0.815" (20.7mm)	0.599" (15.2mm)
Wall Thickness	0.109" (2.769mm)	0.133" (3.4mm)	0.179" (4.6mm)	0.250" (6.35mm)	0.358" (9.093mm)

$$\text{Wall Thickness} = \frac{\text{Outside Diameter} - \text{Inside Diameter}}{2}$$

Illustration #8-1 - Pipe Wall Thickness

ACTUAL AND NOMINAL PIPE SIZES

Actual OD		Nominal Sizes	
Inches	(mm)	Inches	(mm)
0.405	10.3	1/8	6
0.540	13.7	1/4	8
0.675	17.1	3/8	10
0.840	21.3	1/2	15
1.050	26.7	3/4	20
1.315	33.4	1	25
1.660	42.2	1 1/4	32
1.900	48.3	1 1/2	40
2.375	60.3	2	50
2.875	73.0	2 1/2	65
3.500	88.9	3	80
4.000	101.6	3 1/2	90
4.500	114.3	4	100
5.563	141.3	5	125
6.625	168.3	6	150
8.625	219.1	8	200
10.750	273.1	10	250

ACTUAL AND NOMINAL PIPE SIZES

Actual OD		Nominal Sizes	
Inches	(mm)	Inches	(mm)
12.750	323.9	12	300
14.000	355.6	14	350
16.000	406.4	16	400
18.000	457.0	18	450
20.000	508.0	20	500
22.000	559.0	22	550
24.000	610.0	24	600
26.000	660.0	26	650
28.000	711.0	28	700
30.000	762.0	30	750
32.000	813.0	32	800
34.000	864.0	34	850
36.000	914.0	36	900
38.000	965.0	38	950
40.000	1016.0	40	1000
42.000	1067.0	42	1050

Table 8-1 - Actual and Nominal Pipe Sizes

If a pipe on a drawing is 10 inch (250 mm), the actual outside diameter will be 10¾ inches (273 mm), while the inside diameter will vary depending on the wall thickness. However, if the drawing has a 14 inch (350 mm) pipe, the actual outside diameter will be 14 inches (350 mm).

The inside will be considerably less than 14 inches (350 mm), depending on the wall thickness. Experience obtained working with pipe and in reading piping prints will reduce the confusion of this sizing system. See table 8-1 for actual and nominal pipe sizes.

Types of Lines

As noted earlier in this text, drawings are made up of various lines. The common lines are visible or object lines, dimensions lines and extension lines, centerlines, hidden lines, cutting plane lines, and section lines. Pipe drawings use the same lines as other drawings with the addition of flow lines and match or boundary lines. These lines are shown in illustration #8-2.

There are two types of flow lines: primary (major) and secondary (minor). These are used on flow diagrams and piping and instrumentation diagrams (P&ID). Primary lines are shown as thick lines, while secondary lines are medium thick lines about the same weight as object lines.

A match or boundary line is a thick line used as a reference to align two pipe drawings. These are found on flow diagrams, general arrangement, and piping drawings. See illustration #8-3 for an example of flow lines and match lines.

Single Line and Double Line Drawings

It is a common practice to show pipe and fittings on drawings using a single line format. The single line represents the center of the pipe and the center of the fittings . Double line drawings depict the outside diameter of the pipe and fittings, and are easier for the novice blueprint reader to visualize, however, they are time consuming to draw and take up more drawing space.

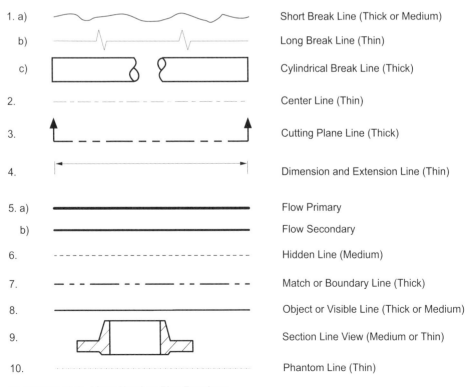

1. a)	Short Break Line (Thick or Medium)
b)	Long Break Line (Thin)
c)	Cylindrical Break Line (Thick)
2.	Center Line (Thin)
3.	Cutting Plane Line (Thick)
4.	Dimension and Extension Line (Thin)
5. a)	Flow Primary
b)	Flow Secondary
6.	Hidden Line (Medium)
7.	Match or Boundary Line (Thick)
8.	Object or Visible Line (Thick or Medium)
9.	Section Line View (Medium or Thin)
10.	Phantom Line (Thin)

Illustration #8-2 - Lines Used on Pipe Drawings

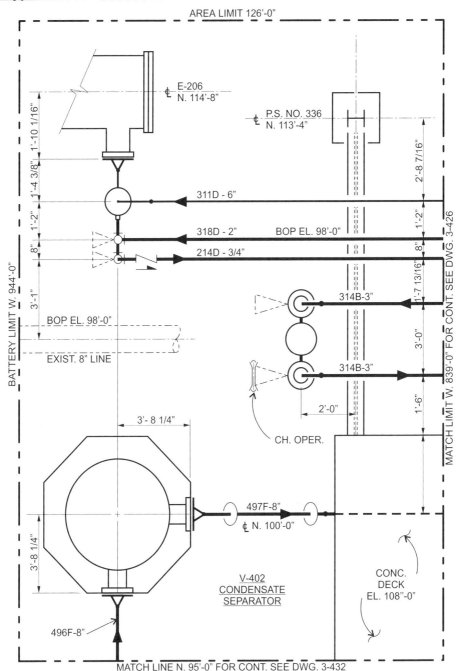

Illustration #8-3 - Flow Lines and Match Lines

Drafters will sometimes illustrate a short section of the pipe or fitting using double lines when it is important for clarity purposes. See illustration #8-4. Note that the single line drawing represents the center of the double line pipe section.

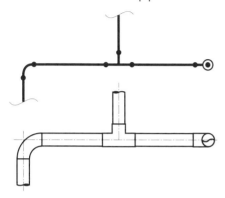

Illustration #8-4 - Single and Double Lines

Line Specification System

Each pipe run on a drawing is identified using a combination of numbers and letters. These combinations of numbers and letters are the name tags of the pipe run, and without them the drawing would be very confusing. illustration #8-5 shows a basic line identification. The symbol is located either directly in line with the pipe or on top of the line.

Illustration #8-5 - Specification of a Line

Pipe drafters congregate these symbols together if room permits. The first number is the nominal pipe size (NPS) of the line, which is 6 inches in illustration #8-5.

The letters WY in the second part are used to indicate what is flowing inside the pipe.

The last number, or set of numbers, is the sequential number used for identification purposes. For example, two or more lines may be the same size and have the same fluid flowing through them, but may start and/or end in different locations thus requiring different identification numbers to reduce any confusion.

A more detailed line identification system

P25 - 82 - HS - 8 - S - IH

Illustration #8-6 - Detailed Specification

is shown in illustration #8-6:
- P25 - is the sequential number (25th. line in the process).
- 82 - denotes the area number of the line. Most plants are divided into areas, and in this example it is area 82.
- HS - represents what is flowing through the pipe. This pipe will contain high pressure steam.
- 8 - is the nominal pipe size in inches.
- S - represents the pipe material specification.
- 1H - insulation type (hot insulation).

The line number will remain with that line until the size changes or the line terminates at a piece of equipment, for instance a process tower or pump.

Additional information may appear beside the line identification symbol. This information may include such things as the volume, temperature, and pressure of the line. The volume is usually given in gallons per minute (GPM) or litres per minute (LPM). The temperature is stated in degrees Fahrenheit (F$^\circ$) or degrees Celsius (C$^\circ$). The pressure is stated in pounds per square inch (PSI) or kilopascals (kPa).

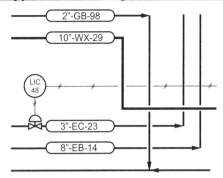

Illustration #8-7 - Line Crossing Precedence

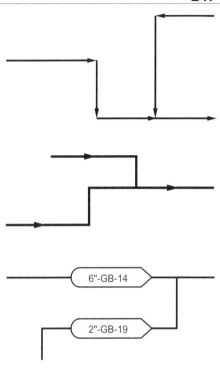

Line Crossings and Terminations

When pipe drawings are produced, line crossings are avoided whenever possible. However, crossings are not always easy to avoid, and when it happens the usual practice is to let primary flow lines take precedence over all other lines. The other flow lines are broken when passing through a major flow. Illustration #8-7 shows the broken secondary lines at the intersection of primary flow lines.

Illustration #8-8 - Flow Direction Indicators

Flow Indicators

Flow direction is usually indicated in a line by adding arrows pointing in the direction of flow. Another flow direction method is included in the line identification symbol.

The symbol is rounded or square on one end and arrow shaped on the end pointing in the direction of flow. See illustration #8-8 for both styles.

Standard Piping Symbols

The standard symbols for fittings, valves and line designations on drawings are shown in illustration #8-9. As a general rule they correspond to the ANSI Z32.23 standard.

However certain companies may modify these symbols to some extent, although generally the symbol is similar. It is difficult to learn all of these symbols, however repeated use of piping drawings and interpretation of the symbols makes the identification easier with time.

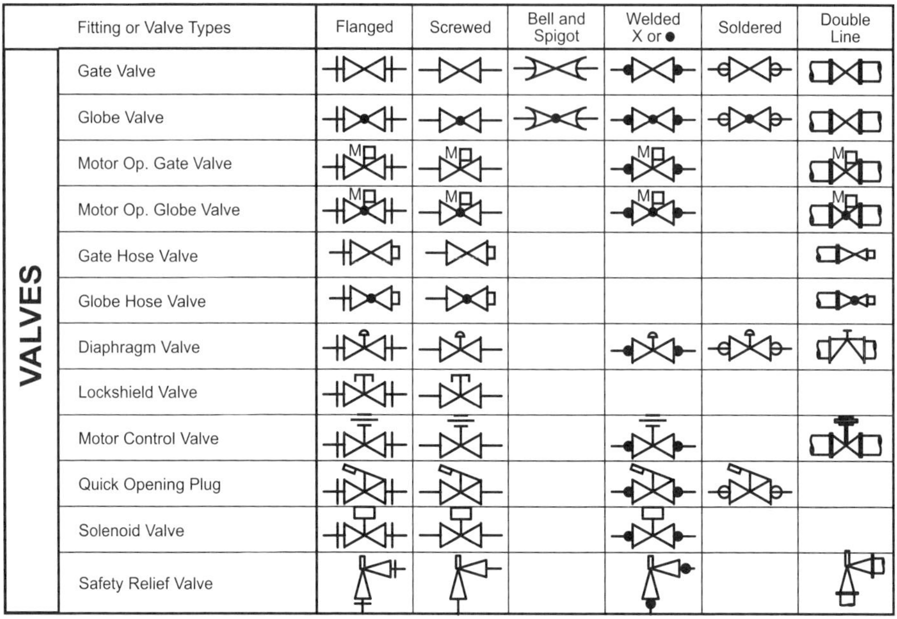

Illustration #8-9 - Standard Piping Symbols (sheet 1 of 5)

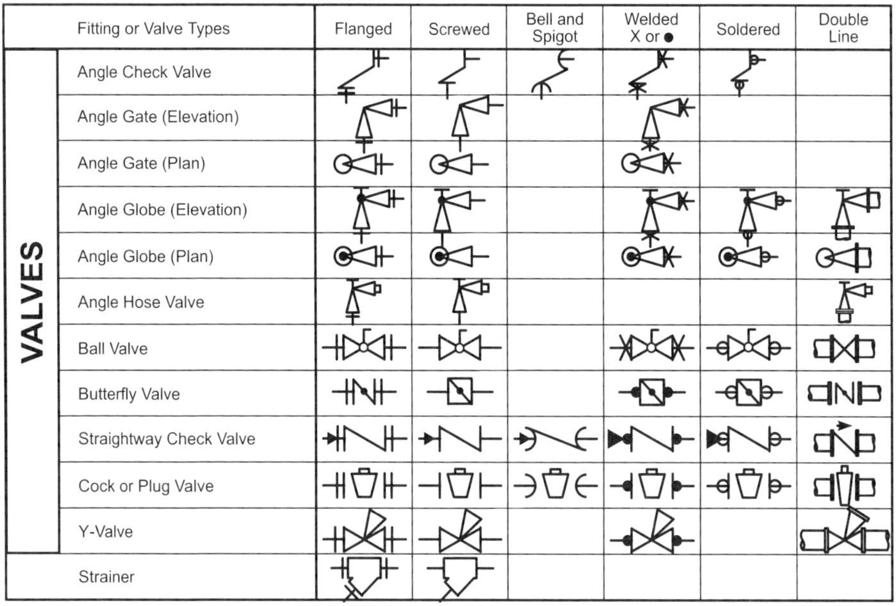

Illustration #8-9 - Standard Piping Symbols (sheet 2 of 5)

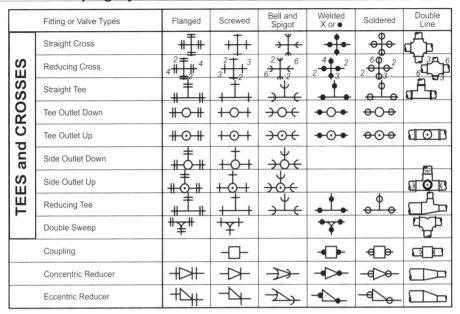

Fitting or Valve Types	Flanged	Screwed	Bell and Spigot	Welded X or ●	Soldered	Double Line
TEES and CROSSES Straight Cross						
Reducing Cross						
Straight Tee						
Tee Outlet Down						
Tee Outlet Up						
Side Outlet Down						
Side Outlet Up						
Reducing Tee						
Double Sweep						
Coupling						
Concentric Reducer						
Eccentric Reducer						

Illustration #8-9 - Standard Piping Symbols (sheet 3 of 5)

Fitting or Valve Types	Flanged	Screwed	Bell and Spigot	Welded X or ●	Soldered	Double Line
ELBOWS 45° Elbow						
90° Elbow						
Elbow Turned Down						
Elbow Turned Up						
Base Elbow						
Long Radius Elbow						
Reducing Elbow						
Side Outlet (Turned Down)						
Side Outlet (Turned Up)						
Elbowlet						
Bushing						
Union						

Illustration #8-9 - Standard Piping Symbols (sheet 4 of 5)

Fitting or Valve Types	Flanged	Screwed	Bell and Spigot	Welded X or ●	Soldered	Double Line
Connecting Pipe Joint						
Expansion Joint						
Lateral Joint						
Sleeve						
Orifice Flange						
Reducing Flange						
Socket Weld Flange						
Weld Neck Flange						
Blind Flange						
Bull Plug						
Pipe Plug						
Cap						

Illustration #8-9 - Standard Piping Symbols (sheet 5 of 5)

Drawing Abbreviations

Drawing notes consist of general notes and specific notes. The general notes refer to the entire drawing and are located on the sides of the drawing, usually near the title block. Specific notes take priority over the general notes and refer to information specific to one part or area of the drawing. Both general and specific notes often use abbreviations.

Illustration #8-10 shows common pipe drawing abbreviations.

Specifications are the written standards referring to the job guidelines, pipe, fittings, valves, and other materials that will be used. This information is located in the project manuals and will become an integral part of the job.

A	Air	AWWA	American Waterworks Association
	Absolute		
AC	Air to Close	BBE	Beveled Both Ends
	Combustion Air	BC	Bolt Circle
AGA	American Gas Association	BF	Blind Flange
AI	Instrument Air	BLE	Beveled Large End
AISC	American Institute of Steel Construction	BLVD	Beveled
ANSI	American National Standard Institute	BOF	Bottom of Face of Flange
AO	Air to Open	BOP	Bottom of Pipe
AP	Plant Air	BSE	Beveled Small End
API	American Petroleum Institute	BW	Butt Weld
ASA	American Standard Association		
ASME	American Society of Mechanical Engineers	C-C	Center to Center
ASTM	American Society of Testing Materials	CFM	Cubic Feet Per Minute
AWS	American Welding Society	CI	Cast Iron

Illustration #8-10 - Piping Drawing Abbreviations

Cr	Chromium		LT	Level Transmitter
CS	Carbon Steel			
	Cold Spring		M	Meter
CS0	Car-Seal Open		Mo	Molybdenum
CTR	Center		MS	Mild Steel
CV	Control Valve			
			N	North
DIA	Diameter		NC	Normally Closed
DS	Dummy Support		NO	Normally Open
DWG	Drawing		NPS	National Pipe Size
				Nominal Pipe Size
E	East		NPT	National Pipe Thread
E-E	End to End		NRS	Non Rising Stem
EL	Elevation		NS	Near Side
ELB	Elbowlet		NTS	Not to Scale
ELL	Elbow			
ERW	Electric Resistance Welding		OD	Outside Diameter
			OS&Y	Outside Screw and Yoke
F	Fahrenheit			
FAB	Fabrication		P&ID	Piping & Instrumentation Diagram
F&D	Face and Drilled		PBE	Plain Both Ends
FF	Face to Face		PC	Pressure Controller
	Flange Face		PCV	Pressure Control Valve
	Flat Face		PE	Plain End
	Full Face (of gasket)		PI	Pressure Indicator
FLG	Flange		POE	Plain One End
FOB	Flat on Bottom		PR	Pressure Regulator
FOT	Flat on Top		PRV	Pressure Reducing Valve
FS	Far Side		PS	Pipe Support
	Field Support		PSI	Pounds Per Square Inch
FTG	Fitting		PSV	Pressure Safety Valve
FW	Field Weld		R	Radius
			RED	Reducer or Reducing
G	Gas		REF	Reference
GALV	Galvanized		REQ.	Required
GPM	Gallon Per Minute		RF	Raised Face
GR	Grade		RJ	Ring Joint
HDR	Header		R/L	Random Length
HEX	Hexagon		RS	Rising Stem
Hg	Mercury			
HPT	Hose Pipe Thread		S	South
HP	High Point			Steam Pressure
	High Pressure		SC	Sample Connection
HTR	Heater			Steam Condensate
HVAC	Heating, Venting and Air Conditioning		SCH	Schedule
ID	Inside Diameter		SCFH	Standard Cubic Feet Per Hour
IE	Invert Elevation		SCFM	Standard Cubic Feet Per Minute
IMP	Imperial		SECT	Section
INS	Insulation		SML	Seamless
INST	Instrument		SO	Slip-On
IPS	Iron Pipe Size		SOL	Sockolet
IS&Y	Inside Screw and Yoke		SP	Sample Point
ISO	Isometric Drawing			Steam Pressure
			SPEC	Specification
LA	Level Alarm		SQ	Square
LC	Level Controller		SR	Short Radius
LG	Level Gage		SS	Stainless Steel
LI	Level Indicator		ST	Steam Tracing
LP	Low Pressure		STD	Standard
	Low Point		SW	Socket Weld
LR	Long Radius		SWG	Swage
LS	Level Switch		SWP	Standard Working Pressure

Illustration #8-10 - Piping Drawing Abbreviations

T	Threaded		V	Valve
	Steam Trap		VC	Vitrified Clay
	Temperature		VERT	Vertical
TBE	Threaded on Both Ends		W	West
TC	Temperature Controller			Water
	Test Connection		W/	With
TE	Threaded End		WC	Water Column
TEF	Teflon		WE	Welded End
TOC	Top of Concrete		WN	Welded Neck
TOL	Threadolet		WOG	Water, Oil, Gas
TOP	Top of Pipe		WOL	Weldolet
TOS	Top of Support		WP	Working Pressure
	Top of Steel			Working Point
TPI	Threads Per Inch		WT	Weight
TYP	Typical		XH	Extra Heavy
			XS	Extra Strong
UNC	Unified National Course		XXH	Double Extra Heavy
UNF	Unified National Fine		XXS	Double Extra Strong

Illustration #8-10 - Piping Drawing Abbreviations

Flow Diagrams

Establishing a measurement on any type of drawing by measuring directly from the print should always be avoided. If a missing dimension is to be established, the tradesperson should consult with a supervisor, or if possible, directly with the draftperson. Flow sheets and P&I diagrams are not drawn to scale and they do not necessarily portray everything in its exact location, however, the drawing will be developed with a sense of proportion and elevation as closely as possible. Illustration #8-11 shows part of the flow sheet of a newspaper recycling process plant. The pumps are located at the bottom of the tanks and the equipment is shown proportionately.

The major flow starts at the upper left and proceeds to the right.

The size of a project often requires more than one flow diagram sheet. When a flow line runs off the edge of the drawing, it is common practice to indicate where the flow is going. The number of the line and the drawing where it continues is stated. These flow lines, when positioned together with the alternate or next drawing, should match up. As mentioned earlier in this section, this continuation is handled by the use of match lines. Illustration #8-12 shows two methods of line continuation, illustration #8-12A when match lines are used, and illustration #8-12B when match lines are not used.

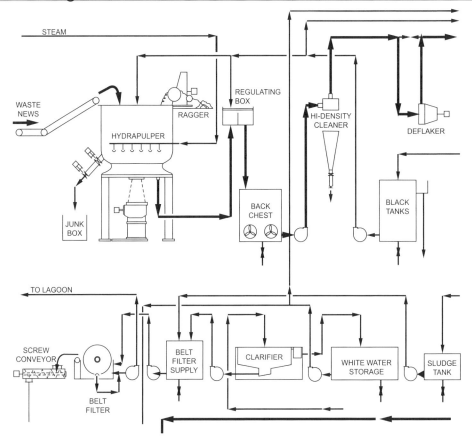

STEAM

WASTE
NEWS

RAGGER

REGULATING
BOX

HI-DENSITY
CLEANER

DEFLAKER

HYDRAPULPER

BLACK
TANKS

JUNK
BOX

BACK
CHEST

TO LAGOON

SCREW
CONVEYOR

BELT
FILTER
SUPPLY

CLARIFIER

WHITE WATER
STORAGE

SLUDGE
TANK

BELT
FILTER

Illustration #8-11 - Flow Diagram

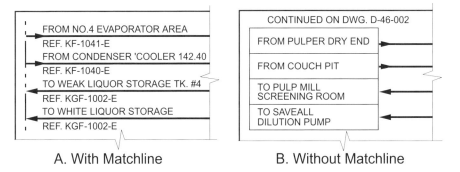

FROM NO.4 EVAPORATOR AREA

REF. KF-1041-E

FROM CONDENSER 'COOLER 142.40

REF. KF-1040-E

TO WEAK LIQUOR STORAGE TK. #4

REF. KGF-1002-E

TO WHITE LIQUOR STORAGE

REF. KGF-1002-E

CONTINUED ON DWG. D-46-002

FROM PULPER DRY END

FROM COUCH PIT

TO PULP MILL
SCREENING ROOM

TO SAVEALL
DILUTION PUMP

A. With Matchline

B. Without Matchline

Illustration #8-12 - Flow Lines Between Drawings

Site Plans, General Arrangements, Piping Plans

Site plans are used to show where buildings, vessels, tanks, and other equipment are located in a plant.

General arrangement drawings zero in on specifics of a major location on the site. For example, looking down on a building without a roof, you can see inside the building and can locate the piping systems and the major equipment such as vessels, tanks and pumps. The piping plan views are developed from the general arrangement drawing.

A piping plan view drawing illustrates the piping system as viewed looking down on it. These plan views are drawn in orthographic projection and can include elevation views, section views and detail views. More detailed pipe drawings are developed from the piping plans.

Sequence of Pipe Drawings

Pipe drawings and blueprints range from general information schematic and flow diagrams to the detailed piping isometric and spool sheets needed for fabrication of pipe sections.

The development of piping drawings usually progresses in the following sequence:

1 . Schematic Diagram
2. Flow Diagram
3. Piping And Instrumentation Diagram (P&ID)
4. Piping Drawing
5. Isometric Drawings
6. Spool Drawings

Note: Some of the drawings may be grouped together or left out depending on the project size and type of piping system.

Schematic Diagram

The schematic diagram or drawing is a theoretical layout of the system and its operation. It is only used in the initial planning stage as a basic guide for the development of the flow diagram. This diagram uses non scale single line flow paths with rectangles or circles representing general system operations and process equipment.

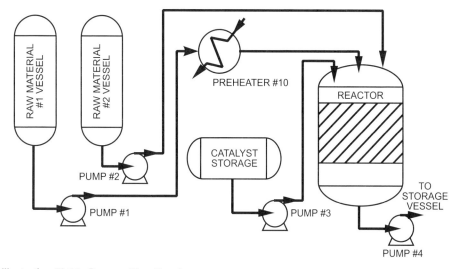

Illustration #8-13 - Process Flow Drawing

Flow Diagram

The flow diagram is a more sophisticated schematic drawing showing equipment layout and the flow of fluids through the system. An example of a typical process flow diagram is represented in illustration #8-13.

The diagram provides an overall perspective of the entire system operation or a specified plant process using basic symbols, flow arrows and single line process runs.

Flow diagrams are not drawn to scale and may be presented as either an elevation or plan view drawing. Installations covering large areas are usually shown as plan view flow diagrams, where less complicated systems are often shown from an elevation view.

Piping and Instrumentation Diagrams

P&ID drawing is the term frequently given to the piping and instrumentation diagram, or it is occasionally referred to as the process and instrumentation diagram. The drawing is essentially a detailed mechanical or process flow diagram in schematic form.

The P&ID drawing is not drawn to scale and equipment on the drawing is located to show major process flow runs from left to right.

A typical P&ID generally includes:
- Major equipment and valves.
- All process lines and pipe sizes for each pipe line.
- Line numbers or codes along with designated flow direction.
- Instrumentation and control devices.

Illustration # 8-14 shows one section of the previous flow diagram (raw material #1 vessel) as it would be developed in a P&ID format.

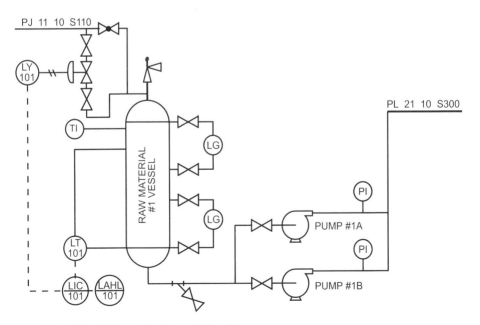

Illustration #8-14 - Piping and Instrumentation Diagram

Instrumentation on P&ID

Most instrumentation on piping and instrumentation diagrams use standardized ISA (Instrumentation Society of America) symbols and identification methods. Balloons or bubbles (circular shaped symbols) are generally used in identifying instruments (see illustration #8-15) with the instrument functions specified by the use of abbreviations within the balloons. Generally, each instrument is first given a functional letter identification followed by a loop identification number.

Locally or Field Mounted Instrument

Board Mounted (Control Room) Instrument

Mounted Behind Board

Instruments Sharing a Common Housing

Illustration #8-15 - Instrument Balloons

The first letter in the abbreviation typically identifies the measured or variable controlled by the instrument.

The first letter will often represent one of the following:
• F Flow
• T Temperature
• L Level
• P Pressure

Table 8-2 shows the first and succeeding letters used in the abbreviation to identify the actual function performed by the instrument.

Piping Drawing (Orthographic Projection)

The piping drawing is the detailed outline to which the piping system is to be fabricated. The true shape and dimensions of equipment are represented on the piping drawings.

INSTRUMENT FUNCTIONS		
Flow		
FI	=	Flow Indicator
FR	=	Flow Recorder
FC	=	Flow Controller
FT	=	Flow Transmitter
Level		
LI	=	Level Indicator
LR	=	Level Recorder
LC	=	Level Controller
LT	=	Level Transmitter
Temperature		
TI	=	Temperature Indicator
TR	=	Temperature Recorder
TC	=	Temperature Controller
TT	=	Temperature Transmitter
Pressure		
PI	=	Pressure Indicator
PR	=	Pressure Recorder
PC	=	Pressure Controller
PT	=	Pressure Transmitter

Table 8-2 - Instrument Functions

Most piping drawings are developed using the orthographic projection method. True orthographic projection drawings consist of six distinct views: top, front, right side, left side, bottom, and rear. However, most drawings find it necessary only to show the top, side and front views. This three view method of orthographic projection is shown in illustration #8-16A. Illustration #8-16B shows a pictoral view of the same object.

In pipe drawing, orthographic projections are referred to as plan, elevation, and sectional views. This type of projection drawing may be used for large and complicated piping systems, piping in buildings, and for some small spool piece drawings. A simple double line orthographic spool sheet drawing showing a plan and elevation view is shown in illustration #8-17.

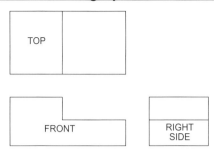

Illustration #8-16A - Orthographic Projection

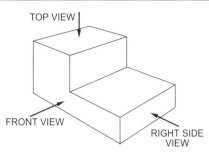

Illustration #8-16B - Actual View of an Object

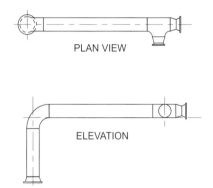

Illustration #8-17 - Plan and Elevation Views

Dimensions, Elevation and Coordinates

Most pipe orthographic drawings are drawn to some scale; with the exception being the spool sheet drawing, which as a rule, relies on written dimensions. Vertical dimensions on large scale plant drawings are specified in elevation designations rather than using dimension lines. The elevation at grade is the normal starting point and typically given an arbitrary elevation of 100 ft. 00 in. (100 m 000 mm).

This dimensioning method provides for a positive number for underground service elevation dimensions and an even number starting point.

In plan view orthographic drawings, co-ordinates are often used to locate structural steel, vessels, tanks and major equipment. Coordinates, as a rule, start from an established reference point at the SouthWest corner of the project. As the distance increases (going north and east from the reference point), the coordinates get larger. In buildings and outlined structures, dimensions are usually given from the structure steel or columns.

Pictorial Piping Drawing

Piping drawings are often shown in a pictorial type of representation for clarity and ease of interpretation, particularly on intricate drawings. The two most common types of piping pictorial drawings are the isometric and the oblique projections.

The oblique drawing is the least common of the two drawings but may be used when an emphasized front view is desirable for clarity. Oblique drawings show the plan or front face of the piping drawing in its true form or plane. All other parts and piping from this plane are then projected back from this view on an angle of 60 degrees, or at 45 degrees on some drawings. Illustration # 8-18 shows parallel tanks and piping layout using an oblique projection.

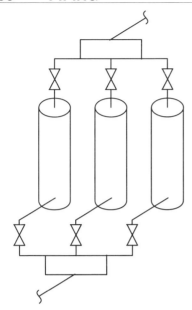

Illustration #8-18 - Oblique Piping Drawing

Isometric or Iso Drawings

The most used pictorial drawing method in the piping industry is isometric projection. The major advantage of an isometric drawing is that three sides of the object are displayed in one practical easy to read view. This ease of interpreting an isometric drawing as compared to an orthographic drawing is shown in illustrations 8-19A and 8-19B. Some companies use isometric projection as their major piping working print, but because of the complexity involved in drawing overlapping multiple pipe runs, it is often only used for fabrications and detail piping work.

Isometric drawing construction uses three axis that are equally spaced at 120 degrees from each other. All horizontal lines are drawn at angles of 30 degrees, while all vertical lines remain vertical. See illustration #8-20.

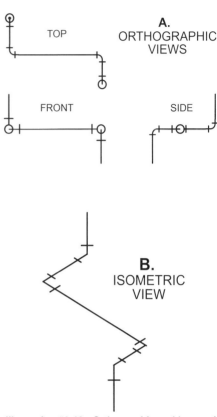

Illustration #8-19 - Orthographic and Isometric Views

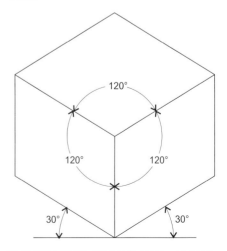

Illustration #8-20 - Isometric Lines and Axes

In piping systems, not all lines run at right angles to each other and when diagonal lines are needed on isometric drawings, they are shown by framing the diagonal line.

The frame is represented by an isometric square or rectangle in the same plane as the offset, shown in illustration #8-21.

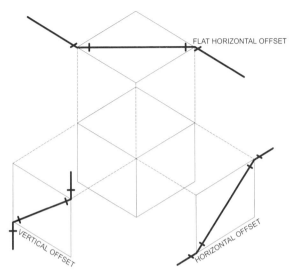

FLAT HORIZONTAL OFFSET

VERTICAL OFFSET

HORIZONTAL OFFSET

Illustration #8-21 - Isometric Rectangle Example

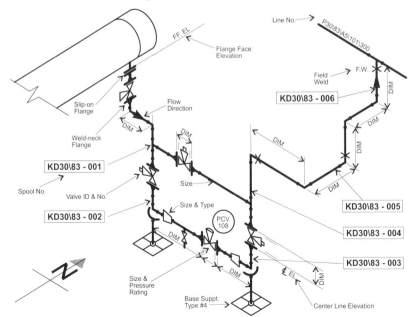

Line No. ➤ P30\83\A5\101\300

FF. EL

Flange Face Elevation

Field Weld

F.W.

KD30\83 - 006

DIM

Slip-on Flange

Flow Direction

DIM

DIM

DIM

Weld-neck Flange

DIM

KD30\83 - 001

DIM

Spool No.

Valve ID & No.

Size

DIM

KD30\83 - 005

KD30\83 - 002

Size & Type

PCV 108

KD30\83 - 004

KD30\83 - 003

DIM

DIM

Size & Pressure Rating

DIM

Base Suppt. Type #4

℄ EL

Center Line Elevation

Illustration #8-22 - Typical Isometric Drawing

Isometric Dimensions

Dimensions on isometric drawings are normally indicated and should not be scaled from the drawing. When drawing isometric piping, the tendency is to give priority to indicating and positioning fittings and valves for clarity rather than scale. The dimensions given are center-to-center for most fittings and face-to-face for flanges and valves.

Hash marks or parallel extension lines using inside dimension lines on flanges and valves indicate that the face-to-face dimension includes the gasket dimension. Illustration #8-22 shows a typical isometric drawing and the basic information that may be found on it.

Pipe Spools

The fabricated components of a particular piping section including pipe fittings, and flanges are referred to as a spool.

The physical size and dimensions of the spool piping section is usually limited to the type of transportation used to deliver the spool from the fabrication location to the actual job site.

Spool drawings, or shop fabrication drawings as they are sometimes referred to, are made up from piping drawings or from detailed isometric drawings. They are a separate drawing incorporating all the dimensions, material specifications and information needed for the complete fabrication of the spool piping.

The spool drawings can be done in orthographic or isometric projection depending on company preference. Isometric spool drawings are generally drawn using the single line method while orthographic drawings are drawn using either single or double lines.

Double line orthographic drawings are usually preferred to the single line projection. Illustration #8-23A, B, and C shows three methods of drawing the same spool.

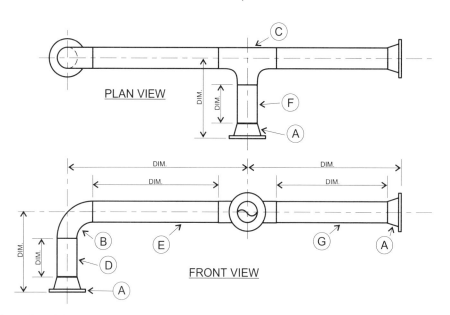

Illustration #8-23A - Doulble Line Orthographic Spool Drawing

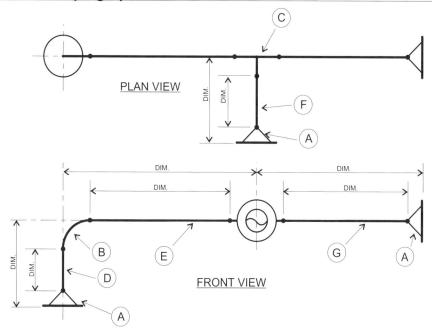

PLAN VIEW

FRONT VIEW

Illustration #8-23B - Single Line Orthographic Spool Drawing

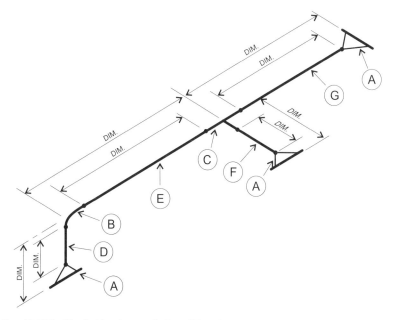

Illustration #8-23C - Single Line Isometric Spool Drawing

Each pipe spool drawing includes a spool number or mark number which is transferred to the finished fabricated pipe spool for identification. The number matches the line number on the piping drawing or isometric drawing to which it belongs. A letter or number is usually added to the end of line number to indicate the position of the spool in the field piping fabrication.

Bill of Material

Each spool drawing includes a bill or list of material specifying the quantity and type of fittings, flanges, bolts, gaskets, and pipe to use in the spool fabrication. An example of the bill of material for the spool drawing in illustration #8-23 is shown in illustration #8-24.

Bill of Materials for Spool Drawing No. KD30\83 - 004		
Item No.	Quantity	Description
Flanges		
A	3	6" (150 mm) 150# R.F. W.N. (STD BORE)
Fittings		
B	1	6" (150 mm) STD. L.R. 90 DEG. ELL
C	1	6" (150 mm) STD. TEE
Pipe		
D	1	6" X 1' - 4" (150 mm X 406.5 mm) SCH 40
E	1	6" X 6' - 10" (150 mm X 2083 mm) SCH 40
F	1	6" X 2' - 0" (150 mm X 609.6 mm) SCH 40
G	1	6" X 5' - 9" (150 mm X 1752.6 mm) SCH 40
Other		

Illustration #8-24 - Bill of Materials for Spool Drawings

General Piping Questions

1. Most pipe used for industrial purposes is primarily made from:
   - ❏ stainless steel
   - ❏ carbon steel
   - ❏ copper alloys
   - ❏ brass or bronze

2. Pipe sizes ranging from ½ inch to 12 inches in diameter are specified as a nominal size, while pipe greater than 12 inches in diameter is specified as an actual outside diameter.
   - ❏ true
   - ❏ false

3. What is the actual outside diameter of a 4 inch (114.3 mm) pipe?

Answer: _____

4. A primary line is shown as a thick line. What type of line is a medium thick line about the same weight as an object line?

Answer: _____

5. What is the name of the line that is used to align two pipe drawings when it is necessary to indicate continuation of a piping system on another drawing?
   - ❏ match or boundary line
   - ❏ grid line
   - ❏ coordinate line
   - ❏ latitude and longitude line

6. On a piping drawing, the first number given on the tag of a piping line used to identify that particular line always refers to the diameter of the pipe used.
   - ❏ true
   - ❏ false

7. What is used on a piping drawing to indicate the direction of flow of the contents of a particular line?

Answer: _____

8. Notes that apply to the entire piping drawing are called specific notes while notes that apply to one particular part or area of the drawing are called general notes.
   - ❏ true
   - ❏ false

9. Piping drawings are not always drawn to scale but are drawn with a sense of proportion and elevation to represent systems as close and practical as possible.
   - ❏ true
   - ❏ false

10. What is the name of the drawing used to show a plan view of the location of buildings, vessels, tanks and other equipment in a plant?

Answer: _____

11. What type of drawing zeros in on specifics of a major location on the plant site?

Answer: _____

12. Piping plan view drawings are developed from:
   - ❏ site plan drawings
   - ❏ general arrangements drawings
   - ❏ isometric drawings
   - ❏ orthographic drawings

13. What type of drawing is a theoretical layout of a piping system and its operation?

Answer: _____

14. What type of diagram is a more sophisticated schematic drawing showing equipment layout and the flow of fluids through the system?

Answer: _____

15. Write out the name of the abbreviation P&ID.

Answer: _____

16. Name the drawing used to illustrate mechanical or process flows in schematic form that includes major equipment, valves and process lines along with their line code and flow direction and any instrumentation and control devices?

Answer: _____

17. What type of piping drawing shows the true shape and dimensions of a equipment and a piping system?

Answer: _____

18. Elevation grades start at 100 feet (100 m) on piping drawings to provide an even number starting point and give underground services a positive number.
   ❏ true
   ❏ false

19. Which pictorial drawing method is most frequently used to develop piping spool drawings?
   ❏ oblique
   ❏ perspective
   ❏ isometric
   ❏ orthographic

20. The dimensions shown on single line isometric spool prints are taken from the center of fittings and flanges.
   ❏ true
   ❏ false

Piping Drawings

The following information refers to IPT's Booster Station Drawings 8-25A to 8-25E.

The following booster station drawings do not make up the complete set of drawings that were used to build the entire station. In addition to the booster pump drawings, the other drawings included in this set are the site plan, building floor plans, and building sections to give the reader a better concept of the building and where the pumps are located. As noted earlier in this section, reference was made to the benefit of having some familiarity with other types of drawings. The ability to read other types of drawings will make it easier to interpret pipe drawings and understand the job requirements.

The first drawing in the set, drawing 8-25A, is the site plan which gives a general idea of the building, its location and its shape. This overview will help understand the drawings that follow.

Drawing 8-25B details the building floor plan and several section views. This drawing shows the building layout and the type of construction used for the building. The location of the pump room is noted, as well as general details of the building including the partition walls and floor layout.

Drawing 8-25C, which is similar to a plan view drawing, is the Pumphouse Flow Schematic diagram. The general location of the pumps, valves and reducers is noted, the flow direction is indicated with arrows, and the pipe sizes are shown.

The drawing does not show any pipe elevation changes. Dimensions are not given as the piping will not be fabricated from this flow diagram drawing, however, it is important to use this drawing in coordination with the other pipe drawings. Drawing 8-25D is the piping floor plan.

This drawing shows the layout of the piping and the pumps as viewed from above. Dimensions are included on this drawing and fabrication of the pipe arrangement could be done from this drawing when combined with piping section drawing 8-25E, although the fabrication of the pipe will most likely be done using smaller individual spool drawings.

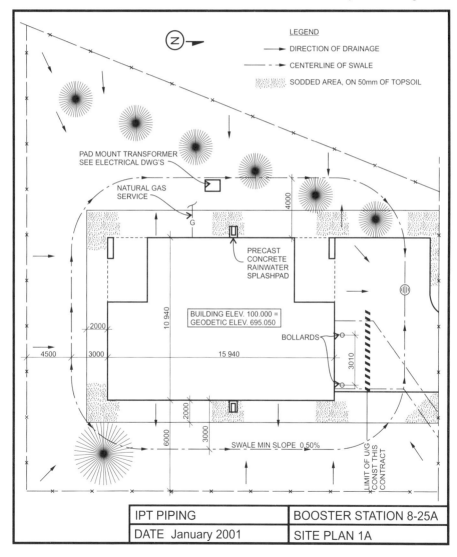

IPT PIPING	BOOSTER STATION 8-25A
DATE January 2001	SITE PLAN 1A

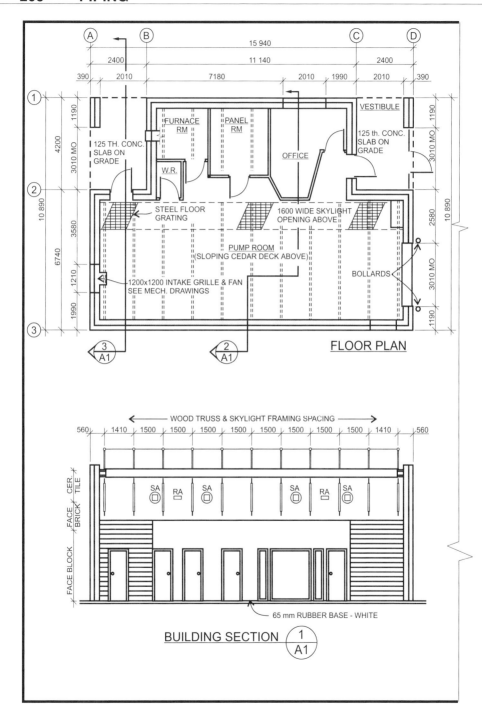

FLOOR PLAN

BUILDING SECTION

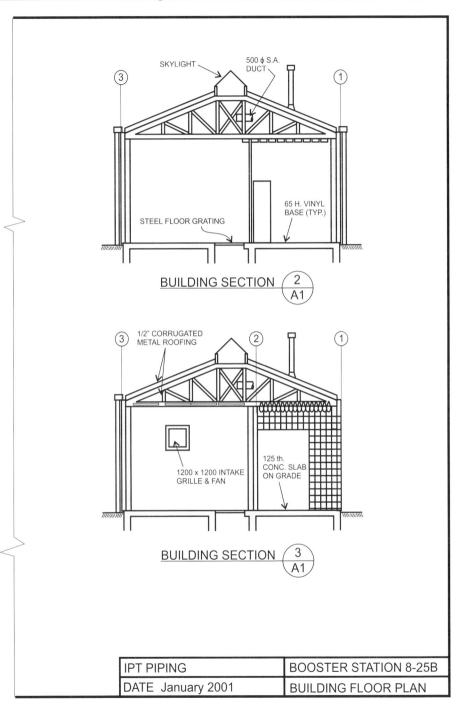

SKYLIGHT

500 φ S.A. DUCT

STEEL FLOOR GRATING

65 H. VINYL BASE (TYP.)

BUILDING SECTION (2 / A1)

1/2" CORRUGATED METAL ROOFING

1200 x 1200 INTAKE GRILLE & FAN

125 th. CONC. SLAB ON GRADE

BUILDING SECTION (3 / A1)

IPT PIPING	BOOSTER STATION 8-25B
DATE January 2001	BUILDING FLOOR PLAN

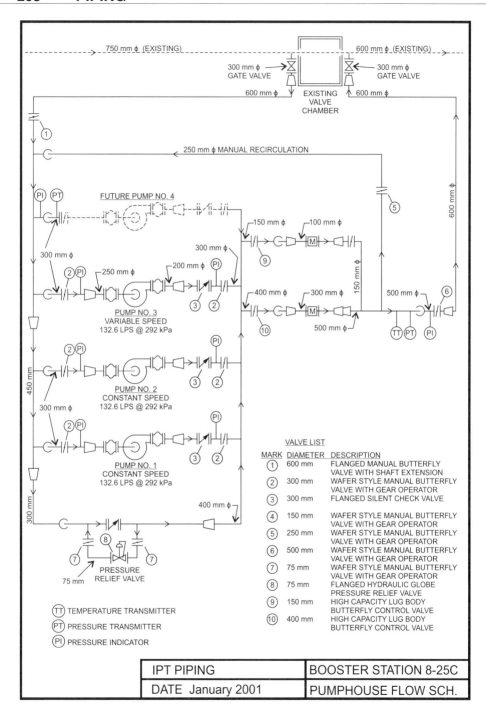

750 mm φ (EXISTING)

300 mm φ
GATE VALVE

300 mm φ
GATE VALVE

600 mm φ

EXISTING
VALVE
CHAMBER

600 mm φ

600 mm φ (EXISTING)

600 mm φ

①

250 mm φ MANUAL RECIRCULATION

⑤

(PI) (PT)

FUTURE PUMP NO. 4

300 mm φ

150 mm φ

100 mm φ

M

300 mm φ

⑨

(PI)

(2)(PI)   250 mm φ   200 mm φ

③   ②

PUMP NO. 3
VARIABLE SPEED
132.6 LPS @ 292 kPa

400 mm φ   300 mm φ

M

⑩

500 mm φ

150 mm φ

500 mm φ   ⑥

(TT)(PT) (PI)

(2)(PI)

(PI)

③   ②

PUMP NO. 2
CONSTANT SPEED
132.6 LPS @ 292 kPa

450 mm

300 mm φ

(2)(PI)

(PI)

③   ②

PUMP NO. 1
CONSTANT SPEED
132.6 LPS @ 292 kPa

300 mm

400 mm φ

⑧

⑦   ⑦

PRESSURE
RELIEF VALVE

75 mm

VALVE LIST

MARK	DIAMETER	DESCRIPTION
①	600 mm	FLANGED MANUAL BUTTERFLY VALVE WITH SHAFT EXTENSION
②	300 mm	WAFER STYLE MANUAL BUTTERFLY VALVE WITH GEAR OPERATOR
③	300 mm	FLANGED SILENT CHECK VALVE
④	150 mm	WAFER STYLE MANUAL BUTTERFLY VALVE WITH GEAR OPERATOR
⑤	250 mm	WAFER STYLE MANUAL BUTTERFLY VALVE WITH GEAR OPERATOR
⑥	500 mm	WAFER STYLE MANUAL BUTTERFLY VALVE WITH GEAR OPERATOR
⑦	75 mm	WAFER STYLE MANUAL BUTTERFLY VALVE WITH GEAR OPERATOR
⑧	75 mm	FLANGED HYDRAULIC GLOBE PRESSURE RELIEF VALVE
⑨	150 mm	HIGH CAPACITY LUG BODY BUTTERFLY CONTROL VALVE
⑩	400 mm	HIGH CAPACITY LUG BODY BUTTERFLY CONTROL VALVE

(TT) TEMPERATURE TRANSMITTER

(PT) PRESSURE TRANSMITTER

(PI) PRESSURE INDICATOR

IPT PIPING	BOOSTER STATION 8-25C
DATE January 2001	PUMPHOUSE FLOW SCH.

Drawing 8-25D is a double line drawing, making it easier to visualize the piping configuration and the location of valves, reducers and other fittings.

Drawing 8-25E represents the piping sections noted on drawing 8-25D. Both are drawn using orthographic projection.

To interpret and understand the orientation of the section views, the reader must first identify the location of each cutting plane line on drawing 8-25D, and then compare it with the corresponding section view on drawing 8-25E.

The next step is to visualize how the section view was rotated from a top view on drawing 8-25D and is now shown as an elevation view on drawing 8-25E.

Imagine physically cutting out a section from drawing 8-25D along the cutting plane line, and then rotating and placing it on drawing 8-25E. For example, try to visualize looking down on a vehicle with a cutting plane line running from left to right, behind the front seat. Then remove the back half of the vehicle starting at that line. Finally, reposition yourself behind the vehicle looking forward. You would see the back of the front seat, the top part of the dashboard, and the rear view mirror attached to the windshield. After this visualization is mastered, interpreting any section view drawn from a main drawing becomes easier.

The following questions refer to Booster Station Drawings 8-25A and 8-25B.

21. State the overall dimensions of the Booster Station building in millimeters.
Answer: _____

22. Noting the direction symbol for north, determine on which side of the building the natural gas service enters.
❏ north
❏ south
❏ east
❏ west

23. What is the bench mark elevation of the building in meters?
Answer: _____

24. On which side of the building are the bollards located.
❏ north
❏ south
❏ east
❏ west

25. What is the Geodetic elevation of the building in meters?
Answer: _____

26. Referring to the Floor Plan, what is the distance between the bollards in millimeters?
Answer: _____

27. Referring to Building Section 2-A1 what is the pump room floor made of?
❏ concrete only
❏ floor grating only
❏ concrete and floor grating
❏ cedar decking

28. State the dimensions in millimeters of the intake grille as noted in Building Section 3-A1.
Answer: _____

29. What is the typical center to center distance in millimeters between the wood trusses as noted in Building Section 1-A1?

Answer: _____

30. What is the thickness of the concrete slab for the vestibule as noted in the Floor Plan?

Answer: _____

31. This building is designed using a grid system.
   - ❏ true
   - ❏ false

32. What is the distance between grid 1. and 2.?
   - ❏ 10 890
   - ❏ 6740
   - ❏ 4200
   - ❏ 2400

The following questions refer to Booster Station Drawing 8-25-C.

33. State the number of the pump that will be installed at a future date.

Answer: _____

34. Which pump is designed to be used at a variable speed?
   - ❏ pump #1
   - ❏ pump #2
   - ❏ pump #3
   - ❏ pump #4

35. What is the rated capacity in liters per second of each pump?

Answer: _____

36. What pump pressure is required to produce the maximum flow rate as noted on this drawing?

Answer: _____

37. What size reducer is used on the inlet side of each pump?

Answer: _____

38. A reducer fitting is used to join the pump outlet pipe to the main flow lines. State the size of this fitting.

Answer: _____

39. What is the mark number as noted in the valve list for the flanged silent check valve?
   - ❏ mark #2
   - ❏ mark #3
   - ❏ mark # 4
   - ❏ mark #5

40. Write out the symbol for pressure indicator.

Answer: _____

41. State the pipe size of the manual recirculation line.

Answer: _____

42. What is the largest size of pipe included on this schematic drawing?

Answer: _____

43. At the outlet side of each pump, what is positioned between the wafer style manual butterfly valve and the flanged silent check valve?
   - ❏ temperature transmitter
   - ❏ pressure transmitter
   - ❏ pressure indicator
   - ❏ future pump #4

44. What is the size of the pressure relief valve?
   - ❏ 600
   - ❏ 300
   - ❏ 150
   - ❏ 75

45. What is the approximate diameter in inches of the 600 mm line?
   - ❏ 30
   - ❏ 24
   - ❏ 16
   - ❏ 8

46. How many different sized valves are required for this schematic?
   - ❏ 10
   - ❏ 7
   - ❏ 5
   - ❏ 3

The following questions refer to Booster Station Drawing 8-25D and 8-25E.

47. What is the center to center dimension between pump no.1 and pump no. 2?

Answer: _____

48. On which drawing is the detail for the 20 mm diameter copper drip pocket drain found?

Answer: _____

49. Determine if this statement is true or false: All steel pipe inside the building 50 mm diameter and smaller is to be galvanized.
   - ❏ true
   - ❏ false

50. State the diameter of the weldolet used for the water return?

Answer: _____

51. Calculate the center to center distance between the pump's inlet header and the outlet header.
   - ❏ 4250 mm
   - ❏ 2350 mm
   - ❏ 1900 mm
   - ❏ 870 mm

52. Referring to section view 21 on drawing 1-E what is the elevation of the main header or manifold?

Answer: _____

53. Calculate the difference in elevation from the centerline of the main header to the center of the 250 mm elbow at elevation 99.585. (see section view 21)

Answer: _____

54. Referring to section view 23 on drawing 1-E, on which Booster Station drawing would a description of mark #8 be found.

Answer: _____

55. In section view 23 the centerline elevation of the 400 mm pipe is noted as 100.475. Calculate the elevation to the center of the 450 x 300 mm. eccentric reducer. (Note: to 300 mm centerline)
   - ❏ 100.475
   - ❏ 99.327
   - ❏ 99.251
   - ❏ 99.125

56. How many drain valves are show in section view 22?
   - ❏ 1 valve
   - ❏ 2 valves
   - ❏ 3 valves
   - ❏ 4 valves

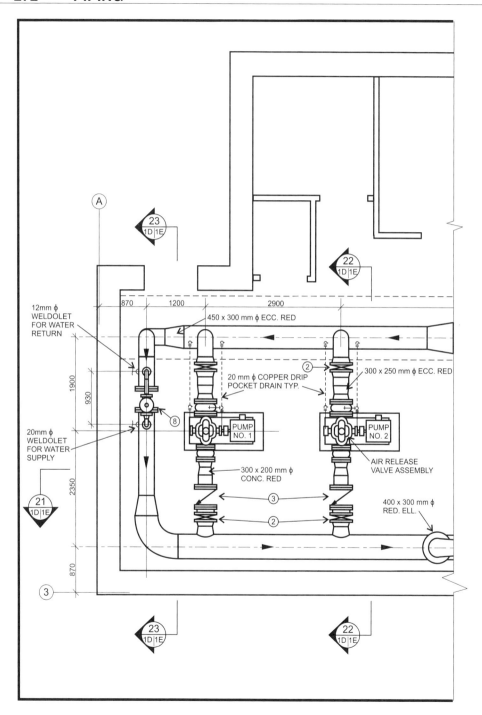

12mm φ WELDOLET FOR WATER RETURN

450 x 300 mm φ ECC. RED

20 mm φ COPPER DRIP POCKET DRAIN TYP.

300 x 250 mm φ ECC. RED

20mm φ WELDOLET FOR WATER SUPPLY

PUMP NO. 1

PUMP NO. 2

AIR RELEASE VALVE ASSEMBLY

300 x 200 mm φ CONC. RED

400 x 300 mm φ RED. ELL.

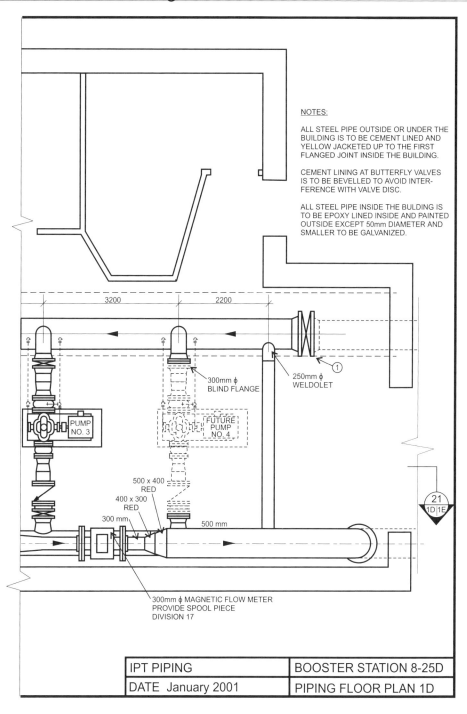

NOTES:

ALL STEEL PIPE OUTSIDE OR UNDER THE
BUILDING IS TO BE CEMENT LINED AND
YELLOW JACKETED UP TO THE FIRST
FLANGED JOINT INSIDE THE BUILDING.

CEMENT LINING AT BUTTERFLY VALVES
IS TO BE BEVELLED TO AVOID INTER-
FERENCE WITH VALVE DISC.

ALL STEEL PIPE INSIDE THE BULDING IS
TO BE EPOXY LINED INSIDE AND PAINTED
OUTSIDE EXCEPT 50mm DIAMETER AND
SMALLER TO BE GALVANIZED.

3200   2200

300mm φ
BLIND FLANGE

250mm φ
WELDOLET

PUMP
NO. 3

FUTURE
PUMP
NO. 4

500 x 400
RED

400 x 300
RED

300 mm

500 mm

500 mm

21
1D 1E

300mm φ MAGNETIC FLOW METER
PROVIDE SPOOL PIECE
DIVISION 17

IPT PIPING	BOOSTER STATION 8-25D
DATE January 2001	PIPING FLOOR PLAN 1D

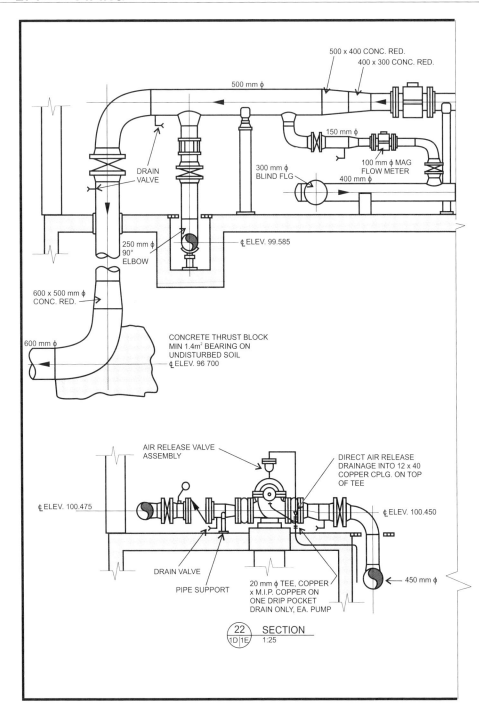

500 x 400 CONC. RED.

400 x 300 CONC. RED.

500 mm φ

DRAIN VALVE

150 mm φ

100 mm φ MAG FLOW METER

300 mm φ BLIND FLG

400 mm φ

250 mm φ 90° ELBOW

₵ ELEV. 99.585

600 x 500 mm φ CONC. RED.

600 mm φ

CONCRETE THRUST BLOCK MIN 1.4m² BEARING ON UNDISTURBED SOIL
₵ ELEV. 96 700

AIR RELEASE VALVE ASSEMBLY

DIRECT AIR RELEASE DRAINAGE INTO 12 x 40 COPPER CPLG. ON TOP OF TEE

₵ ELEV. 100.475

₵ ELEV. 100.450

DRAIN VALVE

PIPE SUPPORT

20 mm φ TEE, COPPER x M.I.P. COPPER ON ONE DRIP POCKET DRAIN ONLY, EA. PUMP

450 mm φ

(22) 1D 1E   SECTION 1:25

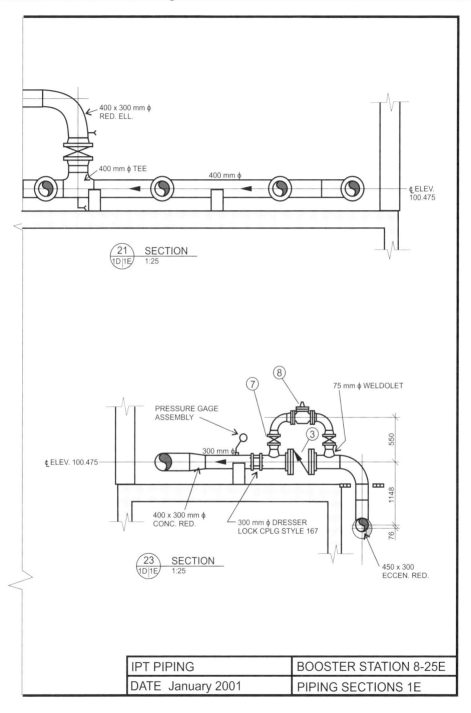

400 x 300 mm φ
RED. ELL.

400 mm φ TEE

400 mm φ

℄ ELEV.
100.475

21 SECTION
1D 1E   1:25

8

7

75 mm φ WELDOLET

PRESSURE GAGE
ASSEMBLY

3

550

300 mm φ

℄ ELEV. 100.475

1148

400 x 300 mm φ
CONC. RED.

300 mm φ DRESSER
LOCK CPLG STYLE 167

76

23 SECTION
1D 1E   1:25

450 x 300
ECCEN. RED.

IPT PIPING	BOOSTER STATION 8-25E
DATE January 2001	PIPING SECTIONS 1E

57. Section view 21, shown on drawing 8-25E, is shown as if viewed from the front.
- ❏ true
- ❏ false

58. The 450 x 300 mm eccentric reducer shown on section view 23 is:
- ❏ above floor level
- ❏ below floor level
- ❏ at floor level
- ❏ none of the above

59. What method is used to reduce the size of the 500 mm pipe down to 300 mm as shown in section view 21 on drawing 25E?

Answer: _____

60. What diameter is the Flow Meter?
- ❏ 500 mm
- ❏ 300 mm
- ❏ 150 mm
- ❏ 100 mm

61. Is there only one Drip Pocket Drain, or one on each pump?

Answer: _____

The following information refers to IPT's Pipe Spool Drawing 8-26

This pipe spool is an isometric single line drawing of a section of pipe. As noted earlier, the single line represents the center of the pipe and all related fittings. This drawing includes a list of materials that will be used to make the spool piece. The list of materials is referenced to the drawing by item numbers ranging from item 1 to item 18. Items 1 to 6 list the pipe that is needed, their nominal size and the cut length for each pipe. The abbreviation BE stands for bevel end.

The standard bevel preparation on manufactured pipe fittings is 37½º, therefore the pipe ends will also be beveled to the same angle. All other fittings are noted in the list of materials. It is common for the fittings to be abbreviated as shown in this drawing.

On the drawing, dimensions are from the center to center of elbows. For flanges the dimensions are from the gasket face of the flange. Pipe handbooks, such as IPT's Pipe Trades Handbook, list the center to face dimension of elbows and the gasket face to end dimensions of flanges. The cut length of any pipe is determined by subtracting the fitting dimensions from the overall length shown on the drawing, and allowing for any weld gap or thread engagement in the case of threaded fittings. The pipe spool will be fabricated using pipe stands and positioners. A procedure called roll welding is used as much as possible to make the job quicker and easier. This method involves the assembly and welding of as many individual straight lengths of pipe and pipe to fittings as is practical. These sub-assemblies or separate pieces are fitted together to make up the spool and the final welds are welded in position. The alternative is to make up the spool piece by piece in its actual position. This is usually more difficult and time consuming.

The following questions refer to IPT's Pipe Spool Drawing 8-26

62. What is the grade of pipe used for this job?
- ❏ A105
- ❏ A234
- ❏ A53-B
- ❏ A106-B

ITM	QTY	SIZE A53-B SMLS Pipe	CUT LGTH
1	1	4-STD (0.237) BExBE	3'-7 1/8"
2	1	4-STD (0.237) BExBE	4'-4 7/8"
3	1	3-STD (0.216) BExBE	5'-1 7/8"
4	1	3-STD (0.216) BExBE	6'-8 1/4"
5	1	3-STD (0.216) BExBE	11'-10 1/8"
6	1	3/4-STD (0.113) PExPE	0'-9 11/16"
		A105 Flanges	Schedule
7	1	4 150# RF Weldneck	STD
8	1	3 150# RF Weldneck	STD
		A234-WPB Fittings	
9	1	4 45 LR BW Elbow	STD
10	1	4 90 LR BW Elbow	STD
11	1	3 90 LR BW Elbow	STD
12	1	3 45 LR BW Elbow	STD
13	1	4x3 BW Red. Tee	STD
		A105 Fittings	STD/STD
14	1	3/4 TH Plug Hex. Hd.	
15	1	3/4x3 150# Sockolet	
		Accessories	Wght
16	1	4 gate valve	
17	1	3/4 ball valve	1#
18	1	shoe	
		Weight 327#	

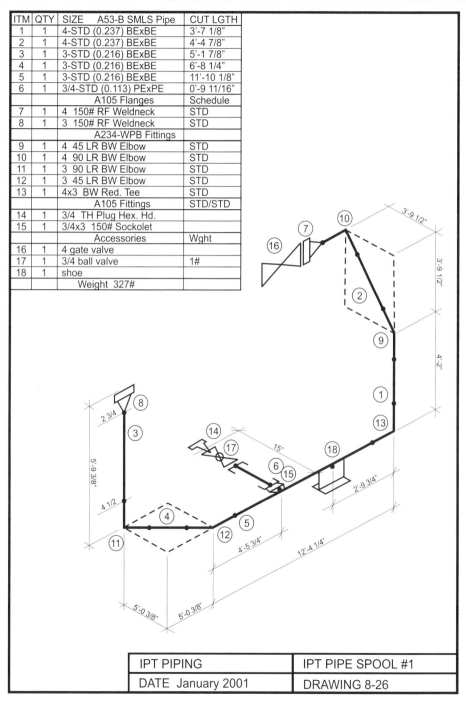

IPT PIPING	IPT PIPE SPOOL #1
DATE January 2001	DRAWING 8-26

63. Calculate how much allowance has been made for weld gap to determine the cut length of item #3 if the face to end length of item #8 is 2¾" and the face to center dimension of item #11 is 4½".

Answer: _____

64. What grade of material is used for the flanges?
   ❏ A105
   ❏ A234
   ❏ A53-B
   ❏ A106-B

65. How far will the center of the shoe be located from the center of item #13?

Answer: _____

66. What will the total weight of this spool be when fabricated?

Answer: _____

67. Which of the listed item numbers refers to the reducing tee?
   ❏ item #6
   ❏ item #8
   ❏ item #11
   ❏ item #13

68. What grade of material is used for the elbows?
   ❏ A105
   ❏ A234
   ❏ A53-B
   ❏ A106-B

69. What is the cut length of item #2?

Answer: _____

70. Determine the amount of 3 inch standard wall pipe needed for this order.

Answer: _____

71. Write out the following abbreviations.

BE _____
PE _____
RF _____
LR _____
BW _____

72. Number 16 is a
   ❏ 4 inch ball valve
   ❏ 4 inch gate valve
   ❏ 3/4 inch ball valve
   ❏ 3/4 inch gate valve

73. Indicate the item number where the pipe size changes from 4 inches to 3 inches.

Answer: _____

74. Item 7 and item 8 are identical weld neck flanges.
   ❏ true
   ❏ false

The following information refers to Depropanizer Reflux Drawings 8-27A and 8-27B

Drawing 8-27A shows a piping plan view, and drawing 8-27B shows two elevations views looking at the unit from the left and right sides at ground level. Plan view drawing 8-27A is a view looking down from the top between match line A and match line C. These two match lines are coordinated with two other drawings. The two vessels, A-575 and C-550, and their related piping are included on both drawings. Drawing 8-27B has the two elevation views, A-A and B-B, as identified in drawing 8-27A. The orientation of elevation A-A and elevation B-B on drawing 8-27B are more easily understood by comparing the direction the arrows are pointing when looking at section lines A-A and B-B on drawing 8-27A.

The general notes on both drawings include the line designations used on the piping. Each line is identified on the drawing by using these abbreviations included in the general notes, then followed by the line number and size.

The following questions refer to Depropanizer Reflux Drawings 8-27A and 8-27B.

75. List the two drawing numbers that correspond to the two match lines identified on drawing 1.

Answer: _____

76. What is the size of the pipe used for line P-526-4"-A150?
   - ❏ 2 inch N.P.S.
   - ❏ 3 inch N.P.S.
   - ❏ 4 inch N.P.S.
   - ❏ 6 inch N.P.S.

77. What do the letters HO in the general notes of drawing 1 refer to?

Answer: _____

78. Determine the direction of flow in line P-578-2"-A150 on drawing 8-27A as the line travels through match line 3.

Answer: _____

79. What is the centerline elevation of vessel A-575?

Answer: _____

80. Do the valve dimensions shown on drawing 8-27B make allowance for gasket thickness?

Answer: _____

81. Calculate the center to center distance between vessel A575 and C550.
   - ❏ 104' - 6½"
   - ❏ 109' - 6"
   - ❏ 4' - 11½"
   - ❏ 5' - 0½

82. Calculate the difference in height between the T.O.S. dimensions shown in Elevation A-A?

Answer: _____

83. What is the centerline elevation of line CW-552-6"-A150 found in Elevation B-B?

Answer: _____

84. What is the height from ground level to the top of steel for the pipe rack?

Answer: _____

85. From elevation B-B, lines BD-552, BD-527, and P-578 are all the same elevation.
   - ❏ true
   - ❏ false

86. How far is line CW-552 from match line 3?
   - ❏ 11 inches
   - ❏ 2 ft. 0 in.
   - ❏ 2 ft. 3 in.
   - ❏ 3 ft. 2 in.

87. What is the center to center distance between items P576 and P577?

Answer: _____

88. What is the outlet line elevation of P576 and P577?

Answer: _____

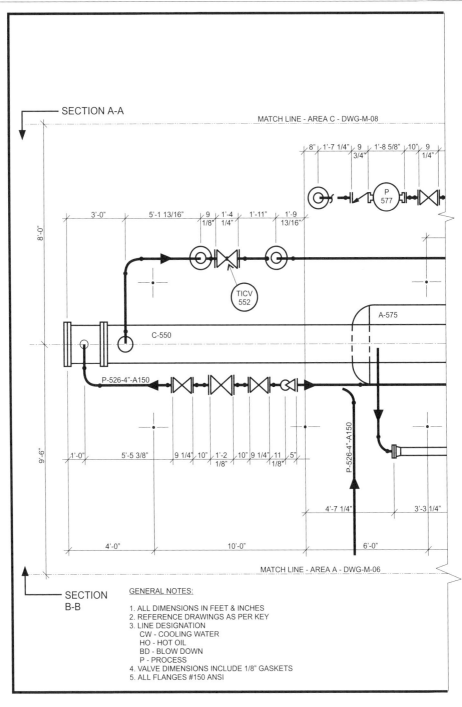

SECTION A-A

MATCH LINE - AREA C - DWG-M-08

8" 1'-7 1/4" 9 3/4" 1'-8 5/8" 10" 9 1/4"

P 577

8'-0"

3'-0" 5'-1 13/16" 9 1/8" 1'-4 1/4" 1'-11" 1'-9 13/16"

TICV 552

A-575

C-550

P-526-4"-A150

9'-6"

1'-0" 5'-5 3/8" 9 1/4" 10" 1'-2 1/8" 10" 9 1/4" 11 1/8" 5"

P-526-4"-A150

4'-7 1/4" 3'-3 1/4"

4'-0" 10'-0" 6'-0"

MATCH LINE - AREA A - DWG-M-06

SECTION B-B

GENERAL NOTES:

1. ALL DIMENSIONS IN FEET & INCHES
2. REFERENCE DRAWINGS AS PER KEY
3. LINE DESIGNATION
   CW - COOLING WATER
   HO - HOT OIL
   BD - BLOW DOWN
   P - PROCESS
4. VALVE DIMENSIONS INCLUDE 1/8" GASKETS
5. ALL FLANGES #150 ANSI

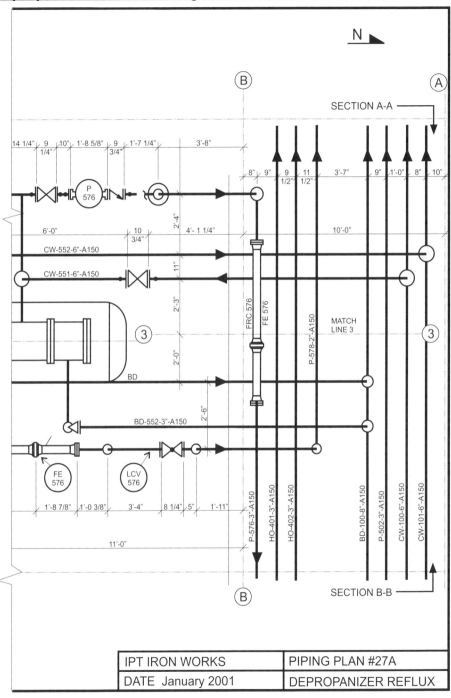

N ▶

Ⓑ

Ⓐ

SECTION A-A

14 1/4" · 9 1/4" · 10" · 1'-8 5/8" · 9 3/4" · 1'-7 1/4" · 3'-8"

8" · 9" · 9 1/2" · 11 1/2" · 3'-7" · 9" · 1'-0" · 8" · 10"

P 576

6'-0"

10 3/4"

2'-4"

4'- 1 1/4"

10'-0"

CW-552-6"-A150

CW-551-6"-A150

11"

FRC 576

FE 576

2'-3"

P-578-2"-A150

MATCH LINE 3

Ⓒ 3

3

2'-0"

BD

BD-552-3"-A150

2'-6"

FE 576

LCV 576

1'-8 7/8" · 1'-0 3/8" · 3'-4" · 8 1/4" · 5" · 1'-11"

P-576-3"-A150

HO-401-3"-A150

HO-402-3"-A150

BD-100-8"-A150

P-502-3"-A150

CW-100-6"-A150

CW-101-6"-A150

11'-0"

Ⓑ

SECTION B-B

IPT IRON WORKS	PIPING PLAN #27A
DATE January 2001	DEPROPANIZER REFLUX

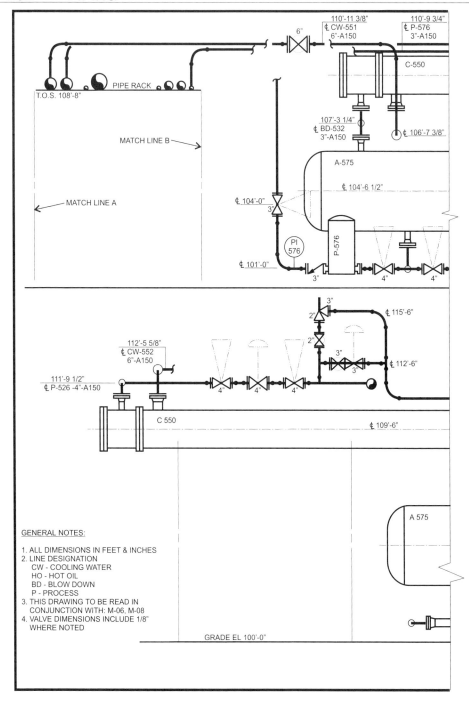

110'-11 3/8"
⌀ CW-551
6"-A150

110'-9 3/4"
⌀ P-576
3"-A150

6"

C-550

PIPE RACK
T.O.S. 108'-8"

107'-3 1/4"
⌀ BD-532
3"-A150

⌀ 106'-7 3/8"

MATCH LINE B

A-575

⌀ 104'-6 1/2"

MATCH LINE A

⌀ 104'-0"
3"

PI
576

P-576

⌀ 101'-0"

3"   4"   4"

3"

2"

115'-6"

112'-5 5/8"
⌀ CW-552
6"-A150

2"

3"

112'-6"

111'-9 1/2"
⌀ P-526 -4"-A150

3"

4"   4"   4"

C 550

109'-6"

A 575

GENERAL NOTES:

1. ALL DIMENSIONS IN FEET & INCHES
2. LINE DESIGNATION
    CW - COOLING WATER
    HO - HOT OIL
    BD - BLOW DOWN
    P - PROCESS
3. THIS DRAWING TO BE READ IN
    CONJUNCTION WITH: M-06, M-08
4. VALVE DIMENSIONS INCLUDE 1/8"
    WHERE NOTED

GRADE EL 100'-0"

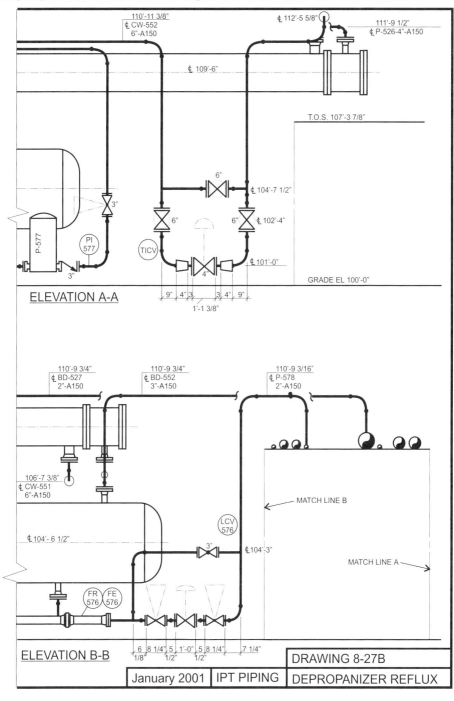

ELEVATION A-A

110'-11 3/8"
¢ CW-552
6"-A150

¢ 112'-5 5/8"

111'-9 1/2"
¢ P-526-4"-A150

¢ 109'-6"

T.O.S. 107'-3 7/8"

6"

¢ 104'-7 1/2"

3"

6"   6"

¢ 102'-4"

P-577   PI 577   TICV

4"

¢ 101'-0"

3"

GRADE EL 100'-0"

9" 4" 3"   3" 4" 9"

1'-1 3/8"

ELEVATION B-B

110'-9 3/4"
¢ BD-527
2"-A150

110'-9 3/4"
¢ BD-552
3"-A150

110'-9 3/16"
¢ P-578
2"-A150

106'-7 3/8"
¢ CW-551
6"-A150

MATCH LINE B

¢ 104'- 6 1/2"

LCV 576

MATCH LINE A

3"

¢ 104'-3"

FR 576   FE 576

6   8 1/4" 5 1'-0" 5 8 1/4"   7 1/4"
1/8"   1/2"   1/2"

| January 2001 | IPT PIPING | DRAWING 8-27B |
| | | DEPROPANIZER REFLUX |

The following information refers to IPT's Pipe Spool Drawing 8-28

Pipe Spool Drawing 8-28 is an isometric drawing of a section of line that will be fabricated on site or in a welding shop. The physical dimension of each spool is governed by the size of the pieces that can be fabricated and shipped, or field fabricated and installed in position.

This particular spool will be made and shipped in three pieces:

- Piece one is the larger Tee shaped section including a tee, several elbows, flanges, and ending at the two 12 inch block valves.
- Piece two is the small piece at G-104 A, which includes the two 12 inch weld neck flanges, one elbow and the short piece of 12 inch line and a ¾" coupling for PI.
- Piece three is the suction piece at G-104 B, also including several elbows and flanges.

Isometric spool drawings of this type include all valves, flanges, instrumentation connections, or any other equipment that connects to it. All the dimensions needed to fabricate the pipe are included. The dimensions for the supports under the 12 inch elbows have been left out. See note: "Field Dim.". The dimensions for the supports will be measured and fabricated on site. A bill of materials is supplied with isometric spool drawings itemizing the parts required to make up the line.

The direction symbol on the drawing indicating North is common for spool drawings. Standard direction compass orientation applies. South is 180° from North, and West and East are 90° either direction from North. Some direction symbols include up and down, although it is understood on this drawing which part of the spool runs up or down.

The following questions refer to IPT's Pipe Spool Drawing 8-28

89. What is the largest nominal size of pipe used for this spool piece?
    - ❏ 12" NPS
    - ❏ 10" NPS
    - ❏ 6" NPS
    - ❏ 4" NPS

90. What is the center of elbow to face of flange dimension shown on the drawing where this line joins components G-104A or G-104B?

Answer: _____

91. State the size and pressure rating of the couplings used as pump casing drains.

Answer: _____

92. The pump casing drain couplings are threaded.
    - ❏ true
    - ❏ false

93. What is the pressure rating of the spectacle blinds used in the 12 inch line?

    ❏ 150#
    ❏ 300#
    ❏ 600#
    ❏ 900#

94. How much clearance is needed between the two 12 inch weld neck flanges for inserting the spectacle blind?

Answer: _____

95. What is the direction of flow in the 12 inch line below the start-up strainer located by component G-104A?

    ❏ north
    ❏ south
    ❏ up
    ❏ down

96. Referring to revision 1, what has been altered or changed on this drawing?

Answer: _____

97. Referring to the Bill of Materials what is the grade, largest diameter and longest length of stud bolts to be used for bolting some of the flanges for this spool.

Answer: _____

98. Referring to the Bill of Materials, what is the pressure rating of the 2 - 1½ inch socket weld 90° elbows?

    ❏ 150#
    ❏ 300#
    ❏ 2000#
    ❏ 3000#

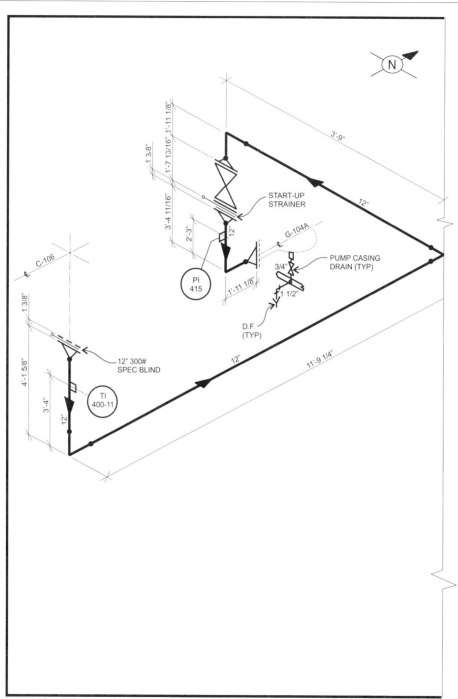

N

3'-9"

12"

1 3/8"
1'-7 13/16"
1'-11 1/8"

START-UP
STRAINER

3'-4 11/16"

2'-3"

12"

G-104A

PUMP CASING
DRAIN (TYP)

3/4"

PI
415

1'-11 1/8"

1 1/2"

C-106

D.F.
(TYP)

1 3/8"

4'-1 5/8"

12" 300#
SPEC BLIND

12"

11'-9 1/4"

3'-4"

TI
400-11

12"

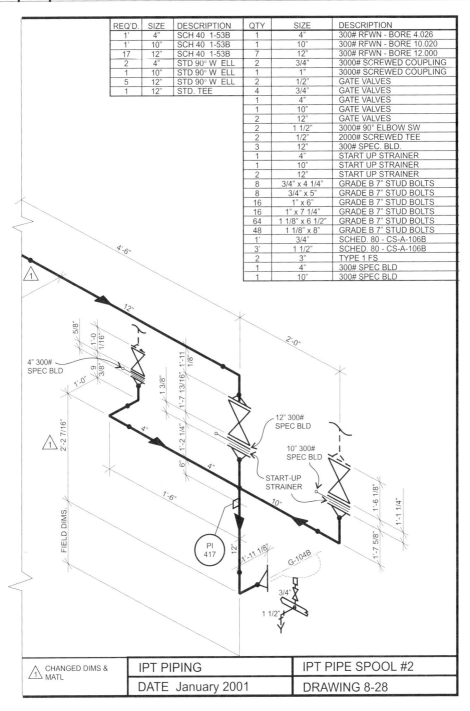

REQ'D.	SIZE	DESCRIPTION	QTY	SIZE	DESCRIPTION
1'	4"	SCH 40 1-53B	1	4"	300# RFWN - BORE 4.026
1'	10"	SCH 40 1-53B	1	10"	300# RFWN - BORE 10.020
17	12"	SCH 40 1-53B	7	12"	300# RFWN - BORE 12.000
2	4"	STD 90° W ELL	2	3/4"	3000# SCREWED COUPLING
1	10"	STD 90° W ELL	1	1"	3000# SCREWED COUPLING
5	12"	STD 90° W ELL	2	1/2"	GATE VALVES
1	12"	STD. TEE	4	3/4"	GATE VALVES
			1	4"	GATE VALVES
			1	10"	GATE VALVES
			2	12"	GATE VALVES
			2	1 1/2"	3000# 90° ELBOW SW
			2	1/2"	2000# SCREWED TEE
			3	12"	300# SPEC. BLD.
			1	4"	START UP STRAINER
			1	10"	START UP STRAINER
			2	12"	START UP STRAINER
			8	3/4" x 4 1/4"	GRADE B 7" STUD BOLTS
			8	3/4" x 5"	GRADE B 7" STUD BOLTS
			16	1" x 6"	GRADE B 7" STUD BOLTS
			16	1" x 7 1/4"	GRADE B 7" STUD BOLTS
			64	1 1/8" x 6 1/2"	GRADE B 7" STUD BOLTS
			48	1 1/8" x 8"	GRADE B 7" STUD BOLTS
			1'	3/4"	SCHED. 80 - CS-A-106B
			3'	1 1/2"	SCHED. 80 - CS-A-106B
			2	3"	TYPE 1 FS
			1	4"	300# SPEC BLD
			1	10"	300# SPEC BLD

CHANGED DIMS & MATL

IPT PIPING	IPT PIPE SPOOL #2
DATE January 2001	DRAWING 8-28

SECTION NINE

RIGGING

Types of Cranes

A crane is a device designed to lift, swing or transport a load to a new position. There are many different types of cranes and lifting devices used for modern day industry. Some crane types are stationary, however most are mobile units operating on wheels or tracks. The lifting capacities of present day cranes are much greater than cranes designed several decades ago, although the appearance, general design, and method of operation is similar. New technolory has advanced the operation of cranes. One example is the use of computerized digital readouts which show the actual lift weight, the load radius, boom length, and the boom angle during the lift. This is extremely beneficial in removing some of the guess work concerning improperly planned lifts. Illustrations #9-1 through #9-6 show the main types of wheeled or track type cranes. These are representations only, not exact models.

Purpose of Rigging Drawings

The purpose of rigging drawings varies from other types of drawings used for fabrication and construction.   Rather than being the guide to make or build something, they are primarily used to show the position of items and to convey all of the important information that is necessary to safely lift an object from one location and reposition it to another location. Rigging prints use the same drawing format as other types of drawings. They have a plan view, an elevation view, and detail views as necessary. All the necessary dimensions will be placed on the drawing including the overall dimensions of the object to be lifted.

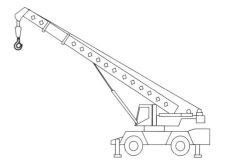

Illustration #9-1 - Rough Terrain Crane

Other information includes the specific location of the crane or cranes, location and height of buildings and other above ground objects that could interfere with the lift. If it is known, the location of underground piping that could affect ground stability is also specified on the drawing.

The purpose of rigging prints is to provide specific data about information that may otherwise be difficult to obtain, and to eliminate possible errors when lifting objects that fall into the critical lift category.

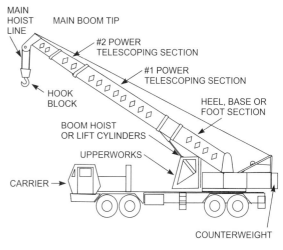

Illustration #9-2 - Carrier Mounted Hydraulic Boom Crane

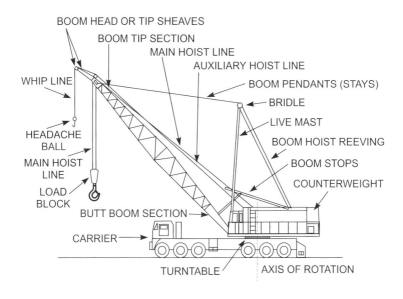

Illustration #9-3 - Carrier Mounted Lattice Boom Crane

Over the years industry has moved in a direction resulting in larger and heavier lifts. Project management companies, government health and safety acts, and insurance companies have placed demands on industry to come up with better ways to guarantee personnel safety and remove any chance of disaster during lifts. Rigging drawings are part of the modern system to remove the "guess work" out of lift preparation, and to improve on the old system of "operate by feel" for hoisting critical lifts.

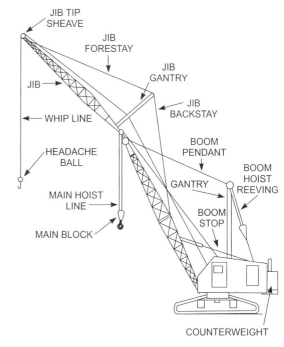

Illustration #9-4 - Crawler Mounted Lattice Boom Crane

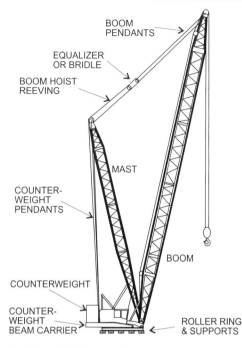

Illustration #9-5 - Ringer Crane

• When special lifting equipment such as non-standard crane configurations will be used.
• The weight of the load exceeds set limits.
• The load weight is close to the crane's lifting capacity, as specified by the crane manufacturer's rating chart.

Criteria other than those listed may be specified to define a critical lift, as one company may have a much lower load weight limit than another. For instance, one company might specify that a lift plan is necessary for any lift over 20 tons in weight, or when a lift is to be made in or around any existing above ground structure.

Designation of a Critical Lift

There are no set rules to define whether a lift is considered critical and thereby requiring a lift study or lift plan. The guidelines will vary from one jurisdiction to another, depending on what is being lifted and where the lift is taking place.

Crane companies and plant owners will often set specific criteria that determines whether a lift study is necessary during new plant construction, or when equipment is being removed or installed in an existing plant.

Some of the factors used to determine whether a lift will be designated as critical are:

• When a load is lifted over or near, operating equipment or electrical power lines.
• When two or more pieces of lifting equipment are required to work in unison.

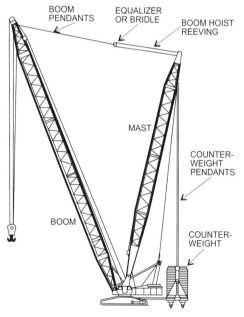

Illustration #9-6 - Trailing Counterweight

Lift Planning Process

The lift plan identifies the requirements needed for the primary areas of every lift. These include:

- The size of crane required and its use to ensure a safe worksite.
- The lift plan identifies what is to be lifted, where it will be lifted from, where it will be placed, and where the lifting crane will be located.
- A lift plan will describe the systematic assessment of important load and site factors. These factors are used to determine the size of crane needed, where it will be located and what site preparations will be required.

A lift plan of some type should be done for all lifts, including those that are non-critical. This plan can be as simple as the supervisor, the crane operator, and the riggers discussing the lift prior to it being made. An ill prepared one ton lift of a neon sign can be more hazardous than a 400 ton lift of a pressure vessel in an operating refinery if something is left unaccounted for and a mishap occurs.

Important Load Factors

Determining the exact weight of the object to be lifted is critical to the development of a safe lift plan. Manufacturing data of rigging hardware, engineering calculations referring to the load weight, shipping manifests, and any other available data should be on hand to determine the weight of the load. The load weight will include all rigging hardware including the crane hook block and hoist lines, spreader bars, slings, and shackles. It is generally acceptable to determine the load weight by including all hardware hanging below the crane boom tip as part of the lift.

In addition, any items that add to the weight of the crane including boom extensions, jibs, etc., are factored in to determine the gross weight of the lift.

The load chart of any crane specifies the gross lifting capacity of that particular crane configuration, at a specific horizontal distance from the center of gravity of the load to the center of rotation or center pin of the crane. It should be noted that the radius of the load determined from the center pin of the crane to the center of gravity of the load refers to a freely suspended load.

Any possible boom or crane component deflection due to the load weight coming off the ground must always be considered when planning a lift. Deflection can cause the load to swing out, thereby changing the initial lifting radius, which in turn affects the ability of the crane to safely pick up a load when it is set up close to capacity at a given radius.

Determination of Important Site Factors

A lift plan will include any site factors that have to be assessed prior to the lift. Soil conditions are always a major consideration for any lift. Even for lighter loads, a crane must be level and stable to work as it was designed. A site may appear to be level and have a solid base, however if there are any underground cavities or soft soil conditions the ground may not be capable of supporting the bearing load. These factors could include such things as; previous ground work, underground ducts, piping, sewers, building backfill, or any number of other things. Reliable information and perhaps a soil inspection may be required to determine the best method to support the crane.

Other site factors, including proximity to above ground structures that may interfere with the load in any way between the lift point and the load destination point must be identified. A determination must be made to see if anything will interfere with the movement of the load or swinging of the crane. Above ground structures like buildings, towers, electrical lines, or working in a plant site with operating equipment, often determines if a lift will be designated as critical. Even a light load suspended on a conventional crane boom can cause the boom to collapse if the boom accidentally touches a structure. Therefore, in confined areas, a lift study must be done to avoid unforeseen hazards.

Note: Rigging Drawings 9-7 through 9-10 are example drawings only, do not transpose this information to any type of similar lift! Information provided courtesy of ProCrane Engineering, a division of Sterling Crane.

Rigging Drawings 9-7A and 9-7B, Installation of Fin Fan Cooler

The following information refers to rigging drawing 9-7, Installation of Fin Fan Cooler. A fin fan cooler is a type of heat exchanger that is not enclosed in a vessel shell. The tubes have spiral fins to allow a better heat transfer for the air blowing through from a large fan or fans. It is somewhat similar in design to an automotive radiator.

This drawing contains a plan view, an elevation view, a perspective view and a rigging detail view. The layout of these rigging drawings is similar to other drawing formats in that it has a title block, general notes, and an area similar to a Bill of Materials. This information itemizes the required rigging hardware and specific information relating to the crane and other lift information.

The plan view shows the crane location in relation to above ground structures, and indicates the initial lift position of the load, the radius, and the final placement of the load. It also shows the swing route of the load.

The elevation view shows specific information about any building steel or structure heights, and the crane and its boom. Drawing 9-7 has a view called the rigging detail and it includes the required slings, shackles, and other rigging components. It also illustrates where each of these components will be used.

The perspective view is a three dimensional view of the area where the lift will be made.

As with many three-dimensional computer produced drawings, this view can be illustrated from any angle resulting in the best perspective of the lift location.

The following questions refer to Rigging Drawing 9-7.

1. What will be the boom length needed to complete this lift, as stated on the drawing?
   - ❏ 39 feet
   - ❏ 133 feet, 6 inches
   - ❏ 137 feet, 11 inches
   - ❏ 145 feet, 10 inches

2. What is the weight of the fin fan?
   - ❏ 51630 lbs.
   - ❏ 54780 lbs.
   - ❏ 57100 lbs.
   - ❏ 66500 lbs.

3. How much does the rigging weigh?
   - ❏ 2320 lbs.
   - ❏ 2840 lbs.
   - ❏ 3150 lbs.
   - ❏ 4580 lbs.

4. When lifting the load, the crane is operating at what percentage of the rated chart capacity?
    - ❏ 100%
    - ❏ 86%
    - ❏ 14%
    - ❏ not stated

5. What is the maximum chart capacity for the crane set up shown on the drawing?
    - ❏ 97000 lbs.
    - ❏ 66500 lbs.
    - ❏ 57100 lbs.
    - ❏ 51630 lbs.

6. What is the weight of the counterweights?

    Answer: _____

7. If, at the time this lift was to be made, there was a wind blowing at 30 mph from the east, would the lift be postponed?
    - ❏ yes
    - ❏ no

8. What is the maximum wind speed allowed according to this drawing?
    - ❏ 10 mph
    - ❏ 15 mph
    - ❏ 20 mph
    - ❏ 30 mph

9. Determine whether this statement is true or false: "Tag lines must be used to control this lift at all times".
    - ❏ true
    - ❏ false

10. The anticipated swing radius measured from the crane center pin to the center of the load or rigging is:
    - ❏ 16 feet,11 inches
    - ❏ 39 feet
    - ❏ 29 feet, 8 inches
    - ❏ 32 feet, 3 inches

11. State in tons the working load limited (WLL) of the largest shackle used?
    - ❏ 2 tons
    - ❏ 10 tons
    - ❏ 12 tons
    - ❏ 25 tons

12. Determine if this statement is true or false. The shackles required to attach the load to the slings are rated at a 12 ton working load limit.
    - ❏ true
    - ❏ false

13. What will be the clearance between the boom and the structure when the load is in the final set position?

    Answer: _____

14. The number of parts of line that the crane load block will be reeved to is:
    - ❏ 2 parts
    - ❏ 4 parts
    - ❏ 6 parts
    - ❏ 8 parts

15. After the crane lifts the load, the boom will swing in a clockwise direction to position the load.
    - ❏ true
    - ❏ false

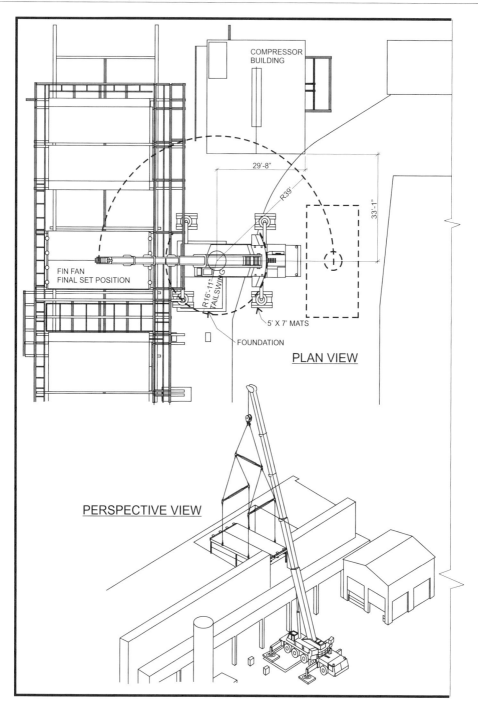

COMPRESSOR BUILDING

29'-8"

R39'

33'-1"

FIN FAN
FINAL SET POSITION

R16'-1"
TAILSWING

5' X 7' MATS

FOUNDATION

PLAN VIEW

PERSPECTIVE VIEW

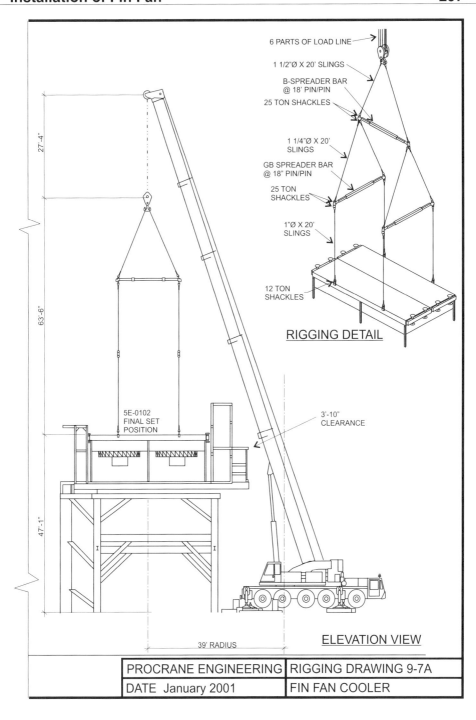

6 PARTS OF LOAD LINE

1 1/2"Ø X 20' SLINGS

B-SPREADER BAR
@ 18' PIN/PIN

25 TON SHACKLES

1 1/4"Ø X 20'
SLINGS

GB SPREADER BAR
@ 18" PIN/PIN

25 TON
SHACKLES

1"Ø X 20'
SLINGS

12 TON
SHACKLES

RIGGING DETAIL

27'-4"

63'-6"

47'-1"

5E-0102
FINAL SET
POSITION

3'-10"
CLEARANCE

39' RADIUS

ELEVATION VIEW

PROCRANE ENGINEERING	RIGGING DRAWING 9-7A
DATE January 2001	FIN FAN COOLER

CRANE/LOAD/LIFT INFORMATION

NOTE: EQUIPMENT SIZE

EQUIPMENT TYPE - FIN FAN COOLER

CRANE INFO.	
CRANE TYPE	DEMAG AC435
COUNTERWEIGHT	97,000 lbs.
BOOM LENGTH	133.5 ft.
MAST LENGTH	-
LIFT RADIUS	39 ft.
CRANE CAPACITY	66,500 lbs.
LOAD INFO	FULL LOAD
EQUIP. WEIGHT	51,630 lbs.
RIGGING WEIGHT	3,150 lbs.
LOAD BLOCK	2,320 lbs.
HEADACHE BALL	-
AUX. HEAD	-
JIB AND BOOM EXT STOWED	-
LIFT INFO	
TOTAL LIFT WEIGHT	57,100 lbs.
% OF CHART CAPACITY	86%

RIGGING LIST

ITEM	QTY	DESCRIPTION
1	2	SLING, 1 1/2 in. DIA X 20 ft.
2	4	SLING, 1 1/4 in. DIA X 20 ft.
3	4	SLING, 1 in. DIA X 20 ft.
4	8	SHACKLE, 25 TON
5	4	SHACKLE, 12 TON
6	1	SPREADER BAR, "B" TYPE @ 18 ft. PIN/PIN
7	2	SPREADER BAR, "GB" TYPE @ 18 ft. PIN/PIN
8		

PROCEDURE:
1. POSITON CRANE AS SHOWN IN PLAN VIEW
2. ATTACH RIGGING TO COOLER
3. HOIST COOLER TO CLEAR OBSTRUCTIONS
4. SWING COUNTER CLOCKWISE UNTIL OVER FINAL SET POSITION
5. LOWER COOLER INTO FINAL SET POSITION AND SECURE
6. DISCONNECT RIGGING

GENERAL NOTES:
1. ENSURE FIRM AND LEVEL FOUNDATION FOR CRANE
2. MAXIMUM WIND SPEED NOT TO EXCEED 20 MPH DURING LIFT
3. TAG LINES MAY BE USED DURING THE LIFT TO CONTROL THE LOAD
4. ALL WIRE ROPE SLINGS TO BE IPS, IWRC

PROCRANE ENGINEERING	RIGGING DRAWING 9-7B
DATE January 2001	FIN FAN COOLER

Rigging Drawings 9-8A and 9-8B, Installation of Heat Exchanger

Rigging Drawing 9-8 is a single crane lift of a heat exchanger. There are a number of above ground obstructions that could interfere with the lift. The drawing consists of a plan view, an elevation view, a perspective view, and a rigging detail. The perspective view is for visual representation only and therefore is not dimensioned. The lift radius will change during the lift, starting with the longer radius at the beginning of the lift, and ending with the shorter radius.

The following questions refer to rigging drawing 9-8.

16. What type of crane is used to make this lift?

Answer: _____

17. State the maximum boom length needed to complete this lift.

Answer: _____

18. What is the weight of the heat exchanger?
   - ❏ 24200 lbs.
   - ❏ 63580 lbs.
   - ❏ 67760 lbs.
   - ❏ 83500 lbs.

19. How much does the rigging weigh including the load block?
   - ❏ 1150 lbs.
   - ❏ 2680 lbs.
   - ❏ 3245 lbs.
   - ❏ 4180 lbs.

20. When lifting the load, the crane is operating at what percentage of the rated chart capacity?
   - ❏ 100%
   - ❏ 81%
   - ❏ 19%
   - ❏ not shown

21. Determine if this statement is true or false. The crane will require a counterweight in excess of 13.5 tons to safely perform this lift.
   - ❏ true
   - ❏ false

22. Determine if this statement is true or false. At a lift radius of 29 feet the crane capacity for this lift is 41.75 tons.
   - ❏ true
   - ❏ false

23. As specified in the rigging drawing, what is the length and diameter of the heat exchanger?

Answer: _____

24. Which of the following terms describes the part of the heat exchanger that the rigging will attach to?
   - ❏ shackle
   - ❏ lifting lugs
   - ❏ heads
   - ❏ support saddles

25. The direction the crane will swing after it lifts the heat exchanger off the back of the truck will be:
   - ❏ clockwise
   - ❏ counter-clockwise

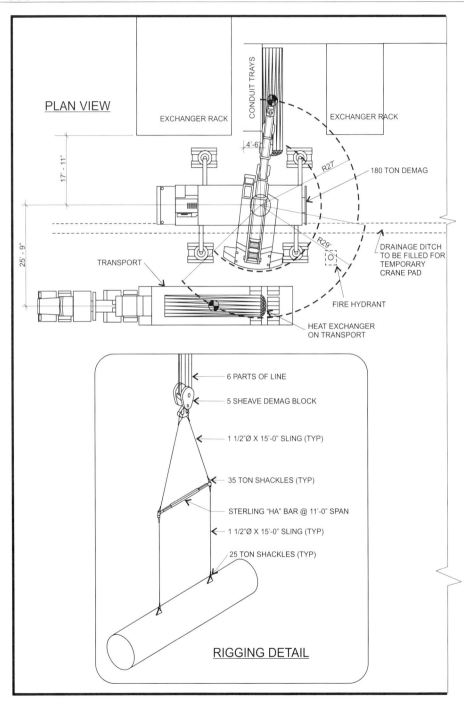

PLAN VIEW

CONDUIT TRAYS

EXCHANGER RACK

EXCHANGER RACK

4'-6"

17' - 11"

R27'

180 TON DEMAG

25' - 9"

R29'

DRAINAGE DITCH
TO BE FILLED FOR
TEMPORARY
CRANE PAD

TRANSPORT

FIRE HYDRANT

HEAT EXCHANGER
ON TRANSPORT

6 PARTS OF LINE

5 SHEAVE DEMAG BLOCK

1 1/2"Ø X 15'-0" SLING (TYP)

35 TON SHACKLES (TYP)

STERLING "HA" BAR @ 11'-0" SPAN

1 1/2"Ø X 15'-0" SLING (TYP)

25 TON SHACKLES (TYP)

RIGGING DETAIL

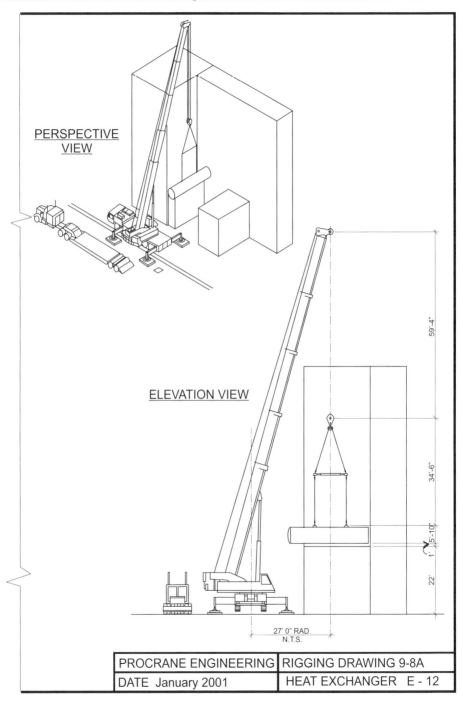

PERSPECTIVE
VIEW

ELEVATION VIEW

59'-4"

34'-6"

5'-10"

1'

22'

27' 0" RAD.
N.T.S.

PROCRANE ENGINEERING	RIGGING DRAWING 9-8A
DATE January 2001	HEAT EXCHANGER E - 12

CRANE/LOAD/LIFT INFORMATION

NOTE: EQUIPMENT SIZE 27' - 10 3/4" X 5' - 4" DIA

CRANE INFO.	
CRANE TYPE	180 TON DEMAG
COUNTERWEIGHT	24,200 lbs.
BOOM LENGTH	115 ft. 3 in.
MAST LENGTH	N/A
LIFT RADIUS	29 ft. 0 in.
CRANE CAPACITY	83,500 lbs.
LOAD INFO.	
EQUIP. WEIGHT	63,580 lbs.
RIGGING WEIGHT	1,500 lbs.
LOAD BLOCK	2,680 lbs.
HEADACHE BALL	N/A
AUX. HEAD	N/A
JIB AND BOOM EXT STOWED	N/A
LIFT INFO.	
TOTAL LIFT WEIGHT	67,760 lbs.
% OF CHART CAPACITY	81%

RIGGING LIST

ITEM	QTY	DESCRIPTION
1	4	SLING, 1 1/2 in. DIA x 15 ft.
2		
3		
4	4	SHACKLE, 35 TON
5	2	SHACKLE, 25 TON
6		
7	1	SPREADER BAR, "HA" TYPE 11 ft. 0 in.
8		

PROCEDURE:
1. POSITON CRANE AS SHOWN IN PLAN VIEW
2. ATTACH CRANE RIGGING TO EXCHANGER
3. HOIST EXCHANGER CLEAR OF TRANSPORT
4. SWING COUNTER-CLOCKWISE ENSURING IT CLEARS THE EXISTING EXCHANGER RACK
5. POSITION EXCHANGER ABOVE FINAL SET POSITION AND LOWER
6. SECURE EXCHANGER AND REMOVE RIGGING

GENERAL NOTES:
1. ENSURE FIRM AND LEVEL FOUNDATION FOR CRANE
2. MAXIMUM WIND SPEED NOT TO EXCEED 20 MPH DURING LIFT
3. TAG LINES MAY BE USED DURING THE LIFT TO CONTROL THE LOAD
4. ALL WIRE ROPE SLINGS TO BE IPS, IWRC

PROCRANE ENGINEERING	RIGGING DRAWING 9-8B
DATE January 2001	HEAT EXCHANGER E-12

26. The term used to describe the piece of rigging equipment which keeps the two vertical leg slings an equal distance apart is:
   - ❏ balance beam
   - ❏ separator bar
   - ❏ spreader bar
   - ❏ equalizer beam

27. State the ground work required to stabilize the drainage ditch for this lift.

Answer: _____

28. Calculate the total vertical height from the ground to the center of the boom tip sheaves of the crane during the lift.
   - ❏ 27 feet 10 inches
   - ❏ 34 feet 6 inches
   - ❏ 93 feet 10 inches
   - ❏ 122 feet 8 inches

29. Determine if this statement is true or false. The crane wheels can remain in contact with the ground as long as the outriggers are fully extended and supporting the crane.
   - ❏ true
   - ❏ false

30. How far is the center of the truck and trailer positioned away from the center of the crane?

Answer: _____

31. Is a constant lift radius of 27 feet maintained throughout the entire lift movement?

Answer: _____

Rigging Drawing 9-9A, 9-9B and 9-9C, Installation of Module

The following information refers to rigging drawings 9-9A, 9-9B and 9-9C, Installation of Module. This drawing details the use of a crane equipped with a superlift attachment. Depending on the intended use, a superlift adds extra counterweight, thus allowing extra boom length for increased lifting height and/or load radius. It can also increase the lifting capacity depending on the configuration. For drawing 9-9, the superlift adds extra counterweight to increase the load radius. The crane type used is a crawler (has tracks rather than tires) with a conventional boom. The term conventional boom relates to non-hydraulic lattice booms. The overall length of this type of boom is increased or decreased by adding or subtracting boom sections.

The following questions refer to Rigging Drawing 9-9.

32. The total mass of the counterweight with the superlift added would be:
   - ❏ 40 tonne
   - ❏ 60 tonne
   - ❏ 120 tonne
   - ❏ 160 tonne

33. State the approximate weight of module 68-B in kilograms.

Answer: _____

34. What will be the lift radius for removal of module 68-B from the transport unit?
   - ❏ 45. 92 feet
   - ❏ 64.32 feet
   - ❏ 72.87 feet
   - ❏ 91.45 feet

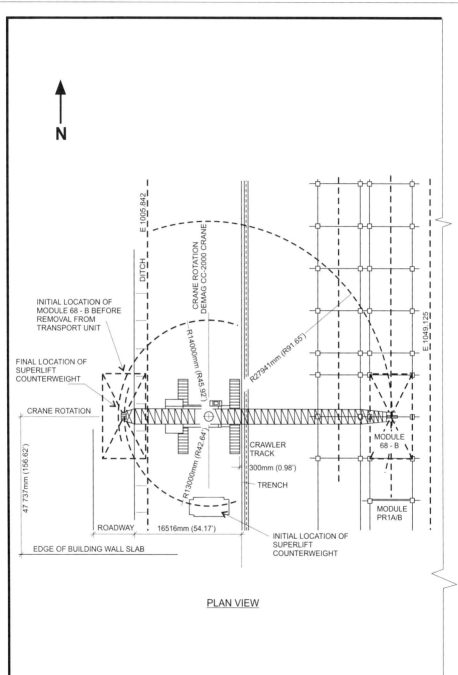

N

E 1005 842

DITCH

CRANE ROTATION
DEMAG CC-2000 CRANE

INITIAL LOCATION OF
MODULE 68 - B BEFORE
REMOVAL FROM
TRANSPORT UNIT

FINAL LOCATION OF
SUPERLIFT
COUNTERWEIGHT

CRANE ROTATION

R14000mm (R45.92')

R27941mm (R91.65')

E 1049.125

R13000mm (R42.64')

CRAWLER
TRACK

MODULE
68 - B

300mm (0.98')

TRENCH

47 737mm (156.62')

ROADWAY

16516mm (54.17')

MODULE
PR1A/B

INITIAL LOCATION OF
SUPERLIFT
COUNTERWEIGHT

EDGE OF BUILDING WALL SLAB

PLAN VIEW

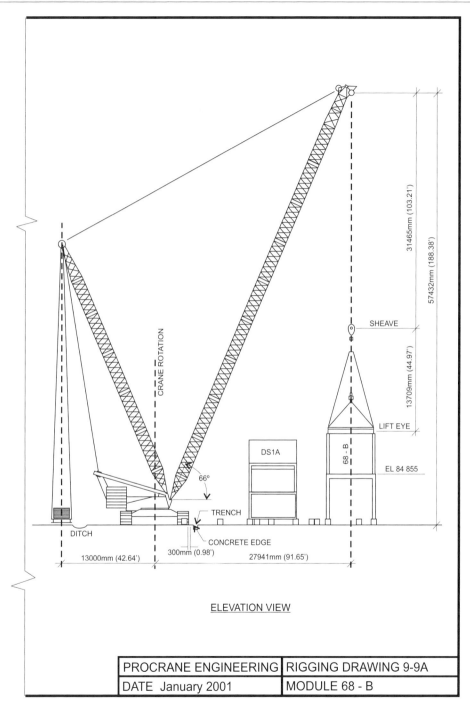

CRANE ROTATION

31465mm (103.21')

57432mm (188.38')

SHEAVE

13709mm (44.97')

LIFT EYE

DS1A

68 - B

EL 84 855

66°

TRENCH

CONCRETE EDGE

DITCH

300mm (0.98')

13000mm (42.64')

27941mm (91.65')

ELEVATION VIEW

PROCRANE ENGINEERING	RIGGING DRAWING 9-9A
DATE January 2001	MODULE 68 - B

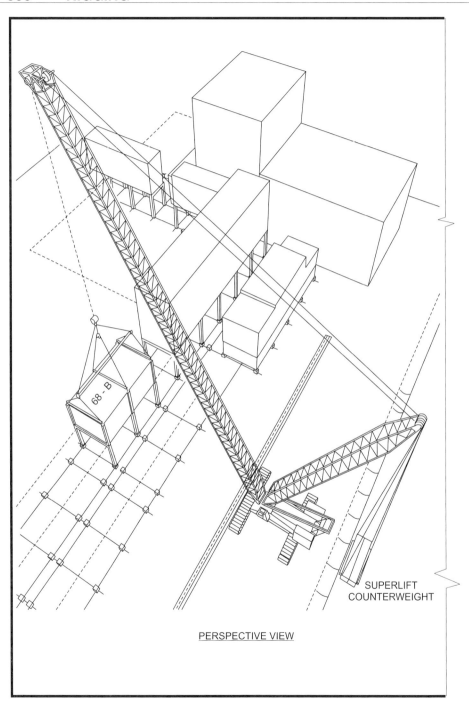

68 - B

SUPERLIFT
COUNTERWEIGHT

PERSPECTIVE VIEW

CRANE/LOAD/LIFT INFORMATION

NOTE: MODULE 68-B WEIGHT 48,637 kg (107,245 lbs.)
MODULE 68-B APPROXIMATE DIMENSIONS: 12 000 mm x 6 500 mm x 5 445 mm
MODULE 68-B APPROXIMATE DIMENSIONS: 40 ft. x 21 ft. x 18 ft. TALL

CRANE INFO.	MODULE 68-B NO SUPERLIFT	MODULE 68-B WITH SUPERLIFT
CRANE TYPE	DEMAG CC 2000 CRAWLER	DEMAG CC 2000 CRAWLER
COUNTERWEIGHT	120 TONNE STD. + 0 TONNE SL	120 TONNE STD. + 40 TONNE SL
BOOM LENGTH	60 m (197 ft.)	60 m (197 ft.)
MAST LENGTH	36 m (118 ft.)	36 m (118 ft.)
LIFT RADIUS	14 000 mm (45.92 ft.)	27 941 mm (91.65 ft.)
CRANE CAPACITY	114 000 kg (251,370 lbs.)	66 207 kg (145,985 lbs.)
LOAD INFO.	ENTIRE MODULE 68-B WEIGHT	ENTIRE MODULE 68-B WEIGHT
EQUIP. WEIGHT	48 637 kg (107,245 lbs.)	48 637 kg (107,245 lbs.)
RIGGING WEIGHT	4 243 kg (9,356 lbs.)	4 243 kg (9,356 lbs.)
LOAD BLOCK	2 721 kg (6,000 lbs.)	2 721 kg (6,000 lbs.)
HEADACHE BALL	N/A	
AUX. HEAD	N/A	
JIB AND BOOM EXT STOWED	N/A	
LIFT INFO.		
TOTAL LIFT WEIGHT	55 601 kg (122,601 lbs.)	55 601 kg (122,601 lbs.)
% OF CHART CAPACITY	49%	84%

RIGGING LIST

REFER TO RIGGING DRAWING #9C

PROCEDURE:
1. POSITON CRANE AS SHOWN IN PLAN VIEW
2. POSITION SUPERLIFT COUNTERWEIGHT SOUTH OF CRANE
3. POSITION TRANSPORT ON ROADWAY SO AS MODULE CENTER OF GRAVITY IS DIRECTLY WEST OF CRANE LOCATION
4. SWING DEMAG CC2000 CRANE BOOM OVER MODULE ON TRANSPORT UNIT
5. ATTACH RIGGING TO MODULE AS SHOWN ON RIGGING DETAIL
6. HOIST MODULE FROM TRANSPORT AND SWING BOOM TO A POSITION DIRECTLY NORTH OF CRANE
7. ATTACH SUPERLIFT COUNTERWEIGHT TO CRANE
8. BOOM DOWN UNTIL SUPERLIFT COUNTERWEIGHT IS CLEAR OF THE GROUND
9. CONTINUE TO SWING MODULE EAST TOWARDS FINAL SET LOCATION
10. HOIST MOODULE AS REQUIRED TO CLEAR OBSTRUCTIONS
11. POSITION MODULE 68-B OVER FINAL SET LOCATION
12. LOWER MODULE TO BENTS
13. ATTACH MODULE TO BENTS -- BY OTHERS
14. REMOVE RIGGING FROM MODULE

GENERAL NOTES:
1. ENSURE FIRM AND LEVEL FOUNDATION FOR CRANE
2. MAXIMUM WIND SPEED NOT TO EXCEED 20 MPH DURING LIFT
3. TAG LINES MAY BE USED DURING THE LIFT TO CONTROL THE LOAD
4. ALL WIRE ROPE SLINGS TO BE IPS, IWRC

PROCRANE ENGINEERING	RIGGING DRAWING 9-9B
DATE January 2001	MODULE 68 - B

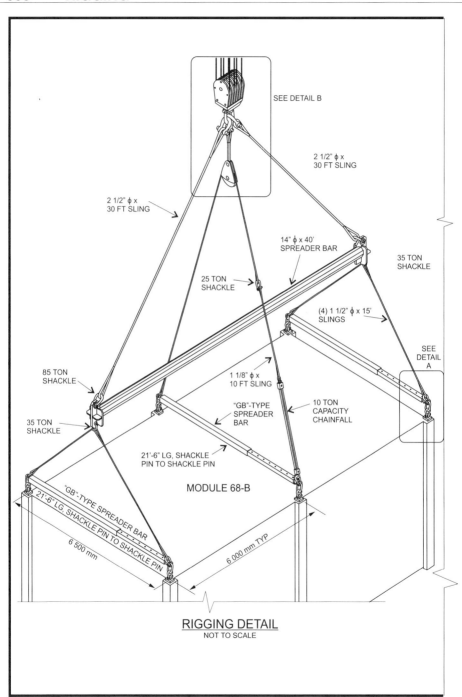

SEE DETAIL B

2 1/2" φ x 30 FT SLING

2 1/2" φ x 30 FT SLING

14" φ x 40' SPREADER BAR

25 TON SHACKLE

35 TON SHACKLE

(4) 1 1/2" φ x 15' SLINGS

SEE DETAIL A

85 TON SHACKLE

1 1/8" φ x 10 FT SLING

"GB"-TYPE SPREADER BAR

10 TON CAPACITY CHAINFALL

35 TON SHACKLE

21'-6" LG, SHACKLE PIN TO SHACKLE PIN

MODULE 68-B

"GB"-TYPE SPREADER BAR

21'-6" LG, SHACKLE PIN TO SHACKLE PIN

6 500 mm

6 000 mm TYP

RIGGING DETAIL

NOT TO SCALE

RIGGING LIST		
ITEM	QTY	DESCRIPTION
1	2	SLING, 2 1/2" φ x 30'-0"
2	1	SLING, 1 1/2" φ x 10'-0"
3	1	SLING, 1 1/2" φ x 50'-0"
4	4	SLING, 1 1/2" φ x 15'-0"
5	1	SLING, 1 1/8" φ x 10'-0"
6	2	SHACKLE, 110 TON
7	2	SHACKLE, 85 TON
8	9	SHACKLE, 35 TON
9	1	SHACKLE, 25 TON
10	3	SPREADER BAR, "GB" TYPE 21'-6" SHACKLE PIN TO SHACKLE PIN
11	1	SPREADER BAR, 14" φ x 40'-0" LG
12	1	SNATCH BLOCK, 40 TON CAPACITY
13	1	CHAINFALL, 10 TON CAPACITY

RIGGING NOTE:

ADDITIONAL SHACKLES MAY BE ADDED AS
REQUIRED TO LEVEL (BALANCE) THE LOAD,
PROVIDING SHACKLE CAPACITY MEETS OR
EXCEEDS THE CAPACITY OF THE ADJACENT
RIGGING.

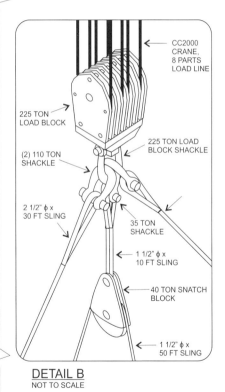

- CC2000 CRANE, 8 PARTS LOAD LINE
- 225 TON LOAD BLOCK
- 225 TON LOAD BLOCK SHACKLE
- (2) 110 TON SHACKLE
- 2 1/2" φ x 30 FT SLING
- 35 TON SHACKLE
- 1 1/2" φ x 10 FT SLING
- 40 TON SNATCH BLOCK
- 1 1/2" φ x 50 FT SLING

DETAIL B
NOT TO SCALE

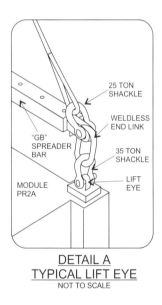

- 25 TON SHACKLE
- WELDLESS END LINK
- "GB" SPREADER BAR
- 35 TON SHACKLE
- MODULE PR2A
- LIFT EYE

DETAIL A
TYPICAL LIFT EYE
NOT TO SCALE

PROCRANE ENGINEERING	RIGGING DRAWING 9-9C
DATE January 2001	MODULE 68 - B

35. What is the rated capacity of the load block in tons?

Answer: _____

36. How many parts of line will be used as the main load line?
- ❏ 4 parts
- ❏ 6 parts
- ❏ 8 parts
- ❏ 10 parts

37. What is the capacity of the snatch block used in the center rigging attachment?
- ❏ 40 ton
- ❏ 35 ton
- ❏ 25 ton
- ❏ 10 ton

38. What is the capacity of the two largest load shackles attached to the load block?
- ❏ 225 tons
- ❏ 220 tons
- ❏ 110 tons
- ❏ 90 tons

39. What is the length of the slings that connect the 40 foot spreader bar to the load block?
- ❏ 10 feet
- ❏ 15 feet
- ❏ 25 feet
- ❏ 30 feet

40. What is the capacity of the shackle used to attach the rigging to any of the module lifting eyes?
- ❏ 25 ton
- ❏ 35 ton
- ❏ 40 ton
- ❏ 50 ton

41. State the center to center distance between the shackle pins on the spreader bars used to attach the rigging to the module.

Answer: _____

42. Referring to the plan view, calculate the difference in the lift radius of the initial pick position and the final location of the module.
- ❏ 45.73 feet
- ❏ 45.92 feet
- ❏ 91.65 feet
- ❏ 137.57 feet

43. Determine if this statement is true or false. The superlift counterweight will be attached to the crane after the module is lifted from the transport and rotated to a position north of the crane.
- ❏ true
- ❏ false

44. Will the crane swing in a clockwise or counter clockwise direction after it picks the module from the transport unit?

Answer: _____

45. What is the weight of all the rigging including the load block in kilograms?

Answer: _____

46. What is the expected boom angle in relationship to the ground after the load is in its final position?

Answer: _____

Rigging Drawing 9-10A and 9-10B, Installation of Fractionator

Rigging drawing 9-10A and 9-10B, Installation of Fractionator, is known as a tandem lift. The term tandem lift is used whenever two cranes are involved in making a lift. It is a common practice when equipment is shipped in the horizontal position and then lifted into the vertical position to use a tandem crane arrangement. The usual procedure is to have one main or primary crane lift the load from a hookup position close to the top, while a tailing or secondary crane lifts the load from a hookup position close to the bottom. As the load is lifted from horizontal to vertical by the primary crane, the secondary crane tails it into position by holding the bottom clear of the ground. The capacity of the primary crane must be sufficient to lift the entire load. On some tandem lifts the load can be lifted and positioned by only swinging the booms, however it is often necessary for one (usually the secondary crane) to travel to reach the final position. Occasionally it is necessary for both cranes to travel.

Another use for tandem lifts is hoisting very long objects into position. This would include loads that remain horizontal from the initial lift through to the final position. In this type of tandem lift, both cranes could be the same capacity, with their combined capacity being capable of lifting the load safely.

Tandem lifts require a lot of pre-planning, as well as good operator and rigging personnel cooperation, and experience. They tend to be more complicated than single crane lifts because of the coordination required from having two cranes connected to the same load and working in close proximity to each other. Any movement by one crane will affect the load distribution on both.

The person in charge of the signaling must know the lifting sequence and be able to anticipate any load movements before signaling the crane operators.

Rigging drawing 9-10A and 9-10B is a tandem lift of a vertical vessel. This vessel will be lifted from the initial horizontal position to the final vertical position. The primary crane has a superlift configuration. This configuration increases the counterweight of the crane, thereby increasing the lift radius. In other applications, a superlift configuration has extra counterweight to increase the load capacity, permit the use of a longer boom, increase the load radius, or a combination of all three. Both cranes in drawing 9-10 are set-up on mats and will be stationary during the lift. The function of the mats is to distribute the bearing pressure from the tracks over a larger surface area, resulting in a lower per square foot of ground pressure. The only crane movements required (besides hoisting the load) are booming up and down, and swinging the load. This lift would require a lot of planning and coordination as there are a number of steps involved between the initial hook up through to the final positioning.

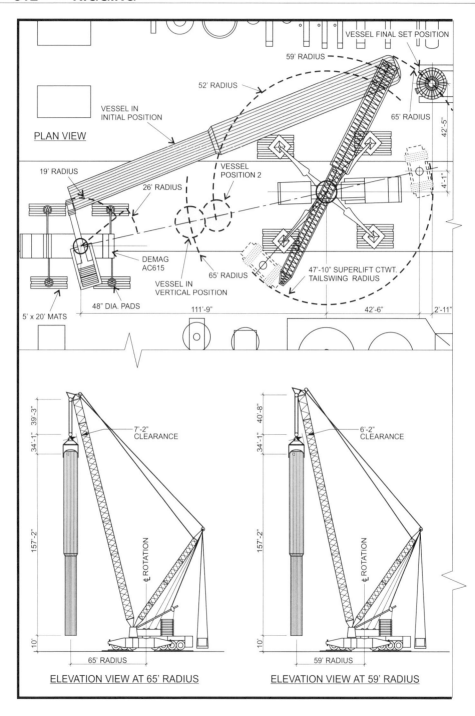

PLAN VIEW

VESSEL FINAL SET POSITION

59' RADIUS

52' RADIUS

VESSEL IN
INITIAL POSITION

65' RADIUS

42'-5"

4'-1"

19' RADIUS

26' RADIUS

VESSEL
POSITION 2

DEMAG
AC615

65' RADIUS

47'-10" SUPERLIFT CTWT.
TAILSWING RADIUS

VESSEL IN
VERTICAL POSITION

48" DIA. PADS

5' x 20' MATS

111'-9"

42'-6"

2'-11"

39'-3"

34'-1"

7'-2"
CLEARANCE

157'-2"

₵ ROTATION

10'

65' RADIUS

ELEVATION VIEW AT 65' RADIUS

40'-8"

34'-1"

6'-2"
CLEARANCE

157'-2"

₵ ROTATION

10'

59' RADIUS

ELEVATION VIEW AT 59' RADIUS

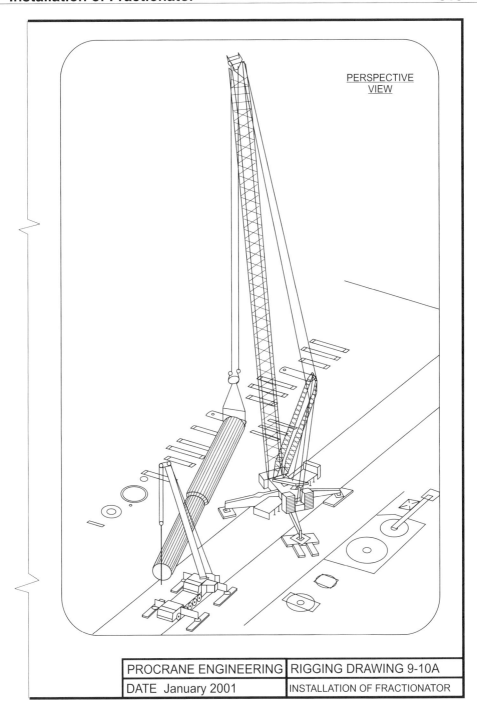

PERSPECTIVE
VIEW

PROCRANE ENGINEERING	RIGGING DRAWING 9-10A
DATE January 2001	INSTALLATION OF FRACTIONATOR

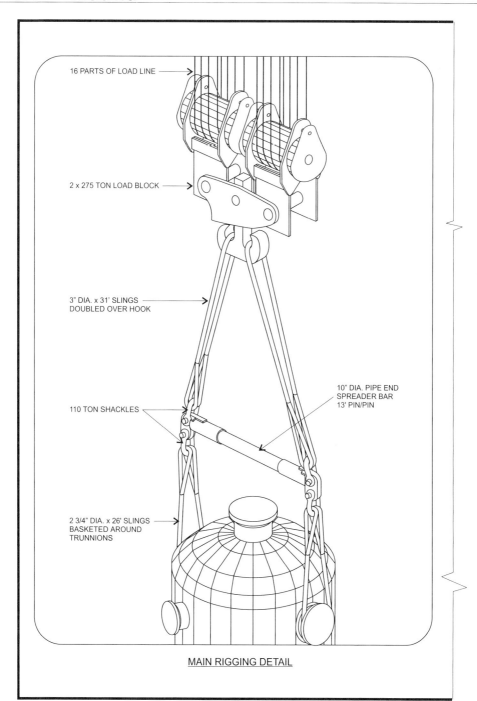

16 PARTS OF LOAD LINE

2 x 275 TON LOAD BLOCK

3" DIA. x 31' SLINGS
DOUBLED OVER HOOK

10" DIA. PIPE END
SPREADER BAR
13' PIN/PIN

110 TON SHACKLES

2 3/4" DIA. x 26' SLINGS
BASKETED AROUND
TRUNNIONS

MAIN RIGGING DETAIL

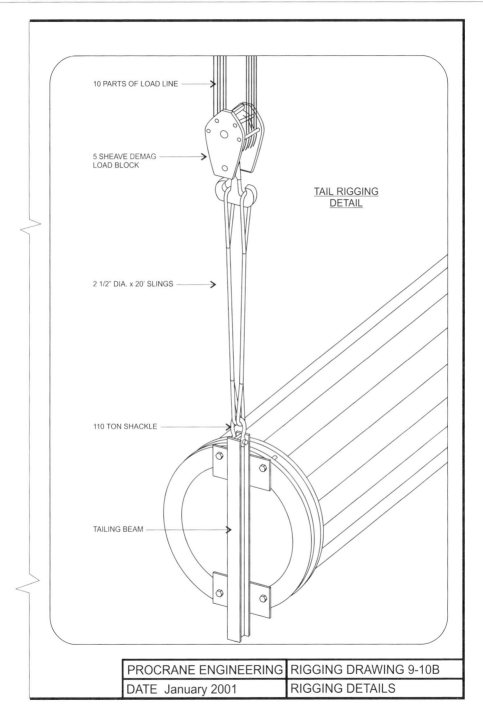

10 PARTS OF LOAD LINE

5 SHEAVE DEMAG
LOAD BLOCK

TAIL RIGGING
DETAIL

2 1/2" DIA. x 20' SLINGS

110 TON SHACKLE

TAILING BEAM

PROCRANE ENGINEERING	RIGGING DRAWING 9-10B
DATE January 2001	RIGGING DETAILS

CRANE / LOAD / LIFT INFORMATION

NOTE:
EQUIPMENT SIZE - NEW FRACTIONATOR
150" ID x 126" ID x 139'-6" TAN/TAN (164'-6" OVERALL HEIGHT)

GENERAL NOTES:

1. ENSURE FIRM AND LEVEL FOUNDATION FOR CRANE.
2. MAXIMUM WIND SPEED NOT TO EXCEED 20 MPH DURING LIFT.
3. TAG LINES MAY BE USED DURING THE LIFT TO CONTROL THE LOAD.
4. ALL WIRE ROPE SLINGS TO BE IPS, IWRC.

CRANE INFO:	MAIN CRANE	MAIN CRANE	TAIL CRANE
TYPE	DEMAG TC3000	DEMAG TC3000	DEMAG AC615
CTWT.	163 T + 193 T SL	163 T + 0 SL	132 000 LBS
BOOM LENGTH	236'	236'	74'
MAST LENGTH	98'	98'	--
MAX. RADIUS	65'	59'	26'
CAPACITY	464 000 LBS	280 200 LBS	194 800 LBS
LOAD INFO:	FULL LOAD	MAIN LOAD	TAIL LOAD
EQUIP. WT.	391 338 LBS	220 569 LBS	170 769 LBS
RIGGING	5 330 LBS	5 330 LBS	4 430 LBS
LOAD BLOCK	22 000 LBS	22 000 LBS	3 086 LBS
HEADACHE BALL	--	--	--
AUX. HEAD	--	--	--
JIB & BOOM EXT.	--	--	--
LIFT INFO:			
TOTAL LIFT WT.	418 668 LBS	247 899 LBS	178 285 LBS
% OF CHART CAP.	91%	89%	92%

PROCEDURE:

1. POSITION CRANES AS SHOWN IN PLAN VIEW.
2. ATTACH RIGGING TO BOTH CRANES AND VESSEL.
3. HOIST VESSEL TO CLEAR SADDLES.
4. BOOM UP MAIN CRANE TO A 52' RADIUS AND SWING COUNTER-CLOCKWISE UNTIL VESSEL IS IN POSITION 2.
5. ATTACH SUPERLIFT COUNTER WEIGHT TO MAIN CRANE (193 TON) AND BOOM DOWN TO A 65' RADIUS.
6. TAIL UP VESSEL TO VERTICAL POSITION.
7. REMOVE TAIL RIGGING.
8. BOOM UP MAIN CRANE TO A 59' RADIUS AND SWING CLOCKWISE UNTIL IN LINE WITH FINAL SET POSITION.
9. BOOM DOWN TO 65' RADIUS, LOWER VESSEL ONTO FOUNDATION & SECURE.
10. REMOVE RIGGING.

RIGGING LIST

ITEM	QTY.	DESCRIPTION
1	2	SLING, 3" DIA. x 31'
2	2	SLING, 2 3/4" DIA. x 26'
3	2	SLING, 2 1/2" DIA. x 20'
4	5	SHACKLE, 110 TON
5	1	SPREADER BAR, 10" DIA. PIPE ENDS w/ 10' SCH 40 PIPE INSERT
6	1	TAIL BEAM

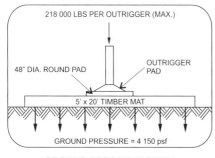

**GROUND PRESSURE DETAIL
FOR DEMAG AC615**

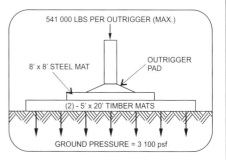

**GROUND PRESSURE DETAIL
FOR DEMAG TC3000**

PROCRANE ENGINEERING	RIGGING DRAWING 9-10C
DATE January 2001	INSTALLATION OF FRACTIONATOR

The following questions refer to Rigging Drawing 9-10.

46. As stated on the drawing, what is the overall height of the vessel to be lifted?

Answer: _____

47. What will be the lift radius of the boom of the main crane before the superlift counterweight is attached?
   - ❏ 65 foot radius
   - ❏ 59 foot radius
   - ❏ 52 foot radius
   - ❏ 26 foot radius

48. Determine if this statement is true or false. The main crane's boom will be at a 52 foot lift radius when the vessel is hoisted clear of the saddles.
   - ❏ true
   - ❏ false

49. State how many times the load radius of the main crane will change after the load has been hooked up.

Answer: _____

50. Calculate the vertical distance from ground level to the center of the main crane's boom tip sheaves after the vessel is lifted to the vertical position and is at a radius of 59 feet.

Answer: _____

51. What will be the center to center distance between the main crane's boom tip sheave and the main load block after the vessel is lifted to the vertical position and at a radius of 65 feet?
   - ❏ 34 feet, 1 inch
   - ❏ 39 feet, 3 inches
   - ❏ 40 feet, 8 inches
   - ❏ 45 feet, 2 inches

52. After the superlift counter weight is attached to the main crane what will the tailswing radius be?
   - ❏ 65 feet, 10 inches
   - ❏ 59 feet, 10 inches
   - ❏ 52 feet, 10 inches
   - ❏ 47 feet, 10 inches

53. What size are the steel mats used under the outriggers of the main crane?

Answer: _____.

54. What is the diameter of the outrigger pads (floats) used on the tail crane?
   - ❏ 24 inches
   - ❏ 36 inches
   - ❏ 48 inches
   - ❏ 60 inches

55. After the vessel is swung in line with its set position the main crane will have to boom down. What is the final lift radius needed to set the vessel over its final position?
   - ❏ 26 foot radius
   - ❏ 52 foot radius
   - ❏ 59 foot radius
   - ❏ 65 foot radius

56. Referring to rigging drawing 9-10B what is the name of the device fastened to the bottom of the vessel that the tail crane rigging will be secured to.

Answer: _____

57. How many parts of line will the main load block of the tail crane be reeved to?
   - ❏ 6 parts
   - ❏ 8 parts
   - ❏ 10 parts
   - ❏ 12 parts

58. The main crane requires two load blocks. How many parts of line will be required per block?

- ❏ 4 parts per block
- ❏ 8 parts per block
- ❏ 12 parts per block
- ❏ 16 parts per block

59. What is the overall length of the slings that will be used in a basket hook up around the lifting trunions at the top of the vessel?

- ❏ 20 feet
- ❏ 26 feet
- ❏ 31 feet
- ❏ 40 feet

60. Determine if this statement is true or false. The lifting eyes for the 31 foot slings used over the main load hook will be secured to the spreader bar with 110 ton shackles.

- ❏ true
- ❏ false

61. Referring to the ground pressure details for the main crane and the tail crane, what type of material are the 5' x 20' mats made of?

Answer: _____

SECTION
TEN

ANSWERS

SECTION ONE ANSWERS

1. Structural steel used in a building is usually fabricated from what type of drawings?
   - ❏ architectural
   - ❏ engineering
   - ❏ heating and ventilation
   - ✔ **shop drawings**

2. Drawings used to assemble components on a jobsite that have been fabricated elsewhere are called:
   - ❏ architectural drawings
   - ❏ fabrication drawings
   - ❏ heating and ventilation drawings
   - ✔ **erection drawings**

3. What type of line has a series of dashes and also has an arrow at each end angled 90 degrees to the line?
   - ❏ hidden line
   - ❏ center line
   - ✔ **cutting plane line**
   - ❏ break line

4. A component that is too long to be shown in full length on a drawing can be shown by using a (an):
   - ❏ object line
   - ❏ center line
   - ❏ section line
   - ✔ **break line**

5. What important symbol, consisting of a triangle containing a number or letter, is often found in various places on a drawing?
   - ❏ mark number
   - ✔ **revision symbol**
   - ❏ centerline
   - ❏ sign size of material symbol

6. What is the name of the symbol that is drawn as a circle with an angled line drawn down through it?
   - ❏ mark number
   - ✔ **round or diameter**
   - ❏ degree of finish
   - ❏ centerline

7. The abbreviation for "thread one end" would be:
   - ❏ THD
   - ❏ TBE
   - ✔ **TOE**
   - ❏ TOL

8. Blueprint dimensions often use a combination of feet and inches, and millimetres.
   - ❏ true
   - ✔ **false**

9. Steel fabrication drawings almost always require drawing measurements to be accurate within ten thousands of an inch.
   - ❏ true
   - ✔ **false**

10. A component measurement, in millimetres, shown as 785 mm (+/- 2), would allow the component dimensions to vary from 784 to 786.
    - ❏ true
    - ✔ **false**

11. With baseline dimensioning, all measurements originate from a common reference point.
    - ✔ **true**
    - ❏ false

12. How many rungs would there be on a ladder if a print indicated the rungs with the measurement note "12 spaces @ 1'-0"?

Answer: 13 rungs

13. The bolt holes on a circular flange are positioned on which of the following?
    - ❏ inside diameter
    - ❏ outside diameter
    - ❏ bolt hole diameter
    - ✔ **bolt circle diameter**

14. The chord distance between bolt holes on a circular flange is the same as the arc distance.
    - ❏ true
    - ✔ **false**

15. The pitch or slope of a surface to a horizontal plane (such as the roof of a building), is known as rise over run.
    - ✔ **true**
    - ❏ false

16. The pitch of a bolt thread is the factor that determines whether the bolt will be fine thread or coarse thread.
    - ✔ **true**
    - ❏ false

17. One steel plate overlapping another plate would be welded with what type of weld?
    - ❏ edge weld
    - ❏ butt weld
    - ✔ **fillet weld**
    - ❏ overlay weld

18. Two plates fitted together to form a tee would have what type of weld?
    - ❏ surface weld
    - ✔ **fillet weld**
    - ❏ edge weld
    - ❏ butt weld

19. A weld symbol placed below the reference line would indicate welding on the arrow side of the joint.
    - ✔ **true**
    - ❏ false

20. What welding procedure is indicated by a flag positioned where the reference line and the arrow join together on a welding symbol?
    - ✔ **weld in the field**
    - ❏ weld in the shop
    - ❏ weld completely around joint
    - ❏ grind joint after welding

21. What welding method or procedure is indicated by a small circle drawn where the reference line and the arrow line join on a welding symbol?
    - ❏ weld in the field
    - ❏ weld in the shop
    - ✔ **weld completely around the joint**
    - ❏ grind joint after welding

22. What symbol is NOT one of the usual welding finish symbols?
    - ❏ C
    - ❏ G
    - ❏ M
    - ✔ **W**

23. Which view is NOT one of the three most commonly used views associated with orthographic projection?
    - ✔ **section view**
    - ❏ top view
    - ❏ front view
    - ❏ side view

24. A perspective view is not suitable for dimensioning as the sides are not drawn to equal length and it is not drawn to scale.
    - ✔ **true**
    - ❏ false

25. The company name and drawing number are found in what area of a print?
   - ❏ general notes
   - ❏ specifications
   - ❏ bill of material
   - ✔ **title block**

26. Which of the following is NOT usually found in the Bill of Materials?
   - ❏ item or mark number
   - ❏ quantity of pieces required
   - ✔ **welding process for components**
   - ❏ description of material

27. Two "mirror image" components are said to be:
   - ✔ **left and right**
   - ❏ section views
   - ❏ top and side views
   - ❏ none of the above

28. The interior construction of an object can be shown with what type of view?
   - ❏ top
   - ❏ side
   - ❏ detail
   - ✔ **section**

29. The details of a sloped surface are best shown using which of the following?
   - ❏ front view
   - ❏ side view
   - ❏ top view
   - ✔ **auxiliary view**

30. What would be the drawing line length of an object 18 ft. 6 in. long, drawn to a scale of 1/4 inch = 1 foot.
   - ❏ 9 ft. 3 1/4 in.
   - ❏ 9 1/4 in.
   - ✔ **4 5/8 in.**
   - ❏ 2 5/16 in.

31. If the 1: 50 metric scale is used, what is the drawing line length of an object 2.5 metres in length?

Answer: 50 mm

32. Blueprints stored in a toolbox should be first in and last out.
   - ❏ true
   - ✔ **false**

SECTION TWO ANSWERS

1. Flat plate heads, rather than ellipsoidal or hemispherical, are more commonly used on pressure vessels?
    - ❏ true
    - ✔ **false**

2. The seam where a vessel head is welded to the shell on a vertical vessel is what type of joint?
    - ❏ longitudinal
    - ❏ vertical
    - ❏ circumferential
    - ✔ **horizontal**

3. The supports for a horizontal pressure vessel are called:
    - ✔ **saddles**
    - ❏ skirts
    - ❏ nozzles
    - ❏ davit arm

4. The anchor bolt chair is welded to the:
    - ❏ top head
    - ✔ **skirt**
    - ❏ manway
    - ❏ demister

5. What is used to seal off a manway opening?
    - ❏ hemispherical head
    - ✔ **blind flange**
    - ❏ wear plate
    - ❏ nozzle neck

6. The orientation view shows the position of items such as nozzles around the vessel circumference in relation to degrees of a circle.
    - ✔ **true**
    - ❏ false

7. The orientation view centerlines usually run in the same clockwise order, 0-90-180-270, regardless of whether the view is positioned on the left or right end of a horizontal vessels elevation view.
    - ✔ **true**
    - ❏ false

8. The first step when laying out a vessel shell is to determine which end to start from.
    - ✔ **true**
    - ❏ false

9. The starting point to lay out a horizontal vessel shell, after determining which end is the reference line, and the order of the centerlines is:
    - ❏ find the position of the largest nozzles first
    - ❏ find how many nozzles are the same size
    - ✔ **establish 0 degrees in relation to the shell weld seam**
    - ❏ establish the length of the skirt

10. An elevation view reference line, established on a vessel head at the point of curvature, is said to be at what point.
    - ❏ reference point
    - ❏ end point
    - ✔ **tangent point**
    - ❏ nozzle point

11. In what area of the drawing is the print number found?

Answer: title block

12. In what area is the grade of material found?

Answer: specifications and B of M

13. Where is the following information found? "All bolt holes to straddle natural vessel centerlines unless noted otherwise."

Answer: general notes

14. What change does revision one refer to?

Answer: added nozzle N3

15. What section of the ASME code is referenced for the fabrication of this vessel?

Answer: section VIII

16. What section of the drawing shows the outside diameter (O.D.) of the nozzle neck for N1?

Answer: nozzle schedule

17. What is the approximate empty weight of this vessel?

Answer: 440 lbs.

18. Calculate the difference between the operating pressure and the hydrotest pressure.

Answer: 62.5 psi

19. What reference line do the location dimensions originate from to dimension the drawing and layout the vessel shell?

Answer: head to shell weld seam

20. The revision is referenced in the nozzle schedule.

 true
❏ false

21. Determine the shell thickness of this vessel.

Answer: 1/4 inch

22. List all the areas of the drawing that show the thickness of the head.

Answer: elevation view, specifications, B of M

23. Calculate the inside diameter of this vessel.

Answer: 23 1/2 inches

24. Coupling C1 is how many degrees from the zero degree centerline?

Answer: 90 degrees

25. How many degrees is the longitudinal seam from the 180 degree centerline?

Answer: 30 degrees

26. Calculate the overall length of this vessel from the flange face of N1 to the flange face of N2.

Answer: 5 ft. 4 in.

27. How far does nozzle N3 project out from the side of the shell?

Answer: 6 inches

28. Determine the weld seam to weld seam length of the shell only.

Answer: 3 ft. 0 in.

29. What is the pressure rating for each of the flanges used on nozzles N1, N2, and N3?

Answer: 150 lbs.

30. What is the design corrosion allowance for this vessel?
   - ❏ 1/4 inch
   - ❏ 1/8 inch
   - ❏ 1/32 inch
   - ✔ **not shown**

31. What is the orientation of the name plate?
Answer: 90 degrees

32. Calculate the length from tangent to tangent between the two heads.
Answer: 3 ft. 4 in.

33. What is the distance from the seam reference line to the center of the hole for nozzle N3 on the elevation view?
Answer: 2 ft. 6 in.

34. Nozzle N3 is located on which of the vessel's quarter lines.
Answer: 270 degrees

35. What is the outside diameter of the pipe used for the neck of nozzle N1?
Answer: 6 5/8 inches

36. Does nozzle N3 have a reinforcing pad?
Answer: no

37. Describe the inside projection requirements for nozzles N1, N2, and N3.
Answer: set flush

38. What is the material grade of the raised face slip-on flanges for nozzles N1 and N2.
Answer: SA-105

39. What is the nominal pipe size (NPS) of coupling C1?
Answer: 1 1/2 inches

40. Will the item installed in C1 be welded or threaded into the coupling?
Answer: threaded

41. Describe what will be done to the inside edge of each nozzle installed in the vessel.
Answer: rounded to 1/8 radius

42. What is the projection from the seam line for nozzles N1 and N2?
Answer: 1 ft. 2 in.

43. The included angle of the weld preparation for the longitudinal and circumferencial seams is 60 degrees.
   - ✔ **true**
   - ❏ false

44. Write out the abbreviations of the two welding processes used to complete the welding requirements for this vessel.
Answer: SMAW and SAW

45. What is the O.D. of the neck for nozzle N3?
   - ❏ 4 inches
   - ✔ **4-1/2 inches**
   - ❏ 6 inches
   - ❏ 6-5/8 inches

46. Calculate the distance from the bottom of the base plate (item #6) to the top of nozzle 2N.
Answer: 10 ft. 1 in.

47. At the intersection points of number 27 and the support legs, which item is cut away?
Answer: item 27 (flat bar)

48. What is the distance from the reference line to the centerline of nozzle 4N?

Answer: 2 ft. 3 in.

49. What is the projection of nozzle 3N from the reference line?

Answer: 1 ft. 0 in.

50. What is the seam to seam distance from the seam of the bottom head to the weld seam of item #3?

Answer: 5 ft. 10 1/2 in.

51. Determine the distance from the top of item #3 to the top of 2N.

Answer: 8 inches

52. What is the distance from the reference line to the bottom of the support legs?

Answer: 2 ft. 11 in.

53. What type of weld is used to attach the support legs to the shell of the vessel?

Answer: fillet

54. What is the leg size of the weld attaching the support leg to the vessel shell?

Answer: 1/4 inch

55. Calculate the elevation from the reference line to the center of nozzle 1CNA.

Answer: 5 ft. 1 in.

56. What is the weld detail describing item 2 being welded to item 3?

Answer: 75 degree vee

57 Refer to the weld that joins #3 to the shell. The bevel angle for the shell and the flange is 37.5 degrees.

✔ **true**
❏ false

58. Describe how the support legs will be prepared to clear the weld seam?

Answer: notch to clear

59. What is the center to center distance between items #3CNA and 3CNB?

Answer: 5 ft. 3 in.

60. The type of weld used to join the bottom head to the shell is called a:

❏ fillet weld
❏ bevel weld
✔ **vee groove weld**
❏ lap weld

61. Nozzles 2CNA and 2CNB are orientated at 90 degrees.

❏ true
✔ **false**

62. Nozzle 1N is how many degrees from the 0 degree centerline?

❏ 45 degrees
❏ 90 degrees
✔ **135 degrees**
❏ 180 degrees

63. Nozzle 2N is located on what center line?

Answer: 0 - 180 degree centerline

64. Nozzle 2N is how many inches off the 90 - 270 degree centerline?

Answer: 7 inches

65. What is the number of support legs (item #5) shown in the orientation view?

Answer: 3 legs

66. Which of the following shows the location of each leg in degrees from the 0 degree centerline?
- ❏ 0, 90 and 270 degrees
- ❏ 30, 90 and 270 degrees
- ❏ 30, 120 and 270 degrees
- ✔ **30, 150 and 270 degrees**

67. The davit arm is located on the 0 degree centerline.
- ✔ **true**
- ❏ false

68. What type of line represents nozzle 3N on the orientation view.
- ✔ **hidden line**
- ❏ object line
- ❏ section line
- ❏ broken line

69. The name plate bracket is located on the:
- ❏ 0 degree centerline
- ✔ **90 degree centerline**
- ❏ 180 degree centerline
- ❏ 270 degree centerline

70. How many nozzles are located on the 45 degree centerline?
- ❏ 1
- ✔ **2**
- ❏ 3
- ❏ 4

71. Nozzle 1N is designated as an inlet nozzle for this vessel.
- ✔ **true**
- ❏ false

72. What nozzle is designated as a spare?

Answer: 1CN

73. What nozzle is used as a level gage?
- ❏ 2N
- ❏ 2CN
- ✔ **3CN**
- ❏ 4N

74. The pressure rating of the couplings is:
- ❏ 150#
- ❏ 300#
- ✔ **3000#**
- ❏ not shown

75. What two nozzles are supplied with blinds?

Answer: M1 and 1CN

76. What is the outside diameter of the pipe that is used for the neck of the manway nozzle?

Answer: 18 inches

77. What is the outside projection for nozzle 4N?

Answer: 8 inches

78. List the Bill of Material item numbers that make up nozzle 1CN.

Answer: 17 and 18

79. As indicated in the weld detail, what is the leg size of the fillet weld required on Nozzle 1N?

Answer: 1/4 inch

80. As shown in the weld detail, how much gap is required between the flange and the neck of 3N?

Answer: 1/16 inch

81. What is the wall thickness of the pipe used for the shell of this pressure vessel?

Answer: .375 inch

82. The end preparation of item 2 is:
- ❏ square cut one end
- ❏ bevel one end
- ✔ **bevel both ends**
- ❏ square cut both ends

83. What is the leg size and thickness of the angle iron used for the support legs?

Answer: 3 x 3 x 5/16

84. Write out the following abbreviations.
- ❏ XXHY double extra heavy
- ❏ RFWN raised face weld neck
- ❏ SMLS. seamless
- ❏ FLG.   flange
- ❏ B.O.E. bevel one end
- ❏ P.O.E. plain one end

85. The nameplate is made of stainless steel.
- ✔ **true**
- ❏ false

86. What is the center to center (c/c) distance between the anchor bolt holes of the fixed saddle and sliding saddle?

Answer: 6175 mm

87. Determine the heel to heel distance between any two of item #57.

Answer: 1274 mm

88. The heel to heel distance between the first and last pipe support brackets (item #57) is:

Answer: 7644 mm

89. The length of the shortest ring section of the shell is:
- ✔ **2819 mm**
- ❏ 3048 mm
- ❏ 6096 mm
- ❏ 8915 mm

90. What is used as the reference line for the elevation view dimensioning of the nozzles?
- ❏ tangent point
- ❏ circumferencial seam
- ✔ **right hand head seam**
- ❏ left hand head seam

91. What is the distance from the left end head seam to the center of the left end lifting lug?
- ✔ **1000**
- ❏ 2000
- ❏ 2819
- ❏ 8915

92. Calculate the distance from the tangent point of the right end head to the center of N1.

Answer: 2631 mm

93. Determine the distance from the horizontal centerline to the center of nozzles N8, N9, and N10.

Answer: 917 mm

94. What is the center to center distance between the holes in the lifting lugs?
- ❏ 1000
- ❏ 3048
- ✔ **6915**
- ❏ 7915

95. How far is the heel of item #45 from the horizontal centerline of this vessel?

    ✔ **767**
    ❏ 817
    ❏ 919
    ❏ 1092

96. The outside diameter of this vessel is:

    ❏ 2135 mm
    ❏ 2154 mm
    ✔ **2173 mm**
    ❏ 2182 mm

97. What is the distance from the reference line to the first of items #57?

    ❏ 530 mm
    ✔ **636 mm**
    ❏ 1274 mm
    ❏ 1370 mm

98. What is the length of ring #1?

Answer: 3048 mm

99. The overall length of the shell rings, not including gap, is 8915 millimeters.

    ✔ **true**
    ❏ false

100. The location of N13 as shown in the elevation view can be described as:

    ❏ near side to the viewer
    ✔ **far side to the viewer**

101. How many nozzles are located on the 0 degree centerline?

Answer: 9

102. The longitudinal seam for ring #3 is located on the:

    ❏ 0 degree centerline
    ❏ 60 degree centerline
    ✔ **180 degree centerline**
    ❏ 300 degree centerline

103. Calculate the number of degrees apart between longitudinal seam #2 and longitudinal seam # 1, starting from ring #2 and rotating in a clockwise direction.

    ❏ 60 degrees apart
    ❏ 120 degrees apart
    ❏ 180 degrees apart
    ✔ **240 degrees apart**

104. The lifting lugs are offset on each side of the 0 degree centerline. What is the distance between them?

    ❏ 57 millimeters
    ✔ **114 millimeters**
    ❏ 45 millimeters
    ❏ 90 millimeters

105. How far is the center of nozzle N10 from the 0 - 180 degree centerline.

Answer: 250 mm

106. What type of weld is required to join item #103 to item #101?

    ❏ bevel weld
    ❏ vee groove weld
    ❏ corner weld
    ✔ **fillet weld**

107. What is the diameter of the hole in item #101 used to install the eye bolt?

Answer: 22 mm

108. The davit arm will be bent to a radius of 500 millimeters.

    ❏ true
    ✔ **false**

109. The length of the lower straight section of pipe on the davit arm, measured from the bottom of the pipe is:

    ❏ 231 millimeters
    ✔ **311 millimeters**
    ❏ 561 millimeters
    ❏ 906 millimeters

110. Referring to the top part of the davit arm, calculate the length of the straight section of pipe measured from the end of item #102 to the start of the bend.

Answer: 202 mm

111. What is the diameter and length of the slotted holes in the saddle base plate?

Answer: 19 x 38 mm

112. What is the center to center distance between the slotted holes in the base plate?

Answer: 1730 mm

113. The wear plate will be rolled to a radius of 1086.5 millimeters.

✔ **true**
❑ false

114. The distance from the horizontal centerline to the upper side of the base plate is:

❑ 1387 millimeters.
✔ **1374 millimeters**
❑ 1065 millimeters
❑ 591 millimeters

115. Which of the following statements best describes the type of weld required to join item #53 to item #51?

❑ 10 millimeter fillet (typical)
❑ 10 millimeter fillet weld arrow side with a vee groove weld on the other side
❑ 10 millimeter bevel groove weld arrow side and a fillet weld on the other side
✔ **10 millimeter fillet weld arrow side with a bevel groove weld on the other side**

SECTION THREE ANSWERS

1. Most tanks are similar to pressure vessels in that they:
    - ❏ have two hemispherical heads
    - ❏ sit horizontal on two saddles
    - ❏ operate at high pressure
    - ✔ **are cylindrical with an elevation and orientation view**

2. Most tanks are vertical with floors that are:
    - ❏ flat
    - ❏ slightly concave
    - ❏ slightly convex
    - ✔ **any of the above**

3. For convenience, what is the usual method of laying out the floor of a tank for welding?
    - ❏ butt joints
    - ✔ **lap joints**
    - ❏ vertical joints
    - ❏ tee joints

4. What type of tank roof is fabricated in a flat position, has a radial cut made in it, and is lifted in the center and welded into a cone shape?
    - ✔ **self supporting**
    - ❏ supported
    - ❏ floating
    - ❏ pressurized

5. The beams that extend from a center column out to the tank shell to hold up roof plates are called:
    - ❏ girders
    - ❏ davit arms
    - ✔ **rafters**
    - ❏ none of the above

6. A rolling ladder is found on what type of tank?
    - ✔ **floating roof**
    - ❏ self supporting
    - ❏ column supported
    - ❏ all of the above

7. On a very large tank, two vertical joints and a horizontal joint can all be positioned together in a cross shape.
    - ❏ true
    - ✔ **false**

8. What protects a floating roof tank against wind damage?
    - ❏ pontoon
    - ❏ column and rafters
    - ❏ reinforcing plate
    - ✔ **stiffening ring**

9. What is the name of the two items that hold up the roof of a supported roof tank?

Answer: columns and rafters

10. What is the inside diameter of the tank?
    - ❏ 3350 mm
    - ❏ 3344 mm
    - ✔ **3338 mm**
    - ❏ 3336 mm

11. What does the abbreviation "T.O. Floor 0-0" mean?

Answer: top of floor at ground level

12. Specify the orientation and the elevation of nozzle N1.

Orientation in degrees = 0 degrees
Elevation in millimeters = 280

13. What is the elevation of the roof angle?

Answer: 4570 mm

14. What is the slope, or pitch of the tank roof?

Answer: 3:12

15. Determine the elevation to the top of the first shell ring.

Answer: 2438 mm

16. How many individual shell plates are required to fabricate the two shell rings?
- ❏ 1 plate per ring
- ❏ 2 plates per ring
- ❏ 2 plates in total
- ✔ **4 plates in total**

17. The orientation to the ladder centerline in a clockwise direction from the 0 degree centerline is 325 degrees.
- ✔ **true**
- ❏ false

18. Describe the orientation and elevation to the manway centerline.

Orientation in degrees = 45° from 0°
Elevation in millimeters = 760

19. In what direction does nozzle N2 face?
- ❏ north
- ✔ **south**
- ❏ east
- ❏ west

20. This tank is classified as a floating roof type.
- ❏ yes
- ✔ **no**

21. The floor of this tank is:
- ❏ concave
- ❏ convex
- ✔ **flat**
- ❏ sloped

22. How many plates make up the tank floor?
- ❏ 1 plate
- ✔ **2 plates**
- ❏ 3 plates
- ❏ 4 plates

23. The diameter of the floor is exactly the same as the outside diameter of the tank.
- ❏ true
- ✔ **false**

24. For the purpose of laying out the pie cut out for the tank roof, the length of the chord is 317 millimeters.
- ✔ **true**
- ❏ false

25. After fit-up to the top of the shell, what is the outside diameter of the tank roof?
- ❏ 3388 millimeters
- ❏ 3452 millimeters
- ✔ **3350 millimeters**
- ❏ 3344 millimeters

26. What is the distance from the top of the tank floor to the center of the drain nozzle?
- ✔ **200 millimeters**
- ❏ 149 millimeters
- ❏ 51 millimeters
- ❏ 40 millimeters

27. Which of the following nozzle flanges is a 4 inch, 300 RFWN?
   - ❏ N1
   - ❏ N2
   - ❏ N3
   - ✔ **none of the above**

28. The neck for nozzle N2 and N6 are both the same length.
   - ❏ true
   - ✔ **false**

29. The "level gage" is item:
   - ❏ N1
   - ❏ N2
   - ✔ **C1A**
   - ❏ C2

30. What is the diameter of the access manway?
   - ❏ 18 inch
   - ❏ 24 inch
   - ❏ 30 inch
   - ✔ **not shown**

31. This tank has three manways. What is the piece mark number for the roof manway?
   - ✔ **M1**
   - ❏ M2
   - ❏ M3
   - ❏ M4

32. Which nozzle is designated for use as a sump?

Answer: N11

33. Which manway is designated as the clean-out?

Answer: M3

34. Referring to the orientation view, what will be the center to center distance between nozzles N14A and N14B after they are installed?

Answer: 305 mm

35. What will be the center to center distance between nozzles C1 and C6 after they are installed?
   - ❏ 203 mm
   - ✔ **1015 mm**
   - ❏ 1676 mm
   - ❏ 2017 mm

36. By how many millimeters do each of the roof plates overlap each other?

Answer: 38 mm

37. Nozzle N2 is how many degrees clockwise from the zero degree centerline?

Answer: 217 3/4 degrees

38. State the roof slope as a rise over run ratio for this tank?

Answer: 1:12

39. Which drawing note refers to the nozzle projection?
   - ❏ note 1
   - ✔ **note 2**
   - ❏ note 3
   - ❏ note 4

40. Determine if this statement is true or false. "All 6 inch nozzles shall project from the outside of the shell to the face of the flange not less than 178 millimeters."
   - ❏ true
   - ✔ **false**

41. State the code and paragraph that specifies the method that will be used to test the bottom of this tank.

Code: AP1650 - note 3

Paragraph: 5.3.2(a) - note 3

42. Determine if this statement is true or false: "The orientation of the first shell plate S1 is 275 degrees clockwise from the 0 degree centerline."

✔ **true**

❏ false

43. Which of these shell plates is the longest, S2 or S2A?

Answer: S2

44. How many shell plates are required to make the first ring of this tank?

❏ 1 plate

❏ 2 plates

❏ 3 plates

✔ **4 plates**

45. State the requirements for hydrotesting this tank.

Answer: Waterfill

46. How many rafters in total are required to support this tank roof?

Answer: 18

47. What structural shape is used to make the rafters?

❏ angle iron

✔ **channel iron**

❏ wide flange beams

❏ flat bar

48. What is the clockwise orientation in degrees from the 0° centerline to the first rafter clip?

✔ **10°**

❏ 20°

❏ 45°

❏ 90°

49. What is the center to center distance in degrees between each rafter clip?

Answer: 20 degrees

50. What is the elevation from the top of the tank floor to the top of the center column?

❏ 4104 mm

❏ 4027 mm

✔ **3897 mm**

❏ 3877 mm

51. What type of weld is used to attach the column gusset plate (item #4) to the column center post?

❏ 5 mm. butt weld

❏ square groove weld

❏ seal weld

✔ **5 mm fillet weld**

52. How many gusset plates (item #4) are spaced evenly around the top of the column?

✔ **6 gusset plates**

❏ 12 gusset plates

❏ 18 gusset plates

❏ 24 gusset plates

53. What is the slope of the slotted holes in the rafters clips stated as a rise over run ratio?

Answer: 1:12

54. What is the height to the top of the rim angle (item #8) from the top of the tank floor?
    - ❏ 4104 mm
    - ❏ 4027 mm
    - ❏ 3897 mm
    - ✔ **3658 mm**

55. Refer to the chain intermittent fillet welding of the gusset plates to the column. What is the required length of each of the welds?
    - ❏ 5 mm
    - ✔ **51 mm**
    - ❏ 102 mm
    - ❏ 125 mm

56. What is the radius from the center of the column to the outside of the tank shell?
    - ✔ **5334 mm**
    - ❏ 5348 mm
    - ❏ 5025 mm
    - ❏ 5279 mm

57. Refer to section A-A. Write out the specific note regarding the welding of the rafter beams to the roof plates.

Answer: do not weld

58. What dimension would be used to position the column rafter clips from the center of the column to the center of the gusset plate hole?
    - ❏ 64 mm
    - ❏ 107 mm
    - ✔ **279 mm**
    - ❏ 444 mm

59. What is the center to center dimension between the two outside holes in the rafter beams?
    - ❏ 4993 mm
    - ✔ **5025 mm**
    - ❏ 5348 mm
    - ❏ 5483 mm

60. The base of the column is not welded to the tank floor, but is held in position with four angle iron supports.
    - ✔ **true**
    - ❏ false

SECTION FOUR ANSWERS

1. The two basic types of heat exchangers are the single tubesheet with a U tube bundle, and two tubesheets with joining straight tubes.
    ✔ **true**
    ❏ false

2. What does the abbreviation TEMA mean in regard to heat exchangers?
Answer: Tubular Exchanger Manufacturers Association

3. The basic function of a heat exchanger is to transfer the heat of one medium and pass it over to another.
    ✔ **true**
    ❏ false

4. Under normal conditions, which of the following heat exchangers would be the most efficient?
    ❏ 1 - 4 inch tube
    ❏ 2 - 3 inch tubes
    ❏ 4 - ¾ inch tubes
    ✔ **40 - ¾ inch tubes**

5. A liquid passing over the outside of the heat exchanger tubes is referred to as:
    ❏ tube side flow
    ✔ **shell side flow**
    ❏ end to end flow
    ❏ circulation flow

6. A liquid passing through the inside of the heat exchanger tubes is referred to as:
    ✔ **tube side flow**
    ❏ shell side flow
    ❏ warming flow
    ❏ circulation flow

7. What is the primary reason for designing a tube bundle that is removable?
Answer: Cleaning and repair

8. All exchangers are designed with two heads.
    ❏ true
    ✔ **false**

9. What is the purpose of a baffle plate in the center of a heat exchanger head?
Answer: To cause the tube side flow to make two passes

10. What word describes the center-to-center distance between tubesheet holes?
Answer: Pitch

11. In a heat exchanger with two heads, what is used to hold the tubesheets and baffles in place before the tubes are installed?
    ❏ gaskets
    ❏ studs
    ❏ flanges
    ✔ **tierods**

12. What is the purpose of tapped holes in the backside of tubesheets?
Answer: Thread in tierods to secure tubesheet and baffles

13. Which heat exchanger would be more efficient?
    ❏ no head baffle or shell baffles
    ❏ no head baffle and one shell baffle
    ❏ one head baffle and two shell baffles
    ✔ **one head baffle and three shell baffles**

14. A kettle reboiler heat exchanger has a space above the tube bundle for venting off vapors.

✔ **true**
❏ false

15. What is the outside diameter of the channel head?

✔ **16 inches**
❏ 20-3/8 inches
❏ 41 inches
❏ 48 inches

16. Calculate the distance from the outside of the channel head to the center of gravity.

Answer: 11 ft. 7 7/8 in.

17. What is the pressure rating of the shell outlet flange?

✔ **150#**
❏ 300#
❏ 600#
❏ 900#

18. Calculate the center to center distance between the two ¾ inch full couplings used for the level gage.

Answer: 2 ft. 5 in.

19. What are the dimensions of the slotted anchor bolt holes in the saddles?

Answer: 1 1/4 X 2 1/4 in.

20. How much does this vessel weigh, including the tube bundle?

❏ 2,400 lbs.
✔ **9,000 lbs.**
❏ 11,400 lbs.
❏ 19,000 lbs.

21. The inlet nozzle for the channel head is larger than the outlet nozzle.

❏ true
✔ **false**

22. What is the total weight of the vessel when full of water for hydro-testing?

❏ 2,400 lbs.
❏ 9,000 lbs.
❏ 11,400 lbs.
✔ **19,000 lbs.**

23. What is the distance from the underside of the channel outlet nozzle to the top of the channel inlet nozzle.

Answer: 3 feet

24. What is the minimum clearance needed to remove the bundle from this heat exchanger?

Answer: 18 ft. 6 in.

25. Determine the measurement from the underside of the saddle baseplate to the top of the 10 inch shell inlet flange.

Answer: 4 ft. 10 3/8 in.

26. What does the tube bundle for this vessel weigh?

✔ **2,400 lbs.**
❏ 9,000 lbs.
❏ 11,400 lbs.
❏ 19,000 lbs.

27. The shell side hydro-test pressure for this vessel is 325 psi.

❏ true
✔ **false**

28. The tubeside fluid will make two passes through the bundle.

✔ **true**
❏ false

29. If the plate thickness of the shell was ½ inch when new, how thick will the shell be after it has corroded to its maximum allowable corrosion allowance?

- ❏ ¼ inch
- ✔ **3/8 inch**
- ❏ ½ inch
- ❏ 5/8 inch

30. From the tubesheet detail, determine the overall thickness of the tubesheet.

Answer: 1 7/8 inches

31. What is the bolt circle (BC) diameter for the bolt holes drilled in the tubesheet?

Answer: 18 3/4 inches

32. What is the height of the weir that controls the liquid level on the shell side of this exchanger?

Answer: 1 ft. 8 in.

33. Determine the distance from the channel side face of the tube sheet to the outside of the tube bends for the tube bundle (bundle length).

Answer: 19 ft. 9 1/8 in.

34. Calculate the distance from the back of the weir to the outside of the shell head on the left end of the exchanger.

Answer: 4 ft. 0 1/2 in.

35. What is the thickness of the partition plate in the channel head?

Answer: 3/8 inches

36. There are two lifting lugs used to install or remove the channel head.

- ✔ **true**
- ❏ false

37. State the amount the tube end protrudes past the face of the tubesheet on the channel head side?

Answer: 1/8 inch

38. What is the leg size and thickness of the angle iron used as the guide rail for installing or removing the bundle?

Answer: 1" x 1" x 1/4"

39. The maximum diameter that the tube holes can measure after completion of drilling and reaming is:

- ❏ .750 in.
- ❏ .752 in.
- ❏ .758 in.
- ✔ **.760 in.**

40. What is the width of the grooves for the tube hole grooving detail?

- ❏ .010 of an inch
- ❏ 1/64 of an inch
- ✔ **.125 of an inch**
- ❏ .375 of an inch

41. What is the distance from the channel head side of the tubesheet face to the center of the second groove in any of the tube holes?

- ❏ 3/8 of an inch
- ❏ ½ of an inch
- ❏ 7/8 of an inch
- ✔ **15/16 of an inch**

42. How many tube holes will be drilled and reamed in the tubesheet.

- ❏ 32 holes
- ❏ 62 holes
- ✔ **124 holes**
- ❏ 128 holes

43. How many holes will be drilled in the tubesheet to accommodate the tierods.
   - ❏ 2
   - ✔ 4
   - ❏ 6
   - ❏ 8

44. The distance from the center of the tubesheet to the center of each of the tierod holes, both horizontal and vertical, is 7 inches.
   - ❏ true
   - ✔ false

45. The center to center distance between horizontal rows 2 and 3 for this tubesheet is 1-1/8 inches.
   - ❏ true
   - ✔ false

46. State the outside diameter of the tubes.
Answer: 3/4 inch

47. The tube pitch for this tubesheet is 1 inch square.
   - ✔ true
   - ❏ false

48. State the number of passes that this exchanger is categorized as:
Answer: 2 pass

49. Calculate the difference between the overall bundle length and the straight length of the tubes.
Answer: 6 1/2 inches

50. What is the minimum gage thickness of the tubes in the bundle?
   - ❏ 75 gage
   - ❏ 62 gage
   - ❏ 16 gage
   - ✔ 14 gage

51. What is the depth of the holes drilled in the tubesheet for the tierods?
Answer: 3/4 inch

52. What is the diameter of the tierod holes drilled in the baffles?
   - ❏ 1/2 inch
   - ✔ 9/16 inch
   - ❏ 5/8 inch
   - ❏ 3/4 inch

53. What is the diameter of the tube holes drilled in the baffles?
   - ✔ 49/64 inch
   - ❏ .758 inch
   - ❏ 3/4 inch
   - ❏ 5/8 inch

54. What is the diameter of all of the baffles, as stated in the drawing?
Answer: 15 1/8 inches

55. How many half baffles will be required for this tube bundle?
   - ❏ 4
   - ✔ 8
   - ❏ 12
   - ❏ 16

56. The height of the 90 degree notches cut in the baffle plates is 1 inch.
   - ✔ true
   - ❏ false

57. What is the straight length of the tubes prior to their being bent for the U shape bundle?
   - ❏ 20 feet
   - ❏ 30 feet
   - ✔ 40 feet
   - ❏ 80 feet

58. What is the center to center spacing between baffles spaced along the length of the tube sheet?

Answer: 2 ft 6 in.

59. View A-A is an end view of the channel head showing the general arrangement of the channel head baffles, orientation of lifting lugs and nozzles.

✔ **true**
❏ false

60. The outside diameter of the shell is:
❏ 64 inches
❏ 59¾ inches
✔ **59¼ inches**
❏ does not specifiy

61. State the overall length of this heat exchanger in millimeters.

Answer: 8503 mm

62. The location of the longitudinal seam for the channel head is on the:

✔ **90 degree centerline**
❏ 180 degree centerline
❏ 270 degree centerline
❏ 360 degree centerline

63. How many individual courses will be needed to make up the shell of the main heat exchanger body (not including the channel cover or rear cover)

❏ one course
❏ two courses
✔ **three courses**
❏ four courses

64. After the channel head is bolted to the shell of the heat exchanger, the distance between the two flanges to accommodate the tubesheet is how many inches?

Answer: 3 5/8 inches

65. What is the distance from the left 0 (zero) reference line to the centerline of the fixed end saddle?

Answer: 32 1/8 inches

66. Which answer indicates the center to center distance between the fixed end saddle and the sliding end saddle in millimeters.

❏ 816 mm
✔ **3816 mm**
❏ 4632 mm
❏ 5448 mm

67. The distance from the left 0 (zero) reference line to the centerline of nozzle D on the channel head is:

✔ **18 inches**
❏ 20 inches
❏ 24 inches
❏ 28 inches

68. How many lifting lugs (item # 9) will be installed on the channel head?

❏ one
✔ **two**
❏ three
❏ four

69. The inside radius of the saddle wear plate will be:

Answer: 29 5/8 inches (752)

70. State the width and length dimensions (in inches) of the saddle base plate.

Answer: 9 in. x 51 5/8 in.

71. What is the leg size of the fillet welds on the saddle?

Answer: 3/8 inch

72. State the dimensions of the slotted holes (in millimeters) in the sliding saddle.

Answer: 38 x 70 mm

73. Referring to the Nozzle Schedule for the oil cooler, what is the nominal pipe size of nozzle C?

    ❏ 8 inch NPS
    ✔ **10 inch NPS**
    ❏ 12 inch NPS
    ❏ 14 inch NPS

74. Determine how many baffle plates and support plates are needed for one tube bundle.

    ❏ 10
    ❏ 12
    ❏ 14
    ✔ **17**

75. State the material thickness of the baffle plates in inches.

Answer: 3/8 inch

76. What is the center to center spacing between any two baffle plates marked number 113 and 114?

    ❏ 10 inches
    ❏ 12 inches
    ✔ **12½ inches**
    ❏ 14 inches

77. How many tubes in total will be installed in this heat exchanger?

Answer: 2216

78. What is the outside diameter of the 14 gage tubes?

    ❏ ¼ inch
    ❏ ½ inch
    ✔ **¾ inch**
    ❏ 1 inch

79. What is the diameter of the tie rod holes to be drilled and tapped in the stationary tubesheet.

    ❏ 1 inch
    ❏ ¾ inch
    ✔ **½ inch**
    ❏ ¼ inch

80. To what depth will the tierod holes be drilled and tapped into the stationary tubesheet,?

    ❏ ¼ inch
    ❏ ½ inch
    ✔ **¾ inch**
    ❏ 1 inch

81. What will be the diameter of the tube holes drilled in the baffles?

Answer: 49/64 inch

82. What is the plus/minus tolerance allowed for the drilling and reaming of the tubesheet holes as indicated in the tube hole detail?

Answer: ± .002 inches

83. What is the face to face distance between the tubesheets?

    ❏ 264 inches
    ✔ **263 3/4 inches**
    ❏ 225 3/4 inches
    ❏ 4 1/8 inches

84. The tie rod holes drilled into the baffles will be 1/2 inch in diameter.

    ❏ true
    ✔ **false**

SECTION FIVE QUESTIONS

1. To what depth is the cope made into the beam web?
Answer: 1 1/4 inches

2. How far back will the fabricator measure from the end of the beam for the cope?
Answer: 2 1/2 inches

3. The flanges of this beam are cut flush on both sides of the beam and on both ends, top and bottom.
   ❏ true
   ✔ **false**

4. Measured from the end of the beam, how far will the flanges be cut for clearance purposes?
Answer: 4 1/2 inches

5. What is the distance from the center of the right end holes to the right end of the beam?
   ❏ 1 inch
   ❏ 1¼ inches
   ✔ **1½ inches**
   ❏ 2 inches

6. What is the diameter of the field bolts used to secure this beam to the connection?
   ❏ ½ inch
   ✔ **¾ inch**
   ❏ 1 inch
   ❏ 1¼ inch

7. What is the overall length of this beam?
Answer: 18 ft. - 2 $^{7}/_{8}$ in.

8. The nominal depth of this beam is 14 inches and it weighs 22 lbs. per foot.
   ✔ **true**
   ❏ false

9. State the diameter of the holes in each end of this beam.
Answer: 13/16 inches

10. How many beams will be fabricated from this drawing?
   ✔ **1**
   ❏ 2
   ❏ 3
   ❏ 4

11. Write out the required beam descriptions.
Answer: 2-W14 x 22 x 30 ft. 5 1/2 in.
             1-W14 x 22 x 27 ft. 4 in.

12. What is the gage distance for all holes in the bottom flange of the beam?
Answer: 3 inches

13. What is the leg size of the fillet welds that join 'aa' to the beam flanges?
Answer: 1/4 inch fillet

14. How many 'Pa's are required for beam B2B?
Answer: 2

15. What is the cut length of items 'Pa'?
Answer: 1 ft. 1 1/2 in.

16. What is the overall length of beam B2C?
Answer: 27 ft. 4 in.

17. Calculate the distance from the left end of beam B2 to the center of plate 'Pa'.
Answer: 15 ft. 8 in.

18. Describe fully the welding required for all plates marked 'Pa'.

Answer: 1/4 fillet - 3 sides

19. How many angles marked 'aa' are required for beam B2A?

Answer: 8

20. What is the heel to heel distance between each angle marked 'aa'?

- ❏ 3 feet
- ✔ **8 feet**
- ❏ 16 feet
- ❏ 24 feet

21. The distance laid out for the first angle 'aa' on the left end of beam B2B is:

- ❏ 4'-10½"
- ✔ **3'-10½"**
- ❏ 2'-8½"
- ❏ 1'-6½"

22. Describe fully the leg size, thickness and cut length of angles 'aa'.

Answer: 2 1/2 x 2 1/2 x 3/8 x 9 1/2 inches

23. How many holes will be drilled in one beam?

- ❏ 6
- ❏ 8
- ✔ **10**
- ❏ 12

24. What is the thickness of item number 'Pa'?

Answer: 3/8 inch

25. Referring to angles 'aa', how far do they protrude from the center of the beam web as shown in the right side view?

Answer: 7 inches

26. Angles 'aa' protrude past the flange on the near side only.

- ❏ true
- ✔ **false**

27. What is the overall length of each beam marked B3?

Answer: 4907 mm

28. What is the plate thickness of P17?

Answer: 13 mm

29. Describe the location of the erection mark to be included on the beam.

Answer: Top Flange - Left End

30. Which of the following piece marks refer to the end plate connections?

- ❏ P73 and P17
- ✔ **P14 and P72**
- ❏ P14 and P17
- ❏ P73 and P17

31. What is the gage distance between web holes located at dimension 4153?

- ❏ 65 mm
- ❏ 75 mm
- ✔ **80 mm**
- ❏ 90 mm

32. How many holes will be made in P73?

Answer: 6 holes

33. What is the gage distance of the holes in end connection P72?

- ❏ 65 mm
- ❏ 75 mm
- ❏ 80 mm
- ✔ **100 mm**

34. How many holes will be made in the web of beam B3?
    - ❏ 8 holes
    - ❏ 12 holes
    - ❏ 14 holes
    - ✔ **16 holes**

35. All dimensions for hole locations in the web of the beam originate from the left side of P72.
    - ❏ true
    - ✔ **false**

36. Referring to the front and top view of the beam, on which side of the beam will all P165's be installed?
    - ❏ near side
    - ✔ **far side**
    - ❏ both sides
    - ❏ top flange

37. The pitch of the web holes at 898 and 4153 is 80 mm.
    - ❏ true
    - ✔ **false**

38. What is the weight of each completed B3?

Answer: 210.5 kg

39. How many columns will be fabricated?

Answer: 2

40. What is the difference between columns C1A and C1B?

Answer: C1A is as shown, C1B is opp. hand

41. What is the cut length of the 6 inch square tubing?

Answer: 23 ft. 11 1/2 in.

42. How thick is the base plate?

Answer: 3/4 inch

43. Describe the size of the angle iron used as a connection.

Answer: 4 x 3 x 3/8

44. What is the distance from the bottom of the base plate to the center hole of the first angle clip?
    - ❏ 10'-10 3/4
    - ❏ 10'-11 1/2
    - ❏ 11'-1 3/4
    - ✔ **11'-2 1/2**

45. Name the size and type of weld used to join the base plate to the square tubing.

Answer: 1/4 fillet

46. Approximately how many inches of weld are required to join the base plate to the column?
    - ❏ 6 inches
    - ❏ 12 inches
    - ❏ 18 inches
    - ✔ **24 inches**

47. Referring to the tail of the welding symbol of the angle iron clips, write out in full the drawing note.

Answer: One inch return both ends typical

48. What is the length of the column including the base plate and the cap plate?

Answer: 24 ft. 0 1/2 in.

49. Referring to the dimensions of the column what does the abbreviation O/A stand for?

Answer: over all length of column

50. State the running dimension needed for locating the angle iron clip closest to the top of the column.

Answer: 23 ft. 2 3/4 in.

51. What is the diameter of the holes in the base plate?

Answer: 1 1/16 in

52. Describe the type of weld used to join the cap plate to the top of the column.

Answer: Square groove all around

53. How many holes will be required in the base plate of the column?
- ❏ 1 hole
- ❏ 2 holes
- ❏ 3 holes
- ✔ **4 holes**

54. Write out the beam size, weight per foot and length of A3.

Answer: W8 x 24 x 30 ft. 3 11/16 in.

55. What is the overall length of this column?

Answer: 30 ft. 4 7/8 in.

56. What are the overall dimensions of plate 'Pa'?

Answer: 8 in x 12 in. x 3/4 in.

57. How many columns A3 will be fabricated from this drawing?
- ✔ **1**
- ❏ 2
- ❏ 3
- ❏ 4

58. State the diameter of the holes drilled in the web of this column.

Answer: 13/16 in.

59. What is the gage outstanding leg for the holes in part 'Ma'.

Answer: 4 1/16 in.

60. State the two running dimensions of plates 'Pc'.

Answer: 3 1/2 in. and 29 ft. 9 in.

61. Which direction will plate Pc face after the column is erected?
- ❏ north
- ✔ **south**
- ❏ east
- ❏ west

62. Calculate the number of holes that will be drilled or punched in the top flange of A3.

Answer: 18

63. What is the diameter of the hole located in plate 'Pc' at location 29'-9"?

Answer: 13/16 in.

64. Determine the number of holes required in plate 'Pb'.

Answer: 4

65. Write out the general note referring to the paint specifications.

Answer: One coat primer

66. Calculate the heel to heel spacing between the third and fourth angles 'Ma' counting from the bottom of the column.

Answer: 2 ft. 7 in.

67. How many holes are required in base plate 'Pa'?
- ❏ 1
- ❏ 2
- ❏ 3
- ✔ **4**

68. What is the diameter of the holes in plate 'Pa'?

Answer: 1 1/16 in.

69. What is the shortest length of bolt required for field connections?
    - ❑ ¾"
    - ❑ 1½"
    - ✔ 1¾"
    - ❑ 2¼"

70. If the hole size is 1/16 inch larger than the diameter of bolt, what is the diameter of the field bolts required for the web hole connections?
    - ❑ 1"
    - ✔ ¾"
    - ❑ ½"
    - ❑ ¼"

71. How many field bolts in total are required as stated on the drawing?
    - ❑ 6 bolts
    - ❑ 16 bolts
    - ❑ 30 bolts
    - ✔ **52 bolts**

72. Determine if this statement is true or false. Plate 'Pb' sits flat on the end of the W8 beam.
    - ❑ true
    - ✔ **false**

73. Calculate the distance from the underside of the base plate to the heel of the last angle 'Ma'.

Answer: 27 ft. 11 in.

74. Determine the cut length of beam W201.

Answer: 7515 mm

75. What is the thickness of the base plate?

Answer: 32 mm

76. Referring to the angle clips 'ma', what is the distance from the heel of the angle to the center of the holes in the angle?

Answer: 50 mm

77. Write in full the abbreviation B/B as it refers to angles 'ma'.

Answer: back to back

78. Write out the rise over run slope for the holes in connector plate 'pb'.

Answer: 250 : 229

79. Calculate the distance from the underside of the base plate to the center of the top hole in connector plate 'pb'.

Answer: 349 mm

80. Which two dimensions would be used to locate the center of the top hole in plate 'pb'?

Answer: 317 mm and 168 mm

81. What is the center to center distance between holes as layed out on the workline for 'pb'?

Answer: 65 mm

82. There are three detail pieces 'mc' required for this column. What is the distance from the center 'mc' to the left end of the beam?

Answer: 4185 mm

83. What type of weld is required to attach plate 'pc' to the beam web?

Answer: 6 mm fillet UNO

84. What is the leg size of the fillet weld required to attach all 'ma's?

Answer: 10 mm fillet

85. What will be the length of the return weld for item 'ma'?

Answer: 20 mm

86. Calculate the running dimension center to center distance between the column web holes located at the top of the column.

Answer: 80 mm

87. The hole gage for the holes noted in the above question is 100 mm center to center.

✔ **true**
❏ false

88. What grade of material is used to fabricate all of the pieces necessary for the column?

Answer: 350 A

89. What is the overall length of this truss?

Answer: 31 ft. 3 1/8 in.

90. The length of each piece 'ma' as stated in the bill of materials is?

Answer: 31 ft. 3 1/8 in.

91. Describe the type, nominal size and weight description of the material used to make the chords.

Answer: W6 x 20

92. What is the size of the square tubing used to make the web members?

Answer: 3 in. x 3 in.

93. What is the wall thickness of the tubing used for the web members?

Answer: 0.188 in.

94. Determine the overall depth of the truss.

Answer: 6 ft. 4 in. with angles

95. Write out the piece mark assigned to the vertical web members.

Answer: mc

96. How many pieces 'mc' are required for **one** complete truss?

Answer: 5

97. What is the approximate angle the ends of 'md' will be cut at?

Answer: 12 : 11 1/8 (approx. 45°)

98. What is the panel point dimension between vertical web members?

Answer: 5 ft. 3 in.

99. What is the center to center dimensions between pieces 'mg'?

Answer: 5 ft.

100. How many holes are in the bottom chord of the truss?

Answer: 8 including flange and web

101. What is the hole gage for the bottom flange of the top chord.

Answer: 3 GA

102. What is the center to center dimension between work points for the diagonal web member 'md'?

Answer: 7 ft. 7 3/4 in.

103. What is the distance measured from the left end of the bottom chord to locate the first hole in the bottom flange?

Answer: 1 1/4 in.

104. Which of these plates will be installed on the near side only of the top chord web?

❏ pc
✔ **pd**
❏ ma
❏ pa

105. Calculate the measurement from the left hand end of the top chord to the heel of the last angle clip 'mg' on the right hand end of the truss.

Answer: 30 ft. 4 1/2 in.

106. How far is the center of the holes in plate 'pb' from the top flange of 'ma'?

Answer: 3 in.

107. What would be the measurement from the left hand end to the second hole center to locate plate 'pd' on the near side of the top chord web ?

Answer: 16 ft. 11 1/2 in.

108. What is the diameter of the holes in plates 'pc and pd'?

Answer: 1 5/16 in.

109. What are the piece mark numbers for the top chord and the bottom chord members?

Answer: ma and mb

110. What is the cut length of the top and bottom chords?

Answer: 18 950 mm

111. What is the center to center distance between panel points?

Answer: 3840 mm

112. Referring to the note for direction marks on the top chord, what is to be marked on the truss?

Answer: west

113. What is the overall depth of this truss?

Answer: 2550 mm

114. Referring to Section B-B, where will pieces Y32 be located?

Answer: midpoint of double angles

115. Referring to Section A-A, what is the dimension from the flange of the top chord to the center of the holes on all pieces Y34?

Answer: 80 mm

116. Describe how the web members are attached to the bottom flange of the top chord.

Answer: welded to gusset plates

117. Write out the leg size of the fillet welds required to secure the web members to the chords.

Answer: 6 and 8 mm

118. The length of the fillet welds noted in question #117 are all the same length.

❏ true
✔ **false**

119. Referring to Section C-C, describe the requirements for welding at the ends of 'md' and 'mg'.

Answer: return 10 @ ends

120. Referring to Section C-C, what is the term most commonly used to describe the fillet welds required to attach 'md and mg' to the bottom chord?

Answer: staggered intermittent

121. What is the running dimension from the left hand end of the truss used to locate 'md' on the bottom chord?

Answer: 11 695 mm

122. On which side of the chord will 'md' and 'mg' be located?

Answer: far side

123. How many holes are in each plate 'Pa'?

Answer: 8 holes

124. Determine how many holes are required in the top chord of the truss.

Answer: 4 holes

125. What is the distance from the flange of the top chord to the center of the first hole in the web?

Answer: 70 mm

126. What is the center to center distance of the web holes in the top chord?

Answer: 65 mm

127. How many full length panel points are required to be layed out on the bottom chord?

Answer: 5

128. What is the typical dimension from the work point in the web of the top chord needed to locate all web members on the connector plate?

Answer: 213 typical, unless noted

129. State the roof pitch for the truss.

Answer: 6 : 12

130. Write out the depth and the weight per foot of the WT used for the bottom chord.

Answer: WT 5 x 8.5

131. Approximately how much WT 8 x 20 is required to make up the entire top chord?

Answer: 43 ft. 9 in.

132. Which of the dimensions shown below relate to the overall span of the truss?
- ❏ 20 feet
- ❏ 20 feet 5 inches
- ✔ **40 feet**
- ❏ 40 feet 10 inches

133. What is the actual out to out dimension of the fabricated truss?
- ❏ 20 feet
- ❏ 20 feet 5 inches
- ❏ 40 feet
- ✔ **40 feet 10 inches**

134. Referring to the welding symbol located at the top of the truss, determine how much gap is required when fitting the two chord halves together.

Answer: none

135. Name the type of weld required that is needed to attach the web angles to the top and bottom chords.

Answer: fillet

136. Which side, "arrow side" or "other side", has the largest weld by size for the web angles to the top chord member joint?

Answer: other side

137. Name the joint preparation required for welding of the two web sections of the WT8's at the peak of the truss.
   - ❑ fillet weld
   - ✔ **vee groove preparation**
   - ❑ bevel groove preparation
   - ❑ double bevel groove preparation

138. What is the name of the weld that is used on the other side of the joint when referring to the weld noted in question number 137?
   - ❑ fillet weld
   - ❑ full penetration weld
   - ✔ **back weld**
   - ❑ butt weld

139. According to this drawing how many steel columns are needed to support beam line C.
   - ❑ 2
   - ❑ 3
   - ✔ **4**
   - ❑ 6

140. Referring to the two center spans of the roof framing plan, write out the complete description of the wide flange beams.

Answer: W460 x 61

141. What size are the columns supporting the wide flange beams?

Answer: HSS 127 x 127 x 7.95 square tubing

142. Are the columns square, rectangular or round?

Answer: square

143. State the dimensions of the base plates used on the columns.

Answer: 280 x 280 x 19

144. Referring to the column base plates, how many anchor bolts are required for each one, and what is their diameter?

Answer: 4 - 19 mm

145. Approximately how many millimeters will beam B10 extend past the center of column C5, for splicing purposes, after it is erected into place?

Answer: 1000 mm

146. Referring to the two beam lines, what is the piece mark number of the beams that will span between grid lines 2 and 3?

Answer: B11

147. What is the depth of the open web steel joists that will span between grid lines C and D?

Answer: 600 mm

148. State the leg size and thickness of the angle iron used on the store front fascia found on grid line 5.

Answer: 75 x 75 x 6

149. Referring to section view 6, what is the clearance allowed for grout between the column base plate and the concrete piling?

Answer: 50 mm grout

150. Will the roof slope down towards the center of the building or slope down towards the outer walls?

Answer: slope into center

151. Determine from section 2 what the thickness of the concrete floor will be.

Answer: 150 mm

152. Referring to section 5, what will be the depth of the front fascia?

Answer: 2166 mm

153. What is the total rise for this stair?
- ❏ 192 mm
- ❏ 250 mm
- ❏ 2496 mm
- ✔ **2690 mm**

154. What is the total run for this stair?
- ❏ 192 mm
- ❏ 250 mm
- ✔ **3250 mm**
- ❏ 4098 mm

155. What is the unit rise for this stair?
- ✔ **192 mm**
- ❏ 250 mm
- ❏ 2496 mm
- ❏ 4098 mm

156. What is the unit run for this stair?
- ❏ 192 mm
- ✔ **250 mm**
- ❏ 3250 mm
- ❏ 4098 mm

157. How many stair treads (pans) will be required for one stair?
- ❏ 11
- ❏ 12
- ✔ **13**
- ❏ 14

158. What is the step length for the rise/run shown for this stair?
- ❏ 178
- ❏ 192
- ❏ 207
- ✔ **315**

159. A note appears at both the bottom and top of the stair stringer and is abbreviated T.O. Conc.. Write out this abbreviation in full.

Answer: top of concrete

160. Name the size of and type of weld used to attach the stair pans to the stringers.

Answer: 4 mm fillet

161. Which of the dimensions listed below refers to the distance the nosing line is measured from the heel of the stringer?
- ✔ **50 mm**
- ❏ 71 mm
- ❏ 147 mm
- ❏ 158 mm

162. What is the vertical height from the floor to the top of the first stair pan?

Answer: 194 mm

163. List the vertical and horizontal dimension used to layout the cut line for the bottom end of the stair stringers.

Answer: 199 and 241 mm

164. What is the work point to work point dimension on the nosing line (work line) when referring to the distance from the nosing of the first tread to the nosing of the last tread?
- ❏ 2496 mm
- ❏ 3250 mm
- ✔ **4098 mm**
- ❏ 4590 mm

165. What is the overall length of the treads for stair A?

Answer: 1050

166. What is the overall length of the treads for stair B?

Answer: 900

167. Including the step to reach the first tread, how many risers are there in total?

Answer: 14

168. What is the total rise of this stair from the floor to the top of the landing?

- ❏ 151 mm
- ❏ 250 mm
- ❏ 2768 mm
- ✔ **3070 mm**

169. What is the total run of this stair from the front of the stringer to the front of the landing?

- ❏ 4480 mm
- ✔ **4556 mm**
- ❏ 4590 mm
- ❏ 7206 mm

170. What is the work point to work point dimension of the nosing line?

- ❏ 5360 mm
- ✔ **5231 mm**
- ❏ 5305 mm
- ❏ 4480 mm

171. What is the rise between any two steps.

Answer: 168.8

172. What is the gage outstanding leg for the hole in piece 'ac'?

Answer: 45 mm

173. Determine which of the distances listed below indicates the individual step length dimension.

- ❏ 151
- ❏ 250
- ✔ **327**
- ❏ 401

174. Using the RD table determine the location dimension for the number 6 tread on the nosing line.

Answer: 1709

175. From the bill of materials, what is the size and length of the channel iron used to make up piece 'mf'?

Answer: C150 x 12 x 970

176. Using the rise over run ratio shown on the drawing, write out the bevel dimensions of the miter cut for piece number 'MC'.

Answer: 141: 250

177. What is the piece mark number of the stair treads?

Answer: ga 29

178. What is the overall width including piece 'pb' of the stair treads.

Answer: 305 mm

179. How many pieces 'pa' in total are fabricated?

Answer: 32

180. What is the purpose of pieces 'pc'?

Answer: support for nosing pb

181. What structural shape is used to fabricate pieces 'ma'?

Answer: square tubing

182. Determine which of the angle irons used for cross bracing between the columns is not full length, and will be cut or coped?

Answer: ab and ac

183. Calculate the edge distance from the center of any of the base plate holes to the outside edge of the base plate.

✔ **40 mm**
❏ 80 mm
❏ 110 mm
❏ 220 mm

184. What does the symbol "do" refer to with reference to pieces 'ab' and 'ac'.

Answer: same size material

185. Is the HSS used to make piece 'ma' square, round or rectanglar?

Answer: round

186. Referring to the plan view shown on this drawing how many vertical support posts will be required for this stair?

Answer: 8

187. How many pieces 'pf' will be installed between any two vertical supports posts for the steps?

Answer: 5

188. Calculate the total length of round HSS needed to fabricate one vertical support post.

Answer: 829 mm

189. Determine how many pieces 'pd' will be installed into the front side platform handrail.

Answer: 5

190. What is the horizontal center to center distance between each vertical post on the stair?

Answer: 1135 mm

191. What will be the total weight in kilograms of the handrail when completed?

Answer: 100 kg

192. What is the center to center distance between each vertical post as layed out along the slope of the stair?

Answer: 1325 mm

193. Name the type of material the ladder side rails are made from.

Answer: HSS tubing

194. What is the center to center spacing of the side rails?

Answer: 510 mm

195. State the overall length of the ladder.

Answer: 10 526 mm

196. How many pieces 'mb' are required and what is the center to center spacing between them?

Answer: 16 and 1200 mm spacing on each side

197. What is the bevel at the intersection of pieces 'ma and mc'?

Answer: 250:250 or 45 degrees

198. How many pieces 'ra' are required and what is the center to center spacing between them?

Answer: 35 rungs @ 300 mm spacing

199. Calculate the difference in diameter between piece's 'pa' and 'pb'.

Answer: 200 mm

200. What is the center to center distance between pieces 'pc' that will be welded to piece 'pb'?

Answer: 265 mm

201. Referring to pieces 'pc', what is the typical angle formed between each piece?

Answer: 40 degrees

202. What size and type of weld is required to attach plate 'pd' to all pieces 'mc?

Answer: 5 mm fillet

203. Is plate 'pd' welded to all pieces 'mb' using a 5 mm fillet weld?

✔ yes
❏ no

204. What size and type of weld is used to attach all pieces 'ra' to the side rails?

Answer: 5 mm fillet

205. Referring to the radius noted for the cage hoops, what does the abbreviation O/S mean?

Answer: outside

206. Describe the purpose for Section A-A.

Answer: top view of lower cage hoop

207. State the diameter of the hole required in piece 'pg'.

Answer: 11 mm

SECTION SIX ANSWERS

1. How many times has drawing 6-4A been revised?
   - ✔ **0**
   - ❏ 1
   - ❏ 2
   - ❏ 4

2. Drawing 6-4A indicates an elevation of 19200 mm or 19.2 meters. If the first floor is at elevation 10 000 mm or 10.0 meters, then how high is floor elevation 19 200 above the first floor?
   - ❏ 10.2 m
   - ✔ **9.2 m**
   - ❏ 8.2 m
   - ❏ 10.0 m

3. What is the overall length and width of the building in meters?

Answer1: 6.4 x 18.4

4. How many columns in total are shown on grid lines 1, 3, and 5 on drawing 6-4A?
   - ❏ 4
   - ❏ 6
   - ❏ 8
   - ✔ **12**

5. What is the width of girder G1 as indicated in the Beam and Girder Schedule for drawing 6-4A?
   - ❏ 200 mm
   - ✔ **250 mm**
   - ❏ 600 mm
   - ❏ 800 mm

6. What is the center of column to center of column distance of girder G1?

Answer: 8075 mm

7. What is the clear span distance for girder G1 from drawing 6-4A?
   - ✔ **7825 mm**
   - ❏ 8000 mm
   - ❏ 8100 mm
   - ❏ 8200 mm

8. What is the clear span distance for the following beams?
   - ❏ B1   5825
   - ❏ B2   5750
   - ❏ B3   5825
   - ❏ B6   5750

9. From the beam schedule for drawing 6-4A, how many of the following beams are required?
   - ❏ B2   2
   - ❏ B3   4
   - ❏ B4   2
   - ❏ B5   2

10. What is the rebar end connection for B1 from the beam schedule?
   - ❏ non-continuous both ends
   - ❏ continuous both ends
   - ✔ **one end continuous, one end non-continuous**
   - ❏ 10 M @ 300

11. From the beam schedule, what is the bottom reinforcement for the following beams?
   - ❏ B2   3 - 25 M
   - ❏ B3   2 - 30 M
   - ❏ B4   2 - 30 M
   - ❏ B5   3 - 20 M

12. What is the difference in depth between the beams and girders?

Answer: 200 mm

13. How far apart are the girder stirrups?
- ❏ 10 M
- ❏ 250 mm
- ✔ **300 mm**
- ❏ 600 mm

14. What size is a #7 rebar?
- ❏ 1/8 inch
- ❏ 3/8 inch
- ❏ 5/8 inch
- ✔ **7/8 inch**

15. When comparing a #7 rebar to a 20 M bar, the 20 M bar will be:
- ❏ larger
- ✔ **smaller**
- ❏ same size
- ❏ will vary depending on manufacturer

16. What is the overall length and width of the building?
Answer: 100 ft. x 83 ft.

17. How many type F3 footings are required?
- ❏ 20
- ❏ 14
- ❏ 6
- ✔ **5**

18. All the plan view grid spacings are the same.
- ❏ true
- ✔ **false**

19. How many 9 ft. x 9 ft. footings are required?
- ❏ 20
- ❏ 14
- ✔ **6**
- ❏ 5

20. What is the thickness for the following footings?
- ❏ F1   1 ft. 11 in.
- ❏ F2   1 ft. 10 in.
- ❏ F3   1 ft. 8 in.
- ❏ F4   1 ft. 7 in.
- ❏ F5   1 ft. 6 in.

21. What is the width of the stairway?
Answer: 8 ft. 0 in.

22. Which footing has the largest diameter rebar?
- ✔ **F1**
- ❏ F3
- ❏ F4
- ❏ All sized the same

23. The bottom of wall elevation is:
- ❏ 92.33 feet
- ❏ 91.33 feet
- ❏ 90.33 feet
- ✔ **89.33 feet**

24. What is the size of the longitudinal reinforcement (parallel to steps) for the stairs on ELEVATION E-E?
- ✔ **#5 @ 6 in.**
- ❏ #4 @ 12 in.
- ❏ 1 1/2 C.L.
- ❏ none of the above

25. What size bar is used for the nosing in each stair tread?
Answer: #4 bar

26. What is the measurement of the rise and run for each step in the stairs?
- ❏ 16 x 16
- ✔ **7 x 10**
- ❏ 10 x 7
- ❏ 9 ft 4 x 14 ft 4

27. The windows have a height of:
   - ❏ 4 ft.
   - ✔ **4 ft. 6 in.**
   - ❏ 5 ft
   - ❏ 6 ft. 6 in.

28. ELEVATION E-E and the FOUNDA-TION PLAN are both drawn to the same scale?
   - ❏ true
   - ✔ **false**

29. The C.L. distance for the rebar at the bottom of the footings is
   - ❏ 1-1/2 in.
   - ✔ **3 in.**
   - ❏ #5 @ 2 ft 6 in.
   - ❏ dowell size not shown

30. Which of the following curtain wall units intersect at grid Y-15?
   - ❏ CW1 and CW2
   - ✔ **CW2 and CW3**
   - ❏ CW3 and CW4
   - ❏ W10 and W15

31. Identify the drawing numbers where the elevation view can be found for:
   - ❏ window type W10   7B
   - ❏ window type W11   7B
   - ❏ curtain wall CW6   211
   - ❏ curtain wall CW2   208

32. Windows W10, and W11 have the same top elevation.
   - ❏ true
   - ✔ **false**

33. What is the elevation for the top of window W11?
   Answer: 102 400, top of block

34. How many windows are required for window types W10 and W11?
   Answer: 7 of each

35. What are the rough opening sizes for windows W10 and W11?
   - ❏ W10   2800 x 810
   - ❏ W11   700 x 1342

36. What is the frame height for windows W10 and W11?
   - ❏ W10   2774.6
   - ❏ W11   674.6

37. What is the frame width for windows W10 and W11?
   - ❏ W10   784.6
   - ❏ W11   1316.6

38. What is the clearance between the rough opening and the frame for windows W10, and W11?
   Answer: 25.4 mm for both

39. What window type is adjacent to window W10?
   Answer: W11

40. If the daylight opening (DLO) dimension is the difference between the outside and inside frame measurements, what is the width of the frame for window W10?
   Answer: 127 mm

41. On drawing 6-7B, elevation W10, there are two details marked as no.1. On which drawings are these details found?
   Answer: 7C and 7D

42. W10 is based on an elevation of 100900. How far above this level does the rough opening start?
   - ❏ 10 mm
   - ✔ **100 mm**
   - ❏ 1000 mm
   - ❏ 2800 mm

43. What is the overhang and projection from the outside wall for the flashing on window W10?

Answer: 40 mm

44. On drawing 6-7C determine the exterior frame width and thickness:

Answer: 63.5 x 19.05

45. On drawing 6-7C determine the interior frame width and thickness:

Answer: 63.5 x 101.6

46. On drawing 6-7C determine the distance between the exterior and the interior frame:

Answer: 33.34 mm

47. On drawing 6-7C determine the thickness of the glass:

Answer: 25.4 mm

48. On drawing 6-7C determine the thickness of the exterior brick:

Answer: 90mm

49. On drawing 6-7D determine the exterior frame width and thickness:

Answer: 63.5 x 19.05

50. On drawing 6-7D determine the interior frame width and thickness:

Answer: 63.5 x 101.6

51. On drawing 6-7C determine the overall measurement from the outside to inside for the window frame unit:

Answer: 153.99

52. There are no revisions to drawings 6-7C and 6-7D.

✔ **true**

❏ false

SECTION SEVEN ANSWERS

1. A pressurized vessel used to produce hot water or steam is called a:

Answer: boiler

2. A boiler has water circulating through the inside of the tubes and hot flue gases on the outside of the tube. Is this a watertube boiler or a firetube boiler?

Answer: watertube boiler

3. A firetube boiler is designed to operate at higher pressures and temperatures?

    ❏ true
    ✔ **false**

4. The pressure part of a watertube boiler in which all water and steam will pass through at least once is the:

    ✔ **steam drum**
    ❏ lower drum
    ❏ economizer
    ❏ superheater

5. The steam drum is never full of water. The reason for this is to allow a steam space above the water.

    ✔ **true**
    ❏ false

6. Is a natural circulation boiler or a forced circulation boiler best suited to meet frequent changes in operating requirements?

Answer: forced circulation

7. Determine if this statement is true or false. Economizers, superheaters, reheaters and airheaters are additional components that increase the efficiency of a steam generator and make steam.

    ❏ true
    ✔ **false**

8. Which of these drums serve as the main distribution point for feeding the individual furnace wall tubes of a water tube boiler?

    ❏ steam drum
    ✔ **lower drum**
    ❏ superheater drum
    ❏ economizer drum

9. The name of the steam generator component that is used to heat the steam to its highest temperature before it goes to the turbine is:

    ❏ steam drum
    ✔ **superheater**
    ❏ reheater
    ❏ economizer

10. After the steam has passed through the first stage of a turbine it is often sent back to the steam generator to be:

    ❏ superheated
    ✔ **reheated**
    ❏ condensed
    ❏ purified

11. This component is used to preheat the boiler feedwater before it enters the steam drum. It is called a/an:

    ❏ superheater
    ❏ reheater
    ❏ airheater
    ✔ **economizer**

12. What is the name of the device used to pre-heat the incoming combustion air?

Answer: air heater

13. The boiler draft fan that supplies the burners and the furnace with combustion air is called:

Answer: forced draft fan

14. The boiler draft fan that is used on the exhaust side of the furnace is called:

Answer: induced draft fan

15. Identify the boiler component that is NOT heated by flue gases passing over it as the gases travel out of the steam generator to the exhaust stack.
- ❏ reheater
- ❏ economizer
- ❏ airheater
- ✔ **steam drum**

16. Which one of the noted boiler pressure parts does this unit **not** have?
- ❏ steam drum
- ❏ superheaters
- ✔ **lower drum**
- ❏ downcomers

17. What is the inside diameter of the steam drum?

Answer: 60 inches I.D.

18. Write out the roof beam description as noted on the drawing.

Answer: W8 x 31

19. Calculate the height to the center of the steam drum from the ground floor.

Answer: 37 ft. 6 in.

20. The distance from the center of the steam drum to the low level alarm is:
- ❏ 6 inches
- ❏ 7 inches
- ✔ **13 inches**
- ❏ 14 inches

21. The distance from the center of the steam drum to the normal water level is six inches.
- ✔ **true**
- ❏ false

22. How far will the steam drum expand away (to the right) from the boiler, as noted on the drawing?
- ❏ 1/16 of and inch
- ✔ **5/16 of and inch**
- ❏ 9/16 of and inch
- ❏ 5/8 of and inch

23. Which of these dimensions refers to the furnace depth, as noted on the drawing?
- ✔ **14'-0"**
- ❏ 16'-0"
- ❏ 24'-0"
- ❏ 38'-0"

24. What is installed over top of the floor tubes to protect them?

Answer: 1 1/2 inch tiles

25. Which dimension represents the vertical distance from the center of the burners to the center of the steam drum?
- ❏ 10'-6"
- ✔ **27'-0"**
- ❏ 39'-0"
- ❏ 42'-3"

26. What is the outside diameter of the upper rear wall header?

Answer: 10 3/4 inches O.D.

27. At what elevation are the observation ports located on both sides of this unit?

       ❏ 100'-6"
       ❏ 117'-0"
       ✔ **121'-0"**
       ❏ 134'-5"

28. If facing the front of the boiler, which statement listed is correct?

       ✔ **this drawing is a right side section view of the boiler**
       ❏ this drawing is a right side view of the boiler
       ❏ this drawing is a left side section view of the boiler
       ❏ this drawing is a left side view of the boiler

29. Referring to the air heater, is the gas flow through the upper or the lower half of the unit?

Answer: upper half

30. How many expansion joints are shown on this drawing for both the air ducts and gas ducts?

       ❏ 3
       ❏ 4
       ❏ 5
       ✔ **7**

31. What is the inside diameter of the steam drum?

Answer: 60 inches I.D.

32. What is the inside diameter of the lower drum?

Answer: 42 inches I.D.

33. What is the wall thickness of the steam drum?

Answer: 4.875 inches

34. What is the wall thickness of the lower drum in inches?

Answer: 3.375 inches

35. Determine if this statement is true or false: "this is a top supported boiler".

       ❏ true
       ✔ **false**

36. Calculate the distance from the floor to the top outside surface of the bottom drum.

Answer: 8 ft. 0 3/8 in.

37. What is the diameter and minimum wall thickness of the furnace tubes as noted in the tube schedule?

Answer: 2 1/2 inches, 0.165 inches

38. Determine if this statement is true or false: "this unit has an economizer that is heated by the flue gases".

       ✔ **true**
       ❏ false

39. What is the diameter and minimum wall thickness of the superheater inlet header?

Answer: 14 inches, 1.375 inches

40. What is the vertical center to center distance between the superheater headers?

Answer: 14 inches

41. Calculate the horizontal distance from the drum centerline to the centerline of the superheater inlet header.

Answer: 4 ft. 6 1/2 in.

42. What is the center to center distance between the steam drum and the lower drum?

Answer: 34 ft. 0 in.

43. Determine the difference between the center to center distance of the side wall headers and the center to center distance of the drums.

Answer: 9 1/2 inches

44. Calculate the distance from the floor to the center of the second buckstay on the right hand side of the boiler.

Answer: 22 ft. 11 in.

45. State the size and weight description of the buckstays as noted on the drawing.

Answer: W18 x 45 (TYP)

46. Determine if this statement is true or false. Cutting plane line A-A as noted on this drawing refers to Sect. A-A of the side elevation drawing.

    ✔ **true**
    ❏ false

47. Which distance noted below refers to the spacing of the frontwall, roof and floor tubes?

    ❏ 2 inches
    ✔ **3 inches**
    ❏ 4 inches
    ❏ 6 inches

48. What is the spacing of the superheater tubes?

    ❏ 2 inches
    ❏ 3 inches
    ✔ **4 inches**
    ❏ 6 inches

49. At what degree or angle from vertical are the gas inlets for the burners installed?

Answer: 45 degrees

50. By observing the expansion symbol on the right hand side, how much side expansion is expected?

Answer: 9/16 inch

SECTION EIGHT ANSWERS

1. Most pipe used for industrial purposes is primarily made from:
   - ❏ stainless steel
   - ✔ **carbon steel**
   - ❏ copper alloys
   - ❏ brass or bronze

2. Pipe sizes ranging from ½ inch to 12 inches in diameter are specified as a nominal size, while pipe greater than 12 inches in diameter is specified as an actual outside diameter.
   - ✔ **true**
   - ❏ false

3. What is the actual outside diameter of a 4 inch (114.3 mm) pipe?

   Answer: 4.5 inches

4. A primary line is shown as a thick line. What type of line is a medium thick line about the same weight as an object line?

   Answer: secondary line

5. What is the name of the line that is used to align two pipe drawings when it is necessary to indicate continuation of a piping system on another drawing?
   - ✔ **match or boundary line**
   - ❏ grid line
   - ❏ coordinate line
   - ❏ latitude and longitude line

6. On a piping drawing, the first number given on the tag of a piping line used to identify that particular line always refers to the diameter of the pipe used.
   - ❏ true
   - ✔ **false**

7. What is used on a piping drawing to indicate the direction of flow of the contents of a particular line?

   Answer: arrow pointing in direction of flow

8. Notes that apply to the entire piping drawing are called specific notes while notes that apply to one particular part or area of the drawing are called general notes.
   - ❏ true
   - ✔ **false**

9. Piping drawings are not always drawn to scale but are drawn with a sense of proportion and elevation to represent systems as close and practical as possible.
   - ✔ **true**
   - ❏ false

10. What is the name of the drawing used to show a plan view of the location of buildings, vessels, tanks and other equipment in a plant?

    Answer: site plan drawing

11. What type of drawing zeros in on specifics of a major location on the plant site?

    Answer: general arrangement drawing

12. Piping plan view drawings are developed from:
    - ❏ site plan drawings
    - ✔ **general arrangements drawings**
    - ❏ isometric drawings
    - ❏ orthographic drawings

13. What type of drawing is a theoretical layout of a piping system and its operation?

    Answer: schematic diagram

14. What type of diagram is a more sophisticated schematic drawing showing equipment layout and the flow of fluids through the system?

Answer: flow diagram

15. Write out the name of the abbreviation P&ID.

Answer: piping and instrumentation diagram

16. Name the drawing used to illustrate mechanical or process flows in schematic form that includes major equipment, valves and process lines along with their line code and flow direction and any instrumentation and control devices?

Answer: piping and instrumentation diagram

17. What type of piping drawing shows the true shape and dimensions of a equipment and a piping system?

Answer: orthographic projection

18. Elevation grades start at 100 feet (100 m) on piping drawings to provide an even number starting point and give underground services a positive number.

✔ **true**
❏ false

19. Which pictorial drawing method is most frequently used to develop piping spool drawings?

❏ oblique
❏ perspective
✔ **isometric**
❏ orthographic

20. The dimensions shown on single line isometric spool prints are taken from the center of fittings and flanges.

✔ **true**
❏ false

21. State the overall dimensions of the Booster Station building in millimeters.

Answer: 15 940 x 10 940

22. Noting the direction symbol for north, determine on which side of the building the natural gas service enters.

❏ north
❏ south
❏ east
✔ **west**

23. What is the bench mark elevation of the building in meters?

Answer: 100 m

24. On which side of the building are the bollards located.

✔ **north**
❏ south
❏ east
❏ west

25. What is the Geodetic elevation of the building in meters?

Answer: 695.050

26. Referring to the Floor Plan, what is the distance between the bollards in millimeters?

Answer: 3010

27. Referring to Building Section 2-A1 what is the pump room floor made of?

❏ concrete only
❏ floor grating only
✔ **concrete and floor grating**
❏ cedar decking

28. State the dimensions in millimeters of the intake grille as noted in Building Section 3-A1.

Answer: 1200 x 1200 mm

29. What is the typical center to center distance in millimeters between the wood trusses as noted in Building Section 1-A1?

Answer: 1500 mm

30. What is the thickness of the concrete slab for the vestibule as noted in the Floor Plan?

Answer: 125 mm

31. This building is designed using a grid system.
   ✔ **true**
   ❏ false

32. What is the distance between grid 1. and 2.?
   ❏ 10 890
   ❏ 6740
   ✔ **4200**
   ❏ 2400

33. State the number of the pump that will be installed at a future date.

Answer: #4

34. Which pump is designed to be used at a variable speed?
   ❏ pump #1
   ❏ pump #2
   ✔ **pump #3**
   ❏ pump #4

35. What is the rated capacity in liters per second of each pump?

Answer: 132.6 lps

36. What pump pressure is required to produce the maximum flow rate as noted on this drawing?

Answer: 292 kPa

37. What size reducer is used on the inlet side of each pump?

Answer: 300 to 250 eccentric reducer

38. A reducer fitting is used to join the pump outlet pipe to the main flow lines. State the size of this fitting.

Answer: 200 to 300 mm

39. What is the mark number as noted in the valve list for the flanged silent check valve?
   ❏ mark #2
   ✔ **mark #3**
   ❏ mark # 4
   ❏ mark #5

40. Write out the symbol for pressure indicator.

Answer: P1

41. State the pipe size of the manual recirculation line.

Answer: 250 mm

42. What is the largest size of pipe included on this schematic drawing?

Answer: 750 mm

43. At the outlet side of each pump, what is positioned between the wafer style manual butterfly valve and the flanged silent check valve?
   ❏ temperature transmitter
   ❏ pressure transmitter
   ✔ **pressure indicator**
   ❏ future pump #4

44. What is the size of the pressure relief valve?
    - ❏ 600
    - ❏ 300
    - ❏ 150
    - ✔ 75

45. What is the approximate diameter in inches of the 600 mm line?
    - ❏ 30
    - ✔ 24
    - ❏ 16
    - ❏ 8

46. How many different sized valves are required for this schematic?
    - ❏ 10
    - ✔ 7
    - ❏ 5
    - ❏ 3

47. What is the center to center dimension between pump no.1 and pump no. 2?

Answer: 2900 mm

48. On which drawing is the detail for the 20 mm diameter copper drip pocket drain found?

Answer: 1E detail 22

49. Determine if this statement is true or false: All steel pipe inside the building 50 mm diameter and smaller is to be galvanized.
    - ✔ true
    - ❏ false

50. State the diameter of the weldolet used for the water return?

Answer: 12 mm

51. Calculate the center to center distance between the pump's inlet header and the outlet header.
    - ✔ **4250 mm**
    - ❏ 2350 mm
    - ❏ 1900 mm
    - ❏ 870 mm

52. Referring to section view 21 on drawing 1-E what is the elevation of the main header or manifold?

Answer: 100.475 mm

53. Calculate the difference in elevation from the centerline of the main header to the center of the 250 mm elbow at elevation 99.585. (see section view 21)

Answer: 890 mm

54. Referring to section view 23 on drawing 1-E, on which Booster Station drawing would a description of mark #8 be found.

Answer: 25C - Pumphouse Flow. Sch.

55. In section view 23 the centerline elevation of the 400 mm pipe is noted as 100.475. Calculate the elevation to the center of the 450 x 300 mm. eccentric reducer. (Note: to 300 mm centerline)
    - ❏ 100.475
    - ✔ **99.327**
    - ❏ 99.251
    - ❏ 99.125

56. How many drain valves are show in section view 22?
    - ❏ 1 valve
    - ✔ **2 valves**
    - ❏ 3 valves
    - ❏ 4 valves

57. Section view 21, shown on drawing 8-25E, is shown as if viewed from the front.
   - ❏ true
   - ✔ **false**

58. The 450 x 300 mm eccentric reducer shown on section view 23 is:
   - ❏ above floor level
   - ✔ **below floor level**
   - ❏ at floor level
   - ❏ none of the above

59. What method is used to reduce the size of the 500 mm pipe down to 300 mm as shown in section view 21 on drawing 25E?
Answer: 500 x 400 reducer and 400 x 300 reducer

60. What diameter is the Flow Meter?
   - ❏ 500 mm
   - ❏ 300 mm
   - ❏ 150 mm
   - ✔ **100 mm**

61. Is there only one Drip Pocket Drain, or one on each pump?
Answer: one on each pump

62. What is the grade of pipe used for this job?
   - ❏ A105
   - ❏ A234
   - ✔ **A53-B**
   - ❏ A106-B

63. Calculate how much allowance has been made for weld gap to determine the cut length of item #3 if the face to end length of item #8 is 2¾" and the face to center dimension of item #11 is 4½".
Answer: 1/8 each end

64. What grade of material is used for the flanges?
   - ✔ **A105**
   - ❏ A234
   - ❏ A53-B
   - ❏ A106-B

65. How far will the center of the shoe be located from the center of item #13?
Answer: 2 ft. 9 3/4 in.

66. What will the total weight of this spool be when fabricated?
Answer: 327 lbs.

67. Which of the listed item numbers refers to the reducing tee?
   - ❏ item #6
   - ❏ item #8
   - ❏ item #11
   - ✔ **item #13**

68. What grade of material is used for the elbows?
   - ❏ A105
   - ✔ **A234**
   - ❏ A53-B
   - ❏ A106-B

69. What is the cut length of item #2?
Answer: 4 ft. 4 7/8 in.

70. Determine the amount of 3 inch standard wall pipe needed for this order.
Answer: 23 ft. 8 1/4 in.

71. Write out the following abbreviations.
BE Bevel End
PE Plain End
RF Raised Flange
LR Long Radius
BW Butt Weld

72. Number 16 is a
    - ❏ 4 inch ball valve
    - ✔ **4 inch gate valve**
    - ❏ 3/4 inch ball valve
    - ❏ 3/4 inch gate valve

73. Indicate the item number where the pipe size changes from 4 inches to 3 inches.

Answer: item 13 - 4 x 3 reducing tee

74. Item 7 and item 8 are identical weld neck flanges.
    - ❏ true
    - ✔ **false**

75. List the two drawing numbers that correspond to the two match lines identified on drawing 1.

Answer: M-08 and M-06

76. What is the size of the pipe used for line P-526-4"-A150?
    - ❏ 2 inch N.P.S.
    - ❏ 3 inch N.P.S.
    - ✔ **4 inch N.P.S.**
    - ❏ 6 inch N.P.S.

77. What do the letters HO in the general notes of drawing 1 refer to?

Answer: hot oil

78. Determine the direction of flow in line P-578-2"-A150 on drawing 8-27A as the line travels through match line 3.

Answer: westerly

79. What is the centerline elevation of vessel A-575?

Answer: 104 ft. 6 1/2 in.

80. Do the valve dimensions shown on drawing 8-27B make allowance for gasket thickness?

Answer: include 1/8 where noted

81. Calculate the center to center distance between vessel A575 and C550.
    - ❏ 104' - 6½"
    - ❏ 109' - 6"
    - ✔ **4' - 11½"**
    - ❏ 5' - 0½

82. Calculate the difference in height between the T.O.S. dimensions shown in Elevation A-A?

Answer: 1 ft. 4 1/8 in.

83. What is the centerline elevation of line CW-552-6"-A150 found in Elevation B-B?

Answer: 112 ft. 5 5/8 in.

84. What is the height from ground level to the top of steel for the pipe rack?

Answer: 8 ft. 8 in.

85. From elevation B-B, lines BD-552, BD-527, and P-578 are all the same elevation.
    - ❏ true
    - ✔ **false**

86. How far is line CW-552 from match line 3?
    - ❏ 11 inches
    - ❏ 2 ft. 0 in.
    - ❏ 2 ft. 3 in.
    - ✔ **3 ft. 2 in.**

87. What is the center to center distance between items P576 and P577?

Answer: 6 ft. 1 3/8 in.

88. What is the outlet line elevation of P576 and P577?

Answer: 101 ft. 0 in.

89. What is the largest nominal size of pipe used for this spool piece?

- ✔ **12" NPS**
- ❏ 10" NPS
- ❏ 6" NPS
- ❏ 4" NPS

90. What is the center of elbow to face of flange dimension shown on the drawing where this line joins components G-104A or G-104B?

Answer: 1 ft. 11 1/8 in.

91. State the size and pressure rating of the couplings used as pump casing drains.

Answer: 3/4 inch

92. The pump casing drain couplings are threaded.

- ✔ **true**
- ❏ false

93. What is the pressure rating of the spectacle blinds used in the 12 inch line?

- ❏ 150#
- ✔ **300#**
- ❏ 600#
- ❏ 900#

94. How much clearance is needed between the two 12 inch weld neck flanges for inserting the spectacle blind?

Answer: 1 3/8 inch

95. What is the direction of flow in the 12 inch line below the start-up strainer located by component G-104A?

- ❏ north
- ❏ south
- ❏ up
- ✔ **down**

96. Referring to revision 1, what has been altered or changed on this drawing?

Answer: changed dimensions and material

97. Referring to the Bill of Materials what is the grade, largest diameter and longest length of stud bolts to be used for bolting some of the flanges for this spool.

Answer: B7 - 1 1/8 x 8

98. Referring to the Bill of Materials, what is the pressure rating of the 2 - 1½ inch socket weld 90° elbows?

- ❏ 150#
- ❏ 300#
- ❏ 2000#
- ✔ **3000#**

SECTION NINE ANSWERS

1. What will be the boom length needed to complete this lift, as stated on the drawing?
   - ❏ 39 feet
   - ✔ **133 feet, 6 inches**
   - ❏ 137 feet, 11 inches
   - ❏ 145 feet, 10 inches

2. What is the weight of the fin fan?
   - ✔ **51630 lbs.**
   - ❏ 54780 lbs.
   - ❏ 57100 lbs.
   - ❏ 66500 lbs.

3. How much does the rigging weigh?
   - ❏ 2320 lbs.
   - ❏ 2840 lbs.
   - ✔ **3150 lbs.**
   - ❏ 4580 lbs.

4. When lifting the load, the crane is operating at what percentage of the rated chart capacity?
   - ❏ 100%
   - ✔ **86%**
   - ❏ 14%
   - ❏ not stated

5. What is the maximum chart capacity for the crane set up shown on the drawing?
   - ❏ 97000 lbs.
   - ✔ **66500 lbs.**
   - ❏ 57100 lbs.
   - ❏ 51630 lbs.

6. What is the weight of the counterweights?
   Answer: 97,000 lbs.

7. If, at the time this lift was to be made, there was a wind blowing at 30 mph from the east, would the lift be postponed?
   - ✔ **yes**
   - ❏ no

8. What is the maximum wind speed allowed according to this drawing?
   - ❏ 10 mph
   - ❏ 15 mph
   - ✔ **20 mph**
   - ❏ 30 mph

9. Determine whether this statement is true or false: "Tag lines must be used to control this lift at all times".
   - ❏ true
   - ✔ **false**

10. The anticipated swing radius measured from the crane center pin to the center of the load or rigging is:
    - ❏ 16 feet,11 inches
    - ✔ **39 feet**
    - ❏ 29 feet, 8 inches
    - ❏ 32 feet, 3 inches

11. State in tons the working load limited (WLL) of the largest shackle used?
    - ❏ 2 tons
    - ❏ 10 tons
    - ❏ 12 tons
    - ✔ **25 tons**

12. Determine if this statement is true or false. The shackles required to attach the load to the slings are rated at a 12 ton working load limit.
    - ✔ **true**
    - ❏ false

13. What will be the clearance between the boom and the structure when the load is in the final set position?
    Answer: 3 ft. 10 in.

14. The number of parts of line that the crane load block will be reeved to is:
- ❏ 2 parts
- ❏ 4 parts
- ✔ **6 parts**
- ❏ 8 parts

15. After the crane lifts the load, the boom will swing in a clockwise direction to position the load.
- ❏ true
- ✔ **false**

16. What type of crane is used to make this lift?

Answer: 180 ton DEMAG

17. State the maximum boom length needed to complete this lift.

Answer: 115 ft. 3 in.

18. What is the weight of the heat exchanger?
- ❏ 24200 lbs.
- ✔ **63580 lbs.**
- ❏ 67760 lbs.
- ❏ 83500 lbs.

19. How much does the rigging weigh including the load block?
- ❏ 1150 lbs.
- ❏ 2680 lbs.
- ❏ 3245 lbs.
- ✔ **4180 lbs.**

20. When lifting the load, the crane is operating at what percentage of the rated chart capacity?
- ❏ 100%
- ✔ **81%**
- ❏ 19%
- ❏ not shown

21. Determine if this statement is true or false. The crane will require a counterweight in excess of 13.5 tons to safely perform this lift.
- ❏ true
- ✔ **false**

22. Determine if this statement is true or false. At a lift radius of 29 feet the crane capacity for this lift is 41.75 tons.
- ✔ **true**
- ❏ false

23. As specified in the rigging drawing, what is the length and diameter of the heat exchanger?

Answer: 27 ft. 10 3/4 in. x 5 ft. 4 in.

24. Which of the following terms describes the part of the heat exchanger that the rigging will attach to?
- ❏ shackle
- ✔ **lifting lugs**
- ❏ heads
- ❏ support saddles

25. The direction the crane will swing after it lifts the heat exchanger off the back of the truck will be:
- ❏ clockwise
- ✔ **counter-clockwise**

26. The term used to describe the piece of rigging equipment which keeps the two vertical leg slings an equal distance apart is:
- ❏ balance beam
- ❏ separator bar
- ✔ **spreader bar**
- ❏ equalizer beam

27. State the ground work required to stabilize the drainage ditch for this lift.

Answer: ditch to be filled

28. Calculate the total vertical height from the ground to the center of the boom tip sheaves of the crane during the lift.
- ❏ 27 feet 10 inches
- ❏ 34 feet 6 inches
- ❏ 93 feet 10 inches
- ✔ **122 feet 8 inches**

29. Determine if this statement is true or false. The crane wheels can remain in contact with the ground as long as the outriggers are fully extended and supporting the crane.
- ❏ true
- ✔ **false**

30. How far is the center of the truck and trailer positioned away from the center of the crane?

Answer: 25 ft. 9 in.

31. Is a constant lift radius of 27 feet maintained throughout the entire lift movement?

Answer: No, a 29 foot radius, then 27 foot

32. The total mass of the counterweight with the superlift added would be:
- ❏ 40 tonne
- ❏ 60 tonne
- ❏ 120 tonne
- ✔ **160 tonne**

33. State the approximate weight of module 68-B in kilograms.

Answer: 48 637 kg

34. What will be the lift radius for removal of module 68-B from the transport unit?
- ✔ **45. 92 feet**
- ❏ 64.32 feet
- ❏ 72.87 feet
- ❏ 91.45 feet

35. What is the rated capacity of the load block in tons?

Answer: 225 tons

36. How many parts of line will be used as the main load line?
- ❏ 4 parts
- ❏ 6 parts
- ✔ **8 parts**
- ❏ 10 parts

37. What is the capacity of the snatch block used in the center rigging attachment?
- ✔ **40 ton**
- ❏ 35 ton
- ❏ 25 ton
- ❏ 10 ton

38. What is the capacity of the two largest load shackles attached to the load block?
- ❏ 225 tons
- ❏ 220 tons
- ✔ **110 tons**
- ❏ 90 tons

39. What is the length of the slings that connect the 40 foot spreader bar to the load block?
- ❏ 10 feet
- ❏ 15 feet
- ❏ 25 feet
- ✔ **30 feet**

40. What is the capacity of the shackle used to attach the rigging to any of the module lifting eyes?
- ❏ 25 ton
- ✔ **35 ton**
- ❏ 40 ton
- ❏ 50 ton

41. State the center to center distance between the shackle pins on the spreader bars used to attach the rigging to the module.

Answer: 21 ft. 6 in.

42. Referring to the plan view, calculate the difference in the lift radius of the initial pick position and the final location of the module.

✔ **45.73 feet**
❏ 45.92 feet
❏ 91.65 feet
❏ 137.57 feet

43. Determine if this statement is true or false. The superlift counterweight will be attached to the crane after the module is lifted from the transport and rotated to a position north of the crane.

✔ **true**
❏ false

44. Will the crane swing in a clockwise or counter clockwise direction after it picks the module from the transport unit?

Answer: clockwise

45. What is the weight of all the rigging including the load block in kilograms?

Answer: 6964 kg

46. What is the expected boom angle in relationship to the ground after the load is in its final position?

Answer: 66 degrees

46. As stated on the drawing, what is the overall height of the vessel to be lifted?

Answer: 164 ft. 6 in.

47. What will be the lift radius of the boom of the main crane before the superlift counterweight is attached?

❏ 65 foot radius
❏ 59 foot radius
✔ **52 foot radius**
❏ 26 foot radius

48. Determine if this statement is true or false. The main crane's boom will be at a 52 foot lift radius when the vessel is hoisted clear of the saddles.

❏ true
✔ **false**

49. State how many times the load radius of the main crane will change after the load has been hooked up.

Answer: 4 times

50. Calculate the vertical distance from ground level to the center of the main crane's boom tip sheaves after the vessel is lifted to the vertical position and is at a radius of 59 feet.

Answer: 241 ft. 11 in.

51. What will be the center to center distance between the main crane's boom tip sheave and the main load block after the vessel is lifted to the vertical position and at a radius of 65 feet?

❏ 34 feet, 1 inch
✔ **39 feet, 3 inches**
❏ 40 feet, 8 inches
❏ 45 feet, 2 inches

52. After the superlift counter weight is attached to the main crane what will the tailswing radius be?

❏ 65 feet, 10 inches
❏ 59 feet, 10 inches
❏ 52 feet, 10 inches
✔ **47 feet, 10 inches**

53. What size are the steel mats used under the outriggers of the main crane?

Answer: 8 ft. x 8 ft.

54. What is the diameter of the outrigger pads (floats) used on the tail crane?
- ❏ 24 inches
- ❏ 36 inches
- ✔ **48 inches**
- ❏ 60 inches

55. After the vessel is swung in line with its set position the main crane will have to boom down. What is the final lift radius needed to set the vessel over its final position?
- ❏ 26 foot radius
- ❏ 52 foot radius
- ❏ 59 foot radius
- ✔ **65 foot radius**

56. Referring to rigging drawing 9-10B what is the name of the device fastened to the bottom of the vessel that the tail crane rigging will be secured to.

Answer: tailing beam

57. How many parts of line will the main load block of the tail crane be reeved to?
- ❏ 6 parts
- ❏ 8 parts
- ✔ **10 parts**
- ❏ 12 parts

58. The main crane requires two load blocks. How many parts of line will be required per block?
- ❏ 4 parts per block
- ✔ **8 parts per block**
- ❏ 12 parts per block
- ❏ 16 parts per block

59. What is the overall length of the slings that will be used in a basket hook up around the lifting trunions at the top of the vessel?
- ❏ 20 feet
- ✔ **26 feet**
- ❏ 31 feet
- ❏ 40 feet

60. Determine if this statement is true or false. The lifting eyes for the 31 foot slings used over the main load hook will be secured to the spreader bar with 110 ton shackles.
- ✔ **true**
- ❏ false

61. Referring to the ground pressure details for the main crane and the tail crane, what type of material are the 5' x 20' mats made of?

Answer: timbers